Victory of Law

Victory of Law

The Fourteenth Amendment, the Civil War,
and American Literature, 1852–1867

DEAK NABERS

The Johns Hopkins University Press

Baltimore

© 2006 The Johns Hopkins University Press
All rights reserved. Published 2006
Printed in the United States of America on acid-free paper
2 4 6 8 9 7 5 3 1

The Johns Hopkins University Press
2715 North Charles Street
Baltimore, Maryland 21218-4363
www.press.jhu.edu

Library of Congress Cataloging-in-Publication Data
Nabers, Deak.
Victory of law : the Fourteenth amendment, the Civil War, and
American literature, 1852–1867 / Deak Nabers.
p.   cm.
Includes bibliographical references and index.
ISBN 0-8018-8350-4 (hardcover : alk. paper)
1. American literature—19th century—Political aspects. 2. Antislavery
movements in literature. 3. Antislavery movements—United States—
History. 4. Rhetoric—Political aspects—United States—History—19th
century. 5. United States. Constitution 14th Amendment. 6. United
States.—Politics and government—19th century. I. Title.
PS217.S55N33 2006
810.9′358097309034—dc22
2005032109

A catalog record for this book is available from the British Library.

CONTENTS

> All persons born or naturalized in the United States, and subject to the
> jurisdiction thereof, are citizens of the United States and of the State
> wherein they reside. No State shall make or enforce any law which
> shall abridge the privileges or immunities of citizens of the United
> States; nor shall any State deprive any person of life, liberty, or
> property, without due process of the law; nor deny to any person
> within its jurisdiction the equal protection of the laws.
>
> *U.S. Constitution, Fourteenth Amendment, Section 1*

At one point in his collection of Civil War poems, *Battle-Pieces and Aspects of the War* (1866), Herman Melville elliptically and ironically describes the Union's success in defeating the Confederacy as a "victory of LAW."[1] It is not hard to see why Melville might have thought that the Union's victory sounded in the domain of law, nor is it hard to see why he might have had some reservations about thinking of it as an uncompromised vindication of the American legal order. The Civil War was indeed an unusually legal military conflict. The Union's war goals were initially articulated in terms of the maintenance of the law: Lincoln called forth the militia in 1861 not to restore the Union but "to cause the laws to be duly executed."[2] And even after it became clear that the North's victory would involve changes in the nation's legal order rather than a mere restoration of it, the champions of those changes tended to think of them as extensions of American law as well as modifications of it. To be sure, the fulfillment of the Union's antislavery agenda required extensive constitutional amendment, but the Reconstruction amendments themselves express an emphatic commitment to the law rather than a departure from it. Many commentators have noted that the phrasing of section 1 of the Fourteenth Amendment, designed to secure "practical freedom" for former slaves,[3] involves little more than the repetition of other pieces of American law; as its author, John Bingham, put it, "every word of this proposed Amendment is today in the Constitution of our country."[4] And if this reaffirmation of previously enumerated constitutional principles transformed the shape of the American constitutional structure, it did so in large part by extending that structure's dependence upon the law—by insisting on the relevance of the "due process of law" and the "privileges or immunities of citizens" to civil standing and civil rights in the nation.

All the same, Melville had good reason to think that there was something ironic about the process whereby the Constitution came to count as a bulwark of antislavery legal principle. It is hard to reconcile Lincoln's commitment to maintaining the laws of the Union with his practice of radically changing the legal landscape of at least half of it. The positive laws secured by the preservation of the Union hardly seem identical to the higher laws enforced in the abolition of slavery: the Union that Lincoln wanted to maintain was, after all, emphatically *not* a union without slaves. In the decades leading up to the Civil War, it was by no means clear that the abolition of slavery could fit so harmoniously into the American legal order as the Reconstruction amendments would imply. Bingham's notion that the civil freedom guaranteed in the Thirteenth Amendment could be secured by something on the order of a reassertion of the nation's already existing Constitution stood at a far remove from William Lloyd Garrison's notion that emancipation would require at least the evisceration of the Constitution and maybe also the elimination of law itself—what he called "the emancipation of our whole race from the dominion of man."[5] This book seeks to explain how a war of slave emancipation could become a "victory of LAW"—a victory of legal process in general and American constitutional law as an expression of that process in particular—by charting the reciprocal relationships between antebellum American literature and the legal notions and arguments that were eventually established as American law in the Fourteenth Amendment. The law of the Union's victory, I suggest, was developed gradually and unevenly throughout the latter part of the 1840s and 1850s, and it was developed in American literature as well as in American courts, legislatures, and political debate.

The historical pedigree of the Fourteenth Amendment is extremely complicated. It has been the subject of intense, and often contentious, historical scrutiny.[6] My goal is not to provide an exhaustive genealogy of the amendment, nor am I under the illusion that the more limited genealogy I will provide will settle all of the outstanding questions surrounding what Jacobus tenBroek has called the amendment's "antislavery origins."[7] I seek only to provide something like the conditions of plausibility of Bingham's constitutional vision.[8] My interest is in reconstructing the argumentative infrastructure that made the Fourteenth Amendment conceivable, not the social and political conditions that made it practical or desirable. Insofar as I explain why the developments considered here took place, I will do so largely in intellectual and legal terms. I will focus on the way certain arguments addressed and confronted rival arguments within a mutually acknowledged context of the American Constitution and the Anglo-American common law. The result will be something like what Paul W. Kahn calls an "internal" history of "reason within law" in the sense that it will be a history of the development of arguments within a structure generated by a set of existing legal forms and practices.[9] But there is at least one important sense in which it will not remain exclusively an internal history—it will focus as much on the legal arguments of nonlegal actors as it will on the legal arguments of judges, legislators, and the like. Chief among these nonlegal actors are writers, whose participation in the legal developments I address was both vigorous and sophisticated.

The book develops one long continuous argument; consequently, the chapters are not entirely self-contained units. Although my argument could be read out of a wide range of works from the 1850s and 1860s, I mean to show the depth of the literary engagement with the legal developments I will be examining, not the breadth of that engagement. My hope is to use intense and focused readings of a few works to lay out the broad parameters in which a wide array of texts might be considered. Works that play a prominent role in one chapter will thus frequently make cameo appearances in other chapters. This tendency is especially pronounced with respect to Melville's *Battle-Pieces,* which is the subject of the first chapter and keeps popping up, like a bad penny, throughout the remainder of the book. I give Melville's Civil War poetry such extensive attention in part because I think it is one of the few remaining unrecognized masterpieces in the canon of the American Renaissance. But, such aesthetic judgments aside, *Battle-Pieces* will command our attention largely because of its acute grasp on the legal implications of the sectional conflict, the Civil War, and Reconstruction. Few works can match the intense rigor with which it processes the significance of the momentous upheavals caused by a civil war. Indeed, it is safe to say that one hundred and forty years of vigorous legal scholarship, careful historical examination, and important adjudication have not produced a more insightful commentary on Bingham's amendment than what is available in Melville's poems.

Like many recent studies of the relationship between literature and law, this book has a foot in two scholarly camps. Assessing the significance of what Andrew Kull has called Bingham's "pleasant phrases" and measuring American literature's contribution to their meaning will require extensive investigation of a wide range of political developments in the 1850s,[10] developments that in some cases no longer arouse much interest in a historiography more concerned with cultural and social development than the old themes of grand political history. I may be the only person left in the academy who thinks that the Freeport doctrine was of momentous import in American history. But if my interests sometimes seem slightly anachronistic, I hope the new light in which I cast them will restore some of their dormant appeal. And if my discussions sometimes veer far and wide from the immediate domain of literary history, I hope they will reveal dimensions of the works I address which have otherwise gone unnoticed.

The book's trajectory is straightforward. The first chapter lays out the principal terms of my analysis by placing Melville's *Battle-Pieces* in the context of the potentially uneasy relations between the Union's two chief aims in the Civil War—union and emancipation. The conservative drive to save the Union would seem to stand in no small tension with the more radical goal of emancipating the South's slaves: insofar as the North pursues freedom as well as union, it would seem less interested in preserving the nation than transforming it. Melville's poetry, I maintain, systematically stresses the ways in which these two goals are incompatible at the same time that it explains how the law, with its capacity to be inflected in both positive and higher forms, is an ideal vehicle for covering over the differences between them. The second chapter examines how slavery's posture in American law encouraged the rigid distinction between higher and positive law which *Battle-Pieces* seeks to enforce. Because slavery had no standing in natural law, its existence required the sanction of positive law. That is what made it a peculiar institution. And it is also what encouraged so many antislavery activists, like Garrison, to devote their energies to attacking the law itself as well as those laws that perpetuated slavery. I contend that this legal skepticism is the organizing principle behind the sentimental antislavery novel (as exemplified by *Uncle Tom's Cabin*) and the narrative of slave revolt (as exemplified by *Dred* and *Clotel*) and that the narrative instability critics have attributed to these literary modes is driven in large part by the works' efforts to imagine an alternative to a slave society independent of the law's coercion.

The third chapter recounts the political developments that gradually reconfigured the relations between slavery and the law over the course of the 1850s as a way of revealing the complexity of Thoreau's political writing and making sense of its evolution from "Resistance to Civil Government" (1849) to "A Plea for Captain John Brown" (1860). Conflicts over the status of fugitive slaves and over the regulation slavery in the United States territories had the effect of aligning legal procedure and statutory power with antislavery outcomes. If positive law counted as a prerequisite for slavery in important Anglo-American slave cases such as *Somerset v. Stewart* (1772), by the end of the 1850s positive law had emerged as a prerequisite for freedom. Operating in continual dialog with this transformation, Thoreau's political essays amount to a systematic elaboration of natural law's *legal* ontology. If Garrison implied that the dominion of God was essentially incompatible with the government of man, Thoreau's great achievement was to reveal the complicated ways in which the dominion of God in fact required the government of man. This reconciliation of positive and natural law, of course, falls far short of reconciling the Constitution with natural law. Because the Constitution certainly had done little enough to advance God's agenda with respect to the peculiar institution, one could align the Constitution with higher law impulses only by imagining that important constitutional provisions had not been enforced. In the fourth chapter I place Hawthorne's lifelong examination of the force of legal language in the context of the emergence of theories of legal interpretation according to which the Constitution could count as much as a statement as an enactment. A remarkable number of major points of constitutional contention in the sectional conflict hinged on debates about whether the law's meaning inheres in its action or in its language. By systematically intertwining the law's power with the law's rhetoric, Hawthorne lays the groundwork for a hermeneutical form of abolition at the same time that he reveals the deep and abiding limits of hermeneutical legal strategies of all kinds.

This latter point was especially significant in the Thirty-ninth Congress, as I show in the final chapter. To those who control the machinery of government, hermeneutical legal activity can only count as a poor substitute for direct legal agency. John Bingham inherited a Constitution whose language could be said to speak of an emancipation it could not deliver. If a variety of political developments in the 1850s began to effect a reconciliation of lower and high forms of law, the Fourteenth Amendment was designed to reunite the Constitution's language with its power. Once abolition requires only the enforcement of national law against state action, the seemingly contradictory Northern war aims fuse into a single enterprise: from Bingham's perspective the effort to enforce the positive law of the Constitution *is* the effort to emancipate slaves and give them civil rights. In bridging these various legal domains, Bingham's amendment and the Constitution it produced also fulfill the ambitions Emerson, Whitman, and others had established for poetry itself. Emerson's poetic theory and Whitman's poetic practice have long been said to revolve around the project of linking the natural and the moral, the categorical and the particular, and the declarative and the symbolic. I seek to measure the poetic achievements of the Republicans and the civic achievements of American poetry in the 1860s by placing Bingham's amendment in the context of Whitman's *Drum-Taps* and Melville's *Battle-Pieces*—each of which embraces the project Bingham set for himself and refuses to see it through. The American Civil War poem most comfortable with its status as a poem, I contend, is ultimately the law for which the Union's victory was gained.

I began thinking about the cluster of issues I explore in this book at the prompting of Allen Grossman, who was surprised to see that several of his off-the-cuff remarks about the relations between lyric and law would ultimately inspire an effort to understand the relations between nature and slavery. All the same, I am grateful for his advice and for his example as both a scholar and a teacher. Stephen Best, Jerome Christensen, Jay Clayton, Florence Dore, Katherine Fusco, John Irwin, Jonathon Kahn, Dennis Kezar, John Limon, Walter Michaels, Sam Otter, and Michael Szalay have each read and commented on portions of the manuscript. This book would be far worse without their recommendations, and worse still had Abigail Cheever not given each chapter her careful scrutiny. Down the stretch, I was fortunate to have Michael Lonegro,

Elizabeth Gratch, and an anonymous reader from the Johns Hopkins University Press help me refine an unwieldy draft into something like a regular book. I wrote most of these pages while teaching at Vanderbilt University, where my students in both the Law School and the English Department were receptive and skeptical in perfect measure. Rebecca Brown, John Goldberg, Bob Rasmussen, and Kent Syverud made me feel very welcome as a visitor at the Vanderbilt Law School, and Colin Dayan, Carolyn Dever, Lynn Enterline, Dana Nelson, Shawn Salvant, Mark Schoenfield, Mark Wollaeger, and Paul Young were inspiring colleagues back in my home department. My most important debts are to Ginia Bellafante and my parents.

A shorter version of chapter 1 appeared in *American Literature*, and parts of chapters 2 and 3 appeared in articles in *American Literary History; Law, Culture and the Humanities;* and *Representations*. I am grateful to the editors and publishers of these journals for permission to reprint this material here.

Victory of Law

Introduction

Emancipation, Universal and Constitutional

It remains a defining image in the history of the American antislavery movement. On July 4, 1854, at the conclusion of an address before a conference of roughly six hundred abolitionist crusaders, William Lloyd Garrison held up a copy of the Constitution of the United States, pronounced it "the source and parent" of the atrocities abolitionists sought to eliminate, and lit it on fire. "So perish all compromises with tyranny," he proclaimed as flames consumed the document. "And let all the people say, 'Amen.'"[1] The dramatic and climactic gesture had been a long time in coming. Garrison had first begun challenging the Constitution some twenty years earlier. As early as 1832, in an essay entitled "The Constitution and the Union," Garrison had questioned "the sacredness of the compact which was formed between the free and slave states, on the adoption of the Constitution." Far from a "sacred compact," Garrison maintained, the Constitution was in fact "the most bloody and heaven-daring arrangement ever made by men for the continuance and protection of a system of the most atrocious villainy ever exhibited on earth" and altogether "null and void" "in the nature of things and according to the will of God."[2] It was for this reason that Garrison was entirely unbothered about the prospect of sectional conflict. "Be assured," he concluded the essay, "that slavery will very speedily destroy this Union, if it be let alone; but even if the Union can be preserved by treading upon the necks and spilling the blood, and destroying the souls of millions of your race, we say it is not worth a price like this. . . . Let the pillars thereof fall—let the superstructure crumble into dust—if it must be upheld by robbery and oppression."[3] By the 1840s Garrison was no longer simply indifferent to the fate of the Union; he came very close to opposing it actively. "Three millions of the American people are crushed under the American Union," he wrote in 1844. And under Garrison's influence that year the American Anti-Slavery Society (AAS) would take "NO UNION WITH SLAVEHOLDERS!" as its slogan.[4]

The object of Garrison's attack on those who would make a "sacred instrument" of "the Constitution of the United States, dripping as it is in human blood," could easily have been Abraham Lincoln, whose major political address of the 1830s (the so-called Lyceum Address) lamented "the increasing disregard for law which pervades the country" and called for a new renewed "reverence for the laws": "Let it become the *political religion* of the nation; and let the old and the young, the rich and the poor, the grave and the gay, of all sexes and tongues, and colors and conditions, sacrifice unceasingly upon its altars" (1:32–33).[5] The early stages of the abolition movement loom ominously in the background of Lincoln's address. Although one of the specific instances of mob violence he describes was actually a lynching carried out against the abolitionist Elijah Lovejoy, the mobs in the Lyceum Address take on a curiously Garrisonian hue: "Having ever regarded the Government as their deadliest bane, they make a jubilee of the suspension of its operations; and pray for nothing so much, as its total annihilation" (1:31). And when toward the end of the address Lincoln conjures the specter of men so ambitious that they would refuse to devote themselves to "supporting and maintaining an edifice that has been erected by others," he immediately associates their strivings for innovation with the end of slavery. "Towering genius," he warns, "thirsts and burns for distinction; and, if possible, it will have it, whether at the expense of emancipating slaves, or enslaving freemen" (1:34).

Needless to say, Garrison would hardly have considered "emancipating slaves" much of an "expense." But even if he had, he still would have had nothing but disdain for Lincoln's strategy for protecting the government against such ambition. Political religion was precisely what Garrison resisted. Lincoln may have thought that it was possible to align what he called "*sound morality*" and "*a reverence for the constitution and laws*" (1:36), but Garrison would never let the two converge. His demand for "Abolitionism" "admits of no compromise," he explained in 1854, because it is "absolute as the Law of God." Reverence is precisely what leads Garrison to see that the Constitution "is to be trampled under foot" and that "no precedent, no example, no law, no compact" can justify it. "How has the slave system grown to its enormous dimensions?" he asked. "Through compromise"—which the Constitution both embodies and inspires.[6] In the ratification of the Constitution the United States had "dethroned the Most High God,"[7] and only by worshipping Lincoln's at false "altars" could the nation keep Him from his rightful place.

It is easy to exaggerate the difference between abolition's greatest spokesman and its ultimate executor. If Garrison condemned the Constitution, he often did so from the vantage of what he called the "heaven-attested Declaration"[8]—a document that also played a central role in the development of Lincoln's political commitments.[9] And if Garrison and the AAS rejected union with slaveholders, they often touted abolition as a means of a more stable sectional compact: as the *Liberator* put it in May 1854, "nothing but the immediate abolition of slavery can make us a united people."[10] Nonetheless, it comes as no small irony that emancipation was as much the result of Lincoln's "political religion" as of Garrison's respect for "the absolute . . . Law of God." There can be little doubt about Lincoln's ultimate allegiances or of the relative priority of the two legal orders in the way he carried out the Civil War. Writing to Horace Greeley in August 1862 about the "policy" he was pursuing with respect to slavery, Lincoln famously insisted, "I have not meant to leave anyone in doubt":

> I would save the Union. I would save it the shortest way under the Constitution. The sooner the national authority can be restored; the nearer the Union will be to the Union "as it was." If there be those who would not save the Union, unless they could at the same time *save* slavery, I do not agree with them. If there be those who would not save the Union unless they could at the same time *destroy* slavery, I do not agree with them. My paramount object in this struggle *is* to save the Union, and it is *not* either to save or destroy slavery. If I could save the Union without freeing *any* slave I would do it, and if I could save it by freeing *all* the slaves I would do it, and if I could save it by freeing some and leaving others alone I would also do that. What I do about slavery, and the colored race, I do because I believe it helps to save the Union; and what I forbear, I forbear because I do *not* believe it would help to save the Union.

To be sure, Lincoln intended "no modification of my oft-stated *personal* wish that all men every where could be free." But he understood his behavior in the "*official*" capacities as president as an instance of the civic religion he had preached, not an abandonment of it (2:358). If Garrison valued the Union only as a means of emancipation, we might say that Lincoln turned to emancipation only as a means of preserving the Union. Fealty to the Constitution "as it was," not a rejection of it as a blood-stained "pact with the Devil," produced American emancipation.

It should not be too shocking that emancipation was realized in the United States as an expression of constitutional necessity rather than a form of constitutional repudiation. Whatever else we might wish to say about Garrisonian abolitionism, we would hardly want to maintain that it was carefully crafted with political feasibility in mind. Historians have long noted the ways in which Garrison's radical and moral crusade was transformed as it acquired a politically viable form over the 1840s and 1850s. "The American anti-slavery movement," Eric Foner observed in one of the classic formulations of the point, " . . . began as a moral crusade, [but] eventually found that it would have to turn to politics to achieve its goals."[11] But there is also a deeper sense in which the actual practice of emancipation in the United States differed from Garrison's vision of it in the decades leading up to the Civil War. The constitutional form in which abolition was realized in the mid-1860s did not merely represent a moderation of Garrison's vision, an accommodation of his radical commitments to the political realities of nineteenth-century America. It also represented something of an assault on his basic constitutional thinking.[12] Emancipation came about not only as a part of a larger effort to preserve the Constitution and the Union but also, at least from the perspective of several of the chief architects of the constitutional amendments that ended slavery in the nation, as a reaffirmation of the Constitution and an extension of the Union it bound together. Lincoln hoped to end the Civil War quickly so as to get "near" "the Constitution 'as it was.'" Some of the framers of the Reconstruction amendments actually seem to have thought that a civil war for emancipation was required to enforce the Constitution as it was.

The key text in this regard is the Fourteenth Amendment, which developed out of what Foner has called "the first [. . .] attempt . . . to define in legislative terms the essence of freedom."[13] The Fourteenth Amendment was, undeniably, an amendment to the Constitution, but its author, John Bingham, insisted that it was more a realization of the old constitutional order than a modification of it. Its passage, Bingham claimed, would embody an expression of the nation's "fidelity to the sacred cause of the Constitution."[14] The claim was not purely rhetorical. Prior to the amendment's passage, the provisions of the Bill of Rights were generally understood to limit the legislative authority of the federal government but not of the states.[15] At least so far as Bingham was concerned, one of the amendment's chief functions was to pull the state governments within the Bill's constitutional umbrella. Controversy continues to surround the question of whether the Fourteenth Amendment "incorporates," as the lawyers put it, the Bill of Rights against the states.[16] There can be little doubt, however, that Bingham and most of the amendment's congressional floor leaders *thought* that the amendment would have that effect. In 1871, several years after the amendment was formally ratified, Bingham explained that "the privileges and immunities of citizens of the United States, as contradistinguished from the citizens of a State, are chiefly defined in the first eight amendments to the Constitution of the United States. . . . Those eight articles . . . never were limitations upon the power of the States, until made so by the Fourteenth Amendment."[17]

"I can hardly believe that any person can be found who will not admit that every one of these provisions is just," Pennsylvania congressman Thaddeus Stevens insisted in a speech given shortly before the House's final vote on the measure. "They are all asserted, in some form or another, in our DECLARATION or organic law. But the Constitution limits only the action of Congress, and is not a limitation on the States. This amendment supplies that defect."[18] There was some justification, then, in Bingham's insistence that the amendment's great purpose was to secure "the enforcement of the Constitution . . . to all the citizens and all the people of the United States."[19] From this vantage the "compromises" that allowed slavery to flourish in the United States were compromises *of* the Constitution, not compromises *by* the Constitution. In translating the question of how the Constitution might be amended so as to prohibit slavery into the question of how the Constitution might be enforced so as to secure freedom, Bingham essentially turned Garrisonian abolitionist constitutional theory on its head.

There is an even further, and more radical, way in which the practice of abolition in the United States in the 1860s departed from the vision of abolitionists in the decades leading up to the Civil War. It might not be too much to say that Garrison's hostility to the Constitution of the United States was really only a subspecies of his larger and more general hostility to the concept of human law itself. Garrison's thinking on this point is extremely complicated, and historians have found it very hard to determine whether he was genuinely committed to the idea that, as Lewis Perry has put it, "a Christian must abstain from government" or, instead, merely deployed that idea as "an instrument of political influence."[20] Yet, however we might sort out the various relations between religious doctrine and political strategy in Garrison's writings, it is easy enough to see that he frequently cast chattel slavery as a small instance of the broader phenomenon of the "dominion of man." The great instance of man's dominion was government itself, which Garrison seldom mentioned without a reminder of its basis in "brute force." Garrison's call for "UNIVERSAL EMANCIPATION" thus entailed something more than the simple emancipation of African-American slaves. It also entailed the displacement of the laws of the state by "the government of the law of love," which amounted to "the dominion of God."[21]

From the perspective of this analogy between slavery and the law, the constitutional measures that secured emancipation in the United States could only look perverse. The instrumentality of the law lies at the heart of the way in which they elaborate civic liberty. What it means to be free, from the perspective of the Reconstruction amendments, is to be subject to the law *rather* than a human master. The Thirteenth Amendment, for instance, does not eliminate slavery altogether; it instead subordinates slavery to legal procedure, prohibiting it "except as a punishment for crime whereof the party shall have been duly convicted."[22] Likewise, the Fourteenth Amendment secures the civil freedom elaborated in the Thirteenth Amendment largely by further insisting upon the former slaves' status as legal subjects—by making them "citizens," affording them all of the "privileges" and "immunities" elaborated already in American law, and guaranteeing that their rights of "life, liberty, and property" would only be compromised by the only force left with enslaving power in the new nation: the due process of law. And indeed, the Fourteenth Amendment was designed to facilitate the exercise of legal power as well as to extend its reach. It did not merely subject states to a broader constitutional authority; it also empowered Congress to pass laws in order to keep the states within that authority. It served, as the *New York Times* summarized one of Bingham's speeches, "to arm the Congress . . . with power to enforce the Bill of Rights."[23] It would be the government's "force" that secured its commitment to freedom. Rather than counting as another form of slavery's oppression, the law here counts as the antidote to it. We might say that constitutional emancipation took place only at the expense of the prospect of Garrison's universal emancipation, or that the end of slavery in the United States counted as much as a repudiation of Garrison's thinking about slavery as a realization of it.

This is not to say, however, that constitutional emancipation betokened something on the order of an unalloyed triumph of Lincoln's "civic religion." Lincoln had initially imagined, after all, that emancipation would come only at the expense of that religion. And while, in 1838 at least, there is something slightly forced about Lincoln's appeal to a civic religion, Bingham's religious reverence for the Constitution seems altogether authentic. Lincoln tells us to revere the law as if it were divine. Bingham's Bill of Rights simply is divine. He needs no invitation to consider the Constitution a "sacred cause." He already thinks that it is a result of "victory" ordained by God, that it provides "all the sacred rights of persons," and that its "essential provisions" are "divine in their justice" and "sublime in their humanity."[24] Nor does he reach this conclusion by ignoring the evils of slavery. He instead thinks that the evils of slavery could persist only because others had ignored the sublimity of their political institutions. The Constitution and laws that needed reverence in the 1830s could command it in the 1860s.

Legal Writings

How did this transformation come to pass? Garrison's complaints about the Constitution and the nature of human law both had reasonably solid bases in American law. The publication of Madison's *Notes* in 1840 confirmed what many reasonable observers had already acknowledged—that slave interests played a considerable role in the shaping of the Constitution and that the document thus at least recognized, if it did not explicitly sanction, the legal status of the peculiar institution in the new nation.[25] And prominent eighteenth- and early-nineteenth-century English cases such as *Somerset v. Stewart* (1772) and *The Slave, Grace* (1827) had dealt with slavery in such a way as to funnel attacks upon it into attacks upon positive law as such. Slavery's standing under the common law and the Constitution had been articulated in such a way that the antislavery judge could hardly avoid "squirm[ing]," as the legal historian

Robert Cover has memorably put it, in the face of his duty.[26] It would take an extraordinary combination of developments to convert the Constitution and the concept of law into abolitionist instruments.

Consider all that is entailed in the belief that the "practical value" of emancipation could result from an amendment providing for the enforcement of the Constitution. There are so many peculiarities implicit in such a notion that it is difficult to list them all. To begin with, Bingham must have had an unusual conception of the Constitution's status in American law: in what sense could we imagine that the Constitution would require an amendment to be enforced? Does the Constitution state the law or enact it? Is the Constitution the "supreme law of the land" or a supremely important *account* of the law? And even if we allow that the Constitution might declare legal principles as well as establish legal norms, we are still left with the problem of identifying the provisions within it which might be incompatible with slavery. Slavery had thrived in the seventy years following the ratification. What had everyone missed? Bingham found what they had missed in the Bill of Rights, and he got around the problem implicit in his needing to enforce already existing constitutional provisions by pointing out that the Bill of Rights had previously only limited the authority of Congress, whereas practical freedom in the nation would require that it limit state governments as well. But why did he think that incorporating the Bill of Rights against the states would count as an enforcement of the Constitution rather than a fundamental transformation of its character? What was it about the Bill of Rights, in other words, which made it plausible for him to treat it as a declaration of general legal principles rather than the establishment of specific constitutional conditions? And why did he think that the Bill, which speaks largely to questions of criminal and civil legal procedure, actually had anything to do with slavery? How could it be that guarantees of "due process of law" could also count as guarantees of civil freedom?

Needless to say, such counterintuitive constitutional thinking could only derive from a wide range of disparate and interacting social, political, and intellectual developments. For the purposes of this study, four items are of particular significance.

1. Over the course of the 1830s and 1840s the Bill of Rights came increasingly to be seen as the repository of exactly those common law principles that had effectively removed slavery from the English legal landscape in the eighteenth century.[27] *Somerset* had insisted that slavery required a foundation in "positive law"; the common law, on its own, recognized no property rights in persons.[28] By the 1850s it was common for the Bill of Rights to be represented as the United States's common law, and it was also common for the American Revolution to be represented as an effort to secure common law rights in the form of the Bill rather than as an effort to secure the rights of self-government for the citizens of American states.[29]

2. At the same time, what Don E. Fehrenbacher has called the "constitutionaliza-tion" of slavery debates in the 1850s tended to fashion the Constitution as a form of written higher law and to treat it as if its relationship to ordinary statutes was identical to the relationship between natural and positive law.[30] If, according to *Somerset,* the common law must give way to the force of positive law, the Constitution provided an alternative legal framework in which legislative positive law could be seen as subordinate to common law alternatives.

3. The 1840s and 1850s saw the development and widespread acceptance of theories of legal hermeneutics under which the Constitution's evasions with respect to slavery could become as significant as its concessions to slaveholders. The Constitution never refers to slavery by name, though the peculiar institution gets some five references by way of other, more benign designations. At one point during the proceedings of the Constitutional Convention, Madison famously insisted that it would be wrong "to admit in the Constitution the idea that there could be property in man."[31] But why did it matter that slavery, as such, goes unmentioned in the Constitution— that, say, slaves are referred to as "other persons" rather than "slaves"? Whatever the Constitution *said,* it would seem, matters less than what it *did,* and what it did, of course, was recognize slavery's significance in the nation's legal, social, and economic makeup. Fehrenbacher disagrees:

> One returns finally to the striking fact that in the . . . clauses dealing with slavery, the word itself was deliberately avoided. This should not be dismissed as mere fastidiousness. The law inheres most essentially in the text of the document, not in the purposes of those who wrote the document, though the purposes may be consulted to illuminate obscure meaning. The sharp contrast here between text and purpose has its own significant effect, whether intended or not. It is as though the framers were half-consciously trying to frame two constitutions, one for their own time and one for the ages, with slavery viewed bifocally—that is, plainly visible at their feet, but disappearing when they lifted their eyes.[32]

As a historical matter, of course, Fehrenbacher is absolutely right: the Constitution was particularly well suited to such bifocal interpretation. But we might say that Fehrenbacher's claims are right only as a matter of history: they are the product of a specific set of historical developments. For whether the law inheres "most essentially" in its text or in the purposes of those who crafted it was itself the subject of crucial debate in the antebellum period, which saw the emergence and dissemination of exactly the textual account of legal ontology on which Fehrenbacher's claim relies. (Note, for instance, that the "significant effect" of avoiding the word might have been "intended or not," even though the word was "deliberately avoided" in the document.)

This understanding of the law's "essential" home was developed in theoretical terms by legal philosophers such as Francis Lieber and in polemical terms by antislavery activists such as Lysander Spooner, and it made it conceivable to think of a constitution as a set of statements in need of enforcement rather than a legal enactment on its own. It even made it possible to think that the enforcement of a constitution would entail radical reversals of that constitution's prior effects.

4. Debates about the status of fugitive slaves and slavery in the United States territories had the effects of reversing the tendencies implicit in *Somerset* and *The Slave, Grace* which led to Garrisonian nonresistance and of generating in their place a legalist, not simply political, form of antislavery. We will see in the third chapter, for instance, that the real force of the famous Freeport doctrine was that it inspired a radical revision of the way in which *Somerset* had configured the legal status of slavery. *Somerset* had insisted that positive law was a prerequisite for slavery; Douglas's response to the *Dred Scott* decision would lead Lincoln to maintain that positive law was a prerequisite for freedom. "Pray what was it that made you free?" Lincoln asked a Cincinnati audience in the summer of 1859. "What kept you free? Did you not find your country free when you came to decide that Ohio should be a free state? . . . Kentucky is separated by this river Ohio, not wide a mile. Kentucky is entirely covered with slavery—Ohio is entirely free of it. What made that difference? . . . Tell us, if you can, in all the range of conjecture, if there be anything you can conceive of that made that difference, other than that there was no law of any sort keeping it out of Kentucky? while the Ordinance of '87 kept it out of Ohio?" (2:78–79). The plight of fugitive slaves effected a similar reversal. Abolitionists often lampooned the idea that human courts had standing sufficient, in Henry Thoreau's terms, to find that a "M A N" was "really a S L A V E." "Does any think that Justice or God awaits [the court's] decision?" But efforts to preserve the freedom of alleged fugitives often embraced legal process as a way of forestalling action under the two fugitive slave acts, and even Thoreau himself would occasionally complain that the men sent back to slavery were in fact "innocent."[33] Defending the freedom of fugitives, as it were, could draw the legalist emancipation of the Thirteenth Amendment from even the most arduous spokesmen for Garrison's more universal variety.

None of these developments alone can account for the ascendance of Bingham's constitutional vision. Taken together, they constitute the conditions of intelligibility for the Fourteenth Amendment. Without them Bingham's proposal would literally have been inconceivable. Many other factors contributed to the amendment's appeal, but these are its most vital legal and constitutional prerequisites. And if constitutional freedom in the United States had its origins, at least in part, in these developments, the developments themselves had their origins, at least in part, in American literature. The point is not that American literature is directly responsible for the developments but, rather, that it played a significant role in the process by which they were initiated, spurred, prodded, debated, challenged, and sustained. The participation is often transparent enough. One does not need to look hard to find legal thematics in the major literary works of the 1850s, and critics have long noted the centrality of legal problems in works ranging from *The Scarlet Letter* to *The Confidence Man,* from *My Bondage and My Freedom* to *Our Nig,* from *Leaves of Grass* to *Walden.* Indeed, the critical history of these works is to a large extent a history of accounts of how they represent the law.

This prevailing literary attention to legal matters in general is part and parcel of the works' slightly more specific interest in the development of constitutional antislavery thinking. It certainly takes no great leap of the imagination to see the persistent relevance of the sectional conflict in major literary developments of the 1850s and 1860s. Abraham Lincoln famously, though perhaps apocryphally, identified Harriet Beecher Stowe as "the little lady who made this big war."[34] Emerson and Thoreau devoted major essays to the fugitive slave controversies that flared in Boston throughout the early 1850s;[35] Melville presented his first volume of poetry as a contribution to the ongoing debate about the "just" terms for the "re-establishment" of the Southern states;[36] Whitman produced a volume of verse about the Civil War and a cluster of major poems devoted to the great champion of "*political religion.*" Recent attention to the significance of the writings of African Americans, especially the narratives of former slaves, has only underscored the relevance of legal debate about slavery to our understanding of the literary culture of the period. Harriet Jacobs's *Incidents in the Life of a Slave Girl* (1861) hinges on a moment in which she parrots, and deforms, one of the crucial passages from *Dred Scott v. Sandford* (1857);[37] Frederick Douglass's literary career developed in long dialog with his struggles within and against Garrisonian abolitionist orthodoxy, and the trajectory of his thinking in many ways flows directly from Garrison's strategies of nonresistance (in works such as *Narrative of the Life of Frederick Douglass, an American Slave,* 1845) to Bingham's strategies of constitutional enforcement (in works such as *The American Constitution and the Slave,* 1860), with appropriate incremental steps between the two along the way (in works such as *My Bondage and My Freedom,* 1855).[38]

American literature's participation in the emergence of Bingham's constitutional vision was by no means confined to works that deal openly and explicitly with slavery, the Constitution, or sectional politics. The legal developments at stake in the emergence of constitutional emancipation were sufficiently momentous to involve matters at quite a far remove from the direct discussion of the status of slavery in American law. Indeed, many of the more powerful literary interventions into the development of a constitutionalist basis for emancipation take place in the context of discussions that might initially seem far removed from the immediate back-and-forth of constitutional debate. Developments in the field of legal hermeneutics, for instance, constitute a significant, though frequently unrecognized, impetus for the series of epistemological puzzles that critics have long located at the heart of the American Renaissance. The scarlet letter, surrounded as it is by questions of whether it has "done its office," stands as a powerfully apt emblem of Bingham's Bill of Rights—those legal provisions with the "defect" of needing further legal security. Hawthorne's initial presentation of "this rag of scarlet cloth" locates the letter precisely at the heart of the questions surrounding legal interpretive practice in the 1840s and 1850s. At issue in those debates was whether legal authority inhered in the law as such or in its interpretation; whether the law was properly interpreted by way of technical and historical analysis or broader registration of more general moral sensibilities; whether the law's ontology was natural or social; and whether the law was properly understood as a wholly human syntax or a human effort to codify a more divine grammar. Hawthorne stages the rag's emergence into language ("This rag of scarlet cloth . . . , on careful examination, assumed the shape of a letter"), insists upon its having a "deep meaning" beyond its status as "a riddle which . . . I saw little hope of solving," suggests that the meaning "streamed forth from the mystic symbol," and locates that meaning somewhere between "my sensibilities" and "the analysis of my mind."[39]

The Scarlet Letter is hardly unique in addressing the pressing issues of the emerging forms of constitutional antislavery from a seemingly remote vantage. Indeed, such a remote vantage is often the very point of the way in which antebellum literary documents engage the legal debates surrounding slavery. Insofar as part of the force of slavery's posture within the Anglo-American legal environment was to raise questions about the status of the law as such, the very generality of many of the legal questions in works from the 1850s could itself make a polemical point. Speaking on the same platform as Garrison on the day of the infamous burning of the Constitution, Thoreau actually condemned the abolition movement for focusing too much on immediate legal controversies. "I lately attended a meeting of the citizens of Concord," he explained, "expecting, as one among many, to speak on the subject of slavery in Massachusetts; but I was surprised and disappointed to find that what had called my townsmen together was the destiny of Nebraska. . . . I had thought the house was on fire, and not the prairie. . . . There is not one slave in Nebraska; there are perhaps a million slaves in Massachusetts" (91). When obedience to the law itself counts as a form of slavery, when the state can no longer "sanction[] the continuance of [the] Union" and "each inhabitant of the state" must "dissolve her union with her" (104), chattel slavery itself represents no more than the tip of slavery's iceberg; the exclusive focus upon slavery's more conspicuous forms only obscures its more pervasive and nefarious manifestations. An engagement with the subjects of Massachusetts can be as important to extricating the nation from slavery as an engagement with the subjects of Tennessee.

Nor is the development of constitutional emancipation merely a topic in American literature of the 1840s and 1850s. It is also a shaping force. We will see, for instance, that William Wells Brown understood fiction itself to constitute an intervention into the legal legacy of *Somerset* and *Slave, Grace,* which is why he produced a self-consciously originary first African-American novel and prefaced that novel with a third-person rendition of his slave narrative. And if, at least from Brown's perspective, the slave narrative and the novel were both crucially *legal* forms, so too was the sentimental novel, which in Stowe's hands embodies and constitutes a particular legal strategy in the domain of the Constitution's compact. Melville explained his decision to devote himself to poetry after the onset of the Civil War in terms of his position with respect to the problems of our finding "just thoughts" about the reestablishment of the Southern states. Thoreau's essays track a complicated relay between poetry and prose as they attempt to work out a rhetorical form appropriate to the "transcendental" interrelation of nature and civil authority he sees in John Brown's preempted revolution (147). Writers from the 1850s were not moonlighting in the arena of constitutional theory. Legal issues lay at the very heart of the *literary* dimension of their engagement with the constitutional crisis brought on by the sectional conflict over slavery.[40]

The Written War

Questions of literary form could so easily acquire legal consequence in part because throughout the body of legal and literary writings we will be surveying the arena of the legal was itself represented in essentially literary terms. The politics of slavery were almost always cast in specifically authorial terms. When Lincoln considered the prospect that ambition might "thirst[] and burn[] for distinction; and, if possible, will have it, whether at the expense of emancipating slaves or enslaving freemen," he claimed to see danger in the way that "towering genius disdains a beaten path. It sees *no distinction* in adding story to story, upon the monuments of fame, erected on the memories of others." The distinction here is between the author who writes *ab ovo* and the author who "treads in the footstep" of a "predecessor" and "serves under" a "chief" (1:34). We might say that the distinction is between those people who produce novels and those who produce chapters, which is to say that it is the distinction between what Ronald Dworkin would have us call the "novelist" and the "judge." Lincoln's civil stability has the same foundation as Dworkin's empire of law—"an artificial genre of literature we might call the chain novel." "In this enterprise a group of novelists writes a novel *seriatim;* each novelist in the chain interprets the chapters he has been given in order to write a new chapter, which is then added to what the next novelist receives and so on."[41] Lincoln's fear of "mob law" was thus in effect a fear of literary creativity (1:31), a fear of an expressive impulse wholly committed, indeed defined by, "the disposition to substitute the wild and furious passions, in lieu of the sober judgment of the Courts" (1:29). And in this regard it should come as no surprise that Lincoln could attribute the coming of the Civil War itself to a book produced by a "little lady." Nor should it be surprising that Thoreau would consider John Brown's revolutionary activities at Harper's Ferry essentially a "written" "work" (150).

But if literature constitutes a threat to civil stability in the Lyceum Address, it is by no means *only* a threat to political institutions. It also stands as something like the origin of those institutions, or, if that is a little bit too strong, the atmosphere within which those institutions thrive. New literary ambition proves threatening precisely because political loyalty is essentially a literary matter. At issue is always the question of how well a given "story" commands our respect, not whether we inhabit a world of judgment rather than a world of stories. Lincoln makes this point emphatically clear toward the end of the address, when he gives us something approaching a concrete account of what it might mean to "erect" stories "on the memories of others." There he addresses the dangers inherent in the prospect that the "scenes of the revolution" might "fade upon the memory of the world, and grow more and more dim by the lapse of time." "Adding of story to story" now appears in the mode of historical writing: "In history, we hope, they will be read of, and recounted, so long as the bible shall be read." (1:35). And Lincoln's concern is now not that such a task is inadequately ambitious but, rather, that it is too difficult, even for the "family of the lion" or the "tribe of the eagle" (1:34). For in literature the scenes "*cannot be* so universally known or vividly felt" as "they were by the generation just gone to rest." Why?

> At the close of that struggle, nearly every adult male had been a participator in some of its scenes. The consequence was, that of those scenes, in the form of a husband, a father, a son, a brother, *a living history* was to be found in every family—a history bearing the indubitable testimonies of its own authenticity, in the limbs of the mangled, in the scars of wounds received, in the midst of the very scenes related. . . . But *those* histories are gone. . . . They *were* a forest of giant oaks; but the all-resistless hurricane has swept over them, and left only, here and there, a lonely trunk, despoiled of its verdure, shorn of its foliage; unshading and unshaded, to murmur in a few more gentle breezes, and to combat with its mutilated limbs, a few ruder storms, then to sink, and be no more. (1:35–36)

We might be inclined to think that Lincoln means to contrast literature to memory, to contrast what is "recounted" in "history" to what is "vividly felt" by actual "participators" (1:36). But it turns out that Lincoln is ultimately interested in the participators not for their memories so much as their bodies. He does not particularly care about *their* knowledge of the past; he cares about how their presence will affect the historical knowledge of others. The participators do not provide the "indubitable testimony" here; history itself does. They are merely its vehicles, if indeed we should not say that their "scars" and "mangled limbs" are its vehicles. In this regard Lincoln poses literature not against experience but against nature itself, a point that becomes clear at the end of the sequence when the "mangled limbs" of the soldiers become the "mutilated limbs" of a tree after the "hurricane has swept over" the forest. Literature poses two distinct challenges to Lincoln's state. On the one hand, literary creativity is strong enough to destroy our political institutions; on the other, our political institutions are frail precisely because they are constituted only by literature.

This is in large part what Emerson meant when he suggested, in "Politics" (1844),[42] that the "law is only a memorandum." "Politics" reads in many ways like a mirror image of the Lyceum Address. Whereas Lincoln worries that political institutions and laws might not be perpetual, Emerson fairly delights in their transience: "Our statute is a currency, which we stamp with our own portrait: it soon becomes unrecognizable, and in the process of time will return to mint" (329–30). Whereas Lincoln fears that the mobs might replace "sober judgments of the Courts," Emerson insists that "the wise know . . . that the State must follow, and not lead the character and progress of the citizen; . . . and that the form of government which prevails, is the expression of what cultivation exists in the population which permits it." Lincoln fears threats to the state, Emerson threats by the state—the threat of "foolish legislation." The default position for Lincoln is intemperate mob rule. The default position for Emerson is something like a just state: "the strongest usurper is quickly got rid of; and they only who build upon Ideas, build for eternity" (329). But despite these divergences in both outlook and temperament, Emerson's vision of the nature of the state is actually quite similar to Lincoln's. Both see it in largely literary terms—a story, a memorandum— and both measure the state's power in terms of the relationship between these writings and nature. Lincoln fears that ambitious newcomers will produce new texts to replace the natural bodies of their forebears; Emerson insists that the texts will never quite override the natural forms they encounter: "With such an ignorant and deceivable majority, States would soon go to ruin, but that there are limitations, beyond which the folly and ambition of governors cannot go. Things have their laws, as well as men; and things refuse to be trifled with" (332).

Ultimately, what saves Emerson's state from ruin is exactly what saves Lincoln's state from the weather. It is the poet: "For, as it is dislocation and detachment from the life of God, that makes things ugly, the poet, who re-attaches things to nature and the Whole,—re-attaching even artificial things, and violations of nature, to nature, by a deeper insight,—disposes very easily of the most disagreeable facts" (225). For a figure like Whitman, of course, Lincoln himself was this poet. But in constitutional terms this function was even more powerfully carried out by John Bingham and his Fourteenth Amendment, which managed to re-tether the various parts of Constitution to their ideal whole, which managed finally to render the Constitution not only the law of the land but also "divine in [its] justice, [and] sublime in [its] humanity."[43]

It has long been an article of faith in American literary criticism that the Civil War was, in Daniel Aaron's provocative phrase, an "unwritten war." "One would expect writers," Aaron maintains, "the 'antennae of the race,' to say something revealing about the meaning if not the causes of the War. . . . [But], with a few notable exceptions, they did not."[44] And to be sure, if one understands war writing largely in terms of accounts of the meaning of battle and military activity, the Civil War did produce few classics. I doubt many of us would want to hold up *Miss Ravenel's Conversion from Secession to Loyalty* (1867) as a rival to *A Farewell to Arms* (1929), *Catch-22* (1955), or *Going after Cacciato* (1978). But if we take Clauswitz seriously enough to understand war as an extension of politics, then it is hard to imagine a war more thoroughly written than the Civil War. Indeed, we might even go so far as to say that the Civil War had been written years before it was actually fought—written in the form of essays like Henry C. Wright's essay "Battle-Field, or Ballot Box" (1842), which suggested that legal emancipation would involve violence no less destructive than slavery itself; and in the form of speeches such as the Lyceum Address, which constituted a "startlingly prophetic" vision, in Edmund Wilson's words, of the future emancipation in which Lincoln himself would play such a multivalent role;[45] and in the form of slave narratives such as *Incidents in the Life of Slave Girl,* which dramatized the enormous difficulty of sorting out human rights from constitutional rights in a post-slavery society. Given the strange alliance between civil and literary vocabularies in these prophetic works, we might even go further and say that the war itself should be understood as a kind of writing, as a part of the work of Emerson's poet or Lincoln's storyteller. It is for this reason, perhaps, that we often miss the complex intellectual work being done in the Fourteenth Amendment: we imagine that that work had already been done by the war itself. An effective history of American literature's engagement with the Civil War requires a detailed excavation of this work and a thorough survey of the terrain—legal, literary, philosophical, even military—on which it took place.

Any reading of the written Civil War must build upon the extensive and challenging body of scholarship that has emerged over the last twenty years around the relationship between legal and literary practices in antebellum America. But that scholarship can be as misleading as it is useful, and it is especially misleading with respect to two particular historical relationships—one having to do with legal authority's relationship to literary practice, the other having to do with its relationship to racial progress. Literary historians have tended to see literary and legal activities as diverging, not converging, in the immediate antebellum period. In his seminal history of the relationship between law and literature in American culture, Robert Ferguson suggested that the political landscape of the early United States was marked by a "configuration of law and letters" which was ruptured by legal and literary developments of the mid-nineteenth century. On his account, indeed, the American Renaissance was constituted in large part by its refusal to engage legal considerations on their own terms. "The new aesthetic of the American Renaissance," he explained, "excludes the legal mind from the literary enterprise."[46] For a generation now scholars have wrestled with Ferguson's argument, and important work by literary historians such as Wai Chee Dimock, Brook Thomas, Gregg Crane, and Priscilla Wald has qualified his position without overturning it altogether. If literature is not "excluded" altogether from the legal mind in the American Renaissance, it remains basically incompatible with it. In the most significant, subtle, and insightful reexamination of Ferguson's position, for instance, Thomas claims that in the 1850s the literary quest for "the universal values" an earlier generation might have "sought in law" entailed "challenging the legal mind, instead of appealing to it."[47]

What powers this sense of literature's opposition to, or distance from, "the legal mind" in the 1850s is the notion that the practice of law became increasingly technical and formal throughout the course of the nineteenth century. As Ferguson puts the point, "Technical competence triumphed over general learning and philosophical discourse as case law accumulated."[48] But this hard and fast distinction between technical competence and philosophical discourse seems as out of place in the world of the 1860s as it would have been in the world of the 1820s. Technical competence was no doubt triumphing at the level of the actual practice of the law at midcentury, but it was not triumphing, or at least not triumphing so clearly, at the level of the way that the law was understood. At least one of the main developments in antebellum American constitutional thinking actually revolved around the task of locating natural law notions of moral justice within America's legal code. The trajectory of this development was to fuse the "universal values" Thomas suggests literature had to find in sources other than law with the positivist legal thinking he suggests excluded them. Rather than abandoning moral and aesthetic concerns in pursuit of autonomous legal forms, the figures who developed the legal thinking ultimately established in the Fourteenth Amendment sought to open formal law up to them. Indeed, as we have already begun to see, the great achievement of that amendment was precisely its capacity to fuse moral, aesthetic, and technical orders of law.

The point here is not simply that Bingham and others were able to give higher law principles positive law form, that they were able to attach human values to a legal order whose formal structure would otherwise exclude them. The fusion effected by the Fourteenth Amendment goes far beyond what Gregg Crane has recently called "higher law constitutionalism."[49] While Crane's higher law constitutionalism is defined chiefly by its hostility to positive law traditions, the most powerful forms of higher law thinking in the antebellum period are themselves highly positivist. The projects that culminated in the Fourteenth Amendment are not projects to invoke a law higher than the Constitution but, instead, projects to locate higher law *within* the Constitution and to codify and enforce the higher law that already inhabits it. In Crane's hands higher law constitutionalism has almost no actual constitutional form; it is as much the thinking of Garrison as of Lincoln. But the higher law constitutionalism of the Reconstruction Amendments is exactly balanced between the appeal of the higher law and the appeal of positive law, between Thomas's universal values and Ferguson's technical competence.

Part of the reason Crane casts his higher constitutionalism in such antiformalist hues is that he implicitly posits an adversarial relationship between positive law and racial justice. In Crane's hands positive law is unfailingly aligned with "such power-based conceptions as slavery and Jim Crow, which attribute the possession of power to a natural or divinely inscribed racial inheritance." The notion that higher law arguments work to "transcend the provincialisms of sect, tribe, and nation" should strike the nineteenth-century historian as oddly one-sided:[50] as Eric Sundquist and others have pointed out, the "natural" in natural law could legitimize claims based on "inscribed" racial characteristics as well as invite more enlightened challenges to such claims.[51] And, as we will see in later chapters, some of Crane's chief examples of legal positivism, such as Taney's opinion in *Dred Scott v. Sandford*,[52] might more accurately be described as expressions of what Fehrenbacher has called "a southern version of higher law" than as expressions of "technical" legal reasoning.[53] But Crane's insistence upon an antithetical relationship between African-American civil rights and positive law is hardly unconventional. The historiography of nineteenth-century civil rights has been decidedly Garrisonian in its orientation.[54] Cultural historians have not merely stressed that the actual practice of nineteenth-century law involved the suppression of black civil rights; they have also expressed intense, if implicit, skepticism that nineteenth-century legal activity could have done anything else.[55] In addition to noting that "the likely operation of law and of race politics in America" would give "no easy quarter to the rights of black freedom," for instance, Sundquist also intimates that "clear enunciations of African American rights" were importantly alien even to "the very notion of the law of nature" in the period. It is for this reason that he can conflate "the mechanics of repression" with the "repressive mechanisms of justice": Garrison's law of love is ultimately no different from Calhoun's law of force. The pursuit of justice in the period does not distinguish repression from the legitimate workings of a body politic; it instead constitutes repression.[56]

Among accounts of nineteenth-century racial politics Sundquist's argument represents an extreme instance of the commitment to an opposition between racial justice and legal thinking. But it is extreme in its commitment to the opposition, not in its invoking it in the first instance. The opposition persists even in the work of those political historians, such as Eric Foner and David Herbert Donald, who are committed to understanding the emergence of a nonrevolutionary politics of antislavery in the 1850s as the outgrowth of an intellectually coherent political project rather than a pragmatist capitulation to the reigning mechanisms of repression.[57] And it also persists even in the work of those literary historians, such as Priscilla Wald, who emphasize what Wald calls "the contingency of personhood upon the law."[58] These scholars represent the very best of nineteenth-century American cultural and political history, but the opposition they posit between civil rights and the agency of the law, whatever its philosophical appeal, merits serious historical reconsideration. At the very least, recent scholarship has tended to overlook the changing relations between positive law and moral claims on behalf of civil rights in the immediate antebellum period. Garrison attacked the law and slavery with equal relish; Bingham celebrated civil rights and the Constitution with equal relish. Until we recognize this shift, and until we come to grips with the ways in which it came to pass, our histories of nineteenth-century emancipation will remain significantly incomplete.[59]

CHAPTER ONE

Victory of LAW

Melville and Reconstruction

Herman Melville famously attached a "Supplement" to *Battle-Pieces and Aspects of the War* (1866) in which he explained that he hoped the volume, among other things, would make a contribution to what he called "just thoughts" about the legal terms on which the "re-establishment" of the Southern states should take place.[1] He hardly needed to articulate this ambition in such explicit terms. From the second line of the volume's opening poem ("The Portent [1859.]"), which refers to the troubling legal status of John Brown's execution, to the penultimate stanza of its final poem, which ponders the force of the claim that "'*The South's the sinner!*'" (243), *Battle-Pieces* repeatedly presents itself as a meditation on the legal implications of the Civil War and Reconstruction. Nor would his prospective audience have needed any warning to pick up on these dimensions of the poems. In 1866, the year the Fourteenth Amendment was proposed by Congress and the year after the Thirteenth Amendment was declared officially ratified by the secretary of state,[2] Melville was alone neither in thinking about the politics of the Civil War and Reconstruction nor in articulating his thoughts about these matters in terms of the status of the law.

But despite the poems' obvious concern with legal issues, and despite the prominence of legal debates in the historical context out of which they emerge, most commentators have been reluctant to account for *Battle-Pieces* in terms of its examination of the legal crisis precipitated by the Civil War. They have tended, instead, to understand the poems in terms of their capacity to capture the tangible horror of the battles they describe or in terms of their relationships the various verse forms they assume.[3] In this chapter I will take *Battle-Pieces* up more or less in the legal terms in which it presents itself;[4] I will approach the volume, that is, chiefly by way of its interest in the contemporary debate about the legal grounds on which the Civil War was fought and the Reconstruction should proceed.[5] There are good reasons for focusing on those matters that have absorbed most of the critical attention *Battle-Pieces* has drawn, and by paying careful attention to the way in which the poems represent the idea of law I will not leave them behind so much as cast them in a new light. But a proper consideration of their relationship to Melville's larger project can take place only after we have narrowed our focus to the somewhat more local problem of what counts as the law in the poems.

This careful engagement with the idea of law in the poems, I submit, will lead us to revise the conventional accounts of both the legal dynamics of Reconstruction and Melville's politics in his later years. Legal theorist and historian Bruce Ackerman has recently claimed that the ratification of the Civil War amendments presents the historian with a series of "legal dilemmas" and "paradoxes" that have been "repressed" and "ignored" by the nation's lawyers, judges, and law professors and to which the "last generation" of Reconstruction historians "has . . . turned a blind eye."[6] These paradoxes and dilemmas derive largely from the liminality of Southern states after the war, from the strange way in which the task of Reconstruction required that the Southern states be imagined both as integral parts of the Union's lawmaking authority and as wholly subject to that authority. Ackerman points out that at the same time that the participation of reconstructed Southern states was necessary to the ultimate passage of the Thirteenth Amendment,[7] their representatives were denied the power to join in the congressional deliberations that led to the proposal of the Fourteenth Amendment. It would seem, he explains, that a legal scholar cannot "successfully vindicate[] the authority of the Thirty-ninth Congress to propose the Fourteenth Amendment . . . in a way that saves the Thirteenth Amendment" from charges of illegitimacy.[8]

Battle-Pieces does not address post–Civil War legal issues chiefly in terms of the relationship between the first two Reconstruction Amendments, but it is devoted, I will argue, to the exposure and evaluation of those largely unacknowledged paradoxes and dilemmas produced by the uncertain legal relations between Southern states and the Union, by the way in which the Civil War raised what Abraham Lincoln would call "the question of whether the seceded States, so called, are in the Union or out of it" as much as it answered it.[9] Both contemporaneous actors and contemporary historians have a tendency to dismiss this "question" as a philosophical conundrum largely irrelevant to the larger questions of how the political crisis brought on by the War should be brought to its resolution. Lincoln himself called it a "pernicious abstraction" (2:699). *Battle-Pieces* will begin to indicate, however, that these questions have been more "repressed" than "ignored" and that the instrument that has allowed them to be repressed is the idea of the law. Melville's Civil War poetry reveals the ways in which the very project of Reconstruction *required* that Southern states assume the "chameleon" form that Ackerman suggests might be so troublesome.[10] It also explains exactly how a political project based on such a paradox might be sustained.

Ackerman's goal is to describe how the Thirteenth and Fourteenth amendments came to be seen as credible and fundamental features of the nation's constitutional order (and to make clear exactly why we should honor their authority today). Melville, on the other hand, works to specify exactly how the dilemmas and paradoxes that might make the amendments' legal status problematic could become central to American politics in the first instance. Ackerman is interested in dispelling the paradoxes he uncovers, Melville in providing their genealogy. So while Ackerman explains how the law might survive the problems generated by the uncertain status of Southern states, Melville actually argues that it is in fact the law itself that allows the Southern states to become chameleons. *Battle-Pieces* dwells on the law's capacity to be inflected in a number of registers, its capacity to receive its content from domains of either political or moral authority. The volume indicates that this dual quality makes the law uniquely suited to the task of suturing together the potentially incompatible Reconstruction projects of restoring the Union (the positive law solution to the problem of secession which required that Southern states count as part of the Union) and re-forming the South (the higher law solution to the problem of slavery which required that Southern states be seen as subject to the Union). The duality of the South's relationship to the Union, as it were, is made intelligible by the duality inherent in the law itself. Paradox and the law are not antithetical forces in *Battle-Pieces;* they are, instead, functionally codependent. The law emerges as politically important precisely because it makes paradox politically viable.

If *Battle-Pieces* will help us bring both the structural dilemmas implicit in Reconstruction and the law's role in preventing them from disabling it into clearer focus, the history of the legal status of Reconstruction will help us clarify the relationship between Melville's poetry and his earlier work. *Battle-Pieces* accounts for the ways in which the law can be mobilized to link together the projects of emancipation and Union, but it does not exactly perform such a mobilization itself. Analogizing the relationship between positive and natural law to the highly awkward relationship between his poems' formal aspirations and their actual content, Melville registers the gap between the just and the lawful with every bit as much force as he registers our tendency to articulate them in terms of one another. In *Battle-Pieces* the law constitutes a functional solution to the dilemmas Reconstruction poses, not a philosophical one. Commentators have generally understood *Battle-Pieces* to mark what Michael Rogin has called Melville's "imaginative rapprochement" with the "authority" of "the state." On this account the Civil War poems signal the emergence of a conservative Melville, one, unlike the author of *White-Jacket; or, The World in a Man-of-War* (1850) and *The Confidence Man: His Masquerade* (1857), wedded to the law's "power to endure and command loyalty."[11] It is certainly the case that law is valorized in *Battle-*

Pieces in ways that have no obvious precedent in Melville's earlier work. It is hard to think, for instance, that the words "Wise Draco" could have appeared in an even remotely unironic context in the earlier fictions, for instance (87), and it is equally hard to imagine the author of such generically unstable works as *Pierre; or, The Ambiguities* (1852) and *Moby-Dick; or, The Whale* (1851) restricting himself to formal rhyme schemes.

But Melville's embrace of the law and celebration of its capacity to inspire loyalty takes place only after the law has become something sufficiently plural as to make the force of its appeal somewhat ambiguous. When we say that we are for "the law" in 1866, are we for Radical Reconstruction (the reform of the South) or presidential restoration (the reincorporation of the South)? *Battle-Pieces* works chiefly to reveal the extent to which a commitment to the law in and of itself cannot distinguish the two forms of Reconstruction from one another. Indeed, it seeks to reveal that it is the very fact that a commitment to the law cannot distinguish the two positions which makes a commitment to law the animating principle of the Union "Cause." Melville's newfound legalism does not represent a retreat from his previous interest in unstable characters and insoluble questions. It is, instead, an extension of it: the law's relationship to God in *Battle-Pieces* is no clearer than the whale's relationship to Him in *Moby-Dick*. And likewise, Melville's newfound commitment to operating in relation to, if not exactly within, the laws of poetic form does not constitute a departure from the legal skepticism coursing through his formally expansive fictions so much as an embodiment of it. By paying careful attention to the way in which the law emerges as a kind of Melvillian figure in the Reconstruction era, we will begin to get a better grasp on what structures the transformations of both American law and Melville's literary practice in the 1860s.

The Crime of Secession

Toward the end of the short poem "Dupont's Round Fight (November, 1861)" Melville explains:

> The rebel at Port Royal felt
> The Unity overawe,
> And rued the spell. A type was here,
> And victory of LAW.   (30)

This suggestion that victories of "The Unity" count as victories of "LAW" recurs throughout *Battle-Pieces*. The cause of the North is repeatedly described in terms of the law. The defeat of the South provides the occasion, we learn in "Lee in the Capitol," the volume's penultimate poem, for "re-established law" (235). When a personi-fied America emerges at the end of the war in "America," the final poem of the vol-ume's first section, she emerges with "Law on her brow" (162). And if the North up-holds, reestablishes, and embodies the law in *Battle-Pieces*, the South is frequently described in terms of its inability to pay legal authorities the proper respect. "Armies of the Wilderness (1863–64)" stresses ways in which the legal has ceased to be an op-erative category among Southern soldiers, who,

In court-houses stable their steeds—
Kindle their fires with indentures and bonds,
And old Lord Fairfax's parchment deeds.   (98)

Indentures, bonds, and deeds are reduced to mere "parchment" in the seceded South. The courthouse stands as merely a dwelling like any other. While Southern court-houses count merely as military facilities, Northern military activity itself counts as a kind of law-giving. Not only is its ultimate effect the reestablishment of laws, but it also expresses the law in its practical operations. In "The Swamp Angel," for instance, Melville claims that a Northern gun "dooms by a far decree" (107). *Battle-Pieces* seems to make the difference between the North and South revolve around their respective relationships to the law: on the one hand we have a population wholly removed from the legal as a category (their courthouses having become military stations), on the other a population wholly immersed within it (their bombs having become legal de-clarations).

Of course, the argument that the Union's cause in the Civil War was the cause of "LAW" already had a long pedigree by the time Melville came to make it in 1866, and with good reason. What makes the "rebel" a rebel, after all, as opposed to a Confed-erate or a Southerner or a Georgian, is precisely that he has rejected the law, that, to deploy the terminology of Justice Grier in his majority opinion in *Prize Cases* (1863), he is a "*traitor*[]" as well as an "*enem*[*y*]."[12] When Abraham Lincoln issued his Procla-mation Calling Militia and Convening Congress on April 15, 1861, he cast his war aims largely in terms of the maintenance of the law. Since "the laws of the United States have been for some time past, and are now opposed, and the execution thereof ob-structed" in Southern states, Lincoln "call[ed] forth [] the militia of the several States of the Union . . . to cause the laws to be duly executed" (2:232). The Civil War, on this account, stands as a war between lawbreakers and law maintainers. It stands as a po-lice action.

There are a number of problems with this account, however, the most notable being that it is hard to think that the various people in the South who advocated, effected, and acquiesced in "secession" thought of their actions chiefly as a kind of treason. Lincoln himself would acknowledge as much in the message he delivered to the special session of Congress he summoned at the same time he called troops forth to "cause the laws to be duly executed." "It might seem, at first thought, to be of little difference whether the present movement in the South be called 'secession' or 'rebellion,'" he explained. "The movers, however, well understand the difference. At the beginning, they knew they could never raise their treason to any respectable magnitude, by any name which implies *violation* of the law. They knew their people possessed as much of moral sense, as much of devotion to law and order, and as much pride in, and reverence for, the history, and government, of their common country, as any other civilized, and patriotic people" (2:254–55). Leaving aside the conspiratorial dimensions of this claim,[13] it should be reasonably clear that Lincoln's ability, or desire, to attribute patriotism to precisely the people he wishes to call traitors begins to make the Civil War less a conflict between loyal and disloyal citizens than a conflict between two different accounts of citizenship. The problem is not that the Southerners have renounced their country but, rather, that they have a bad account of what that country is.[14] The problem is not that Southerners have abandoned the idea of the law (Lincoln himself will insist that they think a state may "*lawfully* . . . withdraw from the union" [2:255]) but, rather, that they have misunderstood it.

And as Southern "rebellion" comes to count as a rebellion against a particular account of the law rather than a rejection of the law as such, the Civil War comes to look less like a police action than a trial. "What is now combated," Lincoln explained in his special message to Congress, "is the position that secession is *consistent* with the Constitution—is *lawful,* and *peaceful*" (2:257). "Several of these States have combined to form a new confederacy, claiming to be acknowledged by the world as a sovereign State," Grier maintained in the *Prize Cases.* "Their right to do so is now being decided by wager of battle" (673). In these moments, tellingly, neither Lincoln nor Grier represents the Southern states as unlawful; they represent them as *allegedly* unlawful. They do not insist that states do not have the legal right to secede; they suggest that that right has yet to be fully adjudicated. The issue for both of them is less whether the Southern states will get away with their unlawful activity than whether that activity is actually unlawful. Grier would eventually go so far as to insist that the only adjudication the question of Southern secession can receive is a military one. After the war, in *Texas v. White* (1869),[15] when the Supreme Court finally held that secession is unconstitutional, Grier would insist in a dissent that the war itself, not the Court, had ruled against the constitutionality of secession. The state of Texas's decision to secede, he explains, "was the sovereign act of a sovereign State, and the verdict on the trial of this question, 'by battle,' as to her right to secede, has been against her" (740). The victory of the North, from this vantage, does not count as the execution of the law so much as the generation of it. And it thus stands as a legal resolution that does not bear any relationship to the relative *legal* merits of the dispute in question: the point of Grier's interest in making the war a trial is to avoid making a strictly legal determination about secession, which is why he makes the notion of trial "by battle" a colloquial expression that he merely quotes rather than a legal expression that he endorses. The war, from this perspective, settles and displaces legal questions, but it does not decide them.

Battle-Pieces carefully registers the ways in which the Union's claim to the mantle of the law might be compromised by Southern assertions of an alternative legal order. Not all of the poems are content to represent Northern victories as victories of "LAW" or to depict Southern soldiers as essentially heedless of legal authority. "Armies of the Wilderness (1863–64)," for instance, consists of a second voice in addition to the one I quoted earlier. At the beginning of the poem we encounter the two voices in a kind of contrapuntal dialog, the one I have already quoted insisting, as we might expect, that Southern soldiers were "The zealots of the Wrong," the other responding:

> *In this strife of brothers*
> *(God, hear their country call),*
> *However it be, whatever betide,*
> *Let not the just one fall.*   (93)

The point here, it would seem, is to issue a prayer on behalf of the North, on behalf of those with "faith" in something other than "the Wrong." But insofar as this voice is marked as separate from the voice that issues the easy condemnation, and insofar as it invokes God on behalf of a set of entities (their country, the just one) whose relationship to the parties would seem to be what the battle would decide rather than something that had been decided before it, it ultimately becomes very hard to understand for whom this prayer is issued. An appeal to the "country" of the "just one," after all, does fairly little to isolate one side from the other: the conflict, at least from the perspective of Lincoln and Grier, is over what will count as the "country" and "the just one"; it is not simply between the country and justice on the one side and something else on the other. And while we might imagine that the speaker's reference to "their" country would move in the direction of his making an appeal for the Northern troops, this tendency would seem to work against the way in which pronouns are used throughout the poem.[16] In the first stanza it is the Southern troops, not the Northern ones, who stand as a "they," and in the next stanza we will encounter Northern soldiers in the form of an "our." The sequence's ambiguity is further enhanced by its open admission of its uncertainty, its invoking a "whatever" and a "however" in its plea, and by its refusal to designate the "just one." The passage seems to stand for a principle (just ones should win), not a side—indeed, insofar as it stands for a principle, it seems to renounce its capacity to stand for a side.

Even as the poems gesture in the direction of understanding the war in terms of its restoration of the law, they begin to suggest that "the law" that is being restored counts only as one legal realm out of several. In "Lee in the Capitol," for instance, we learn that many Southern soldiers understand the war to have imposed Northern law instead of restoring American law: "some distrust your law," the general explains (232). Lee himself is far more generous than his cohorts. He suggests that the war's "reestablished law" could count as a "sound core" for the restoration of national unity. But the poem itself understands the end of the war in the skeptical terms of Lee's army, not the accommodating terms of their general. At the beginning of the poem we learn that Lee "His doom accepts, perforce content, / And acquiesces in asserted laws" (229). The war here seems merely to "assert" laws rather than restore them; or if it restores them, it does so only by asserting them, not by producing a general awareness of their inherent lawfulness.[17] Lee is "content" in the new order of things, from this perspective, less because he has come to recognize that he was "wrong" than because the Union's "force" has overwhelmed him.

In this regard we might suggest that *Battle-Pieces* repeatedly connects the end of the war with the reestablishment of law precisely by way of denying the law that is reestablished at least part of its legal authority. If, as we learn in the inscriptive or memorial verse "Presentation to the Authorities: by Privates, of Colors captured in Battles ending in the Surrender of Lee," the effect of the war was to allow Northern troops to "go / To waiting homes with vindicated laws" (182), we are also repeatedly reminded that it is force, and force alone, which allows for such a sense of vindication. As Melville explains at the close of "The Fall of Richmond: tidings received in a Northern Metropolis (April, 1865)":

Well that the faith we firmly kept,
And never our aim foreswore
For the Terrors that trooped from each recess
When fainting we fought in the Wilderness,
And Hell made loud hurrah;
But God is in Heaven, and Grant in the Town,
And Right through might is Law—
God's way adore.

(136)

"Might" emerges here as the chief vehicle of "Law," and as we think of "might" as making Law, we come to revise our initial understanding of what it means for the speaker to claim that "God is in Heaven, and Grant in the Town." At first glance we might be inclined to read the line as affirming the inevitable power of right in the world. We might take it to mean that it is precisely because God is in Heaven that Grant is in the town. But by the end of the sequence it seems less that Melville wishes to assert a causal connection between the two facts than that he wishes to insist upon the difference between earthly and heavenly domains of law: God's domain is in heaven, Grant's is in the town. The good news is that the "loud hurrah" Hell might make is irrelevant to the Law on earth, where might will rule; the bad news is that what makes it irrelevant is not God but Grant's earthly power. Hence, the weirdly hyperbolic italicized command to "*God's way adore.*" By the end of the poem it is not entirely clear why we would adore God's way or even why we would think that it was remotely relevant to Grant's victory. Why, after all, should a demonstration of the force of might on earth be an occasion for religious celebration? But the poem's refusal to demonstrate God's value goes hand in hand with its having to tell us that we should adore Him. As the poem makes us revise our sense of God's way, as it makes us think that that way revolves less around producing heavenly law on earth than allowing the laws of the two places to remain distinct, it forces us to encounter a divine way that we will have to be told to adore.

This relativizing drive in *Battle-Pieces* exposes the inherent tension in understanding a war as a trial. In his majority opinion in the *Prize Cases* Grier defines war in precisely the terms that emerge in "The Fall of Richmond." War, he explains, is "that state in which a nation prosecutes its right by force" (666). But the idea that the Union prosecuted its right by force during the Civil War seems only to raise the question of why it did not prosecute its right by more conventional trials. Why was the war not conceived as the police activity necessary in order to begin the trial of those who had violated the law, rather than being described as secession's trial in and of itself?[18] The replacement of the court of law by the battle of law would seem to announce the collapse of the legal order rather than a vindication of it. Insofar as we understand Southern secession to be devoted to the project of making Union law inapplicable in some places, the very fact that Southern secession ever comes to count as a thing against which the state will have to wage what, in his annual message to Congress in 1862, Lincoln called "civil war" means that the South will have succeeded (2:393): efforts to overcome secession will operate at least partially in terms of the abeyance of the very law from which the seceders wished to escape.

And if the fact that the Southern rebellion presented itself as a secession rather than a rebellion worked to compromise the notion that the war revolved simply around the maintenance of the law, the fact that the prosecution of the war effort led the Union into awkward relationships with the very constitutional order it claimed to be defending ultimately made the notion seem entirely far-fetched. The problem with identifying the Union with the law was not simply that secession had the effect of relativizing the very laws the Union wished to claim were absolute; it was also that the Union's response to secession had the effect of leading the Union itself into a posture that, at least from the perspective of many prominent contemporary legal scholars, was itself unconstitutional. The most awkward of these awkward postures, of course, had to do with Lincoln's decisions to suspend habeas corpus, first along the military line between Philadelphia and Washington (on April 27, 1861) and then throughout the nation (on September 24, 1862)[19]—decisions that, as Chief Justice of the Supreme Court Roger Taney explained in his review of the 1861 decree while riding circuit in Baltimore in *Ex Parte Merryman* (1861), "thrust aside the judicial authorities and officers to whom the constitution has confided power and duty of interpreting and administering laws, and substituted military government in its place, to be administered and executed by military officers."[20]

The notion that Lincoln's prosecution of the war itself represented a revolution against the nation's legal order was hardly confined to Democrats and conservatives such as Taney. As late as the late summer of 1861, an abolitionist no less radical than Wendell Phillips was willing to declare Lincoln's administration a "fearful peril to democratic institutions," and Joel Parker (at the time a law professor at Harvard) was willing to claim it had become "an absolute, . . . uncontrollable government, a perfect military despotism."[21] Nor was Lincoln himself unwilling to admit that his efforts to save Union might come at the expense of some of the provisions of the Constitution in which he imagined it to be consecrated. In his special message to Congress in 1861 he insisted that the issue of the war "embraces more than the fate of these United States. It presents to the whole family of man, the question whether a constitutional republic, or a democracy—a government of the people, by the same people—can, or cannot, maintain its territorial integrity, against its own domestic foes." "Must a government," he continued, "be too *strong* for the liberties of its own people, or too *weak* to maintain its own existence?" (2:250).

The problem here is that there might be a deep tension between the republican and constitutional parts of a "constitutional republic" and that republic's capacity to maintain its "territorial integrity." And given the dilemma, Lincoln chose to side with territorial integrity instead of legal integrity. At various moments Lincoln almost seemed willing to acknowledge that his suspension of habeas corpus was unconstitutional, that the only thing that would make it lawful was the fact that without it there would be no legal order whatsoever: "I felt that measures, otherwise unconstitutional, might become lawful, by becoming indispensable to the preservation of the constitution, through the preservation of the nation" (2:251). At other times Lincoln seemed more interested in defending his decision to suspend habeas corpus than excusing it, and he produced a number of impassioned defenses of the legality of his actions.[22]

But even as he produced these defenses, he repeatedly acknowledged that he was entering controversial constitutional terrain. His arguments tended to hinge on the claim that narrow constitutional considerations were not exactly relevant to the proper evaluation of executive decisions in wartime, not that the suspension of habeas corpus was clearly a matter of the president's prerogative. As he explained in his special message to Congress in 1861, with the Constitution under assault by secession, it seemed odd to worry so much about the legality of those actions that are devoted to preserving it. "Are all the laws," he queried, "*but one,* to go unexecuted, and the government itself go to pieces, lest that one be violated?" (2:253).

Lincoln's suggestion that the suspension of habeas corpus counts simply as the violation of "one" law like any other is somewhat disingenuous. The right of habeas corpus is precisely the right to be subject to the law rather than more arbitrary forms of coercion. Suspending habeas corpus may or not have been a legal mistake, but whether or not Lincoln had the legal right to do it, the suspension, as Taney's objection had already made clear, had the effect of suspending the law itself. To put it slightly differently, war might be a lawful activity, but regardless of the state's legal right to engage in it, it seems to be an activity that suspends the ordinary mechanisms of the law. And indeed, two of the most important sets of decisions in the immediate Reconstruction period revolved around restoring the judicial branch to its status as the arbiter of the law.[23] Consider *Ex Parte Milligan* (1866), a case that revolved around the constitutionality of a death sentence imposed on a civilian (Milligan) by a military court in Indiana. "The Constitution of the United States," Justice David Davis began his famous majority opinion, "is a law for rulers and people, equally in war and peace, and covers with the shield of its protection all classes of men, at all times, and under all circumstances. No doctrine, involving more pernicious consequences, was ever invented by the writ of man than that any of its provisions may be suspended during any of the great exigencies of government."[24] Johnson thought of Reconstruction largely in terms of the restoration of national law in the former South. "The full assertion of the powers of the General Government," he explained in his first inaugural address, "requires the holding of circuit courts of the United States within the districts where their authority has been interrupted" (2045). Cases such as *Ex Parte Milligan* suggest that these districts were not merely Southern districts and that the force that interrupted their authority could be the Union army as much as the Confederate one. The fact that Northern guns count as "decrees" can mark either the Union's immersion within the law or its need to be returned to it.

Nor was the Union army the only obstacle to the operation of the law after the war. The Congress and Northern state legislatures themselves also served a similar function—or so at least the Court claimed in two decisions it rendered in 1867. In the so-called Test Oath cases (*Cummings v. Missouri* and *Ex Parte Garland*) the Court declared unconstitutional both federal and state requirements that citizens seeking to carry on specified professions (providing religious and legal counsel) subscribe to an oath that they had never given aid to the rebellion.[25] There are a number of ways in which the Court might have approached the constitutional problems posed by these laws, but Justice Field's majority opinions cast the issue in question in terms of the constitutional relationship between legislative and legal authority.[26] Since disqualification from an occupation was a traditional punishment for a crime, he reasoned, the laws requiring the oaths in effect constituted ex post facto laws and bills of attainder, each of which is prohibited under Article I of the Constitution. The requirement that one swear an oath to take up some public duty, however, is hardly a textbook example of either of the two proscribed kinds of legislation (ex post facto laws seek to punish persons for acts unlawful at the time of their performance; bills of attainder are acts of legislative punishment usually, Justice Miller pointed out in his dissent, directed at a specific individual and imposing death upon him). And consequently, in order to make the oath requirements under consideration plausibly fall within the class of laws proscribed by the Constitution, Field felt compelled not only to invoke the Constitution's prohibitions of ex post facto legislation and bills of attainder but also to provide an account of their purpose and rationale. Bills of attainder and ex post fact legislation, he explained, both revolve around the replacement of the judiciary by the legislature. Each constitutes "a legislative act which inflicts punishment without a judicial trial," a moment in which "the legislative body, in addition to its legitimate functions, exercises the powers and office of judge" (323). Relief from test oaths here stands as a guarantee of the law itself, of "judicial trials" rather than political ones. The war's having been a kind of trial once seemed to endow the North's victory with a legal content. *Ex Parte Milligan* and the Test Oath cases cast the decreeing Northern army in a wholly different light. They would deprive the North's victory, on the battlefield and in the legislative halls rather than before a "legitimate" judge, of its legal content. The war devoted to the restoration of the law has itself generated a need for the law to be restored.[27]

The Crime of Slavery

Not everyone involved in the Union cause accepted the Supreme Court's arguments about the lawfulness of these prominent Reconstruction measures, of course. The Test Oath cases were decided by a pure party line vote, and in *Ex Parte Milligan* only one Republican joined the majority opinion. For many Northerners the Court itself was what had betrayed the law, not the military tribunal that sentenced Milligan to death or the congresses of Missouri and the United States which attempted to prevent people like him from being able to follow certain professions. Hence, for instance, John Jay Jr. would write to Chief Justice Chase: "I cannot yet consent to believe that we are brought into this dilemma—& that appointees of Mr. Lincoln are ready to imitate the Late Chief Justice in making the Court the chief support of the advocates of Slavery & the Rebellion," and the *Alton Telegraph* would insist that "one thing is certain . . . and that is that the American people have determined to preserve our free institutions, the unity of the states, and the free rights of men, and . . . the Supreme Court will [not] long be permitted to stand in the way of these great ends."[28] In calling these decisions Dred Scott II and III,[29] the Northern press committed itself to the unlawfulness of the judiciary rather than acquiescing in the judiciary's claim about the legal problems implicit in executive and legislative usurpations of judicial authority.

From this perspective we might become more sensitive to the ways in which at least one dimension of the Union cause was wedded to a critique of American law rather than a commitment to its continued operation. I am thinking, of course, about the legal history of abolition, a history, as it is usually understood, which revolved around a hostile relationship to American legal authority. As Robert M. Cover has famously demonstrated in *Justice Accused* (1975), antislavery jurists such as Lemuel Shaw, John McLean, and Francis Lieber constantly worked through the dilemma presented by the fact that their political and moral commitments stood opposed to a law they felt obliged to enforce; they repeatedly found themselves subordinating their consciences to what they took to be the law's demands. "We look to the law and only the law," McLean explained. "In these matters, the law, and not conscience, constitutes the rule of action." Or as Lieber put the point, "Not I but the law, which is given to me, and which is my master says this."[30] On this account freedom bears an antithetical relationship to the law in two ways: the law calls for pro-slavery activity (in the various allowances to slavery made in the Constitution and various state statutes), and it enslaves the judges who are required to enforce it ("my master"). And the Civil War is therefore valuable precisely because it suspends the law, because it provides a moment in which "conscience" and antislavery sentiment can be operative. Thaddeus Stevens welcomed Reconstruction, for example, precisely because of the legal instability that came with it. "In my youth, in my manhood, in my old age," he explained in announcing his decision to vote for the Fourteenth Amendment, "I had fondly dreamed that [some] fortunate chance should have broken up for awhile the foundation of our institutions, and released us from obligations the most tyrannical that man ever imposed in the name of freedom."[31]

It would not exactly be fair to say, however, that when the antislavery adherents welcomed the war's having broken up "for awhile the foundation of our institutions" they were actually welcoming the repeal of law itself. Indeed, it would make more sense to suggest that they thought that breaking up the nation's formal legal institutions instead afforded the nation an opportunity to better align itself with a more substantial law than what had previously bound judges. McLean's decision to follow what he called "the law" involved his setting aside not only his "conscience" but also "the immutable principles of right" and, most crucially, "the law of nature."[32] What initially looks like a tension between the Union's commitment to law and the Union's celebration of anarchy might be redescribed as a tension between the Union's simultaneous commitment to two different kinds of law, its simultaneous commitment, to deploy terms from an 1845 decision by Judge Read of Ohio, to "positive laws and institutions" and to higher law "principles of natural justice and right."[33] If at first it looks like a problem that the Union seems completely willing to violate the legal order it claims it wishes to maintain, we can now see that the problem has less to do with the Union's hypocrisy than with the fact that it was committed to different kinds of law whose ends do not always overlap.

These two commitments structure and make intelligible the very project of Reconstruction. Simply put, were the Union to excise the "crime" to which it was wedded in the sense of detaching itself from the South's slavery, the Civil War would produce nothing to reconstruct, only, as Thaddeus Stevens would put it, "conquered territory."[34] And likewise, were Southern states understood simply in terms of the crime of secession there would be no need to reconstruct them, only a need, as Johnson was fond of insisting, to "restore" their relations to the nation (2044). We might say that Reconstruction is nothing more than the name we give to the effort to reconcile these essentially incompatible visions of the post-secession nation. And we might further say that proper accounts of crucial Reconstruction measures such as the 1866 Civil Rights Act and the Fourteenth Amendment must begin by addressing the ways in which they sought to effect such a reconciliation. In the introduction I provided an outline of how we might understand the Fourteenth Amendment in these terms, and in later chapters I will flesh out that outline in considerable detail. Before turning to the larger issue of the Fourteenth Amendment, however, I would like to devote the remainder of this chapter to the small portion of the overall problem that Melville engages most intensely in the *Battle-Pieces*—namely, that the North's simultaneous commitment to two separate orders of law has the effect of producing two separate, and two potentially incompatible, accounts of exactly what crime the South may be said to have committed in the early 1860s; and that as a consequence the precise relationship between the South and the Union becomes essentially and inherently unstable.

Another way of making the point I have been driving at over the last several pages is to say that while the Union's two chief war aims—unity and emancipation—can both be articulated in terms of a defense of the law, neither of the two actually makes very much sense in terms of the legal order that makes the defense of the other intelligible. Melville casts this point in stark form in the second poem of *Battle Pieces*, "Misgivings (1860)," by describing what he calls "my country" as "the World's fairest hope linked with man's foulest crime" (13). Here the South emerges in the context of both the criminal and the "linking" that undergirds the idea of the Union. But the crime of which the South seems guilty is not exactly the crime of treason, and the role the war plays in regard to this Union is not exactly to restore it. If we understand the South's "crime" to be the crime of secession, it is easy enough to see how the war could revolve around "union" and the constitutional law that supports it. But as we begin to imagine that what separates the South from the North is the South's guilt with respect to the crime of slavery, rather than the crime of secession, it becomes increasingly hard to desire that the two halves be unified: why should we want to link man's fairest hope to his foulest crime? Or, to put the point slightly differently, as the South is understood chiefly in its relation to its slaves rather than the North, then the "unity" the War seeks to produce will revolve around changing the law, eliminating the crime of slavery from the nation's legal order (by protecting, in the words of the *Alton Telegraph*, "the free rights of men"), rather than enforcing it. It is as if by having slaves the South had already seceded from the moral order of the nation and by allowing slavery the nation's law had participated in the secession rather than stood as the ground of opposing it. The justice defended by a commitment to the Union is precisely the justice accused by a commitment to emancipation.

"It is enough," Melville writes in his "Supplement," "for all practical purposes, if the South have been taught by the terrors of civil war to feel the Secession, like Slavery, is against Destiny; that both now lie buried in one grave; that her fate is linked with ours; and that together we comprise the Nation" (260). So long as secession and slavery are seen as inextricably linked, as they are here, there is little difficulty in making the war's purposes look reasonably compatible. But what unites secession and slavery here, tellingly, is not their illegality but, rather, their incompatibility with the teleological narrative Melville thinks the war has just vindicated: destiny unites the causes in a way that a particular account of the law cannot. The rest of *Battle-Pieces* shows us what happens when destiny is not available to perform this service. The poems in the volume juxtapose the Union's two war aims only to distinguish them. They routinely hint at a connection between the nobility of the Union's "Cause" and "the laws," only eventually to reveal that connection to be wholly illusory. In "Inscription: for Graves at Pea Ridge, Arkansas," for instance,

Melville explains in the voice of one of the slain Union soldiers that death in the battle was:

> Better than tranquil plight,
> And tame surrender of the Cause
> Hallowed by hearts and by the laws.
> We here who warred for Man and Right,
> The choice of warring never laid with us.
> There we were ruled by the traitor's choice.   (166)

Here, at least at first, the "Cause" seems to be "hallowed . . . by the laws." But insofar as the speaker understands himself as warring "for Man and Right," he understands himself to be warring for precisely what McLean and others had insisted the law must bracket and ignore. And the poem itself seems to recognize as much when it goes on to make it look as though the relevant laws for the encounter between North and South are in fact produced by the South itself: "There we were ruled by the traitor's choice." On one account, of course, the North is compelled to fight here because the South revolted: they fight in order to vindicate or enforce the rule of Union law. But from the perspective of the ambivaience surrounding the idea of law in the early Reconstruction period, the North is compelled to "war" against the South not so much because of Southern treason as because the law itself seems to side with such "treason": one of the South's crimes, as it were, is legal. The conversion of secession into slaveholding becomes the movement from the law to the right, becomes the movement from upholding Northern law (union) to overcoming Southern law (slavery).

If before, say in Lincoln's special address of 1861, it seemed awkward that the South could look as though it were both seceding and rebelling, now we can see that this dual identity is in fact inevitable and fundamental to the Union's project in the Civil War. This duality allows the commitment to transform the law to look like a commitment to preserve it. Toward the end of the final poem of the first section of *Battle-Pieces,* "America," Melville produces an image of the personified nation, emerging from the gloom of the war, with "Law on her brow and empire in her eyes" (162). I have already quoted the first part of this image, and it should now seem as though it was deeply unfair and misleading of me to have omitted the second part at the time. The relationship between America's "brow" and her "eyes" can only seem contradictory. The commitment to "empire" requires an assault on the laws of other places. While one might say that a nation with a commitment to "its" laws could be imperial or that a nation with a commitment to "the natural law" could be imperial, it is hard to see how a nation committed to the law as such could start an empire. But we have already seen that the force of the Union's prosecution of the Civil War is to tie the former categories of law (its law, the law) to the latter (law as such) in a single project. The Union's project in the war, that is, entails that it be both imperial (insofar as it must transform Southern laws) and a defense against empire (insofar as it prevents the South from destroying its legal authority); it entails the South's being located both inside and outside of the nation. To produce a new union of free states which will replace the old union of freedom and slavery, the nation will have to have "Law on her brow and empire in her eyes."

Nowhere do these matters emerge more clearly than in the case in which the Supreme Court eventually held that secession was unconstitutional, *Texas v. White*. The jurisdictional questions at issue in the case quite literally revolved around the questions of whether Texas had remained a state throughout the Civil War and whether it continued to be one in the midst of Reconstruction. Since, as Chief Justice Salmon P. Chase put the matter in his majority opinion, the Supreme Court has "original jurisdiction of suits by States against citizens of other States" but "States entitled to invoke this jurisdiction must be States of the Union" and "no jurisdiction has been conferred upon [the Supreme Court] of suits by any other political communities than such States" (719), the Court could consider the case only so long as it was satisfied that Texas was in fact a state both at the time in which the contested transactions took place (1865) and at the time in which the proceedings were being adjudicated (1868). The first and crucial question, then, was whether "in consequence of" its secession, Texas had in fact seceded. Chase answered this question quickly, if somewhat arbitrarily, by claiming that because the Articles of Confederation had declared the Union of American states to "be perpetual," the Constitution's assertion that it was devoted to producing "a more perfect Union" meant, among other things, that the more perfect Union it produced would be no less dissoluble than its antecedent. "It is difficult to convey the idea of indissoluble unity more clearly than by these words," Chase explained. "What can be indissoluble if a perpetual Union, made more perfect, is not?" (725).

I imagine that many of us can think of clearer expressions of indissolubility than those we find in the Constitution.[35] There are a number of fairly obvious problems with Chase's reasoning: why should we think that a guarantee of perfection counts as a guarantee of perpetuality? But whether or not it is plausible for Chase to claim that the Constitution could not be clearer about the matter of secession, we might well expect that the matter of the Court's jurisdiction would be settled at this point: Texas had never seceded; the Union is perpetual. "Considered therefore as transactions under the Constitution," Chase explained, "the ordinances of secession, adopted by the convention and ratified by a majority of the citizens of Texas, and all the acts of her legislature intended to give effect to that ordinance, were absolutely null." "It certainly follows," he went on, "that the State did not cease to be a State, nor her citizens to be citizens of the Union. If this were otherwise, the State must have become foreign, and her citizens foreigners. The war must have ceased to be a war for the suppression of rebellion, and must have become a war for conquest and subjugation" (726).

Put this schematically, matters seem pretty clear. But matters do not remain clear for all that long. For while Chase was insistent that the "obligations" of states that attempt to secede "remain unimpaired," he acknowledged that "the relations which subsist while these obligations are performed are essentially different from those which arise when they are disregarded and set at naught." And this change of "relations" turns out effectively to overturn the claim that "the State did not cease to be a state." Chase understood the consequences of these changing relations in a number of different ways, but for our purposes it is sufficient to note the two "new duties" he thought the changing relations "impose[]" on the United States and to note further that that there are two new duties is itself a little bit surprising, especially so in light of Chase's account of what constitutes the first one: "The first was that of suppressing the rebellion." One would think that the suppression of the rebellion would itself constitute the entirety of the government's duty. If secession alone changes the relations between the State and the Union, then the end of the secession would seem to be the end of the problem. Or to put the point in Chase's terms, if the problem is merely that "the government and citizens of the State, refusing to recognize their constitutional obligations, assumed the character of enemies," then it would seem that the suppression of the enemies is all the reconstruction Texas needs (727).

But of course, secession is not the only way in which Chase understood the Texas legislature of the mid-1860s to have violated the law of the Union: it also violated that law in its commitment to slavery. Since "Slaves, in the insurgent States, with certain local exceptions, had been declared free by the Proclamation of Emancipation," "the restoration of the government which existed before the rebellion, . . . was obviously impossible; . . . it was necessary that the old constitution should receive such amendments as would conform its provisions to the new conditions created by emancipation." (728–29). Eventually, Chase would decide that the United States had carried out its two "duties" sufficiently well so that Texas had the right to appeal to the Supreme Court's jurisdiction, but he would do so only after essentially abandoning his initial claim that Texas had always remained in the Union. For as the Union comes to transform the state of Texas rather than suppressing the rebels who took it over, Chase's distinction between a "war for the suppression of rebellion" and a "war for conquest and subjugation" effectively collapses. Chase himself was quite happy to admit that the "suppression of rebellion" was only "the first" of the government's tasks. Rather than standing as an elaboration of the way in which the seceding States remain in the

Union throughout the war, Chase's opinion actually reveals ways in which those States must be said both to remain in the Union and to have exiled themselves from it. As Grier pointed out in his dissent, Chase's argument has the effect of turning a state into a "chameleon, assum[ing] the color of the object to which she adheres"; it has the effect of maintaining that "she is in the Union and was never out of it, and yet not a state at all for four years" (740).

In the chameleon Southern state we encounter a particularly graphic instance of what James G. Randall called "the dual status theory of the war." "The conflict," he explained, "was . . . conceived as a war and as rebellion; the Southerners were 'rebels,' yet belligerents; the legal relations might be at once international and municipal."[36] But coming from the perspective of Melville's sense of the Union's *needing* to blend legalism with imperialism, we approach this dual nature from a vantage that allows us to revise substantially what has come to be the ordinary account of the origins and significance of the "dual status theory." As the ordinary account would have it, the South could be imagined to be both inside and outside of the Union at the same time precisely because it did not matter very much how its relationship to the Union actually was described.[37] It is certainly the case that many of the principal figures in the debates over Reconstruction seemed to care pretty little how the conflict was described. "Our case is double," Sumner explained, "and you may call it rebellion or war as you please, or you may call it both."[38]

Figures such as Sumner could be so cavalier about the question in part because as a practical matter the issue seemed already to have been resolved. As Justice Grier explained in the *Prize Cases,* insofar as the Confederate states had "occup[ied] and [held] in a hostile manner a certain portion of territory; [had] declared their independence; [had] cast off their allegiance; [had] organized armies; [had] commenced hostilities against their former sovereign, the world acknowledges them as belligerents, and the contest a *war.*" Regardless of their status *de jure,* they constitute an alien state "*de facto*" (667). It did not matter which way Northern lawmakers chose to describe the problem: they were in a war no matter how often they said that they were merely putting down a rebellion. This argument was aided by the fact that many of those, like Grier, who devoted much attention to the question of the exact relationship between the South and the Union seemed to think that little hinged on the distinction. They did not merely say the distinction between a war and a rebellion was of no practical importance. They also insisted that it was of no theoretical importance. Hence, in the *Prize Cases* Grier would claim that it made no sense to think "that insurgents who have risen in rebellion against their sovereign, expelled her Courts, established a revolutionary government, organized armies, and commenced hostilities, are not *enemies* because they are *traitors*" or that "a war levied on the Government by

traitors, in order to dismember and destroy it, is not a war because it is an 'insurrection'" (670). And if Grier could act as though there was no incompatibility between
the status of enemy and traitor, others, such as Francis P. Blair, would maintain that
there was actually a causal relationship between the two: "It is because . . . they are belligerents," he pointed out, "that they become traitors."[39]

Indeed, by 1866 an interest in the status of Southern states had come to count
merely as a mark of one's conservative tendencies. In a speech on Reconstruction
given on April 11, 1865, Lincoln confessed that he had "been shown a letter . . . in which
the writer expresses regret that my mind has not seemed to be definitely fixed on the
question whether the seceded States, so called, are in the Union or out of it" (2:699).
But though he had "found professed Union men endeavoring to make that question,"
he had "*purposely* forborne any public expression upon it. As it appears to me that
question has not been, nor yet is, a practically material one, and that any discussion
of it, while it thus remains practically immaterial, could have no effect other than the
mischievous one of dividing our friends." The relationship between the Southern
states and the Union was, he concluded, "a merely pernicious abstraction" (2:699).

In this world where it comes as a surprise that "professed Union men" would even
ask whether Southern states had actually seceded, where the very posing of the question seems to cast doubt on one's status as a Union man, Johnson's claim in his First
Annual Message that "whether the territory within the limits of [Southern] states
should be held as conquered territory" should be "the first question that presented itself for decision" in the war's aftermath would stand as an early sign of the problem
he would later pose for the Reconstruction project (2042–43). But it is telling that Lincoln himself had once insisted that it was vitally important to clarify precisely the matter he now "*purposely*" avoided addressing. In a passage in his special message of 1861
which I have already quoted, he admitted that "it might seem, at first thought, to be
of little difference whether the present movement at the South be called 'secession' or
'rebellion'" and then went on to stress how much difference the exposure of the "ingenious sophism" animating the Confederacy made in the articulation of Northern
war aims (1:254–55). What had changed in the interim, of course, is that the Union
had acquired a new war aim that made the exile of the Southern states as appealing
as their incorporation. And it is for this reason that by 1865 the question Lincoln had
once thought the war would settle emerges as an obstacle to the completion of the
war. It is for this reason, in other words, that Lincoln thinks not only that the question he had been avoiding is not "practically material" but also that posing it would
be downright "mischievous." The dual status theory of the war was not available because a precise account of the South's actual constitutional status was unnecessary to

the project of Reconstruction; it was, instead, generated precisely because an amorphous account was necessary to that project.

Obviously, I do not mean to make the claim that this duality was *theoretically* necessary. It is easy enough to see how one could argue that the war was simply about the expansion of the "free soil" empire into the South (this would be the point of Stevens's argument that the Southern states should be treated merely as "conquered territory" or Sumner's argument that through their secession the Southern states had committed what he called "state suicide" [6:301]). And it is equally easy to see how one might maintain that the war was simply about the restoration of the Southern states as a part of the Union (this would be the point of Johnson's efforts to handle Reconstruction by way of treason trials). My point is that the duality is *politically* necessary, that it is necessary so long as one wants to keep these two distinct war aims (law and empire) wholly compatible with one another. And my further point is that the glue that keeps the two strains of the dual theory together is the idea of law, an idea whose capacity to be inflected in either a formal (or positivist or lower) or a substantive (or higher or natural) manner allows it to serve as the mechanism for restoration of law by way of the expansion of the Northern empire.

Parenthetical Combinations

The law's duality in the Reconstruction period is the primary subject of *Battle-Pieces*, and the work engages the idea most forcefully in the poem with which I began, "Dupont's Round Fight." We have already seen that Melville's poems frequently separate formal law from higher law. What is interesting about "Dupont's Round Fight" is the way in which it insists upon keeping the two legal realms juxtaposed at the same time that it reveals the differences between them. On first glance the poem reads as a simple statement of legality of the Northern moral cause. After having declared that the North "warred for Right," the speaker goes on to say that its victory is a "victory of LAW" (30). But careful attention to the way in which the ideas of LAW and right intersect in the poem begins to make them look less fully intertwined than the first glance would indicate. The victory of LAW which emerges at the end of the poem ultimately turns out to be less a victory of legal substance than of legal form. The poem opens by claiming, in a set of lines which will soon be my focus, that "All art whose aim is sure" "In time and measure perfect moves," and it is in this context of the formal dimensions of successful aesthetic productions that we are first told that Dupont's fleet warred for right. Such art, we learn in the second stanza, informs the nautical practice of Dupont's fleet:

Nor less the Fleet that warred for Right,
And warring so, prevailed,
In geometric beauty curved,
And in an orbit sailed.   (30)

This sequence stages the conversion of a number of concerns about the ends of various practices (aim is sure, warred for right) into concerns about those practices' methods. Warring *rightly* replaces warring *for* right as the grounds for the poem's account of why the Union's victory is a victory "of LAW." And as a result, when, as we learn in the final stanza, "The rebel at Port Royal felt / the Unity overawe," then, he is not being overawed by the rightness of the North's Cause; he is being overawed by the aesthetic unity of the Northern battle plan—its "geometric beauty." The Unity valorized in the last lines of the poem attaches to the Unity of the fleet, not the Unity of the nation. We have a victory of law not in the sense that right is victorious nor even in the sense that the law is upheld by the battle but, rather, in the sense that those who conform to *some* law vanquish their enemies. Even as the poem ultimately seems to empty out the notion of LAW of any of its substantive content, however, it also remains committed to connecting right to the LAW: "warring so" is still aligned with "warring for Right." This connection is made at the expense of the content of rightness. Indeed, we might say that the poem begins to indicate that it is only by emptying right of substance that it can continue to look like LAW. But the poem prefers this emptying to the out-and-out exclusion of substantive law from its purview. The poem both juxtaposes and separates right and LAW. To put the point in terms of "The Fall of Richmond," God may be in heaven and Grant in the town, but the fact that they are not in the same place is not the occasion for Melville to lose sight of either one. And from this perspective we might even say that what is most remarkable about *Battle-Pieces* is its commitment to keeping God and right present in poems that seem to be devoted to wholly marginalizing them.

We can begin to register the force of this point by observing that in the opening lines of the poem this multivalent relationship between right and law is presented in a slightly different register. This other register is the register of aesthetic production. "The Fleet that warred for Right," as I just indicated, is specifically analogized in the poem's opening lines to "All Art whose aim is sure":

In time and measure perfect moves
All Art whose aim is sure;
Evolving rhyme and stars divine
Have rules, and they endure.   (30)

Just as the poem eventually tries to establish a connection between what Dupont's fleet fights for and the way it goes about that fight, here it establishes the same connection between the methods of good Art ("In time and measure perfect moves") and their results ("whose aim is sure"). But just as the effect of Melville's description of the fleet's technique is to marginalize the fleet's cause, to make the relevant "LAW" look purely technical rather than in any way substantial, here the effect of his interest in the "rules" of art tends to displace concerns about the accuracy of its "aims." Which is simply to say that while we learn that there is a connection between formal adherence to the rules and aesthetic success, we are never given a reason to value aesthetic success independent of formal rules: the aim is "sure"; it is not "true." And, furthermore, even the sure aim is bracketed off from the stanza's interest in enduring rules. Forms themselves (i.e., the "evolving rhyme"), not aesthetic products constructed out of them, are what "Have rules," and they are also what "endure."[40] If the stanza opens with an interest in something that might look like aesthetic accuracy (aim is sure), it eventually drops the matter and moves into a space where technique alone stands as all that is of consequence. Just as Dupont's cause eventually disappears behind his method, so too is art's aim eventually occluded by its procedures. But just as the poem's relative indifference to the rightness of Dupont's cause does not cause the idea of rightness to be jettisoned from the poem altogether, so too does its relative indifference to matters of poetic accuracy fail to prevent matters such as aim from entering its mix. Melville insists upon both the proximity and the distinction between right and law.

Not all of the poems in *Battle-Pieces* which explicitly take up the relationship between poetic form and content are as eager as "Dupont's Round Fight" to suggest that poetic content can follow from "perfect" poetic form. Most of the poems in the volume actually understand such poetic form to be antagonistic to their artistic aims. If "Dupont's Round Fight" tries to hold out the hope that formal propriety in some way guarantees aesthetic integrity, other poems, such as, to take only one example, "A Utilitarian View of the Monitor's Fight," seem to suggest that the important aesthetic work lies in matching one's form with one's aim, not in assuring the accuracy of one's aim by committing oneself to the LAW of form:

Plain be the phrase, yet apt the verse,
More ponderous than nimble;
For since grimed War here laid aside
His Orient pomp, 'twould ill befit
Overmuch to ply
The rhyme's barbaric cymbal.   (61)

Here the chief concern is with the "aptness" of rhyme rather than its necessity, the way in which forms "ply" to various conditions in the world rather than the way in which a commitment to them, in and of itself, assures artistic success. "Dupont's Round Fight," as it were, moves in the direction of something like McLean's insistence that law need be applied independent of its relationship to "natural law" (but without his explicit insistence that such a movement leaves more substantial matters behind); "A Utilitarian View of the Monitor's Fight" suggests that law should only count as meaningful insofar as it is powered by a meaningful correspondence to natural law. And in this shift we see the emergence of what counts as LAW in the former poem as something "barbaric" in the latter one. We see, as it were, how McLean's lawfulness could come to count as the abolitionists' gross injustice.

But just as Melville's interest in the value of aesthetic law never wholly displaces the matter of aesthetic aim, so too does his interest in aesthetic aim leave open some space for a commitment to aesthetic form. Even as "A Utilitarian View of the Monitor's Fight" comes to revise the account of the relationship between legal form and legal substance which we encounter in "Dupont's Round Fight," it never actually wholly abandons the idea that "phrases" should "move" in "time and measure perfect." It merely establishes a new set of criteria for determining what "time and measure" are appropriate—or, rather, it simply provides a set of criteria in the first place: instead of saying that our forms should be perfect, it actually tells us how they could be made perfect. Even to characterize the shift in these terms is to characterize it as a meaningful shift. In providing no criteria, "Dupont's Round Fight" seems actually to suggest that none, other than purely formal ones, would ever be necessary. But insofar as "A Utilitarian View" at least continues to operate as if aesthetic form and aesthetic content are reconcilable, we might see some continuity between it and the earlier poem: it does not suggest that formal criteria alone could count as effecting the reconciliation, but it also does not suggest that the two should be understood as wholly distinct and irrelevant to each other either.

There are other sequences in the *Battle-Pieces*, however, in which Melville seems less interested in providing a framework for reconciling the formal and the substantive than in staging how difficult such a task would be—sequences, that is, in which he seems most interested in distinguishing between the two categories at precisely those moments in which they come to be aligned. Perhaps the most important and conspicuous way in which Melville effects this sense of clash between the substantive and the formal lies in his frequent, not to say obsessive, deployment of parenthetical expressions—there are three parenthetical expressions, for instance, in the fourteen-line first poem alone. From one perspective parentheses would seem to work principally in the direction of bracketing ordinary syntactical requirements, of introducing material into an utterance without actually locating it syntactically within the utterance. But parenthetical expressions also produce a gap between the formal syntactical procedure of a sentence and its substantive content from the opposite direction as well. For parentheses do not only allow for a certain bracketing of formal needs in the face of substantive demands; they also serve as the form by which material of marginal substantive import is incorporated into sentences that would otherwise disregard it. The parenthetical can serve as a formal way of bracketing substance as well as a way of bracketing form in the face of substantive imperatives.

Melville's use of parentheses works to animate both of these accounts of parentheses at the same time. The parenthetical expressions generally appear in contexts that foreground their relationship to the formal dimensions of poetic artifacts, in moments in which the parenthetical expressions make sense in terms of poetic form even if they do not make sense in terms of syntactical form. Consider, for instance, these lines from "Malvern Hill (July, 1862)":

> The battle-smoked flag, with stars eclipsed,
> We followed (it never fell!)—
> In silence husbanded our strength—
> Received their yell;
> Till on this slope we patient turned
> With cannon ordered well;
> Reverse we proved was not defeat.   (68)

The question here is, what is the relationship between the parenthetical utterance and the rest of the passage? The question emerges, at first, because the parentheses seem to contain no information, or at least no information that we need to be told. It is, of course, the very premise of the poem that the flag "never fell," that "reverse" is not exactly the same thing as "defeat." From this perspective the chief work of the parenthetical phrase seems to be to produce a word to rhyme with *yell*: the phrase would seem, that is, to be motivated formally but not substantially. And this point gathers a little bit of force when we notice that the poem as a whole seems to be about the process by which formal distinctions (the difference between retreating and being defeated) can be made to have substantive content (the retreating army itself comes to do the defeating at the poem's end): hence, although it would seem at first either to be of very little substantive import whether the flag "never fell" (who cares if your flag falls if you end up winning the day?) or to go without saying that it did not (how can you win the day if you've already been defeated?), what the sequence begins to reveal is that my initial dismissal of the parenthetical claim came precisely because I was too committed to the substantive content of formal properties, because I assumed that a surviving army retained its flag. Or to put the point slightly differently, the seemingly redundant reference to the flag is necessary precisely because there is an inadequate connection between form and substance in the world: hence, it counts as a triumph to demonstrate that form followed content. And from this perspective, we might say that the sequence stages what looks like a reconciliation of formal dimensions of the flag with its substantive content (it makes the utterance look as though its doing something other than formal work) but that it does so only by way of insisting upon the crucial difference between the formal and the substantive, between those things that might rhyme and those things that might mean. The poem dramatizes the *need* for the reconciliation between the two as much as it stages the reconciliation itself.

Similar work also takes place in the first four lines of the first poem in the volume, "The Portent (1859.)":

Hanging from the beam,
Slowly swaying (such the law),
Gaunt the shadow on your green,
Shenandoah.   (11)

Here the syntactical form of the sentence cannot be reconciled with the formal demands of the poem's rhyme: the interruption of the syntactical form is necessary to the operation of the poetic one. And this point is all the more telling because it happens precisely because of the emergence of the idea of law into the poem. When law appears as the poem's subject, it also begins to answer to its form. Again we get something like a reconciliation of the formal and the substantive, and again that reconciliation is only powered by an initial distinction between the two of them, by the staging of the intrusion of the law into an utterance that seems neither to be about the law (hence, law only appears parenthetically) nor to conform to poetic laws (hence, the maintenance of them requires its appearance). We might say that the reconciliation of the formal and the substantive here is purely a parenthetical part of the poem. It happens at the expense of both the form (the sentence is interrupted by an intrusive parentheses) and the content (the parentheses summons a topic removed from, not to say contrary to, the sense of the stanza as a whole) of the nonparenthetical portions of the sentence. We get something like "Dupont's Round Fight" inserted parenthetically into another poem: two sets of laws, laws that can be placed into close proximity to one another put cannot wholly be folded into each other—a point that is vividly confirmed once we recall that the North's victory of LAW will entail the subordination of the particular Southern legal regime that here appears so marginal.

We can now profitably return to the chief issues raised by the critical history of *Battle-Pieces*. Melville's relationship to poetic form has been at the center of criticism of *Battle-Pieces* throughout the work's critical history. The concern goes back as far as William Dean Howells's sense that Melville's poems bear no relationship to anything external to them (they are, he explained, "filled with . . . , not words and blood, but words alone"), and it has emerged in most of the major readings of *Battle-Pieces* since then, even those, such as Michael Rogin's, which are less concerned with the work's literary merit than its political content.[41] There are, of course, good biographical reasons for critics to be especially attentive to form in this work. *Battle-Pieces* was, after all, Melville's first published volume of poetry, and its appearance seems to have marked definitively his shift from novelist to poet: from 1866 until his death he would produce some twelve hundred pages of verse but only one extended work of prose fiction. And the work's location in the trajectory of Melville's career is hardly the only reason critics have for being interested in its relationship to its own formal properties. As we have begun to see, the volume constantly makes that relationship the object of its own attention. It is almost impossible not to notice that the poems in *Battle-Pieces* spend an enormous amount of time explicitly thematizing the relationship between their own poetic syntax and the war they seek to describe.

Approaching the poems from the perspective of their interest in the complexity surrounding the idea of "the LAW" immediately after the Civil War allows us to place this old object of critical attention in a new light, however, or, at the very least, it allows us to see that the problem of literary form which the poems thematize and embody is actually part of *Battle-Pieces'* larger interest in the relationship between form and law. Critics have been right to notice that Melville's poetic practice frequently interferes with his realist pretensions, and they have also been right to notice that his poems at best only partially embody the forms they attempt to assume. But what we have begun to see is that the poems are actually *about* these two problems: their subject is the incompatibility between form and content and the way in which that incompatibility poses problems for a commitment to the idea of the law. In discussing these matters, critics have not been describing the poems so much as summarizing them.[42] And crucially, they have not been avoiding the poems' interest in the political context in which they obviously locate themselves by focusing on matters of poetic form; they have, instead, been describing it. For what the poems ultimately take as their subject is a world in which formal laws are seen as both necessary and obstructive, a world in which higher aims are both required and diverting. We might call this world the world of poetry, especially the world of poetry as seen by a writer of prose. Or we might call it the world of Reconstruction. If Melville's poetry's status as poetry seems forever to arrest our attention, it does so precisely because of its peculiar capacity to stand as an analog for the political matters that constitute its content.

CHAPTER TWO

Shadows of Law

Somerset and the Literature of Abolition

States of Slavery

The remainder of this book will be devoted to specifying how the legal system that counts as doubled and unstable for Melville might be unified and stabilized. As a first step in this process, I will need to generate a far more specific account of the way in which slavery and the idea of law interact in antebellum American legal thinking. And at least at first, this account will only emphasize the legal duality and instability that so interests Melville in *Battle-Pieces*. To say that slavery was lawful in the United States prior to the Civil War is only to begin to hint at the extent to which slavery and the law were intertwined with one another in antebellum Anglo-American jurisprudence. Slavery was not merely lawful in antebellum America; it was essentially lawful. Not only, that is, was slavery sanctioned by the laws; its existence required such a sanction. Unlike all other social institutions recognized in the law, slavery could not exist unless it was specifically legally licensed. It was in this sense that slavery was a *peculiar* institution, and this peculiarity was absolutely central to the way in which slavery was understood, protected, and confronted before the Civil War.

In the first, and most famous, description of the general nature of slavery in *Uncle Tom's Cabin* (1852), Harriet Beecher Stowe claims that "the shadow of *law*" secures the slave's subordination.[1] Stowe's association of slavery with the law, of course, was hardly unusual. Her association of slavery with the *shadow* of law, however, was a little bit more idiosyncratic, and it was an idiosyncrasy she shared with Melville, who explored the relationship between slavery and legal shadows in a range of works from *Benito Cereno* (1855) to *Battle-Pieces*.[2] *Battle-Pieces* engages the shadows of slave law with particular enthusiasm. The collection's opening poem begins with an image of the "shadow" of an abolitionist (xi); its third poem contains an account of how "Dominion (unsought by the free)" flows from the capacity of the "Iron Dome" of the state to "fling her huge shadow athwart the main" (17); and its first and longest section concludes with an image of a triumphant personified America's revival from the "trance" of the Civil War as "the shadow . . . fle[es]" from her presence (161, 162).

But if the shadow of law lies at the heart of slavery's abuses of the civil rights of African Americans in *Uncle Tom's Cabin,* in *Battle-Pieces* the retreat of the law's shadow does not occasion the rise of African-American civil rights so much as signal the arrival of a new set of grounds for their suppression. At the same time that Melville represents the end of the Civil War as the culmination of a long battle against the shadow of a slave state, he also represents it as the realization of the United States as a racially unified nation, a "natural brotherhood" that no longer "sanction[s]" the "sin of blood" (241). Insofar as he imagines that "Africa" might bear some debt to the United States for the war that liberated African Americans ("Can Africa pay back this blood / Spilt on Potomac's shore?" [242]), Melville begins to jettison Africans from civil standing in the nation that emerges after the ordeal of emancipation. When the shadow of slave law recedes in *Battle-Pieces,* slaves become African rather than Africans becoming American.[3] What stands as the chief obstacle to black civil rights in *Uncle Tom's Cabin* thus emerges in *Battle-Pieces* as something like a prerequisite for their recognition.[4]

Although the movement from *Uncle Tom's Cabin* to *Battle-Pieces* would seem to invite us to chart the shifting relations between the law and African-American civil rights in the 1850s and 1860s, such a project bears a contentious relationship to most recent cultural histories of black civil rights in the nineteenth century. As I pointed out in the introduction, the very idea that the relationship between the law and African-American civil rights was unstable in the mid-nineteenth century has been largely alien to the usual understanding of the period—which is simply to say that the historiography of black civil rights, at least the cultural and literary historiography of black civil rights, has been so concerned with works such as *Uncle Tom's Cabin* that it has been largely blind to works such as *Battle-Pieces.* Upcoming chapters will use the historical emergence of the Reconstruction amendments to question the prevailing consensus that legalism was somehow incompatible with projects devoted to racial justice in the nineteenth century. In this chapter, however, I mean to show what makes the consensus position plausible rather than what makes it limited and misguided. I will suggest that our customary sense of the antagonism between civil rights and legal power derives from a particular and historically specific account of the relationship between slavery and the law, an account that flowered in the abolitionist thinking of figures such as William Lloyd Garrison and which received its definitive literary elaboration in *Uncle Tom's Cabin.* On this account slavery's dependence upon the support of positive law ultimately taints the very idea of the law. For Garrison and for the Stowe of *Uncle Tom's Cabin,* we will see, nineteenth-century law does not simply allow slavery; it ultimately embodies it, just as it does for many recent historians of the period.

For all of his rhetorical and cultural eminence, of course, Garrison's most radical assaults on slavery never exactly represented mainstream American antislavery thought. There is some question, indeed, as to whether they actually represented Garrison's own thoughts about slavery. Not only did his positions on the matters I will be addressing fluctuate from the 1830s to the 1860s, but it is often difficult to determine whether Garrison was more committed to the constative matter of the arguments he prosecuted or the performative matter of the social and political effects those arguments might have had in the immediate contexts in which he delivered them.[5] I will make no effort to specify the exact range of Garrison's influence. Nor will I try to sort Garrison's inner conviction from his outward bluster. Instead, I will suggest that Garrison gave forceful voice to a powerful tendency implicit in slavery's standing in Anglo-American law and that this tendency can also be registered even in accounts of slavery which lack either Garrison's particular political commitments or his rhetorical intensity. "Any evaluation of antislavery thought or action," David Brion Davis writes in his magisterial and highly influential book *The Problem of Slavery in the Age of Revolution* (1975), "must take account of specific social and historical contexts."[6] Without in any way discounting the significance of these contexts in the development of American antislavery thinking, I hope to supplement the analysis of Davis and his descendants by recalling the *legal* context in which that thinking developed. That legal context plays a pivotal role in the development of the nation's ultimate response to chattel slavery—the Reconstruction amendments. And it also plays a foundational role in the development of an American literature of abolition. As a way of approaching this literature of abolition, I will now turn to the peculiar institution's peculiarity.

"Resistance to Civil Government," or Radical Abolition

By far the most important antebellum ruling on the legal nature of slavery was the English case *Somerset v. Stewart* (1772), in which Lord Mansfield held that any slave who became a resident of England would cease to be a slave. A number of legal authorities had reached this conclusion before Mansfield had an opportunity to rule on the question. The most significant version of the argument had appeared in the first volume of William Blackstone's *Commentaries* (1765), in which the English "constitution" was said to possess something along the lines of the positive power to emancipate the bondsman. "And this spirit of liberty is so deeply rooted in our constitution, and rooted even in our very soil," Blackstone explained, "that a slave or negro, the moment he lands in England, falls under the protection of the laws; and so far becomes a freeman." Blackstone was emphatic about the general tendency of English law, its "spirit" we might say, but vague about the exact legal provisions that lead to his desired emancipatory results: hence, the invocation of British "soil," as well as "the laws," as a bulwark of English constitutional liberty. Indeed, the ultimate authority for English constitutional liberty in the *Commentaries* turns out to be "reason" and "natural law" rather than any clearly identifiable common law tradition. "It is repugnant to reason, and the principles of natural law, that such a state [i.e., slavery] should subsist anywhere," Blackstone noted. And it is "upon these principles," rather than anything more concrete, that "the Law of England abhors, and will not tolerate the existence of slavery, within this nation."[7]

Perhaps sensing the nebulous character of the law at work in Blackstone's vision of liberating soil, Mansfield traced the resident slave's freedom to slightly different sources. Rather than imagining that the English constitution expressed affirmative antislavery principles, he instead derived English freedom from the *absence* of any specific legal recognition of slavery. "The state of slavery is of such a nature," he claimed, "that it is incapable of being introduced on any reasons . . . but only by positive law. . . . It is so odious, that nothing can be suffered to support it, but positive law."[8] We might at first take Mansfield's argument to be simply another version of Blackstone's: insisting on slavery's incompatibility with "natural right," both give it no purchase in England. We might even say that Mansfield extends Blackstone's argument: whereas Blackstone made slavery incompatible with a nebulously defined English law, Mansfield makes it incompatible with *any* legal scheme in which it is not given explicit standing. But it is crucial for us to recognize that Mansfield buys his thoroughgoing abjection of slavery at the expense of the normative authority of the realm of natural right: paradoxically, freedom becomes man's default condition in *Somerset* only at the moment that moral standing is wholly subordinated to legal will. Robert Cover has maintained that "*Somerset's Case* vindicated Blackstone" (17), and David Brion Davis has said that Blackstone's authority "seemed to validate Lord Mansfield's reported statement" (473). But in many crucial respects Mansfield's opinion represented an *inversion* of Blackstone's thinking rather than an extension of it. Whereas Blackstone would derive the law from nature, Mansfield's ruling implied, to quote Cover, "that there was nothing necessary or inevitable about law's harmony with nature." Indeed, Cover goes on, "where positive law sanctioned slavery, Mansfield explicitly conceded the supremacy of such positive law" (17). If Blackstone had suggested that slavery was essentially illegal ("the Law of England abhors, and will not tolerate the existence of slavery, within this nation"), Mansfield maintains that it is essentially legal—a product, that is, of positive law and of positive law alone. And it was

Mansfield's configuration of the relations among slavery, nature, and the law, not Blackstone's, which would become controlling for the future development of the Anglo-American law of slavery.[9] By the 1850s it had become axiomatic in American courts that, as Justice Benjamin Curtis put it in his dissent in *Dred Scott*, "slavery, being contrary to natural right, is created only by municipal law."[10]

Somerset's doctrinal preeminence should not trick us into thinking that Mansfield demonstrated any particular insight about how the institution of slavery had developed in the English colonies. Mansfield seems to have thought that his account of slavery's formal legal standing followed from its history: "it [slavery] *must* take its rise from *positive* law; the origin of it can in no country or age be traced back to any other source: immemorial usage preserves the memory of positive law long after all traces of the occasion, reason, authority, and time of its introduction are lost."[11] But as a historical claim this is almost surely false. As Davis has explained, "Negro slavery had been established in the New World not by positive law but by impromptu decisions" (473–74). The development of a plausible form of constitutionalist antislavery doctrine would require the rediscovery of the history *Somerset* effectively effaces. And if Mansfield's formulation obscured the actual history of slavery in the New World, it also inspired an unfortunately empty and befuddled account of the status of the nature with which slavery was allegedly incompatible. Insofar as slavery was alien to natural right, it was possible to imagine that the laws occasioning it involved fiction, if not an out-and-out effacement of reality. Anthony Benezet, for instance, endorsed the claim that the "doctrine" of "higher law," properly understood, implied that "no Legislature on Earth . . . can alter the Nature of things, or make that to be lawful, which is contrary to the Law of God."[12] Everything here hinges on a systematic misunderstanding of the relationship between natural law and the laws of nature, a misunderstanding, of course, which critics of natural law had long maintained to be more or less unavoidable. One would think that we might be able to make laws even if we cannot change nature. Despite such commonsense objections, however, this line of thinking retained its force up through the 1850s. "Again it happens that the Boston Court House is full of armed men," Thoreau lamented at the beginning of "Slavery in Massachusetts" (1854), "holding prisoner and trying a M A N, to find out if he is not really a S L A V E." The problem with such considerations is not simply that they are unjust, Thoreau insisted; it is also that they are "ridiculous."[13]

In the next chapter I will address in greater detail *Somerset*'s implications for the way in which antislavery thinkers understood nature. Here I will take up the question of the way in which it shaped their conception of the state. Mansfield's notion that slavery could only exist in places where it had been legally authorized was central to the development of American antislavery discourse in both its constitutional and its anticonstitutional forms. For radicals such as William Lloyd Garrison and Wendell Phillips the very existence of slavery in the nation came to be a mark of the nation's fundamental legal commitment to it: how else, given *Somerset*, could it exist? Hence, as we have seen, Garrison would feel entirely comfortable burning the Constitution for dramatic effect in the midst of his antislavery addresses. And hence, likewise, Phillips would entitle his most important abolitionist work *The Constitution: A Pro-Slavery Compact* (1844) and would include in the volume the resignation letter of Francis Jackson—a letter that insisted that "the oath to support the Constitution of the United States is a solemn promise to do that which is a violation of the natural rights of man, and a sin in the sight of God."[14]

It is in the same spirit that Thoreau, to pick an abolitionist at a slight remove from the Garrisonian inner circle, would leaven his political essays from the 1840s and 1850s with a series of assaults on the Constitution. In "Resistance to Civil Government" (1849) he insists that "the very constitution" of "the State" "is evil" (74); in "Slavery in Massachusetts" he contends that justice can only be derived from "a higher law than the Constitution" (104). From this perspective Daniel Webster can be condemned simply for his loyalty to the nation's legal order; the terms of Webster's valor are also the terms of his failure. "He well deserves to be called, as he has been called, the Defender of the Constitution," Thoreau explains. But given "the sanction which the Constitution gives to slavery" (87), that defense—Webster's inability "to take a fact out of its merely political relations" (88)—is precisely what Thoreau considers his problem. The route to success in this environment is the route away from constitutions, which is why Thoreau ultimately ends up advancing the cause of resignation with a vehemence Phillips himself might have admired. "If the tax-gatherer, or any other officer, asks me, as one has done, 'But what shall I do?' My answer is, 'If you really wish to do any thing, resign your office'" (76–77).

Garrisonians actually went beyond simply suggesting that governmental officials should dissociate themselves from the nation's legal machinery. The fact that positive law could be separated from natural right for them represented more than the occasion, or even the obligation, for legal reform. It also represented the prospect that positive law was at its very essence an obstacle to the realization of God's justice. *Somerset* suggested something about the nature of law as well as the nature of the American legal code. Figures such as Garrison were ultimately less concerned with the particular features of American law than with the very fact that the United States had laws in the first instance. In the 1830s and 1840s, at least, they were often as devoted to abolition of the state ("the emancipation of our whole race from the dominion of man," in Garrison's terms) as they were to the abolition of slavery.[15] It is for this reason that *voting* would emerge as such a crucial point of contention in the Garrisonian abolitionist camp. In his now famous 1842 *Liberator* essay "Ballot-box and Battle-field," for instance, Henry C. Wright claimed that he would never vote in the United States—not even if his vote would emancipate all of the nation's slaves.[16] Why? Voting entails an implicit acquiescence before the state's commitment to slavery, and it also grants an implicit license to the execution of what Garrison called that "law which I think is wrong." In voting each citizen in effect takes the place of the judge who must resign. When the abolitionist citizen votes in a pro-slavery society, Garrison explained, he "means either to undertake myself to execute the law which I think is wrong, or to appoint another to do so."[17] It is according to this logic that Thoreau would ultimately apply Phillips's resignation imperative to the entire citizenry of the state rather than only its judicial officers. As his anticonstitutionalism extends to a critique of accommodating citizens as well as political operatives, Thoreau finds himself imagining a "revolution" that will only be "accomplished" "when the subject has refused his allegiance, and the officer has resigned his office" (77). "Let each inhabitant of the State dissolve his union with her," he announces in "Slavery in Massachusetts," "as long as she delays to do her duty" "to dissolve her union with the slaveholder" (104).

These passages raise the question of whether the problem lies at the practical level of the particular legal arrangements (which might be "wrong" or fail in their "duty") or at the theoretical level of the power implicit in the law as such. Voting in antebellum America, Garrison announced in 1842, "[is] of Satanic origin, and inherently wicked and murderous. We must cease to sanction it. . . . voting for men to have discretionary power over the lives and liberties of their fellow-men must be put in the same category with rum-drinking, profanity, lewdness, and every evil work."[18] We might initially think that Garrison is issuing two, and two potentially incompatible, complaints at once here: one about a particular kind of voting (voting for men to have discretionary power) and one about voting in and of itself (inherently wicked). Would one's voting be evil if it worked to prevent slavery rather than allow it? But this dilemma is resolved once we see that, at least so far as Garrison is concerned, it would be impossible to vote without participating in the world he condemns. Regardless of whether you vote for a pro-slavery figure and regardless even of whether you vote in a state that has laws authorizing slavery, you will be voting in a pro-slavery legal world. Implicit in the idea of law is the power to make slavery. Legislators will always have discretionary powers "over the lives and liberties of their fellow-men," and positive law can always, despite the dictates of natural law, institute slavery. If *Somerset* could seem to configure slavery as a positive law exception to a world generally organized in terms more or less compatible with natural right, Garrison understands the power to enslave to be the paradigmatic instance of the authority of positive law itself: what positive law *is* is the establishment of a political order that deviates from natural right.

And it thus little matters for him if the man who has "discretionary powers" over another is the slave master or the politician, which is why he can simply elide the two figures as he goes along. Does the representative or the slaveholder hold "discretionary powers" over his "fellow-men" in this sequence? If slavery is essentially legal, from this perspective, the law is also, and equally, essentially enslaving.[19]

Hence, while Thoreau seems to suggest that the "inhabitant" need only dissolve his union with the state so long as the state is implicated in slavery, he, too, ultimately seems as worried about the very existence of something like a state as the existence of improper state policies and laws. We might recall, for instance, that after announcing that he "heartily accept[s] the motto,—'That government is best which governs least,'" at the outset of "Resistance to Civil Government," Thoreau goes on to gloss the motto by suggesting that it "finally amounts to this, which I also believe,—'That government is best which governs not at all'" (63). Thoreau's concern is not so much with good governance as with good governments—a point that emerges clearly enough from his interest in the status of governments (whether they are good) rather than their performance (whether they govern well). And this shift is in some sense required by his commitment to the idea that government itself is the chief problem that governments face, that what makes a good government is precisely the absence of any governmental agency ("governs not at all").[20] To be sure, Thoreau quickly qualifies his opening remarks about the value of governments that do not govern. "But, to speak practically and as a citizen, unlike those who call themselves no-government men," he explains after rattling on about how progress is possible only to the extent that government manages to stay out of "its way," "I ask for, not at once no government, but *at once* a better government" (64). But even here Thoreau stops short of saying that he is not a "no-government man"; he only announces that he will be adopting another role, speaking in another idiom, on the present occasion. The essay's title, after all, is "Resistance to Civil Government," not "Reforming our Civil Government" or even, as it is so often called, "Civil Disobedience." And as it turns out, Thoreau's vision of a "better government" is entirely consistent with that title. Thoreau invokes his "right to refuse allegiance to and resist the government" in the context of the prospect that he may be asked to recognize as "*my* government" "that political organization . . . which is the *slave's* government also." Over the course of "Resistance to Civil Government" the category of the "better government" shrivels to the point where it no longer includes anything that we could comfortably call a government, while the category of the "*slave's* government" expands to the point where it is impossible to keep any recognizable political institution from falling within it (67).[21]

What makes a government a slave's government? Not slave laws but the army. Thoreau represents the army as both the instrument of the nation's coercion and as an example of it—an instrument insofar as the army "put[s] down an insurrection of the slaves" or "march[es] to Mexico" (71); an example insofar as Thoreau can imagine civil authority, at least civil authority in the United States, only in terms of military hierarchy. At the beginning of "Resistance to Civil Government" he proceeds from his famous opening lines about the value of the government that "governs not at all" to an account of the analogy between active governments and standing armies. "The objections which have been brought against a standing army, and they are many and weighty, and deserve to prevail, may also at last be brought against a standing government" (63). He keeps this analogy before his reader throughout the essay, especially in the moment in which he suggests that the relationship between the citizen and the state is essentially no different than the relationship between the soldier and the state: "and behold a marine, such a man as an American government can make, or such as it can make a man with its black arts, a mere shadow and reminiscence of humanity, a man laid out alive and standing, and already, as one might say, buried under arms of funeral accompaniments. . . . The mass of men serve the State thus, not as men mainly, but as machines, with their bodies" (66). This marine returns in "Slavery in Massachusetts"; once again he stands for the problems of the civilian who accepts the state's authority; and in this later appearance his status as a slave is not merely implied, as it is when Thoreau talks about the ways in which the state converts its "men" into "machines," but is actually announced: "I am compelled to see that they put themselves, or rather, are by character, in this respect, exactly on a level with the marine who discharges his musket in any direction he is ordered to. They are just as much tools and little men. Certainly they are not the more to be respected, because their master enslaves their understandings and consciences, instead of their bodies" (103).

One does not have to be *in* this army to be enslaved by it. Even the democratic state is nothing more than a war machine in "Resistance to Civil Government." "After all," Thoreau explains, "the practical reason why, when the power is once in the hands of the people, a majority are permitted, and for a long period continue, to rule, is not because they are most likely to be right, nor because this seems fairest to the minority, but because they are physically the strongest" (64). The "rule" of this group seems nothing more than the "discretionary power" Garrison wishes to remove from the world. "The State," Thoreau insists, "never confronts a man's sense, intellectual or moral, but only his body, his senses. It is not armed with superior wit or honesty, but with superior physical strength" (80). Majoritarianism simply counts as a "brute force" like any other. Civil authority is simply another form of martial command.

We should hardly be surprised, then, that Thoreau avoids being a no-government man only by valuing governmental arrangements in which the government itself is absent. Garrison collapses the state into slavery by imagining that the relationship of the state to the citizen will always be like the relationship of a master to a slave. Thoreau resurrects the state from slavery by casting his image of the proper government in terms that insist upon an equality between the citizen and the state. At the end of "Resistance to Civil Government," for instance, after insisting that the state "can have no pure right over my person and property except that which I concede to it," Thoreau "pleases [himself] with imagining a State at least which can afford to be just to all men." What makes this state just is that it "treats" its citizens (Thoreau calls them "individual[s]") as "neighbor[s]." It is only when the state does not make laws for any man that it can count as a "just" state for "all men" (89). Thoreau makes this same point even more forcefully in "A Plea for Captain John Brown," in which he suggests that Brown, in "knowing himself for a man," understood himself to be "the equal of any and all governments." What it means to be American, from this perspective, is not to be equal before the law but to be equal to the law: "In that sense he was the most American of us all" (125).

Within this framework it makes perfect sense for Thoreau to claim that the "better government" he demands at the beginning of "Resistance to Civil Government" "commands his respect," rather than his loyalty. And it also makes perfect sense for him to dwell, as he does, on the moments in which he meets "this American government" "directly, and face to face" (74). Emerson famously began his essay "Politics" (1844) by reminding us that, "in dealing with the State, we ought to remember that its institutions are not aboriginal, though they existed before we were born," by which he meant "that they are not superior to the citizen."[22] Thoreau does not reduce the government to the *status* of the citizen; he makes it into a citizen. Governments are not simply personified by their representatives; they also exist, in some important sense, at the level of the person. "I am as desirous of being a good neighbor as being a bad subject," Thoreau explains. Insofar as he is his government's "good neighbor," he will necessarily fail to be its "subject." This is why the essay concludes with Thoreau's leaving prison to join "a huckleberry party" rather than a political movement (84). Far from marking a turn "inward" in the face of "social confrontation,"[23] the gesture is instead a form of polemic, an exemplification of the essay's overarching political premise.

At the end of "A Plea for Captain John Brown," when Thoreau contemplates a world in which Brown will be recognized for the hero Thoreau takes him to be, Thoreau imagines a world not in which there will be *no* slavery but, rather, one without "at least the present form of Slavery." The reason that he cannot exactly imagine a future of abolition is that he cannot imagine a future without a state, without a government: his contemplation of this world is figured in terms of "some future national gallery" (138). This almost metaphysical alliance of the state with slavery constitutes abolitionism's radicalism. From the perspective of an essay such as "Resistance to Civil Government," what is radical about radical abolitionism is not that it was opposed to the idea of moderate reform or opposed to accommodations to established sources of power or opposed to efforts to produce constitutional or immanent accounts of the way in which the nation might be transformed. It is not even that radical abolitionists were, as they have often been described, utopianists or perfectionists or that they imagined that the only acceptable state was the ideal one.[24] What is radical about radical abolitionism is, instead, that it imagined that there was no conceivable legal solution to slavery in the first place, that slavery and the law were not only inextricable but also identical.

If this point emerges somewhat obliquely in "Resistance to Civil Government" and some of Thoreau's later antislavery essays, it receives direct and precise expression in *Battle-Pieces*. Melville has his own version of Thoreau's "future national gallery," and like Thoreau, he associates this gallery with both the elimination and the persistence of slavery. In the first poem of the first section of *Battle-Pieces*, "The Conflict of Convictions (1860–61)," Melville prophesies some imaginable happenings of the war:

> Power unanointed may come—
> Dominion (unsought by the free)
> And the Iron Dome,
> Stronger for stress and strain,
> Fling her huge shadow athwart the main;
> But the Founders' dream shall flee.
> Age after age shall be
> As age after age has ever been.   (17)

We have already seen that a large part of the anxiety that pervades *Battle-Pieces* results from Melville's inability to feel entirely comfortable with the power of the national state that emerges from the Civil War, his inability, to put the point in the terms of this sequence, to see the newly empowered federal government as "anointed" by any legitimate authority.[25] For our present purposes, however, Melville's anxiety about the "Dominion" of the new "Iron Dome" is less important than his willingness to draw a connection between the strength of the Iron Dome and the persistence of slavery. That we should associate the dome's shadow in "The Conflict of Convictions" with the *end* of slavery seems clear enough. The shadow we see here is merely an enlargement of the shadow *Battle-Pieces* presents us in its opening epigraphic poem, "The Portent." That shadow is John Brown's ("Hanging from the beam, / . . . Gaunt the shadow on your green!" [11]), and from the perspective of its transformation into a "huge shadow athwart the main," the Northern war effort would seem to count as an extension of

Brown's slave uprising. It is only by linking the war effort to emancipation, after all, that it becomes plausible for Melville to think that the dome's power might be so "unanointed" that the "Founders' dream shall flee." The "Founders' dream" of a united nation would not be compromised by the restoration of the Union, nor would it be compromised by the shadow of slavery itself. What could compromise it is the notion that political entities within the restored Union might not allow slavery. Melville thus links the end of slavery (the emergence of the shadow) with the persistence of slavery (the presence of "Dominion [unsought by the free]"). The death of slavery becomes a kind of enslaving, an enslaving of the formerly slave nation (slave in the sense that slavery was possible within it) by the newly free one (free in the sense that no one is free to hold slaves).

This transformation of emancipation into enslavement is grounded, only seemingly paradoxically, in the most radical form of abolitionist legal thinking. This passage does not merely present us with the imperial, and improperly dominating, state. It also presents us with the state as a form of domination. The "Power unanointed" and the "Dominion" here operate almost entirely independent of the dome's agency. The dome's "shadow," in and of itself, entails dominion, and entails dominion despite the absence of the dome's doing anything such as deploying force. Melville claims that the Iron Dome "flings" "her huge shadow," but surely there is a sense in which the shadow will fall against the "main" regardless of the Dome's intentions and aspirations. And indeed, the whole force of the poem is to make precisely this point— even emancipation entails slavery. Thoreau's "present form of Slavery" has become Melville's claim that, even if the Founders' dream has fled, nothing will have changed: "Age after age shall be / As age after age has been." So long as slavery is seen as an inevitable result of the existence of the state, changes in the nature of the state will never eliminate it.

Melville graphically reinforces this point in those moments in *Battle-Pieces* when the state that emerges from the Civil War seems more attractive than the dome in "The Conflict of Convictions." Ultimately, the more attractive state merely conceals its slavery rather than avoiding the perils of Dominion altogether. We might imagine that the pessimism of "The Conflict of Convictions" is tempered in some important regard when Melville returns to this set of images in "America," the poem that closes the first section of *Battle-Pieces*. "America" ends in a moment in which the "shadow" itself is forced to "flee" by the "light" it once seemed to overrun: "While the shadow, chased by light, / Fled along the far-drawn height, / And left her on the crag" (162). From this vantage the war has converted Brown's shadow into America's light. But by the same token, it is not at all clear that it has thereby dispelled the problems of Power unanointed and Dominion which were initially associated with him. For the "America" that emerges in the place of the shadow is herself marked as an imperial force, or at least as a site at which the law cannot be detached from Dominion and power. She appears, Melville explains, with "Law on her brow *and* empire in her eyes" (162; my emph.). Shadows and light may alternate positions over the course of *Battle-Pieces,* but Melville refuses to count the triumph of the light as the defeat of the problems with which the shadows were once associated.[26] Age after age shall be, indeed, as age after age has ever been.

Stowe's Rules of Slavery

Even this brief account of *Battle-Pieces* suggests that the most radical critiques of the pro-slavery constitution might ultimately run toward more conservative ends than we might first expect. We can begin to generate a more politically concrete image of the conservative ends in question—begin to flesh them out in an atmosphere less relentlessly abstract than Melville's poetry of Domes and Founders' dreams—by turning to *Uncle Tom's Cabin. Uncle Tom's Cabin* is almost certainly the most thorough antebellum consideration of the potential identity between the state and the slave master. But while it has become a critical commonplace that the novel presents a sentimental critique of the law and the legalism that served as the foundation of antebellum slavery, the intensity and extent of the novel's critique of the idea of law have seldom been fully recognized.[27] Critics have generally understood Stowe to have slavery as her primary object of concern and have thus taken the novel's interest in legalism to be a side effect of its interest in slavery. As Brook Thomas explains, "The problem for Stowe is . . . [not] the law. It is slavery."[28] But, as we have already begun to see, in a post-*Somerset* world law could not merely be said to aid and abet slavery; it could also be said to constitute slavery. In *Uncle Tom's Cabin* the problem of slavery ultimately proves to be indistinguishable from the more general problem of the law—indeed, in *Uncle Tom's Cabin* the problem of slavery merely serves as an example of the more general problems of law. Insofar as critics have neglected to locate Stowe within the context of what Gregg Crane has called the "jurisprudential crisis provoked by the law of slavery,"[29] they have been unable to register the extent of her *systematic* aversion to normative legal authority.

My point, it should be clear, is not that Stowe was an unthinking and uncritical follower of Garrison. Over the course of the 1850s their relationship was notoriously turbulent, in large part because Stowe ultimately proved far more supportive of pragmatist and legalist responses to the peculiar institution than the Garrisonians who most emphatically articulated the antislavery thinking I locate at the core of *Uncle Tom's Cabin.* Even as early as *The Key to Uncle Tom's Cabin* (1853), Stowe would begin to elaborate an abolitionist politics based on an account of the moral obligation of citizens to deploy the law to terminate slavery.[30] Nor, indeed, is *Uncle Tom's Cabin* itself altogether unequivocal in its alignment of legal authority and human bondage. One need not deny either Stowe's versatility or the novel's occasional inconsistency, however, to recognize that a deep-rooted legal skepticism quite literally organizes *Uncle Tom's Cabin*. If *Uncle Tom's Cabin* is somewhat erratic in the way it explicitly addresses the law, it is far more resolute in the way it implicitly configures the law's relationship to justice. For many recent commentators *Uncle Tom's Cabin* amounts to a series of contradictions, tensions, and paradoxes. The novel's sturdy coherence resurfaces, however, the minute we acknowledge the structural significance of its legal skepticism.

We can begin to reconstruct this coherence by noting that if it is not entirely clear in *Uncle Tom's Cabin* that there can be slavery without law, it is equally unclear that there can be law without slavery. Exactly what constitutes the essence of slavery has been the subject of a great deal of scholarly attention over the last half-century, and the best recent accounts of it have tended to de-emphasize the importance of the law in its construction. Orlando Patterson, for instance, in the course of elaborating his influential claim that slavery should be understood in terms of a social death that is structured around "*the permanent, violent domination of natally alienated and generally dishonored persons*," blithely announces that the notion that a slave is someone "without a legal personality" is merely "another fallacy that we can quickly dispose of."[31] Stowe, however, repeatedly insists upon the legal dimension of slavery—indeed, insists upon it precisely because of the irrelevance of the social considerations Patterson locates at slavery's heart: the law matters in *Uncle Tom's Cabin* because some masters, and all readers, will recognize slaves as members of the human community, with "beating hearts and living affections"; and will thus provide them with some social acknowledgment, with "kind protection and indulgence" (13). Stowe goes out of her way to separate the social exclusion Patterson makes central to slavery from the legal exclusion she makes central to it. Think, for instance, of the way in which she stresses that those with whom George works interact with him as a worker, rather than a slave, and thereby indicates that the master-slave relationship might actually be marginal to the slave's actual quotidian life: "'I think you're altogether right, friend,' said Mr. Wilson; 'and this boy described here *is* a fine fellow—no mistake about that'" (152–53).[32]

From this perspective slavery requires not that slaves be socially dead but that their social lives not be legally recognized. And indeed, *Uncle Tom's Cabin*'s first, and most famous, account of the evil of slavery works precisely to make this point: "Whoever visits some estates there . . . might be tempted to dream the oft-fabled poetic legend of a patriarchal institution . . . ; but over and above the scene there broods a porten-

tous shadow—the shadow of *law*. So long as the law considers all these human beings, with beating hearts and living affections, only as so many *things* belonging to a
master,— . . . so long it is impossible to make anything beautiful or desirable in the
best regulated administration of slavery" (13–14). The idea here, of course, is that social life is no compensation for legal death: no matter how well slaves may in fact be
treated at any particular juncture ("the best regulated administration of slavery"), the
very fact that they are slaves will always guarantee that their condition is unacceptable. But Stowe does not say that "the shadow of *the* law" looms over the slave. She
says that the shadow of *law* itself does. The effect of the formulation, and we will soon
see that this effect is produced throughout *Uncle Tom's Cabin*, is to suggest that the
problem is not with a particular legal order; it is, instead, with legal orders as such.

Of course, we might imagine that the problem of the "shadow of law" in this context stems from problems of the law's jurisdiction, from the law's inability to recognize slaves as legal subjects. This is at least part of the force of Stowe's claim that slaves
live in the "shadow" of the law, their access to it presumably blocked by their masters'
mediation. What is left implicit in Stowe's image of the shadow of law is made somewhat more explicit slightly later on in the passage when she complains that slaves are
treated as "so many *things* belonging to a master," rather than as "human beings, with
beating hearts and living affections." And it is made even more explicit later on in the
novel when George refuses to acknowledge the authority of the law that has enslaved
him because it does not recognize his status as such a being: "I know perfectly well
that you have the law on your side. . . . But . . . we don't own your laws; we don't own
your country" (281–82). But in *Uncle Tom's Cabin* the movement from the local laws
of "you" and "them" into the space of a more generally inclusive realm of the human
does not necessarily take us out of either the shadow of law or the problems Stowe associates with it.[33] The "beating hearts" that should lead to the inclusion of slaves in a
legal order of rights actually themselves constitute something of a legal order, one that
is every bit as detrimental to the health and happiness of the slaves as the one to which
it seems to be opposed. Simon Legree claims that slaves survive—"generally last"—
"'cordin' as their constitution is" (484). George and Stowe may present George's body
as an alternative to the force of slavery's law, but it is hardly clear that its legal order
is any more forgiving to him. He will cease to be a slave only when he escapes his constitution—political or biological.[34]

It is not even certain, moreover, that he will cease to be a slave then. The end of the
person's constitution seems only to invoke the authority of yet another one: God's.
Tom claims that Legree cannot buy his "soul": "No! no! no! my soul an't yours, Mas'r!
You haven't bought it,—ye can't buy it!" His soul is secure from Legree's acquisitive
aspirations not so much because souls, in principle, cannot be bought but, rather, be-

cause Tom's soul, in practice, has already "been bought and paid for by one that is able to keep it." From this vantage God does not represent an alternative to slavery so much as a better form of it. The Pauline implications of this form of self-abnegation are readily apparent, but Stowe clearly means for us to understand God's mastery in socioeconomic terms as well as spiritual ones. It is for this reason that while Stowe certainly represents death as a kind of release from earthly slavery, she does not exactly represent heaven as a release from it. Heaven is the place Tom "want[s] to go" not because he will be free there but because he will be reunited with his proper master there (509). And when George, who of course has no interest in returning to his proper master, imagines death as a solution to his difficulties, he describes its value in terms that make no recourse whatsoever either to heaven or to God. "All men are free and equal *in the grave,* if it comes to that" (163). It is one thing to imagine that all are "equal" in the grave and quite another to say that they are all "free" there. Free from what? Free to do what? What marks George's freedom is not so much the prospect of agency as the absence of constitutions—the state's, his body's, or God's.

Critics have long wondered exactly how effectively *Uncle Tom's Cabin*'s critique of slavery could inform an actual political project of abolition, but George's bleak vision of liberty might actually lead us to question the extent to which the novel amounts to a critique of slavery in the first instance.[35] Like *Battle-Pieces, Uncle Tom's Cabin* often seems bent on representing the abolition of slavery as the extension of slavery. Every plausible alternative to slavery in the novel seemingly becomes just another form of slavery. Death, especially death in the sense of being in the grave as opposed to death in the sense of returning to our maker, would hardly seem to count as an acceptable solution to the problems slavery poses. If the closest we can get to free and equal is "free and equal in the grave," freedom and equality might begin to seem pretty much irrelevant. What would Stowe consider a true alternative to slavery? Here the key figure is Ophelia, who, as we learn early on in our acquaintance with her, "was the absolute bond-slave of the '*ought.*'" More than any other figure in the novel she embodies the prospect of a tyrannical religiosity: "Her theological tenets were all made up, labelled in the most positive and distinct forms, . . . And, underlying all, deeper than anything else, higher and broader, lay the strongest principle of her being—conscientiousness" (227).

What makes Ophelia's relationship to morality both anomalous and slavish is precisely her willingness to transform moral considerations into specific codified "theological tenets." This point is made just as emphatically in Stowe's representation of Tom's relationship to God. For at least as Tom understands it, what makes God his master is that Tom treats God as a source of law: "but my soul I won't give up to mortal man. I will hold on to the Lord, and put his commands before all" (541). It is as if God would not count as a master to Tom if he were not responsible for the "commands" Tom puts before "all," if he could not be apprehended as a source of rules as well as a source of inspiration. What it means to accept theological tenets and put God's commands before all becomes clear in Ophelia's responses to the moral abuses that arise in the daily maintenance of slavery as a social institution. After learning that "those folks have whipped Prue to death!" she expresses amazement at the idea that there are no political forces that work to prevent such a moral outrage: "an't you going to *do* anything about it? . . . Haven't you got any *selectmen,* or anybody, to interfere and look after such matters?" (312). Ophelia's slavery would thus seem to stem from the way in which she understands moral considerations as the occasion for action, Tom's from the way he takes God's commandments as actual commands.

From this perspective morality can be saved from slavery only when it is removed from the realm of behavior ("*do* anything about it"). It may be possible to be against slavery, but it is impossible to oppose it (by passing laws or "holding on to God") without also reproducing it—which is why Stowe can locate freedom, as well as equality, in death: freedom for her entails one's being removed from the world of action, not one's possessing the capacity to act.[36] Philip Fisher has noted that the "time schemes of sentimental stories involve moments when action is impossible" and has suggested that the true mark of Stowe's sentimentalism is her deep fascination with moments in which characters possess "unendurable knowledge in the absence of the power to act."[37] In light of Stowe's interest in the connection between action and slavery, we can expand Fisher's analysis by saying that Stowe embraces the sentimental because it is only within such a frame that she imagines slavery to be escapable.[38] Stowe is less interested in *fighting* slavery with sentiment than in *avoiding* slavery with it.[39] Critics have long noted what seems like an uneasy relation in *Uncle Tom's Cabin* between the intensity of Stowe's critique of slavery and the gingerly way in which she sidles up to antislavery political action.[40] But since any translation of the novel's critique of the legal order of slavery into a legal alternative to slavery would, from Stowe's perspective, simply count as the restoration of slavery, what looks like the novel's political quiescence is actually a function of its commitment to its radical premises. There is no "contradiction" (to use Joseph Bellin's terms) between Stowe's vigorous "judgment" of slavery and her tentative embrace of any "action" that might eliminate it, no "tension" (to use Gregg Crane's terms) between her "jurisprudence of feeling" and her ambivalence about "revolutionary anger."[41] Stowe's judgment precludes action; her jurisprudence of feeling forbids revolution. The question for her is not how effectively her sentimentalism translates into a radical politics of antislavery so much as how effectively her sentimentalism retains its radical character by being untranslatable into a politics of any kind whatsoever.

It is in these terms that we can best make sense of Stowe's infamous "concluding remarks," in which she tells her readers "what any individual can do" about the horrors her novel has depicted: "But, what can any individual do? Of that, every individual can judge. There is but one thing that every individual can do,—they can see to it that *they feel right.* An atmosphere of sympathetic influence encircles every human being; and the man or woman who *feels* strongly, healthily and justly, on the great interests of humanity, is a constant benefactor to the human race. See, then, to your sympathies in this matter! Are they in harmony with the sympathies of Christ? or are they swayed and perverted by the sophistries of worldly policy?" (632). The usual recent emphasis on Stowe's commitment to "feeling" in this sequence is perhaps a little bit misleading:[42] it is clear from context that her interest in feeling here is a result of her effort to produce a policy that "every individual" can follow, not simply one available to the figures, such as "Christian men and women of the North" (who can "*pray*" as well as "*feel*"), whom she addresses in the paragraphs surrounding this one. It is nonetheless useful to note that Stowe's account of what people should "do" focuses so much on an action that looks almost wholly internal to prospective reformers, for it begins to train our eyes on the immense difficulty she has in formulating an affirmative politics of antislavery. The difficulty becomes especially conspicuous at the paragraph's end, where Stowe tells her readers to "see . . . to your sympathies in this matter" without specifying exactly what sympathies we should have. At this point we might become aware that her order to "feel right" neither includes nor entails a description of what "right" feeling is, and we might also go on to notice that her instructions for carrying out our "seeing" about our sympathies invokes a normative standard—"the sympathies of Christ"—without either giving that standard any content or insisting that we accommodate our sympathies to it. We are told to put our feelings "in harmony" with those of Christ, not to follow his example or his instruction: this Christ is not another version of Tom's God. Along these lines it is not hard to register that what Stowe tells her readers to "do" does not ultimately involve any direct interaction with the problem in question. What the readers should do is exist and by existing produce an "atmosphere." Not only is feeling not very active, but Stowe channels the feeling through an intermediary before talking about "benefactors": the readers hardly look like agents of this beneficence. If the goal is to avoid "the sophistries of worldly policy," Stowe does so by making her advice avoid both the realm of the "worldly" *and* the realm of "policy."

Tom takes Stowe's advice. In Tom's death Stowe finds what she calls a "*victory*" for "Africa," a victory that comes less from anything Tom does than from the way he feels ("When we can love and pray over all and through all, the battle's past, and the victory's come") and which manifests itself in terms of positive influence in the world (in the conversion of Cassy) only indirectly: "The deep fervor of Tom's feelings, the softness of his voice, his tears, fell like dew on the wild, unsettled spirit of the poor woman" (564). Tom's power lies in his "feelings," not his "words"; indeed, insofar as Stowe sandwiches her account of those words between two descriptions of his feelings and insofar as she refuses to disclose what his words were, the words seem less to express his feelings than simply to indicate that he has them. From this standpoint it is hardly surprising that Tom ultimately produces an atmosphere ("dew") within which change takes place rather than wielding an instrument for effecting it. This is a kind of "reign[ing]" so removed from "worldly policy" that Stowe can endorse it.[43]

Even this kind of victory, however, is somewhat awkward. We can begin to see as much by placing the scene of Cassy's conversion in the context of *Battle-Pieces*, in which, you will recall, Melville's account of the persistence of slavery was linked to the notion that the mere existence of the state itself constitutes a form of Dominion. For the point of Melville's image of the dome in "The Conflict of Convictions" is that there is no difference between the emergence of an atmosphere in which change occurs and the production of normative standards that compel change to take place. Like Tom, the dome does not seem to act at all; like Stowe's readers, it works through an intermediary (the sun's light) and indeed seems less to work through an intermediary than to be worked through by the medium in which its actions are elaborated. But Melville's attenuation of the dome's agency, unlike Stowe's attenuation of Tom's, does almost nothing to lessen his apprehension about its authority, and Stowe herself is sensitive to the ways in which what might look like Tom's victory for Africa could come to count as a defeat for Cassy's liberty. When victories like Tom's threaten to emerge in the domain of Melville's domes rather than the domain of Cassy's heart, *Uncle Tom's Cabin* is no more tolerant of them than *Battle-Pieces*.

Tom is not the only figure who attains something like a victory and the prospect of "reign[ing]" at the end of the novel. George's fate is also associated with an African victory over slavery, and though on its surface George's ultimate course has a more straightforward relationship to political action than Tom's, Stowe nonetheless ensures that even his victory will not involve the production of law. George's desire to be free is integrally linked to the desire, as he puts it, to have "a country, a nation, of my own" (616): "I haven't any country, any more than I have any father. But I'm going to have one." But the country he thinks he will have here ("when I get to Canada where the laws will own me and protect me, *that* shall be my country") turns out to be just another of the countries he feels he has to abandon (161). His ambition to have a country of his "own" is systematically frustrated in *Uncle Tom's Cabin*. His career is, in effect, nothing more than a record of the repudiation of jurisdiction after jurisdiction—the South, the North, Canada, England, France—before he finally finds one in which he is willing to live.

It is telling in this regard, moreover, that what makes Africa an acceptable final destination is precisely the fact that there are, at least as George sees it, no fully developed countries there. In Africa he will participate in a "new enterprise" rather than being assimilated into an old one. Indeed, it is ultimately somewhat unclear if the new enterprise of which he will be a part should really count as a nation in any straightforward civil or political sense. We can get a glimmer of the problem in his suggestion that he wishes to have "a country, a nation, of my own." These terms might seem to be interchangeable, but for George there is an important difference between them. He is interested in being a part of the "republic" of Liberia and the "African *nationality.*" And it is his commitment to the difference between the two which allows him to want to be a part of both a single national organization and the proliferation of multiple political enterprises: "A nation starts, now, with all the great problems of republican life and civilization wrought out to its hand;—it has not to discover, but only to apply. Let us, then, all take hold together, with all our might, and see what we can do with this new enterprise, and the whole splendid continent of Africa opens before us and our children. *Our nation* shall roll the tide of civilization and Christianity along its shores, and plant there mighty republics" (615).

We might well wonder if George wishes to be part of a political entity like a republic or a racial entity like a people. Over the course of this sequence he moves from an interest in "an African *nationality*" and "a people that shall have a tangible, separate existence of its own" to an interest in "a country, a nation, of my own." George's final destination may be to a nation that has no political form, to a nation made simply of his "people."[44] The "grand council of free nations" he envisions will provide a forum for "appeal[s]" and "remonstrat[ions]" rather than opportunities for government (615). Stowe would later repudiate the project of African colonization which marks *Uncle Tom's Cabin*'s conclusion, and many critics have concluded from Stowe's later hostility to colonization that the novel's interest in colonization was essentially a detachable "matter of anti-slavery politics" subject to easy revision down the road.[45] But given the novel's systematic efforts to oppose liberty to the state, George's ultimate fate looks more like an integral outgrowth of novel's core commitments than a tangential postscript. George claims that he wants to be "owned" by the laws of the country in which he lives (161). For Stowe the story of George's emancipation requires the infinite postponement of his arriving in such a place. Like *Battle-Pieces, Uncle Tom's Cabin* can replace the dominion of darkness with the dominion of light, but, also like *Battle-Pieces,* it cannot replace dominion with freedom.

Thwarted Revolutions

Up to this point I have been addressing works that *sought* to intertwine the law and slavery. They set about demonstrating the extent to which the taint of slavery can attach to the law. But the connection they elaborate between the law and slavery also appears in a variety of works that are not so devoted to elaborating that connection, even in some that seem committed to contesting it. And it is in these resistant works that we can feel the full force of the abolitionist reading of *Somerset*. Melville wants to condemn the law as a form of slavery, but someone like William Wells Brown, we will see, wants to use the law as a means of attacking slavery. That a work such as *Clotel; or, The President's Daughter: A Narrative of Slave Life in the United States* (1853) presents its legalist condemnation of slavery as a call for a new form of "bondage,"[46] that it casts the laws that might eliminate slavery as a set of "fetters," gives Garrison's reading of Mansfield an almost tyrannical quality largely absent from such relatively compliant expressions of that reading as *Battle-Pieces* and *Uncle Tom's Cabin*.

The most salient evidence of *Somerset*'s more unwelcome pull lies in the antebellum literature of slave revolution. This literature is internally divided at its very core—yearning on the one hand to command the law as an instrument for social transformation, uncomfortable on the other about the moral implications of such political reform. The tension has not gone unrecognized in recent criticism, in which it has been generally characterized as a tension between a revolutionary impulse and a recoil from the violence such a revolution would unleash.[47] But the literature of slave revolution is ambivalent about the political results of revolutions as well as the violence required to bring those results about—indeed, it is more ambivalent, or at least more conspicuously ambivalent, about the political implications of revolutions than their practical consequences. Consider *Dred: A Tale of the Great Dismal Swamp* (1856),[48] for instance, a novel that is generally regarded as a marked departure from the political quiescence implicit in Stowe's earlier best-seller.[49] About three-quarters of the way through *Dred*, after experiencing the horrors of slavery in countless ways over a nearly countless number of pages, Harry has finally had enough. Invoking the Declaration of Independence and its claim that "it is [the] *right* and [the] *duty*" of those "reduce[d] . . . under absolute despotism" "to throw off such government," he gathers a group of fellow slaves around him and issues, "in earnest and vehement language," a plea for revolutionary action. His plea is in some senses nothing more than the plot of *Dred* itself: "Harry then . . . narrated the abuse which had been inflicted upon Milly; and then recited, in a clear and solemn voice, that judicial decision which had burned itself into his memory, and which had confirmed and given full license to that despotic power. He related the fate of his own contract—of services for years to the family which he had labored, all ending in worse than nothing. And then he told his sister's history, till his voice was broken by sobs" (455–56). Harry gives an impressive rhetorical performance. It resonates with his fellow slaves, who quickly link their own life histories to his complaint; and perhaps more important, it clearly meets the revolutionary standards implicit in his introductory remarks about the Declaration. Harry's "full[y] license[d] despotic power" obviously echoes Jefferson's "absolute despotism." The case might seem to have been fully clinched even before the gathering receives word of yet another example of the despotism he invokes: Hark's murder ("Dey's all last night a killing of him" [457]). Dred only seems to confirm the obvious when he responds to the news by saying: "The harvest groweth ripe! The press is full! The vats overflow!" (458).

Yet something funny happens as Dred continues to talk about how "the day of vengeance is in my heart, and the year of the redeemed is come!" (459): he decides that the press is not quite full enough and that the vats might still hold a little more. "Brethren," he concludes, "the vision is sealed up, and the token is not yet come! The Lamb still beareth the yoke of their iniquities. . . . And there is silence in heaven for the space of half an hour! But hold yourselves in waiting, for the day cometh!" What Dred demands, and what he has not quite received, is something other than "silence" from the heavens. "When the Lord saith unto us, Smite," he explains, "then we will smite" (460). In the absence of such an explicit divine intervention, the revolution would teeter perilously close to something on the order of revenge. Dred hears Harry's remarks as an appeal to God: "Hear ye the word of the Lord against this people" (458). But others in the audience, such as Hannibal, hear them as a demand for a more immediate, and perhaps more primitive, form of justice: "We will reward them as they have rewarded us! In the cup that they have filled to us we will measure to them again." "God forbid," Dred responds, "that the elect of the Lord should do that!" (460). And in effect He does forbid such "vengeance" by remaining mute even in the face of such overwhelming evidence of the "people's" suffering (461).

Dred's momentary reticence should not be confused with any reservation about the moral right of revolutionary force. Although the night's proceedings come to a close, in "dead silence" (462), after Milly's plea that the gathering "love yer enemies" and "leave de vengeance to" "de Lord" (461), Dred makes it clear that he thinks that the group is putting off its revolt, not abandoning it. Her "prayers have prevailed" only "this time" (462). At another time he openly acknowledges, "we will slay them utterly, and consume them from off the face of the earth" (460). But Dred's requirement— that God actually say something to the revolutionaries, that the revolution proceed not only in accordance with God's will but also in obedience to his direct command—might seem so rigorous as to preclude in practical terms the revolution he fully embraces in moral terms. Stowe herself seems to have reached this conclusion. *Dred* constitutes something of a repudiation of Dred's commitment to proceeding only on God's explicit instruction. Later on in the novel Clayton condemns his uncle for waiting for "*the Lord* to raise up a standard" before he commits himself to "necessary reforms": "What would you think, if a man's house were on fire, and he should sit praying that the Lord in his mysterious providence he would put it out?" (491). *Dred* refuses to leave the task of eliminating slavery entirely in God's hands. At times Stowe even goes so far as to imagine that it must lie wholly within ours.

Of course, this sequence is somewhat equivocal. These "necessary reforms," unlike Dred's revolution, will be done in "a way perfectly peaceable and lawful." Indeed, Clayton is as concerned about the violence a mob might do to a reformer ("who is cloven down under the hoof of a mob") as he is with the reforms themselves (491). And his example of the fiery house blurs the distinction between Dred's resistance to Harry's appeal and Milly's. Clayton begins by condemning the notion that we should await God's *sign;* he ends by condemning the notion that we should await God's *agency.* This equivocation is ultimately built into the larger fabric of *Dred* as a whole. If the novel repeatedly reminds us that God alone will not solve the problems of slavery, it never quite specifies what will. The successful antislavery actions in the novel involve neither revolution nor reform so much as what Stowe calls "Flight" (541). And even the strongest advocates of the right of slave revolt fall short of making such a revolt seem truly justified. Harry might invite the Lord to "judge between us" and the nation's Founding Fathers, "if the laws that they put upon us be not worse than any that lay upon them" (455). But he does not seem to think all that much rides upon the comparison. Neither the American Revolution nor anything modeled upon it ultimately gets his full approval. "Whatever my course may be," he writes to Clayton, "remember my excuse for it is the same as that on which your government is built" (436). Natural law arguments "excuse" violence rather than justify it—no wonder Dred is so concerned that Harry's invocation of the Declaration of Independence would lead to revenge rather than revolution. In this regard it should hardly come as a surprise that Stowe gives the antislavery "township" Clayton forms at the end of *Dred* only the thinnest of political foundations (534). The locale "is the richest and finest in the region," not the most democratic; and if it provides excellent civic facilities such as schools, its chief contribution to the surrounding area seems to have been to "nearly double[] the price of real estate in the vicinity" (544). Whatever else Clayton has done in Canada, he has not led a democratic or natural rights revolution. He has not even established what George might call a political "enterprise."

As we have already been able to gauge, recent studies of Stowe have revolved around efforts to specify the nature of her relationship to the politics of antislavery in the 1850s. It is indeed difficult to determine whether Stowe shies away from the political interventions *Dred* so often seems to invite because of deep philosophical misgivings about forceful responses to the injustices of slavery (as when the right of revolution becomes merely an excuse) or because of deep practical misgivings about their likely effectiveness (as when Clayton "admit[s] the right of an oppressed people to change their form of government, *if they can*" [442]). But in many respects the question of *where* Stowe stood with respect to the politics of antislavery is less interesting than the prior question of *why* she would have felt the need to choose between political calculation and moral purity in the first instance. What pressure occasions Dred's immense dependence upon God's actual word before he begins his cleansing bloodshed? Harry invokes the model of the Founding Fathers, after all, and they seem to have gotten by without an extra gesture from the Almighty—even though, as both Harry and Dred both point out, they faced even less oppression than their slave progeny. What would make a revolution for slave emancipation in the 1850s repudiate the rationale for the Founders' "government" even as it lays claim to extending it? Why should the Founders' practice be both exemplary and unacceptable?

Obviously, at least part of the problem here can be laid at the feet of the legacy of *Somerset* and its implicit suggestion that positive law amounts to the record of man's deviation from God's natural order. Such a regime puts a great deal of pressure on the moments in which men intervene in their own affairs, if it does not essentially preclude them from doing as much. Nonetheless, Stowe's assault on the integrity of the American Revolution still seems somewhat extreme. Even figures such as Garrison, after all, tended to celebrate the Declaration of Independence; indeed, Garrison claimed to derive his antislavery position in part from Jefferson's natural rights rhetoric. "I am a believer," he said in the 1854 address in which he burned the Constitution, "in that portion of the Declaration of Independence in which it is set forth, as among self-evident truths, 'that all men are created equal; that they are endowed by their Creator with certain inalienable rights; that among these are life, liberty, and the pursuit of happiness.' Hence, I am an Abolitionist."[50] His complaint was with the Constitution, the law itself, not the principles of the Revolution, to which he paid as much homage as even religious Unionists such as Lincoln. Why was Stowe unable, or at least unwilling, to make a similar distinction?

In the remainder of this chapter I will explain exactly what inspires Stowe to invoke the model of the American Revolution in the context of slavery and what prevents her from embracing it as a model for antislavery agitation. I will lay out my argument largely in terms of a reading of Brown's novel *Clotel*, which probably constitutes 1850s America's most profound rethinking of the meaning of the Revolution. Brown, we will see, provides a startlingly clear genealogy of Dred's demand and a visionary account of how it might be met. I am aware that few readers are likely to associate *Clotel* with that tradition of antebellum narratives about slave revolts in which *Dred* plays such a central role.[51] Political revolution seldom breaks through into the purview of the novel's extended accounts of romantic difficulty, and when it does break through it is treated with something on the order of contempt. Late in *Clotel* Dred himself makes an appearance, and Brown could hardly represent him with less sympathy. In *Clotel*'s account of the revolt of the Dismal Swamp, the "large, tall, full-blooded negro, with a stern and savage countenance" and "marks on his face [which] showed that he was from one of the barbarous tribes in Africa," *pursues* pure revenge rather than tempering it: "from revenge [he] imbrued his hands in the blood of all the whites he could meet" (202). When, in response, "the whites massacred all blacks found beyond their owners' plantations" and "the negroes, in return, set fire to houses, and put those to death who attempted to escape the flames," Brown sees simply the operations of slavery, not a reasonable protest against it: "The carnage was added to carnage, and the blood of the whites flowed to avenge the blood of the blacks. These were the ravages of slavery" (203). But even as Brown refuses to *represent* a slave revolt as anything more than carnage, his novel itself *constitutes* a more successful revolutionary effort—albeit one that is severely, and self-consciously, circumscribed by the legal scaffolding that had come to surround slavery in Anglo-American law. It is indeed Brown's point, even when matters of political revolution seem far from his immediate attention, to provide an outline of that scaffolding and an example of the terms in which it could be overcome.

Shifting the locus of my analysis from what *Clotel* represents to what it embodies will allow me to address the formal considerations that have long lay at the center of the novel's critical interest.[52] I will, for example, be able to say exactly why the first published African-American novel is a novel. But while I see *Clotel* as a brilliant demonstration of the possibilities and limitations of political authority within the regime constructed around slavery in Anglo-American law, critics have usually seen it as a hodgepodge of half-baked narrative threads. For many of Brown's most recent readers *Clotel* constitutes an aesthetic disaster, not a political revolution. Robert Reid-Pharr, for instance, begins his analysis by admitting that *Clotel* is simply incoherent: "Brown never establishes the authorial control that is so very apparent in the novels of twentieth-century (Black) America."[53] There are, to be sure, good reasons to question exactly what authority Brown exercises in the book. Few works of literature match the novel's self-conscious staging of its own dependence upon its sources. *Clo-tel* often seems little more than a patchwork of citations and borrowings. Whole chunks of its narrative come from stories published by other hands, and Brown's prose swarms with quotations from a broad range of writers and politicians. But we will see that this conspicuous intertextuality is not the mark of Brown's inability to control his novel so much as a dramatization of how much power he has within it. Indeed, the entire point of the novel is to reveal Brown's authorial control and to demonstrate that, at least within the world of *Clotel*, Brown himself possesses such control that a Dred-style sign from God would be either unnecessary or redundant. If anything, Brown has too much control in *Clotel*. Throughout the novel there looms the subtle but not entirely muted prospect that there is something vaguely improper about the authority he wields over his narrative and characters. Brown may be able to avoid re-venge only by engaging in blasphemy.

It will be important that we recognize the nature of Brown's authority in *Clotel* as well as the centrality of that authority to his enterprise as a whole. In his notes to what remains the most important single piece of Brown scholarship, the Bedford edition of *Clotel*, Robert Levine insists that Brown was no mere "documentary historian." Brown did not seek to document "the white supremacist culture" he inhabited but to "contest" it by way of "a massive, complex, often brilliant effort to recontextualize his source materials," an effort that "raise[ed] questions about the ways in which mean-ings are produced in a white racist culture, and ultimately suggest[ed] news ways of reading that culture" (233). Levine's Brown comes across as something on the order of a cultural historian, with no greater task before him than that of producing frameworks in which we might understand the intellectual and social landscape he inhabits. But *Clotel* is far more devoted to contesting than it is to recontextualizing— which is to say that what it means to contest are the actual institutions and practices of nineteenth-century American culture, not the way in which those institutions and practices were represented and understood. In his "Conclusion," in describing his en-terprise in the terms Levine associates with the documentary historian, Brown refers to the various "sources" and "scenes" that constitute "my narrative" as "my resources" (226), and throughout the novel he systematically subordinates considerations of truth to considerations of action. *Clotel* repeatedly eschews the enterprise of under-standing the "evil of slavery" so as to take up the more pressing question of how to effect the institution's removal. In the pages that follow we will examine why Brown thought *Clotel* could help "proclaim[] the Year of Jublilee" throughout the Anglo-American world and exactly why he thought the novel form was central to the task at hand (227). The first step in making sense of these unexpected commitments is to come to terms with Brown's understanding of the American Revolution.

The Government of Men

As a number of commentators have recently observed, a striking Anglophilia per-
meates the major antislavery African-American works of the 1850s and 1860s.[54] Consider, for instance, this sequence from the last pages of William Craft's *Running a
Thousand Miles for Freedom* (1860),[55] the published version of one of the many slave
narratives Brown cribs in *Clotel:*

> [We are grateful] to the Vigilance Committee of Boston . . . for the very kind and noble
> manner in which they assisted us to preserve our liberties and to escape from Boston, as
> it were like Lot from Sodom, to a place of refuge, and finally to this truly free and glori-
> ous country; where no tyrant, let his power be ever so absolute over his poor trembling
> victims at home, dare come and lay violent hands upon us or upon our dear little
> boys . . . and reduce us to the legal level of the beast that perisheth. Oh! May God bless
> the thousands of . . . abolitionists in America, who are laboring . . . to restore to every
> bondman his God-given rights; may God ever smile upon England and upon England's
> good, much-beloved, and deservedly-honoured Queen, for the generous protection that
> is given to unfortunate refugees of every rank, and of every colour and clime. (732)

The basic terms of this appeal are hardly surprising: as a practical matter, the *Commentaries* and *Somerset* had in their various ways established English "soil" as a more
powerful guard against slavery than any American personal liberty law. There is nonetheless something slightly hyperbolic in Craft's devotion to England and in his condemnation of the United States. It is strange, after all, to think of *Boston* as the Sodom
of slavery or to see in it an apt image of a tyrant with "absolute" "power" over "trem-
bling victims." To be sure, the passage of the Fugitive Slave Act 1850 served as a powerful reminder of the limits of local antislavery authority in the United States—a topic
I will take up in more detail in the next chapter. But the idea that the restoration of
"Godgiven rights" entails a repudiation of Boston, that iconic emblem of the Revolution allegedly devoted to such rights, remains somewhat jarring, as does Craft's inti-
mation that African Americans would need to "escape" that city as if it were no different from the plantation itself. And the pointed peculiarity of this alignment of Boston
and tyranny only becomes more emphatic in light of the figure Craft opposes to the
American tyrant Boston somehow embodies: England's good and deservedly honored queen. The image of the queen, not to put too fine a point on the matter, rather
obviously summons the prospect of the personal authority of the tyrant as much as
the personal protection of the benefactor. Why not focus on the English tradition of
parliamentary government, the canonical documents that established that tradition,

or, following Blackstone, the English soil and the air? Given the trajectory tradition of abolitionist thinking we have been charting, however, Victoria's appearance as an emblem of God-given rights makes perfect sense. For the English monarch here seems to stand as a model of government without governing authority, as an embodiment of a state that exercises no will other than the negative energy devoted to "protect" its inhabitants from the legislative innovations of other regimes. The monarch, that is, stands as something like the institutional form of Blackstone's more metaphorical "soil." It is precisely because she no longer exercises the government's power—because, like Thoreau's neighbor, she is "loved" and "honored" but not exactly obeyed— that she can represent the state of natural right.

Discarding Boston for the "protection" of the English throne, Craft effectively insists that freedom entails something along the lines of a reversal of the American Revolution. And though that claim is cast in conspicuously polemical tones in *Running a Thousand Miles for Freedom,* it nonetheless played an important role in the antislavery imagination more broadly, a role that is sometimes obscured by the ease with which emancipation can be represented as an extension of the Revolution rather than its repudiation. David Brion Davis suggests that there was what Davis calls a "logic" of the Revolution, a logic that tended in the direction of emancipation and which was effectively tempered or contained by the Constitution in which the Revolution culminated: "The logic of the Revolution suggested that [antislavery] principles might have prevailed at the Constitutional Convention" (322). This claim that the Constitution thwarted the emancipatory impulses looming within the Revolution has a long and distinguished pedigree in abolitionist polemic, dating back at least as far as Garrison's 1832 essay "The Great Crisis." "By the infamous bargain which they [the Founders] made between themselves," Garrison maintained, "they virtually dethroned the Most High God, and trampled beneath their feet their own solemn and heaven-attested Declaration, that all men are created equal, and endowed by their Creator with certain inalienable rights—among which are life, liberty, and the pursuit of happiness."[56] But the Declaration did more than "clearly and accurately define[] the rights of man,"[57] and some of its other tendencies were not so clearly heaven-attested as Garrison or Davis would imply. From the perspective of the antislavery 1850s, the Revolution's logic could be far more nuanced and multivalent than we might first expect.

Pinpointing an antislavery logic in the Revolution, of course, is an easy task. Antislavery sentiment so clearly pervades the rhetoric of the Revolution that most commentators find themselves astonished that the revolutionary leaders themselves seemed not to recognize the ultimate implications of their claims. "How is it," Samuel Johnson famously quipped, "that we hear the loudest *yelps* for liberty from the drivers of negroes?"[58] Historians have indeed had a hard time avoiding the inference that what Davis called a "cruel[] irony" (285) attends a revolution that celebrated the rights of man while at the same time countenancing the persistence of slavery. The point is not that there is some simple contradiction between the revolutionary impulse and the practice of slavery. Even if one grants Edmund Morgan's claim that Americans "bought their independence with slave labor," he is still left to cope with the yawning gap between what Morgan calls a "political language that magnified the rights of freemen" and a sociopolitical infrastructure that had been constructed around the peculiar institution.[59] Davis's *Problem of Slavery in the Age of Revolution* amounts to the classic treatment of this chasm between revolutionary discourse and colonial social practice, and he sees in it something "more . . . than irony." "If the American Revolution could not solve the problem of slavery," he maintains, "it at least led to a *perception* of the problem" (285). And what Davis adduces as an *effect* of the Revolution could be described in the 1850s as the *intention* of the Revolution—or at least the intention of the Declaration of Independence. With the Declaration the Founders, Abraham Lincoln explained in his 1857 "Speech on the 'Dred Scott' Decision," "meant to set up a standard maxim for a free society which should be familiar to all: constantly looked to, constantly labored for, and even though never perfectly attained, constantly approximated and thereby constantly spreading and deepening its influence and augmenting the happiness and value of life to people, of all colors, everywhere."[60]

It is against this backdrop that we can best understand Brown's deployment of Jefferson in *Clotel*.[61] Jefferson's most telling appearance in the novel coincides with his daughter's suicide outside of the nation's "capital": "Thus died Clotel, the daughter of Thomas Jefferson, a president of the United States; a man distinguished as the author of the Declaration of American Independence, and one of the first statesmen of that country" (207). Obviously, at least part of the point here is to deny the Revolution the indirect and direct benefits Davis and Lincoln, respectively, attribute to it.[62] For Brown the relationship between Jefferson and his slaves remains essentially ironic: the Revolution does not lead to the perception of the problem of slavery; *Clotel* does.[63] To focus exclusively on the irony of Jefferson's daughter's dying as a slave outside of Washington, however, is to miss the force of Brown's more subtle point. With *Running a Thousand Miles* in mind, we might notice that Brown undermines the moral standing of the United States's founding document even as he reveals the irony in the nation's being unable to live up to its commitments. Brown insists upon, indeed conjures, the national particularity of Jefferson's declaration of human rights: "Declaration of *American* Independence." Whereas Lincoln sees an expression of a "standard maxim for a free society which should be familiar to all," Brown sees a specifically nationalist, not to say ethnocentric, expression of power. The problem of slavery thus seems to derive less from the fact that the United States is failing to meet the Declaration's standard than from the fact that she is governed by that document in the first instance. And in this regard *Clotel* begins to suggest that American slavery was the *result* of the American Revolution rather than an embarrassing legacy of a prior, and less liberal, regime.

Such a notion might initially seem somewhat farfetched, but in narrowing the Declaration's scope to a finite, slaveholding sect, Brown was merely anticipating what would become a prominent line of argument in the sectional crisis of the 1850s. Historians have long noted the Declaration's emerging prominence in immediate prewar political culture and stressed the way in which it shaped what David Donald has called the "political philosophy" of the era.[64] I will discuss some of the more technical legal implications of the Declaration's new salience in chapter 4. For now it is enough for us to note that Chief Justice Taney devoted several crucial paragraphs of his *Dred Scott* opinion to the Declaration, despite its having no obvious legal bearing on, or authority with respect to, the matter at hand; and that Stephen Douglas located it at the heart of his doctrine of popular sovereignty, which meant that it would play a central role in the Lincoln-Douglas debates of 1858 and in the gradual fragmenting of the Democratic Party in 1859 and 1860. It is hardly surprising, of course, that political leaders would invoke such a revered document in times of crisis. But there were also more substantial reasons for the Declaration's salience in the period. The most obvious of these reasons is that by the 1850s Jefferson's truths were finally, or were once again, leading to the "perception" that slavery constituted a "problem" in a nation ostensibly dedicated to freedom. And in this regard the very project of figures such as Taney and Davis was to detach the document from the irony that might to seem to attend it.

Taney's reading of Jefferson's self-evident truths openly confronts the prospect that "the conduct" of the Framers would be "utterly and flagrantly inconsistent with the principles they asserted."[65] And Douglas's commitment to reading the Declaration through the lens of racial exclusion was developed largely in response to Lincoln's effort to turn the document to antislavery purposes. "Mr. Lincoln is very much in the habit of following in the track of Lovejoy in this particular, by reading that part of the Declaration of Independence to prove that the negro was endowed by the Almighty with the inalienable right of equality with white men," Douglas complained on September 15, 1858, during the third Lincoln-Douglas debate at Jonesboro. "Now, I say to you, my fellow-citizens, that in my opinion the signers of the Declaration had no reference to the negro whatever when they declared all men to be created equal. They desired to express by that phrase, white men, men of European birth and European descent, and had no reference either to the negro, the savage Indians, the Fejee, the

Malay, or any other inferior and degraded race, when they spoke of the equality of men" (1:598). Douglas's Declaration without "reference" to the "negro" or the "Fejee," of course, is nothing more than Brown's "Declaration of American Independence." It sits comfortably alongside the practice of American slavery precisely because it is devoted less to human rights than to American sovereignty. As Davis himself observes, the Founding Fathers were not simply fighting on behalf of natural rights. They were also fighting, "after all, for self-determination. And it is now clear that slavery was of central importance to both southern and national economies, and thus to the viability of the 'American system'" (256).

From this vantage the Declaration and the Revolution did not merely fail to solve the problem of slavery; they actually contributed to the problem of slavery. Davis casts the point in largely socioeconomic terms, but it also had important theoretical implications. Taney did not have to defend slavery from the principles of the Revolution; he could actually *derive* it from them. The "obstacles to emancipation" "raised" by "demands for self-determination" existed at the level of political theory as well as the level of social practice and reality (259), and indeed the political implications of self-determination are probably more important than the socioeconomic ones Davis adduces. We might tweak Davis's claim by noting that the Founders were fighting for the *right* of self-determination as well as the maintenance of their familiar social and political structures. And this form of self-government, at least from the perspective of the Garrisonian reading of *Somerset,* was precisely what constituted slavery: the consent of the governed is also the dominion of man. The Revolution could thus seem to take away with democratic practice exactly those rights it extended as a matter of democratic theory. It certainly did not have to be seen in these terms. In a classic reading of the Lincoln-Douglas debates, Harry Jaffa has maintained that the force of Lincoln's position in 1858 was to insist that self-government, properly understood, required a recognition of natural rights.[66] But this point was hardly as clear to Lincoln's contemporaries as it is to Jaffa, and it is easy to find figures such as Douglas who could derive slavery from popular sovereignty and derive popular sovereignty from Jefferson's Declaration of American Independence. "This government," Douglas announced in the final Lincoln-Douglas debate at Alton, "was made upon the great basis of the sovereignty of the States, the right of each State to regulate its own domestic institutions to suit itself" (1:776). In a culture where the sovereignty of the state came at the expense of the sovereignty of God, where man's "suit[ing] himself" involved his abjuring his Maker, Douglas's defense of democracy, with its implicit concessions to the sovereignty of man, amounted to a defense of slavery—whether or not that peculiar "institution" seemed appropriate to the men seeking their "happiness" through "regulations."

This tendency in Douglas's thinking, or at least the susceptibility of his thinking to this kind of reading, effectively reverses the considerations that organize the usual accounts of the "problem of slavery" in American history. A long and dutiful career of service to the rights of slaveholders should not necessarily make us question what Davis calls the "genuineness" of Jefferson's liberal beliefs (174). Nor should it lead us to decry the "limits" of enlightenment in actual American social and economic life. It should, instead, lead us to recognize that Jefferson's liberalism, at least from the perspective of the 1850s, was essentially Janus-faced—looking toward both the rights that slavery compromised *and* the rights that it implied. Pointing out that "American colonists were not trapped in an accidental contradiction between slavery and freedom," Davis reminds us that "demands for consistency between principles and practice . . . were rather beside the point" (262). But what makes the relationship between slavery and freedom in the United States "not accidental" is precisely the fact that the two could not be simply divided as principle and practice. The Declaration's principles include self-government as well as natural rights; we might even say they include the natural right of self-government. And thus slavery's persistence could be said to mark the new nation's commitment to "liberty" every bit as much as its commitment to "the public order" (260).[67]

Which is, in the end, the primary force of Craft's invocation of the queen as a symbol of freedom. It is not that Craft is unaware that slavery could be challenged from within an American political tradition. On the page before he writes his celebration of Victoria, he quotes a letter in which Samuel May laments that "the shadow of the British throne" guarantees "life, liberty, and the pursuit of happiness" far better than America, the self-proclaimed "land of the free" (731). But from Craft's perspective the nation's problem was not so much that it failed to be "the land of the free, and the home of the brave" as that it *was* a land where man felt free to rule, where the relevant crimes would be defined by man rather than God. Victoria could make no such claim. The throne's authority, being in the end nothing more than a "shadow," nothing more than an expression of the status of the soil itself, preserves freedom in a way that no legislative body could ever hope to emulate.

The end of *Running a Thousand Miles for Freedom* is useful for the way in which it indicates that the association of American rights with the persistence of slavery was by no means the exclusive property of figures whose political identities were forged largely in resistance to the burgeoning antislavery sentiment in the United States in the 1850s. The association played a central role in the antislavery imagination as well, especially in the thinking of Brown himself, who, as we have already seen, configures the Declaration as a particularly national document rather than a more broadly philosophical one. Brown also gives over a considerable part of *Clotel* to what ultimately emerges as a critique not simply of slavery but of democratic self-government more broadly:

> We say much against European despotism; let us look to ourselves. That government is despotic where the rulers govern the subjects by their own mere will—by decrees and laws emanating from their uncontrolled will, in the enactment and execution of which they have no right except at the will of the rulers. Despotism does not depend upon the number of rulers, or the number of subjects. It may have one ruler or many. . . . In this government, the free white citizens are the rulers—the sovereigns, as we delight to be called. All others are subjects. There are, perhaps, some sixteen or seventeen millions of sovereigns, and four millions of subjects. (176–77)

To be sure, Brown directs most of his ire toward the systematic exclusion of one class of the population from any participation in the "enactment and execution" of the laws. But in the course of elaborating this point, he also outlines another, more radical critique of American democracy. In casting his complaint about the exclusion of African Americans from civil standing in the United States as a critique of majority rule ("despotism does not depend upon the number of rulers, or the numbers of subjects"), Brown ultimately attacks sovereignty as such as well as the uneven distribution of it among the population ("the sovereigns, as we delight to be called"). Mere democratic participation, after all, does not in any way guarantee, in and of itself, that the decrees and laws of the government will be "controlled" or that they will have their origins in something other than "mere will." The solution to these problems lies as much in limitations upon self-government as in an inclusive franchise. And from this perspective we might begin to reconfigure our understanding of Brown's seemingly scathing references to "slavery, with its democratic whips, republican chains, and bloodhounds" (57). Not merely expressions of Davis's "cruel irony," these juxtapositions record slavery's capacity to render democratic self-government itself a form of the tyranny we imagine republics and democracies to have superseded.

Chains of Freedom

It comes as no surprise, then, that Brown suggests early on in *Clotel* that Horatio Green's betrayal of Clotel is facilitated by the fact that Horatio encountered the "strong temptation of variety in love" "unfettered by the laws of the land" (102). This linking of the land's laws and the fetters of slavery was an almost syllogistic outgrowth of the abolitionist reading of *Somerset* I have been tracing, and it lies at the very heart of the way in which Brown elaborates the nature of marriage in *Clotel*. This single reference to the "fetters" of marriage law might seem merely rhetorical but for the fact that, by the time we learn of Horatio's difficulties, the status of his relationship with Clotel has already been described extensively in terms of the fetters of formal marital commitment. "The tenderness of Clotel's conscience," Brown has already explained, "and the high value she placed upon virtue, required an outward marriage; though she well knew that a union with her proscribed race was unrecognized by law. . . . But her high poetic nature regarded reality rather than the semblance of things. . . . 'If the mutual love we have for each other, [she said] and the dictates of your own conscience do not cause you to remain my husband, and your affections fall from me, I would not, if I could, hold you by a single fetter.' It was indeed a marriage sanctioned by heaven, although unrecognized on earth" (100). This sequence reads as a veritable blueprint of the natural law critique of slavery: certain conditions exist in "reality," which the law, with its strange fixation only upon mere the "semblance of things," may or may not "recognize." Indeed, we might even say that the force of the sequence is systematically to detach "virtue" and "conscience" from legal institutions such as "outward marriage" and to locate them exclusively at the level of moral sentiment. Brown begins by suggesting that Clotel's "virtue" "required" marriage; he concludes by reporting that such constraints would effectively compromise the purity of her moral sentiments. Romantic relations dependent upon the recognition of the law can only be the product of a coercion unworthy of decent, "high," and "poetic natures." It is hard not to get the impression that Clotel's marriage was sanctioned in heaven precisely because it was not recognized on earth.

If this point is only implicit in *Clotel*, it is given more direct expression in *Dred*, in which Clayton openly announces that "there can be no true love without liberty" and Nina tells Harry that she is concerned that their sibling affection might constitute a "chain" on his freedom: "Well, Harry," said Nina, after a moment's thought, "my love shall not be a clasp upon *any* chain; for, as there is a God in heaven, I will set you free!" (131, 146). Stowe's point is not to divorce love altogether from the domain of political authority. Even as she suggests that "true love" requires "liberty," she also casts love as the foundation of any proper interpersonal hierarchy. By the end of the novel, for instance, Clayton's sister emerges as a sort of American Victoria—as a "queen" on "her own plantation." Her reign there is justified, like Victoria's in *Running in a Thousand Miles to Freedom*, because it is based on what Stowe calls "the strongest of all powers, that of love" (306). The danger in *Dred*, however, is that love can easily turn into chains. Instead of representing an alternative political order based on conscience and affections, it can be "recognized" by the state and turned precisely into one of the tyrannical fetters we might hope that it would lead us to escape.

While Stowe insists that love constitutes the "strongest of all powers," however, Brown suggests that its force is almost negligible in relation to the fetters of legal form.

Given Horatio's weak commitment to "his own inward convictions" and to "moral principle" (103), his love for Clotel clearly stands no chance at withstanding the temptations around him without reinforcement from the state. And though Brown's emphasis upon his weakness might incline us to consider that weakness somewhat unusual, it turns out that love "unrecognized" in marriage almost never survives in *Clotel*. The marriage with which the novel culminates, based as it is on George's persistent commitment to the "dictates of his conscience," is merely the exception that proves the rule: "But the adherence of George Green to the resolution never to marry, unless to Mary, is, indeed, a rare instance of fidelity of man in the matter of love" (225). One way to understand Brown's pessimism, of course, would be to say that the power of the state simply overcomes the power of conscience: perhaps without any hope of recourse to the law's fetters, "man" would not be so subject to temptation. But the corruption Brown locates at the center of the male tendency to infidelity does not simply derive from distortions built around reality by human government, and as a result his solution to the difficulty conscience and sentiment face in the modern world is somewhat different from Stowe's. Here are his remarks about the importance of marriage and love:

> Marriage is, indeed, the first and most important institution of human existence—the foundation of all civilisation and culture—the root of church and state. It is . . . for many persons the only relation in which they feel the true sentiments of humanity. It gives scope for every human virtue, since each of these is developed from the love and the confidence which here predominate. . . . As husband and wife through each other become conscious of complete humanity, and every human feeling, and every human virtue; so children in their first awakening in the fond covenant of love between parents, both of whom are tenderly concerned for the same object, find an image of complete humanity leagued in free love. The spirit of love which prevails between them acts with creative power upon the young mind and awakens every germ of goodness within it. . . . [W]hat must be the moral degradation of that people to whom marriage is denied? . . . Reader, when you take into consideration the fact that no safeguard is thrown around virtue and no inducement is held out to slave women to be chaste, you will not be surprised when we tell you that immorality and vice pervade the cities of the Southern States. (83–84)

There are certainly overtones of Stowe's celebration of the "reigning" power of "free love" here. But unlike both Stowe and his heroine, Brown is interested in marriage as an "institution," not a sentiment. And indeed, rather than thinking that the institution is responsive to various sentiments, he seems to think that it is generative of them. It is the "foundation" of "all civilisation and culture" in large part because it is the foundation of those sentiments on which they rely. Those sentiments do not lead people to marry; they are occasioned because people marry. Hence, "complete humanity" finds not its expression but its *realization* in marriage, and hence, Brown dwells at greater length on what marriage does than on what it is. The most spectacular instance of the tendency, but only the most spectacular instance of it, comes when Brown addresses the "moral degradation of that people to whom marriage is denied" and deploys the phrase *moral degradation* entirely sincerely: in depriving slaves of the chance to marry, Southern states are not denying them a human right so much as a moral opportunity, the moral opportunity, in fact, to be fully human in the first instance. Moral degradation is a consequence of Southern legal practices as well as a characteristic of them. Horatio's weakness, from this vantage, is a social and political condition rather than a personal and moral one: men need the fetters of slavery, which here become "safeguards" and "inducements," in order to realize their moral aspirations. Brown thus effectively reverses what we might take to be the ordinary account of the relationship between love and marriage, and in so doing, he also begins to tweak the post-*Somerset* account of the relationship between freedom and the law. If lovers are "free" in marriage, they are also being "prevailed" upon, which is simply to say that their freedom derives from their submission to a social arrangement rather than their inhabiting social arrangements that proceed from their sentiments.[68]

It is hard to overstate the significance of this shift in the relations between freedom and the law's fetters, which inspires in *Clotel* something on the order of a desire for slavery. Horatio needs fetters in order to become a moral agent, and as it turns out, men need chains in order to claim "true freedom." In the midst of his third-person slave narrative introduction, Brown approvingly quotes a poem that declares:

No! true freedom is to share
All the chains our brothers wear,
And with heart and hand to be
Earnest to make others free.   (66)

Within *Clotel* men are not "created" free or equal; freedom and equality are their creation. True freedom derives from shared "chains" rather than the transcendence of all forms of coercion. It is therefore no wonder that Brown is as concerned about the systematic displacement of African Americans from civil standing as he is about slavery itself. In *Clotel* that displacement, that insistent denial of the capacity of Africans to "share" a government with whites, *is* slavery. And it is also no wonder that Brown tends to reverse Mansfield's insistence that freedom involves the absence of legal displacement of the natural condition of freedom. There is *no* natural condition of freedom in *Clotel* for the law to displace. Consequently, when it comes time for Brown to give his account of the sources of English freedom, he follows Blackstone rather than *Som-*

erset. British soil, he explains, "confers and inspires" freedom (51). It does not merely offer protections from external invasions of natural right.

This reading will no doubt strike many readers as exaggerated or overemphatic, and I have no interest in denying that *Clotel* sometimes invokes the natural rights discourse that characterizes so many of its companion volumes in the literature of antislavery. One of *Clotel*'s chapters is entitled "Death Is Freedom" (204), which, as we have seen, would be a disturbingly apt summary of the trajectory of Stowe's thinking in *Uncle Tom's Cabin*. And Brown does at times posit what looks like a naturalist ontology for political freedom. "You may place the slave where you please," Georgiana tells Carlton, and "debase and crush him as a rational being; you may do this, and *the idea that he was born free will survive it all.* It is allied to his hope of immortality; it is the ethereal part of his nature, which oppression cannot reach; it is a torch lit up in his soul by the hand of Deity, and never meant to be extinguished by the hand of man" (155). But what God gives "the slave" here is not the "torch" of freedom itself but the "idea" of freedom, or the "hope" that it might be realized. We are not endowed with liberty so much as with the conviction that we were so endowed.

These modulations and equivocations illuminate the subtle parody that suffuses Brown's deployment of natural rights rhetoric in *Clotel*. To the extent that Brown contemplates the idea that political institutions might recognize human freedom rather than producing it, he generally does so in an idiom that actually undermines the natural rights discourse he seems to be invoking. "No sooner was I on British soil," he explains at one point in his introductory narrative, "than I was recognized as a man and an equal. The very dogs in the streets appeared conscious of my manhood" (73). Here British soil coincides with the recognition of Brown's manhood—rather than, say, the conferring of civil status upon him. But the way Brown registers this recognition only serves to emphasize the positivist nature of the manhood he has in mind. For as the behavior of dogs comes to signify Brown's manhood, it becomes hard not to conclude that the category of man is in some sense essentially nonnatural. What distinguishes the man and the slave before a dog? The whole point of the appeal to nature is to stress the artificiality of slavery, to stress, that is, that dogs can know no slaves. In imagining that dogs might respond to the civil transformations "confer[red] and inspired" by British soil, Brown suggests that the category of the man is no more independent of human formulation than that of the slave. Not content simply to challenge the notion that freedom is the natural condition of man, Brown even undermines the premise that authorizes that notion—that human beings are men in the first instance.

The manhood sniffed out by England's discriminating dogs can hardly have a divine or natural ontology, and Brown makes this point even more emphatically in the slightly more personal setting of his pre-*Clotel* slave memoir *Narrative of William W.*

Brown, a Fugitive Slave, Written by Himself (1847). In the midst of his initial slave narrative Brown had suggested that his arrival in the North and his consequent realization of the status as a free man constituted a transformation, as much as a realization, of his identity as a man: "The fact that I was a freeman—could walk, talk, eat and sleep as a man, and no one to stand over me with the bloodclotted cowhide—all this made me feel that I was not myself." That he goes on to be christened in his new identity at the bottom of the page only underscores the essentially determinative status of civic identity within his conception of liberty and bondage:

> "Well," said he, "thee must have another name. Since thee has got out of slavery, thee has become a man, and men always have two names."
>
> I told him that he was the first man to extend the hand of friendship to me, and I would give him the privilege of naming me.
>
> "If I name thee," said he, "I shall call thee Wells Brown, after myself."
>
> "But," said I, "I am not willing to lose my name of William. As it was taken from me once against my will, I am not willing to part with it again upon any terms."
>
> "Then," said he, "I will call thee William Wells Brown." (420)

This sequence appears, with only one variation, in the narrative that prefaces *Clotel* (63). The variation, of course, is that by *Clotel* the "I" of Brown's first narrative has morphed into the person/character/figure of "William." This shift in narrative modes is surely the most peculiar feature of *Clotel*'s preface, and from the perspective of the earlier account we can begin to see why Brown would come to think that third-person narrative was appropriate to the tale of his emancipation: that emancipation literally involved his having become "not myself," a man where he had once been a slave.[69]

Brown's relatively cavalier attitude toward this external "christening" as a man may be usefully contrasted to the intricate, not to say overwrought, way in which Frederick Douglass stages his emergence into manhood in the *Narrative of the Life of Frederick Douglass, an American Slave* (1845), the work that established the narrative template that Brown's *Narrative* rather obviously appropriates. Douglass's position on the relationship between manhood and freedom is an enormously complicated subject; a full treatment of it would involve careful attention to the development of Douglass's autobiographical technique over his three autobiographies, the role of masculinity in the construction of political subjectivity in the mid-nineteenth century, the gender valences of mid-nineteenth-century reform movements, and Douglass's shifting attitudes toward the nature of slavery and its relationship to the various legal orders—natural, constitutional, and positivist—in which it was given political standing in antebellum America.[70] All that need concern us now is Douglass's intense and conspicuous reluctance to trace any dimension of manhood to the external registers that generate it in Brown's work. Douglass frames his famous description of his confrontation with Covey within what might seem to be the narrative trajectory of Brown's *Narrative*. The "battle with Mr. Covey," he explains (331), represents the story of "how a slave was made a man." But this story of Douglass's emerging manhood is itself situated within a larger narrative frame that begins with the story of "how a man was made a slave" (326): "My natural elasticity was crushed, my intellect languished, the disposition to read departed, the cheerful spark that lingered about my eye died, the dark night of slavery closed in upon me; and behold a man transformed into a brute" (324).

The point is clear: if Douglass is "made a man," he is so made in part because he *begins* as a man. The confrontation with Covey "revived within me a sense of my own manhood"; it does not generate that sense in the first instance. The "embers of freedom" and the "heaven of freedom" are indigenous to Douglass, in need of "rekind[ling]" or "resurrection," not construction or conferral (331). And as it turns out, freedom and manhood are no more native to Douglass than elaborate philosophical critiques of slavery. *The Columbian Orator* does not introduce him to arguments that might help him "meet the arguments brought forward to sustain slavery." Instead, its contents "gave tongue to interesting thoughts of my own soul, which had frequently flashed through my mind, and died away for want of utterance." "The reading of these documents" does not teach him anything; it "enable[s]" him "to utter my thoughts" (308). Brown's men are born with the "hope" and "idea" that they were born free; Douglass is born free and with the "thoughts" of the antislavery orator. He embodies what they imagine to be true.

This distinction explains the differences between Douglass's christening and Brown's. Although Douglass also stages the process whereby he receives a name from a white patron upon his arrival in the North, he turns the scene to a radically different end from the one we find in Brown's *Narrative*. When Douglass offers Mr. Johnson "the privilege of choosing me a name," he insists that he retain "the name of 'Frederick'" so as to "preserve a sense of my identity" (358), not as a tribute to the new power of his "will." Indeed, Douglass's "identity" is so strong in the *Narrative* that it is hard to imagine that it could ever have been in need of preservation. He goes on to "use the name as my own" because he is "more widely known by that name than by either of the others" (359). This formulation stresses precisely the contingent relationship between persons and names which Brown's christening, involving as it does an entirely new person, would seem to foreclose. While it is almost as if Brown's name *determines* his identity, Douglass's name is essentially a matter of convenience. The sources of his identity lie elsewhere.[71]

Ethical Consequences

In chapter 6 of *Clotel* Brown produces what amounts to a debate among three ways of evaluating the morality of slavery. One method, represented by Mr. John Peck, holds that man's natural rights must come from "some authority" in the Bible and notes that since Adam and Eve only had alienable rights it is hard to see a foundation for inalienable rights in the Bible's elaboration of the condition of man. Another, represented by Mr. Carlton, one of Peck's "old-school fellows," maintains that "rights and wrongs," being the creations of man in his "gregarious state," are "necessarily the creatures of society" and that they are therefore both "artificial and voluntary" (107). Neither of these positions, obviously enough, is especially hostile to slavery—Peck's biblical commitments allow "our rights" only in relation to "our duties" and goes no farther than calling for slaves to have some access to the Gospel; Carlton may be "no great admirer of . . . slavery," but he is also no great admirer of "the Bible," and his derivation of "my duty" from merely his "conscience" and his "heart," though it may seem slightly more amenable to an antislavery orientation than Peck's pure scholasticism, in no way entails a commitment to emancipation (108).

Both of these positions, however, are clearly superseded over the course of the chapter by a third one, put forth by Peck's daughter Georgiana. Unlike her father, Georgiana holds that "the Bible was both the bulwark of Christianity and of liberty." Why it would even be necessary to say that the Bible is a bulwark of Christianity will become clear later on; Georgiana makes it a bulwark of liberty by shifting the ground of ethical evaluation from considerations of metaphysics to considerations of consequences. "To judge justly the character of anything," she explains, "we must know what it does. That which does good is good, and that which does evil is evil." What this means in the context of slavery is that rather than determining whether there is "some authority" for an inalienable right to freedom in the Bible, we should instead examine whether, "in its proper tendency," slavery accomplishes "the manifest design of God" (109). That Brown would establish such a clear link between our "respecting the rights of the slave" and considerations of tendencies and institutions rather than rights should not surprise us. We have already seen that he takes a similar position with respect to marriage, which he values for its effects as much as for its nature. And we have also already seen that Brown tends to represent the various metaphysical categories whose integrity antislavery sentiment sought to protect, such as "man," as themselves nothing more than the products of various tendencies and institutions. What might surprise us, from this vantage, is that Brown does not altogether endorse the moral thinking Georgiana embodies. "If true greatness consists in doing good to

mankind," Brown announces upon Georgiana's death, "then was Georgiana Carlton
an ornament to human nature" (185). What makes her moral status merely hypo-
thetical? Why should greatness inhere in anything other than doing good to mankind?

We can begin to get at what is at stake in this equivocation by examining the moment in which Georgiana meets her father's argument about the Bible's tolerance of
slavery head on and provides an extended account of the incompatibility between human bondage and the word of God. Several features of Brown's presentation of this
argument are worth noting. For starters, Georgiana presents her argument in the context of another agenda. Her primary goal is not to persuade her father of the truth of
her position with respect to the Bible; it is, rather, to persuade him not to discuss his
understanding of the Bible with Carlton. Her argument is part of an impassioned plea
to her father not to "speak of the Bible as sustaining" slavery in his conversations with
Carlton because Carlton is "on the stool of repentance, if he has not already been received among the elect," and "nothing would be more dangerous to the soul of a young
convert than to satisfy him that the Scriptures favored such a system of sin" (128). Her
"first object," Brown explicitly acknowledges, "was to awaken in Carlton's breast a love
for Jesus Christ." Vindicating "the Bible from sustaining the monstrous institution of
slavery" takes on the subordinate status of merely "her next aim" (127). It is for this
reason that she can so happily disavow any claim to persuasion. She makes a request,
not a case: " 'Believe me, dear papa,' she replied. 'I would not be understood as wish-
ing to teach you, or to dictate to you in the least; but only grant my request, not to al-
lude to the Bible as sanctioning slavery, when speaking with Mr. Carlton' " (131). She
has a far more tangible project in mind than Levine's recontextualization.

Moreover, while Brown's formulation of "first object" and "next aim" would seem
to imply that Georgiana's has two separate and essentially distinct goals, it turns out
that there is an important sense in which she conceives of her next aim as a *means* to
her first object rather than an independent enterprise in its own right. She is, in fact,
perfectly willing to sacrifice the moral standing of the Bible to save her future husband's soul: "He, you know, was bordering on infidelity, and if the Bible sanctions
slavery, then he will naturally enough say that it is not from God; for the argument
from internal evidence is not only refuted, but actually turned against the Bible. If the
Bible sanctions slavery, then it misrepresents the will of God. Nothing could be more
dangerous to the soul of a young convert than to satisfy him that the Scriptures favored such a system of sin" (128). The status of the Bible matters here only insofar as
it might have some effect on the "soul of a young convert." Georgiana would happily
discard the Bible should it prove inconvenient: "if the Bible sanctions slavery, then it
misrepresents the will of God." It happens that in this instance discarding the Bible is
decidedly inconvenient, so she proceeds to vindicate Scripture instead of dismissing

it, but her commitment to Carlton is so great that it wholly absorbs the value of the Bible.

The Bible's subordinate status in Georgiana's practical theology helps prepare us for the way in which Brown dismisses her claims about the Bible in his representation of her ultimate rhetorical success. Georgiana's biblical pleading works. At the very least she accomplishes her first object—her father agrees not to talk to Carlton about the Bible's relationship to slavery. And she also seems to accomplish her next aim as well. After her long explication of the Bible's antislavery tendencies, Peck responds, "Now Georgiana, . . . I must be permitted to entertain my own views on this subject, and to exercise my own judgment" (130). No longer casting himself as a normative biblical authority, he can only ask for room for the forms of private judgment which had initially been province of his daughter and other antislavery churchgoers aspiring to blunt the impact of official pro-slavery ecclesiastical pronouncements.[72] But Brown is quick to note that Georgiana achieves this rather remarkable "noble work" less because of the force of her argument than because of the endearing way in which she presents it. If "no one was better able than herself to impress" her antislavery "view upon the hearts of" others, it is because she is "modest and self-possessed, with a voice of great sweetness, and a most winning manner" and can therefore "engage their attention" "with the greatest ease" (131). Georgiana's persuasive success stands as an incident of her charm. Brown concentrates on her "voice of great sweetness" and "winning manner," not her knowledge of the Bible. He pointedly does not actually say that Georgiana's position is the right one: it is her "view," not the truth. Her achievement is a matter of presentation rather than insight.

There is something strange, not to say cynical, about Brown's willingness to represent such moments of religious instruction in the terms of flirtation—a point that only receives a more emphatic iteration in the way he couples the moment in which Carlton becomes saved with the moment in which he falls in love with Georgiana. This cynicism has suffused his account of Georgiana's argument from the very beginning. If it is hard to accept the notion that the best religious teachers are the most alluring ones, it is even harder to accept the idea that the Bible needs "vindication." To be sure, Georgiana maintains that it needs vindication from human error: the fault lies with man, not Scripture. But she is hardly deferential in her efforts to rescue it from our misapprehensions. She openly acknowledges that a devotion to God *could* occasion the dismissal of his biblical word: the Bible does not necessarily guide us to God; we choose whether we think it adequately corresponds to Him. And even if Georgiana maintains that it does represent Him accurately, we should not overlook the way in which she presents the beliefs of a man who is merely on the "stool of repentance" as a standard the Bible must meet. She seems more willing to acknowledge that the Bible is out of alignment with God than that Carlton would be. It stands in greater need of salvation than the sinners on earth.

This sense of nascent blasphemy follows Georgiana wherever she goes in *Clotel*. "With respect to her philosophy," Brown announces in the chapter recounting Georgiana's death, "it was of a noble cast. It was, that all men are by nature equal; that they are wisely and justly endowed by their Creator with certain rights, which are irrefragable; and that, however human pride and human avarice may depress and debase, still God is the author of good to man—and of evil, man is the artificer to himself and to his species" (181). The remarkable insertion here is "wisely and justly," as if God's judgment is a fit subject for Georgiana's evaluation. And along these lines, it is worth noting that what Georgiana praises God for doing is exactly what Brown praises Georgiana for doing: being an author of good to man. At the end of this very chapter he will praise his heroine for "doing good to mankind" (185). Georgiana usurps God's function as well as his judgment. We can now see at least one of the reasons for Brown's ambivalence about Georgiana's ultimate standing. She becomes an "ornament to human nature" only to the extent that she can be substituted for God.

Georgiana's philosophy and practice are only relatively minor examples of human usurpations of seemingly divine functions in *Clotel*. The greatest example of such a usurpation is, in fact, the novel itself. Here is Brown's account of the moments leading up to Clotel's suicide:

> She had only to pass three-fourths of a mile across the bridge, and she could bury herself in a vast forest, just in time when the curtain of night would close around her, and protect her from the pursuit of her enemies. . . . But God by his Providence had otherwise determined. He had determined that an appalling tragedy should be enacted that night, . . . which should be an evidence wherever it should be known, of the unconquerable love of liberty the heart may inherit; as well as fresh admonition to the slave dealer, of the cruelty and enormity of his crimes. (205)

The "author" of whatever good this "appalling tragedy" might occasion, of course, is Brown himself, not "God by his Providence." Clotel's death is Brown's plot, and the juxtaposition of her tragic life and the "President" is the very premise of his book. This substitution is hardly subtle, nor does Brown enact it without any reservation. For the moment in which he assumes the role of God in becoming, quite literally, the author of good to mankind is also a moment in which he is an "artificer of evil" to one of his "species," whose life is traded for its use-value in carrying out Brown's greater design. It will have been noted that Georgiana's noble philosophy differs very little from Jefferson's. What *Clotel* stages is the impossibility of man's *implementing* such a philosophy: engineering the Declaration of Independence puts Brown in exactly the same slaveholding position as Jefferson; it requires that he displace God every bit as effectively as the United States of America once had.

There is, of course, a great irony in the trajectory I have charted throughout this chapter. For however much Brown may present himself as an antislavery activist, *Clotel* certainly did far less actually to bring about the great Jubilee than *Uncle Tom's Cabin*. We might well say that Brown ultimately provides something on the order of the theory to Stowe's practice, or that Stowe's novel enacts Georgiana-style persuasion while Brown's only describes it. More important than the wide disparity between the two novels' respective cultural impacts, however, is a core set of concerns that they both share—that the law is itself a form of slavery, that legal prerogative challenges divine authority, that political action involves a kind of blasphemy. This set of concerns is a product of many social and political factors, but it is most centrally a product of slavery's peculiar standing in Anglo-American law. The "year of Jubilee" in the United States would ultimately involve a substantial reconfiguration of the relations between the law, slavery, and God. We can feel an impulse, albeit a thwarted impulse, toward such a reconfiguration in *Clotel*. We will soon encounter works that do more than gesture in the direction of such a reconfiguration. But before we can properly take their measure, we must first get a grasp on the historical conditions that enabled Brown's ambivalence about the law to become Lincoln's ambivalence about nature.

CHAPTER THREE

Constitutional Disobedience

Thoreau, Sumner, and the Transcendental Law of the 1850s

"But hold yourselves in waiting, for the day cometh! When the Lord saith unto us, Smite, then we will smite."[1] How can a revolution requiring God's approval ever take place? In the last chapter we saw why Dred establishes such a lofty standard for revolutionary political action, and we observed, in William Wells Brown's *Clotel; or, The President's Daughter,* at least one way in which that standard might be met. Brown's solution to the problem, however, is hardly an unalloyed success; one would hope that our choice is not between quiescence and blasphemy. We might expect Dred's standard to play a less important role, therefore, in works such as Martin Delany's *Blake: or, The Huts of America, a Novel* (1859–62) and Thoreau's militant antislavery essays which are comparatively more receptive to the idea of antislavery revolution than *Dred: A Tale of the Great Dismal Swamp.*[2] But God's approval is no less important in a work such as *Blake* than it is in *Clotel.* Delany simply finesses the difficulty of imagining that God has given the revolution the go-ahead in the form of a direct address by locating divine utterance in nature rather than "heaven." When Andy and Charles wonder how slaves will know that they have a right to rebel against their masters and how they will know what role they are to assume in that rebellion, Henry explains that those matters are "so simple that the most stupid among the slaves will understand it as well as if he had been instructed for a year. . . . So simple is it that the trees of the forest or an orchard can illustrate it; flocks of birds or domestic cattle, fields of corn, hemp, or sugar cane; tobacco, rice, or cotton, the whistling of the wind, rustling of leaves, flashing of lightning, roaring of thunder, and running of streams all keep it constantly before their eyes and in their memory, so they can't forget it if they would." From this perspective, in which both the impulse to and the justification for "the general insurrection of the slaves in every state" is literally written into the natural order, it is as if Dred were willfully blind to God's will rather than particularly scrupulous about it.[3] God saith, but Dred does not know where to hear his speeches.

It is not self-evidently clear, however, that Delany's solution to the problem that obstructs Harry's revolution completely meets all of the objections someone like Brown might put to it. For one thing, nature's comments on political arrangements have often eluded even those who were out looking for them. If the revolutionary plan and justification are simply written in the natural order, why is Henry needed to inspire and lead the revolution? Why has the revolution not already happened? To put the point slightly differently, why would we be inclined to think that freedom is a natural condition for man, natural in the sense that the "flock" is the natural condition for a bird? While we might say that freedom is a natural condition for men in moral terms, it seems awkward to say that it is not also essentially a political condition. This is precisely Emerson's point, in his great address on the emancipation of the British West Indies, when he celebrates emancipation as "an event singular in the history of civilization; a day of reason; of clear light; of that which makes us better than a flock of birds and beasts."[4] Our freedom may in some sense be visible in the flocks of birds and beasts, but attaining it requires a kind of behavior and insight they are unable to exemplify. In Delany's terms we need Henry as well as nature—which only serves to raise the question again of how we know that Henry is following God's will rather than his own. Nature alone will not tell us that.

This point becomes clear in Thoreau's use of nature to authorize something on the order of revolution at the end of "Slavery in Massachusetts": "[A white water-lily] is the emblem of purity. It bursts up so pure and fair to the eye, and so sweet to the scent, as if to show us what sweetness and purity reside in, and can be extracted from the slime and muck of earth. . . . It suggests what kind of laws have prevailed longest and widest, and still prevail, and that the time may come when man's deeds will smell as sweet. . . . We do not complain that [slavery and servility] *live,* but that they do not *get buried.* Let the living bury them; even they are good for manure" (108–9). This amazingly complicated sequence illuminates the difficulty of deriving theological sanction from nature. To begin with, Thoreau acknowledges a division in nature itself—the world is made up of foul-scented matter (like slime and slavery) as well as sweet-scented matter (like flowers). And consequently, though Thoreau introduces his call to arms as if it simply follows from his description of the flower, there is a sense in which slavery is no less at home in the world than freedom. Indeed, there are a number of moments in which freedom seems to require slavery rather than simply representing its transcendence: the flower grows from slime; slavery becomes manure. Natural laws may have "prevailed longest and widest," then, but we can hardly be sure *which* natural laws—the ones that bring flowers from the slime or the ones that allow slime to emerge? Hence, natural laws cannot be placed in any simple opposition to human laws—slavery accords with a natural condition no less than freedom, which ultimately means that freedom will require human behavior and agency every bit as much as slavery. The living must *act,* not simply avoid obstructing. God may well make it clear that there is no life in slavery and that we are morally bound to "bury" it, but the message does not emerge from a simple glance at the natural world.

This chapter seeks to account for the series of ironies and contradictions on display in this sequence and in Thoreau's 1850s antislavery essays more generally. These essays constitute a stunningly precise and insightful record of a multivalent process whereby the relations between slavery and nature, on the one hand, and slavery and law, on the other, were reversed as the impending crisis pressed on to civil war over the course of the 1850s. The first part of the chapter is devoted to exploring the relations between slavery and legal authority in Roger Taney's *Dred Scott* opinion and in the political debates that inspired it and which it inspired. We will see that these debates effectively inverted the structure in which *Somerset* had located slavery and nature. Whereas Mansfield had seemed to suggest that, independent of the law, man would necessarily be free, the major sectional controversies of the 1850s generated an emerging consensus that man's freedom actually required the law. Garrison's nature is "the dominion of God"; Thoreau's nature contains slime. Having charted these reversals and explicated the central role they play in Thoreau's "Slavery in Massachusetts," I then turn to the ways in which they lead to the emergence of an invigorated account of natural law in Thoreau's great essays from the late 1850s, especially his essays on John Brown. These later essays elaborate the complicated and surprising prerequisite conditions for nature to serve as a genuine source of moral authority in a world in which slavery can be a default political condition. They indicate the extent to which natural law is an essentially *legal* institution and systematically examine the pressures that lead it to lose either its moral or political authority.

The chapter concludes with an exploration of the way in which the structure of Thoreau's legalized nature could be redeployed in terms of the American Constitution as a forceful antislavery instrument. Thoreau is more or less uninterested in American legal code. He cares more about nature's abstract relationship to legal command than the Constitution's relationship to the statutes of Massachusetts. But the basic legal structure he begins to outline had enormous potency as a form of constitutional thinking. By transforming the relationship Thoreau establishes between nature and legal edict into a relationship between the Constitution and local law, Charles Sumner was able to convert Thoreau's project of legalizing nature into a project of naturalizing American legal code. In Sumner's antislavery addresses what might look like the natural law commitments of the American Revolution become the common law commitments of ordinary Englishmen, who, rather than adopting a new Constitution in 1787, instead provide the old English Constitution its firmest foundation in their revolution for the rights of man. Natural law emerges in these arguments only as a form of already existing human law: the foundational positive law of a constitution. Making the "Supreme Law" of God also the "supreme law of the land," Sumner restores to natural law the normative power it would seem to have lost in the wake of *Somerset*.

In many ways I will be describing a steady progression in Thoreau's thinking about natural law, from the relatively Garrisonian "Resistance to Civil Government" (1849) through the highly ambivalent "Slavery in Massachusetts" (1854) to the unexpectedly litigious John Brown essays (1859). The progression is not entirely seamless: intimations of the more formal natural law to come may be found in "Resistance to Civil Government," and strands of something on the verge of what Lewis Perry would consider abolitionist anarchism persist even in the later essays.[5] What is important for my purposes is the general trajectory of Thoreau's thought, a trajectory that has gone almost entirely unrecognized in Thoreau studies. Whereas my Thoreau ends up vigorously insisting upon our need to interweave the world of nature with the world of man, we will see that the Thoreau most commonly on display in recent Thoreau scholarship seeks to protect nature from man's deforming grasp. Most of this difference derives, no doubt, simply from the fact that I approach Thoreau through his antislavery essays instead of *Walden* or *The Journal*. But at least part of the difference derives from the fact that it is easy to overlook nature's enormously complicated and shifting relations to human freedom in the 1850s, and indeed especially easy to overlook the complexity of those relations if one comes across "Slavery in Massachusetts" by way of *Walden* rather than by way of the fugitive slave controversies.[6] In order to understand the full force of the natural law that emerges in Thoreau's later political essays, we will need a comprehensive grasp of the larger political context in which he elaborated it, and it is to that context that I now turn.

Dred Scott and the Nature of Slavery

A strange affinity exists between *Uncle Tom's Cabin* and Taney's now infamous *Dred Scott* opinion.[7] The point here is not simply that the most radical forms of abolitionist thinking seemed to make the Constitution into the pro-slavery document Southerners wished it to be—a point that was clear even with the publication of Wendell Phillips's 1844 work, *The Constitution: A Pro-Slavery Compact; or, Extracts from the Madison Papers*, which some Southerners thought suitable for circulation in the Cotton Kingdom as Southern propaganda.[8] *Dred Scott* does not merely concur with *Uncle Tom's Cabin* that the Constitution is essentially committed to slavery; the two texts also share a vision of the civic status of Africans in the United States. What is striking about this congruent vision, of course, is that it can straddle what might seem an unbridgeable gap between the abolitionist and the defender of slavery. But strange though it may seem, precisely what counts as the grounds of freedom for Stowe could be made to count as the grounds of slavery for Taney: the factors that Stowe sees as central to the emancipation of African Americans actually become in *Dred Scott* the necessary conditions of their continued enslavement.

In order to understand how Stowe's notion of freedom becomes Taney's assurance of slavery, we need only look at the way political agitation with respect to slavery in the 1850s interacted with the old *Somerset* paradigm. The "purpose" of "the Compromise of 1850," David Potter has written, "was to put a stop to the agitation on the slavery question," but the measure proved unsuccessful.[9] Its "futility" lay in the fact that it exacerbated, rather than disarming, conflict over the two issues that most clearly divided the North and the South—the status of fugitive slaves and the status of slaves in the territories.[10] Neither of these conflicts involved a direct challenge to the existence of American slavery, and historians have often wondered how they could have generated sufficient animosity to precipitate a secession movement and a four-year civil war.[11] But both of them did involve a challenge to the customary alignment of slavery and the law, and in each of them the law emerged as a vehicle of liberty rather than slavery. The principal project of Taney's *Dred Scott* opinion was to reverse that tendency, in effect to produce a higher law of slavery to counter an emerging positive law of freedom. If it made no sense to fight over the status of slavery in territories where it might never go, it made more sense to fight over slavery's emergence as a higher law principle. In his February 1860 address at Cooper Union, Lincoln in fact identified precisely this point as the single decisive factor in the growing secession movement of the last years of the 1850s. "The question recurs," he announced, "what will satisfy them? . . . This, and this only: cease to call slavery *wrong*, and join them in calling it *right*. And this must be done thoroughly—done in *acts* as well as *words*."[12] Historians, especially Don Fehrenbacher and William Freehling,[13] have carefully registered this emergence of slavery as "*right*," as a principle of higher rather than positive law. They have been less sensitive to the ways in which its emergence in this capacity transformed the status and meaning of legalist responses to the problem of slavery in the United States.

Fugitive Slavery

The fugitive slave controversies most clearly reveal the changing relationship between the law and slavery in the 1850s, and it is in terms of these conflicts that it is easiest to see, and understand, the convergence between Stowe and Taney. The very nature of fugitive slave proceedings tended to put pressure on Stowe's legal skepticism.

While Stowe's account of the relationship between the law and slavery flows from her sense that the law is the foundation of slave conditions, in fugitive slave cases the law is not asked to uphold slavery so much as to determine whether a given figure is a slave. And this shift from a world in which the law *enforces* slave status to the world in which it *adjudicates* it resulted in a profound transformation in the relationship between law and freedom. In fugitive slave cases the law actually could quite literally take the authority that Wright denies himself—the right to make men and women free.

Of course, one might suggest that the law did not really possess this power—a court could not actually free a slave; it could only determine whether a given person was a slave. But by the 1850s the distinction between a court's ruling on whether someone was a slave and its ruling against slavery by simply emancipating him had begun to break down under pressure from two distinct but compatible and interrelated sources. First, as a matter of practice, Northern juries were reluctant to rule that any given alleged fugitive was a slave. In what might look like a kind of jury nullification, they sometimes simply declared that anyone who came before them was free. And in order to produce opportunities for such moments of court-based, but not necessarily strictly legal, acts of emancipation, many Northern states, most notably Massachusetts, guaranteed alleged fugitives comprehensive procedural rights—the writs of habeas corpus and personal replevin, jury trial, and appointed counsel—in various so-called personal liberty acts.[14] Second, at the same time that juries were unwilling to find that any given person was a slave and Northern states were providing them with opportunities to express that unwillingness, there was a developing current of opinion in the North that it would actually be unlawful for juries to make such a finding, a developing current of opinion that no master could meet even the most minimal burden of proof in a case involving an alleged fugitive. The acts of Northern juries, from this perspective, did not entail the nullification of the law so much as the application of its finer points.

Interestingly, this developing current of opinion was no less shaped by the legacy of *Somerset* than Stowe's or Garrison's sense that the law was fundamentally corrupt. It was based on an argument, first given currency in Alvan Stewart's speculative 1837 essay "A Constitutional Argument on the Subject of Slavery," that most slaves were unlawfully enslaved, but unlawfully enslaved not so much in the sense that their being slaves violated natural law as in the sense that they had become slaves as a result of mechanisms other than those of the Constitution's positive law. According to Stewart, the Fifth Amendment established that no person could become a slave "except by the indictment of a grand jury, and trial by a petit jury, and the judgment of a court thereon." In what amounts to a radicalization of *Somerset*, Stewart insisted that in the United States slavery requires not merely legal sanction but also legal *process*. Since

American slaves had not become slaves as a result of the "due process of law" which the Fifth Amendment guarantees all "persons," he reasoned, "there are no persons in this land" who "could legally" be considered slaves under the Constitution.[15]

Stewart's argument rested on somewhat shaky legal and historical grounds,[16] but it dovetailed nicely with fugitive slave agitation. For insofar as he in effect made every slave, whether or not she had fled from her master, into a kind of fugitive slave, Stewart made efforts to obstruct the maintenance of slavery into efforts to emancipate all slaves. In converting the procedural *interference* with slavery into a procedural *requirement* for slavery, to put it slightly differently, he provided the groundwork for the transformation of what might have been considered occasions for expressions of hostility to the law from the perspective of natural justice into a framework for an essentially legal form of emancipation. And both tellingly and unsurprisingly, this perspective was ultimately installed as the American legal principle of emancipation in the Thirteenth Amendment, which does not abolish slavery so much as it subjects it to legal procedure.

The ease with which legal nullification could become law enforcement in the 1850s is graphically visible in Thoreau's "Slavery in Massachusetts," which counts at one and the same time as an attack on the law as essentially enslaving ("The law will never make men free") and as a critique of the state for failing to apply the law ("They are lovers of law and order, who observe the law when the government breaks it" [98]). We might think that the law Thoreau means to defend here is a kind of natural law; he suggests as much when he exhorts us to obey "that eternal and only just CONSTI-TUTION, which [God], . . . has written in [our] being" (103). But Thoreau is ultimately as concerned with what he calls "the laws of the State" as he is with "the laws of humanity" (94). Just as the refusal to obey the positive law of slavery could emerge over the 1840s and 1850s as an expression of a commitment to the idea that legal procedure must always be followed, so too does Thoreau's embrace of the Godly emerge over the course of "Slavery in Massachusetts" as a form of allegiance to the courthouse. Thoreau laments the prospect that what he calls "a perfectly innocent man" would be taken "into slavery" (95), not simply the fact that slavery itself exists. If at times he suggests that no man could ever be judged a slave ("Again it happens that the Boston Court House is full of armed men, holding prisoner and trying a MAN, to find if he is not really a SLAVE. Does any one think that Justice or God awaits Mr. Loring's decision?" [92]), he also repeatedly stresses the fugitive's innocence in his pleas on the fugitive's behalf ("I feel that my investment in life here is worth many per cent. less since Massachusetts last deliberately sent back an innocent man . . . to slavery" [106]). Thoreau's position is as much the position of the Thirteenth Amendment as it is the position of the *Liberator* (in which, in fact, "Slavery in Massachusetts" first appeared).

Or rather, "Slavery in Massachusetts" enacts the transformation of the position of the *Liberator* into the position of the Thirteenth Amendment, the transformation of natural justice into legal proceduralism.

Thoreau's "Slavery in Massachusetts" is hardly the only place in which we can witness such a transformation. The association of legal procedure with liberty appears at a wide variety of sites in the 1850s, not least in the trajectory of Stowe's antislavery thinking itself. As we have seen, in *Uncle Tom's Cabin,* which first appeared in print in 1852, slavery and the law seem so inescapably linked as to be identical. Four years later, however, in *Dred,* "the nature of the institution . . . of slavery" is linked less to "the law" as such than to a particular legal order in which slaves have no access to the courts (358): "We cannot allow," Judge Clayton explains, "the right of the master to be brought into discussion in the courts of justice" (354).[17] If *Dred* is torn about how to repair the problem of slavery, it is torn in large part because Stowe had begun, however ambivalently, to cast the law as a necessary instrument of freedom.

Historians have long associated the failure of the Compromise of 1850 with the Fugitive Slave Act, which having, as David Potter put it, "passed after a surprisingly small amount of debate," "contained a number of gratuitously obnoxious provisions," such as "den[ying] the alleged fugitive any right to a jury trial" and "permit[ting] his case to be removed from the ordinary judicial tribunals."[18] The act's hostility to due process is almost inevitably labeled "gratuitous." In their description of the problems that surrounded the implementation of the act in the 1850s, Harold Hyman and William Wiecek could almost be quoting Potter: "The Act of 1850 was gratuitously offensive to northern whites—to say nothing of northern blacks."[19] But from the perspective of "Slavery in Massachusetts" and *Dred* we can begin to see that there was nothing at all gratuitous about Southern efforts to remove questions of slavery from the domain of established legal procedure: the adjudication of matters such as slave status was precisely what slavery's defenders sought to avoid. And likewise, we can also begin to see that Northern efforts to resist the implementation of the act were not simply efforts to keep slavery confined to the South (and away, say, from Massachusetts). Antislavery legislators such as Charles Sumner were neither missing the point nor accommodating themselves to the "Slave Power" when they focused their ire on the Fugitive Slave Act. Over the course of the 1850s Stowe's "shadow of *law*" was fast emerging as what Sumner would call the "shield of Law and Constitution" in his important "Freedom National, Slavery Local" address of August 1852.[20] As legal process became an instrument of emancipation and a grounds on which to discredit slavery, the jurisdictional and procedural matters on which Sumner dwelled could be said to include "the whole war" he was often criticized for avoiding.[21]

Denying Dred Scott access to legal procedure could thus be as important to Taney as keeping him from the shadow of slave laws might have been to the Stowe of *Uncle Tom's Cabin*. And so while *Uncle Tom's Cabin* is chiefly interested in keeping the law away from persons, Taney is interested in keeping slaves away from the law. The first half of his opinion amounts to little more than an elaboration of a set of federal jurisdictional principles that would wholly preclude any federal legal proceeding over the status of any slave.[22] Taney's chief goal in this part of the opinion, as is now well-known, was to insist that, at least in a constitutional sense, African Americans, even free African Americans, were not a part of the "people" of the United States and were consequently unable to file suit in its federal courts.[23] Taney's opinion in effect confirms George's complaint that he is not acknowledged by American law ("What laws are there for us?" [158–59]): "The question before us is, whether the class of people described in the plea in abatement [African Americans] compose a portion of [the] people, and are constituent members of this sovereignty. We think they are not, and that they are not included, and were not to be included under the word 'citizens' in the Constitution, and can therefore claim none of the rights and privileges which that instrument provides for and secures to citizens of the United States" (404–5).

This conclusion has been subject to criticism on a number of grounds,[24] but my concern here is less with the accuracy of the chief justice's argument than with its effects. By placing African Americans outside of the domain of "citizens," of course, Taney effectively blocks their access to the federal courts and the emancipating authority that many were beginning to associate with them. More important, in so doing he effectively redefines the *nature* of citizenship in the United States as well as black Americans' relationship to it. For in shifting the relevant jurisdictional issue in *Dred Scott* from the question of whether Dred Scott was a slave to the question of whether he is one of the slave *class*, Taney rewrites civic status in the United States as a racial property. Slaves, as we have seen, are made by the law—but the slave class must be made by something else. Taney thus replaces, as Don Fehrenbacher has noted, the Constitution's distinction between "free persons" and "other persons" with what the chief justice calls "the line of division which the Constitution has drawn between the citizen race and . . . the African race" (419–20).[25] The point here is not that Taney allows for discrimination against African Americans at the level of the law or that he insists that African Americans do not happen to be American citizens; it is, instead, that he imagines race to be essential to civil status in the nation. And from this perspective the most remarkable feature of Taney's *Dred Scott* opinion is not its racism so much as its racialism; it is not so much that the chief justice might concur with those—he calls them the nation's Founders—who believe that "they [African Americans] had no rights which a white man was bound to respect," as that he effectively rewrites race-based slavery as the enslavement of a race (407).

It is for this reason that Taney is not only willing but also downright happy to conflate "the people of the United States" with the "citizens of the United States" at the outset of his opinion: "The words 'people of the United States' and 'citizens' are synonymous terms, and mean the same thing" (404). Such a potential alignment of citizens and persons in a "political body" might seem to work in the direction of Stowe's interest in beating hearts and living affections. It might seem, that is, to produce a citizenry wholly unmarked by unnatural grounds of discrimination. But as it ultimately turns out, the conflation of the civil and the biological ultimately works for Taney, just as it works for George at the end of *Uncle Tom's Cabin,* as a way of summoning the racial rather than transcending it.[26] Classes do not disappear once we think of people as citizens; they merely appear in biological rather than political terms: "They [African Americans] were at that time considered as a subordinate and inferior class of beings, who had been subjugated by the dominant race, and, whether emancipated or not, yet remained subject to their authority, and had no rights or privileges but such as those who held the power and the Government might choose to grant them" (404–5). Over the course of this sentence the "political body" of white "citizens" eventually becomes "the dominant race." As it emerges as the dominant race, those excluded from it begin to look less than entirely human, becoming, in Taney's words, "subordinate and inferior beings" wholly excluded from any human or natural rights—this is, after all, what it means to be without "rights or privileges" except insofar as the state chooses to grant them to you. And at the moment Taney becomes comfortable bracketing Africans from the human, he also becomes comfortable subordinating their civil status to their racial status and treating them all alike, "whether emancipated or not." By making citizens of the people, he can make slaves of the race.

Commentators have often called attention to Taney's "trick," as Fehrenbacher describes it, of "lumping free Negroes with slaves."[27] Far from resulting from trickery, however, the conflation of the free and the slave Negro counts almost as a syllogistic inevitability given Taney's systematic undermining of the civil basis of the nation's racial slavery. Taney notes at one point that in colonial America "no distinction" "was made between the free negro or mulatto and the slave" with "respect" to "the intermarriages between white persons and negroes or mulattos" (409). He often acts as though "no distinction" was made between the free and the enslaved African with respect to any feature of civic life, not just with respect to marriage. Indeed, we can already see how little he values the category of "free" with respect to the "negro" here in the way in which he aligns the "free negro" with the "mulatto" as if they were somehow similar entities—as if freedom was proportionately accorded with respect to one's biological relationship to Africa. Needless to say, the operations associated with the so-called one-drop rule rendered such considerations comically inaccurate, if not downright absurd. But as citizenship becomes a matter of "race," it would seem entirely plausible to think of one's relationship to a race as being in some sense on the same order as one's relationship to freedom.

A similar set of moves also takes place in *Uncle Tom's Cabin*. Not only does George join Taney in thinking that his status as a citizen is connected to his joining a racial population of his "people," but he also ultimately comes to understand his status as a slave less as a legal phenomenon than as a hereditary one. His formulation of the matter actually has the effect of distinguishing these two grounds of slave identity and stressing the latter: "but what country have *I*, or any one like me, born of slave mothers? What laws are there for us?"[28] Although George is referring here in part to the fact that only one of his parents was a slave, he nonetheless implies that, legally speaking, his being a slave is less important than his having been the descendant of one. Ancestry replaces the laws that are not "for" George as the mechanism of his oppression, or to put a somewhat finer point on the matter, the primacy of ancestry to the law allows George to insist that his civil status will not be defined in legal terms.

For the chief justice the fact that "a negro['s] . . . *ancestors* were imported into this country and sold as slaves" ensured that he could not "become a member of the political community formed and brought into existence by the Constitution of the United States" (403; my emph.).[29] George would seem to concur, and indeed he spends most of *Uncle Tom's Cabin* seeking a place where the race of *his* people are *the* people. Stewart had imagined that the replacement of ancestry by legal procedure would generate emancipation: "No matter what evidence you produce to show that you own the slave, if your title be unbroken through five generations of men, and if you have a bill of sale from him who claimed the fugitive's mother and grandmother, that will not answer" the demand that you produce evidence that a "court has pronounced judgment" that a person is your slave (288). But neither George nor Taney will allow the law to displace ancestry. And it is precisely by insisting on the necessary and primary relevance of ancestry to Africans' relationship to the law that they guarantee the potential slaves' subordination, that they secure the slave state from the law's liberating capacities.

The most egregious effect of this line of thinking in the chief justice's opinion is almost certainly Taney's willingness to contemplate the legal enslavement of African Americans simply because they are African. At one point he claims that in colonial America "the negro might justly and lawfully be reduced to slavery for [the white man's] benefit" (407). To be sure, Taney contemplates this prospect only in historical terms, but the prospect was as inappropriate to the historical context in which he presents it as it would have been to the 1850s. As is now and was then well-known, it was a long-standing principle in American law that free men became slaves only in Africa (where, as Taney, notes, the "English government" and the "English people" had "seized them on the coast of Africa, and sold them or held them in slavery for their own use" [408]). Even Southern courts, lax though they might have been with respect to the evidentiary requirements imposed upon those who asserted that a given African American was a slave, refused to recognize a right to enslave in the United States.[30] But having located Africans beyond the legal distinction between slave and citizen, Taney in effect leaves them no grounds on which they could appeal such a kidnapping—as well, of course, as no forum in which to present such an appeal. Counting as "beings" rather than persons, defined by race rather than law, African Americans are virtual slaves even when they are not actual slaves. In *Dred Scott* the entire black race assumes the formal status of Stowe's slaves: no matter how well they may be treated, even to the point of being freed, they may still be sold down the river.

I have been discussing *Dred Scott* as if it were primarily a case about legal standing and due process, and I have suggested that Taney preserves the Constitution as a proslavery document in large part by denying procedural rights to African Americans. To represent *Dred Scott* as hostile to due process rights, however, might seem slightly disingenuous. Many legal historians have suggested that the most significant passage in Taney's opinion involves an application of the Fifth Amendment's due process clause. The passage appears in Taney's discussion of the constitutionality of the Missouri Compromise:

> Thus the rights of property are united with the rights of person, and placed on the same grounds by the fifth amendment to the Constitution, which provides that no person shall be deprived of life, liberty and property, without due process of law. And an act of Congress which deprives a citizen of the United States of his liberty or property, merely because he came himself or brought his property into a particular Territory of the United States, and who had committed no offense against the laws, could hardly be dignified with the name of due process of law. (450)

These sentences are frequently taken to be what David A. Currie calls "at least very possibly the first application of substantive due process in the Supreme Court, the original precedent for *Lochner v. New York* and *Roe v. Wade*,"[31] and for this reason *Dred Scott* more frequently stands in legal history as a pioneering expansion of due process rights than as an aggressive circumscription of them. It is not at all clear, however, that this argument can carry, or was meant to carry, the weight that legal history has assigned it. For starters the due process claim makes up only a tiny portion of Taney's argument against the Missouri Compromise's antislavery provisions. The vast majority of that part of the opinion is devoted to a tendentious reading of the Constitution's provisions for congressional government of the territories, a reading designed to deny Congress legislative authority, of any kind other than that directly necessary to admit new states into the Union, over the nation's territorial holdings. In 1828 Chief Justice John Marshall had maintained that "in legislating for" the territories under the territories clause "Congress exercises the combined powers of the general, and of a state government."[32] Taney insisted that Congress's power was only to "admit" states from the territories and that consequently it could not constitutionally act as a state government in relation to them with respect to issues of slavery. The implication, though Taney never makes his reasoning on this point absolutely explicit, is that the only "power" to prohibit slavery is the power of a "state government." The force of most of Taney's argument about the Missouri Compromise is thus to deny Congress's authority with respect to slavery altogether as a matter of enumerated powers, not to maintain that Congress's exercise of its legitimate legislative power in the territories is limited by the Bill of Rights.[33]

And if Taney's due process argument only bears an oblique relation to the preponderance of his opinion, it is itself so truncated and telescopic as to seem as much an afterthought as a carefully elaborated and crucially important foundation for his ultimate holding. In light of the earlier parts of the opinion the key term in the passage I quoted earlier is *citizen*. By insisting that the Fifth Amendment applies to citizens, not persons, Taney can rewrite what Stewart would consider the "liberty" interests of the slave as the "liberty and property" interests of his master. Of course, the Fifth Amendment happens to apply to persons, not citizens: "nor shall any person . . . be deprived of life, liberty, or property, without due process of law." That is a small matter. And it is also a small matter that it is almost impossible to figure out exactly how the Missouri Compromise's prohibition of slavery deprives any slaveholder of property. The law simply insisted that slavery was "forever prohibited" in a certain territory; it did not provide any enforcement mechanism for that provision. Yet, even if we take the law to deprive slaveholders of their property, it is still unclear how they are deprived of it without due process of law. Taney says that the slaveholders in question would "have committed no offense against the laws," which makes sense only if we imagine that the laws prohibiting slavery somehow do not count as laws. To be sure, forfeiture through emancipation was a standard penalty for violations of slave prohibitions, but a slaveholder could only suffer such a fate by violating the law. Without even raising the still further question of whether the Bill of Rights was applicable in the territories in the first instance,[34] it is probably safe to conclude that Taney's due process arguments are, if anything, even less sensible than Stewart's were. They were so feeble, indeed, that many scholars have concluded that even Taney did not take them seriously. The Taney Court's most thorough historian, Carl Swisher, for example, argues that this passage constituted a "suggestion, rather than . . . a necessary link in his argument."[35] "Perhaps Taney was so tentative and sketchy in his use of the [due process] clause," Fehrenbacher speculates, "because he realized how inadequate it was as a basis for nullifying congressional power to prohibit slavery in the territories."[36]

The flimsiness of Taney's due process claims, especially the flimsiness of his insistence that the slaveholder in the Louisiana territories has "violated no law," underscores the sense in which *Dred Scott,* far from deploying due process as a way of protecting *rights,* actually deploys some deeply abstracted notion of the sanctity of slave property as a way of dismissing *laws.* And its most important historical effect, the splitting of the Democratic Party over the so-called Freeport doctrine, would make this point crystal clear.

Territorial Powers

Had Abraham Lincoln been assassinated, as many feared would happen, on his way to Washington in 1861, his most famous oratorical accomplishment would be the "House Divided" speech of 1858. But that speech is often considered substantially less important in his rise to the presidency than a single question he posed in his second debate with Douglas later that year in Freeport: "Can the people of a United States Territory, in any lawful way, against the wish of a citizen of the United States, exclude slavery from its limits prior to the formation of a State Constitution?" (1:541–42). According to historical lore, this question, and the answer Douglas would give to it, drove the major political developments of the latter half of the 1850s. As Don Fehrenbacher has summarized the matter, the Freeport exchange "is said to have 1) secured his [Douglas's] re-election to the Senate, but 2) destroyed much of his support in the South, and 3) divided the Democratic Party, thus 4) contributing decisively to Lincoln's victory in 1860."[37] Lincoln's question, on the usual account, forced Douglas to choose between popular sovereignty and the portion of the *Dred Scott* opinion overturning the Missouri Compromise. Douglas could save himself in Illinois, we are told, only by distancing himself from Taney, but in so doing he rendered himself no longer viable as a major figure in the increasingly sectionalized Democratic Party.

Careful attention to the matter, however, has made it hard to sustain the common image of "the tall, awkward prairie lawyer pin[ning] his distinguished opponent upon the horns of a dilemma."[38] For starters this particular question was hardly at the center of Lincoln's thinking during this campaign. He had already raised the issue casually, without following up on it, in a speech in Chicago earlier in the summer. This version of the interrogatory was hardly less casual. The so-called Freeport question was in fact only the second of four questions Lincoln offered, in a listed sequence, for

Douglas's consideration during his opening address at the Freeport debate. Of the four questions it did the least to advance Lincoln's primary agenda during the canvas at hand—linking Douglas with a pro-slavery conspiracy ("The real issue in this controversy . . . is the sentiment on the part of one class that looks upon slavery *as a wrong*, and of another class that *does not* look upon it as a wrong" [1:807]). Nor would Lincoln's broaching of the matter have come as a daring bolt out of the blue. Douglas had already given the basic outline of the answer he would give at Freeport, without major political fallout, in the summer of 1857. And Lincoln's Freeport question had been posed, and posed repeatedly and forcefully, by Illinois's *other* senator, Lyman Trumbull, in the acrimonious Senate debates regarding Kansas's bid for statehood.[39]

To be sure, Southern Democrats were not enamored of Douglas's performance throughout the Lecompton affair, but they complained about his stance with respect to the Lecompton Constitution, not his stance with respect to popular sovereignty and *Dred Scott*. With respect to the latter, indeed, they would have very little to complain about. As late as two weeks *after* the debate at Freeport, in an address in Maine, no less a fire-eater than Jefferson Davis himself would attack what he characterized as "the oft repeated fallacy of forcing slavery upon any community" in terms that could hardly be separated from Douglas's soon-to-be infamous Freeport doctrine.[40] It was only after Davis saw that that position was causing him to be aligned with Douglas that he came to repudiate it. Ultimately, it is hard to deny the truth of Fehrenbacher's claim that though we tend to think that "the Freeport Doctrine made Douglas unacceptable in the South, . . . it would be more accurate to say that Douglas made the Freeport Doctrine unacceptable in the South" (500).

Scholarly history has thus come to dismiss the importance of the Freeport exchange as much as folk history once celebrated it. Because "Lincoln was not the first to ask it, and Douglas had already answered it repeatedly," and because it raised a question that was not "a major issue of the debates," David Potter claims, "the Freeport question was one of the great nonevents in American history."[41] That the usual story about Freeport is misleading, however, does not mean that nothing significant was at stake in the exchange. Lincoln's question, and the replies it elicited, may have been a "nonevent" in the political terms that interest Potter and Fehrenbacher, but they constituted a crucial event in the history of the American law of slavery, a historical moment in which a fundamental tenet, indeed the fundamental tenet, of American slave jurisprudence was effectively discarded. The Freeport exchanges are in many respects worthy of mythology; we just constructed the wrong mythology around them.

To see what was at stake in Lincoln's question we need to focus not on the question itself, or even on Douglas's response to it, but, rather, on Lincoln's response to Douglas's replies. Here is Douglas's answer, the Freeport doctrine:

I answer emphatically, as Mr. Lincoln has heard me answer a hundred times from every stump in Illinois, that in my opinion the people of a territory can, by lawful means, exclude slavery from their limits prior to the formation of a State Constitution. . . . It matters not what way the Supreme Court may hereafter decide as to the abstract question whether slavery may or may not go into a territory under the constitution, the people have the lawful means to introduce it or exclude it as they please, for the reason that slavery cannot exist a day or an hour anywhere, unless it is supported by local police regulations. Those regulations can only be established by the local legislature, and if the people are opposed to slavery they will elect representatives to that body who will by unfriendly legislation effectually prevent the introduction of it into their midst. . . . Hence, no matter what the decision of the Supreme Court may be on that abstract question, still the right of the people to make a slave territory or a free territory is perfect and complete. (1:551–52)[42]

Douglas is advancing two arguments here, conveniently switching back and forth between them. On the one hand, he makes the practical point that populations will always be able to get around unwanted constitutional mandates not to forbid slavery, simply by doing "effectually" what they cannot do officially: the refusal to supply "local police regulations" and the passing of actively "unfriendly legislation" will "prevent the introduction of slavery into [the] midst" of the territories as effectively as any Wilmot Proviso. Having the *capacity* to block the introduction of slavery, however, is not quite the same as having the *right* to do so. Lincoln had asked whether the territorial legislature had "lawful means" at its disposal to prevent the introduction of slavery, not whether it had "effectual" ones. So Douglas supplements his arguments about territorial power with arguments about territorial right. The power to produce unfriendly legislation in the face of unpleasant constitutional demands thus becomes the "perfect and complete" right to do so. Constitutional questions become merely "abstract" exercises without any normative authority over those jurisdictions we might imagine to be bound by them.

How one shaded this argument ultimately proved to be crucial to how well one survived the ever-expanding Southern demands for national recognition of their slave rights. In dispensing with the "oft repeated fallacy of forcing slavery upon any community" in Maine, Davis tended to emphasize the first half of Douglas's doctrine:

If the inhabitants of any territory should refuse to enact such laws and police regulations as would give security to their property or his, it would be rendered more or less valueless, in proportion to the difficulty of holding it without such protection. . . . Therefore, though the right would remain, the remedy being withheld, it would follow that the owner would be practically debarred by the circumstances of the case, from taking slave property into a territory where the sense of the inhabitants was opposed to its introduction. So much for the oft repeated fallacy of forcing slavery upon any community.[43]

Here we only get claims about the power of territorial inhabitants. The "rights" lie altogether with the slaveholder; the territory is simply left with the capacity to "withhold" remedies in their breech and to "refuse" adequately to secure and protect them. Of course, given the political circumstances in which they were delivered, the whole tenor of Davis's remarks is to accept, if not exactly sanction, such exercises of local decision making. In speaking about the prospect that a community might have slavery "forced" upon it, he connects the expansion of slavery to power as well as right and thereby hints that the community would be meeting simply another form of power rather than a claim originating from a deeper and higher authority. But it was easy enough for Davis to withdraw from even this implicit acceptance of the prospect of territorial self-protection. Once he found himself too tightly connected to Douglas, he retreated by insisting that he was interested only in describing the unlawful shenanigans available to those who would not allow the Constitution to stand in the way of their hostility to Southerners and their rights. "The difference between us [Douglas and Davis]," Davis explained, "is as wide as that of one who should assert the right to rob from him who admitted the power. It is true, as I stated at that time, all property requires protection from the society in the midst of which it is held. This necessity does not confer a right to destroy, but rather creates an obligation to protect."[44] Historians have characterized this "retreat" as a reversal of "the reasoning of [Davis's] utterance at Portland" and a "contradict[ion]" of that earlier speech's "stated purpose."[45] But it is important to see that this retreat is in some senses built into the Freeport doctrine itself, built into its equivocations on the subject of whether territorial governments retained the right to prevent the introduction of slavery into their jurisdictions or instead simply had certain measures at hand with which they could defend themselves from the implications of *Dred Scott*.

In many ways Lincoln's response to the Freeport doctrine in the 1858 debates was to pave the way for Davis's retreat. With characteristic incisiveness Lincoln immediately latched on to the way Douglas seemed to be deriving right from power rather than the other way around. If *Dred Scott* is right, he maintained in the next debate at Jonesboro, and "the Constitution of the United States expressly recognizes property in slaves, and prohibits any person from being deprived of property without due process of law" (1:617), then from what perspective would a territorial legislature retain "the right" to keep slave property from its jurisdiction? "I will ask you my friends, if you were elected members of the Legislature, what would be the first thing you would have to do before entering upon your duties? *Swear to support the Constitution of the United States*. . . . There can be nothing in the words 'support the constitution,' if you may run counter to it by refusing any right established under the constitution" (1:619). "Why this is *monstrous* sort of talk about the Constitution of the United States!" Lincoln continued in the final debate at Alton: "*There has never been as outlandish or lawless a doctrine from the mouth of any respectable man on earth.* I do not believe it a constitutional right to hold slaves in a Territory of the United States. I believe the decision was improperly made and go for reversing it. Judge Douglas is furious against those who go for reversing a decision. But he is for legislating it out of all force while the law itself stands. I repeat that there has never been so monstrous a doctrine uttered from the mouth of a respectable man" (1:812–13). Indeed, Lincoln's last words in the debates sought to reveal the implications of Douglas's willingness to elide claims about right and power. "And the man who argues that by unfriendly legislation, in spite of that constitutional right, slavery may be driven from the Territories cannot avoid furnishing an argument by which Abolitionists may deny the obligation to return fugitives, and claim the power to pass laws unfriendly to the right of the slaveholder to reclaim his fugitive [tellingly, not "slave"]. . . . Why there is not such an abolitionist in the nation as Douglas, after all" (1:813–14).

Later we will see that the exact obligations and powers conferred by the fugitive slave clause were anything but clear in the 1850s and that Lincoln had good jurisprudential reasons, as well as good political reasons, for bringing up the subject in the context of the territories' authority with respect to slavery. For now, however, we need only note that Lincoln certainly did not raise his second interrogatory at Freeport as a way of establishing that Douglas was the nation's leading abolitionist. As tempting as it was to ridicule Douglas's cavalier acceptance of the notion that a constitutional right might go unenforced, Lincoln was actually more interested in pointing to the inadequacy of the power with which Douglas left the territories than in suggesting that such a power could never be reconciled with Taney's opinion. Douglas was able to evade much of the force of Lincoln's charge that he was advancing a "*monstrous* doctrine" by separating the territorial legislature's power to pass "unfriendly legislation" from its power not affirmatively to protect slave property. "Is Congress bound to pass every act that is constitutional?" he asked at Galesburg (1:728). Of course, if *Dred Scott* held that, as Lincoln would paraphrase, "the right of property in slaves is distinctly and expressly affirmed in the Constitution" (2:52), then Taney would not have been giving Congress (or the territorial legislatures it authorized) an opportunity to protect slavery so much as an obligation to do so. But inaction always looks less unlawful than action, and Lincoln himself would have to admit that Douglas's post-Freeport versions of the Freeport doctrine "escape[] to some extent the absurd position I have stated." Although Lincoln would sometimes contend that Douglas's later responses merely cast the same "sense" in "different language" (2:50), he generally stressed the weakness of the power Douglas vested in the territorial legislatures rather than its unlawfulness.

Even in his very first response to the Freeport doctrine, at the third debate, in Jonesboro, Lincoln opened his critique on historical rather than constitutional grounds. "I hold," he explained, "that the proposition that slavery cannot enter a new country without police regulations is historically false. It is not true at all." Slavery has always spread, Lincoln pointed out, "*without* these 'police regulations' which the Judge now thinks necessary for the establishment of it" (1:618). What the Freeport doctrine amounts to, from this vantage, is something like a restatement of *Somerset*, or, to put it more precisely, a translation of *Somerset* into practical rather than formal terms. Douglas's claim that the "absence of" "a slave code or police regulations" "excludes" slavery from a territory "as positively as a constitutional prohibition" could easily pass as a summary of Mansfield's great opinion (1:757). And Lincoln's repeated efforts, in speeches such as the one he gave in Cincinnati in the summer of 1859, to locate the positive law provisions of the Northwest Ordinance at the center of the history of American free-soil expansion ("in Missouri there was no law to keep that country from filling up with slaves, while in Illinois there was the Ordinance of '87" [2:80]) amount to a simple reversal of Mansfield's old formulation. If Mansfield had suggested that the "nature" of slavery made it "incapable of being introduced . . . but only by positive law," Lincoln replied that "there is vigor enough in Slavery to plant itself in a new country even" without the protection of positive law. And if Mansfield had said that "nothing can be suffered to support" slavery "but positive law," Lincoln insisted that "not only law but the *enforcement* of law" was necessary to "keep it [slavery] out" of a territory (1:618). We will see in the next chapter why Lincoln felt a need to supplement the demand for "law" itself with a second demand for law "*enforcement*," but for now we need merely register the way in which the law, having once been wholly tethered to, indeed almost subsumed within, slavery, becomes in the course of the debate surrounding the Freeport doctrine the last and only recourse of freedom.

"Slavery in Massachusetts" is no less acute about these developments than it was about the transformation of the status of legal proceduralism in the debates about fugitive slaves. Indeed, it is easy to see the essay as a kind of inverted Freeport debate, with the law's capacity to "forc[e]" freedom "upon any [unwilling] community" in question, and with Thoreau sliding back and forth between the positions Douglas and Lincoln would lay out in the late 1850s. "The law will never make men free," Thoreau insists at one point, as if the community will always stand immune from what Douglas might call the law's abstract holdings. In practically the same breath, however, Thoreau goes on to complain that "they are the lovers of law and order, who observe the law when the government breaks it" (98). The law in this second passage may initially look a lot like the natural law from which Mansfield separates the "positive law" of slavery, but the relationship between these two laws is slightly more complicated in "Slavery in Massachusetts" than it is in *Somerset*. The key here lies in Thoreau's sense that the government "breaks" the law. In *Somerset* the two legal domains are essentially distinct; in "Slavery in Massachusetts" they are mutually informing. And consequently, Thoreau worries about violations of "the laws of State" as much as violations of "the laws of humanity" (94). What counted in "Resistance to Civil Government" as an eagerness for a state that "governs not at all" turns (63), in "Slavery in Massachusetts," into a critique of the state for not governing enough.

Much of the polemic in "Slavery in Massachusetts" is directed at the state for failing to be a state. During Boston's fugitive slave controversies, Thoreau laments, "it appeared to be forgotten that there was such a man" as the governor, "or such an office" as the one he occupies. The governor only "endeavor[ed] to fill the gubernatorial chair" during the controversies. "He was no governor of mine. He did not govern me" (93). This intense desire for government leads Thoreau into precisely the forms of "constitutional" blindness he often finds so exasperating in others: "I had thought that the Governor was in some sense the executive officer of the State; that it was his business, as a Governor, to see that the laws of the State were executed; while, as a man, took care that he did not, by so doing, break the laws of humanity; but when there is any special important use for him, he is useless, or worse than useless, and permits the laws of the State to go unexecuted" (94). If anything, the "laws of humanity" and the Governor's status as a "man" are less important here than the "laws of the State" and the governor's status as "the executive officer of the State." Thoreau comes very close to relegating the laws of humanity to a merely private space; he certainly cares more about the governor's public behavior than about his actual moral beliefs. Like Douglas and Davis, Thoreau might claim that the "true resources of justice in any community" lie in the "sentiment of the people," not "the legal tribunals of the country." At the same, however, it is easy to feel this position subtly sliding away as "Slavery in Massachusetts" unfolds, and, as Lincoln would maintain, the actual "administration of justice" comes by the essay's close to be as important to the maintenance of freedom as the "sentiment" that would animate it ("Slavery in Massachusetts," 97).

"Slavery in Massachusetts" represents only a tame instance, however, of the emergence of law *enforcement* as the foundation for freedom in the United States. The most telling and graphic instance of that emergence is Melville's *Battle-Pieces* itself.[46] Written some fifteen years after *Uncle Tom's Cabin* and ten years after *Dred Scott*, Melville's Civil War poetry sees what *Uncle Tom's Cabin* seems to miss altogether and what Thoreau would only gradually come to recognize: the law's power might be presented as a solution—indeed, a necessary solution—to American civil rights problems. The racialism of *Uncle Tom's Cabin* seems almost inadvertent; its full impact clearly surfaces only in the context of Taney's more strenuous effort to mine the condition in which Stowe tends to leave her African-American characters for its racialist potential in *Dred Scott*. By the mid-1860s, however, it was quite a bit easier for Melville to grasp the ways in which the law served as the most effective check on the racialist abuses it might have once seemed to facilitate.[47] He simply refuses to let it perform that function in *Battle-Pieces*. The collection repeatedly stages, if it is not indeed structured around, his unwillingness to let the law do the civil rights work to which Reconstruction efforts were turning it.

In order to get at this dimension of Melville's Civil War poetry, we must first grasp the way in which he understands the relationship between African Americans and the nation that emerges from the bloody confrontation of the early 1860s. That African Americans would be no more at home in his postwar nation than they were in Taney's Revolutionary America should hardly be surprising. Part of the force of Melville's connecting emancipation with enslavement, after all, lies in the notion that the emergence of African Americans as rights-bearing subjects counts as a subordination of the white nation that had previously allowed their enslavement. Melville insists that he opposes, and for that matter has always opposed, slavery.[48] But in opposing slavery he does not exactly embrace the idea of a multiracial United States. Indeed, he imagines that the war for emancipation could easily count as a war for a nation other than the United States, that a victory for African Americans is not a victory for Americans. Hence, in *Battle-Piece*'s final poem, "A Meditation," he gives voice, even if the voice is not precisely his own, to the idea that emancipation can only be seen as a collateral effect of the Civil War, not one of its legitimate accomplishments: "Can Africa pay back this blood / Spilt on Potomac's shore?" (242). Rather than being a war for the union of Africa with the United States, a war for the civil rights of Africans within the United States, Melville's Civil War is a war in which African rights rupture the union of white "brothers" within the United States. If there is a "darker side" to the war, as Melville suggests at the end of "A Meditation" (243), it lies only in part in the immense violence that the aftermath of the war will never quite undo. It also lies in the fact that the war was not exclusively devoted to keeping the nation's white brothers together.

Given *Dred Scott*, of course, the notion that African Americans were not exactly Americans was hardly altogether outlandish or remarkable. Part of the point of the Fourteenth Amendment, after all, was to dispose of this account of American citizenship, an enterprise that would have hardly seemed pressing in a world in which Melville's position was unusual. What is notable about Melville's thinking about the relationship between Africa and the United States is his interest in connecting the usurpation of American interests by African benefits with the deployment of the law—or, as we might say, following the reading of "The Conflict of Convictions" I outlined in the last chapter, with the inevitable tyranny that the deployment of the law entails. We can begin to get at this point by noting the way in which Melville connects the emergence of the state as a form of domination with the emergence of the state in the form of an African. It is ultimately as hard to distinguish the United States that emerges over the course of *Battle-Pieces* from the Negro as it is to distinguish light from shadows under the domain of law. As Michael Rogin and Carolyn Karcher have observed,[49] Melville's interest in "shadows" has a history that precedes even "The Portent," and in their earliest incarnations Melville's shadows represented not a political enterprise so much as the persons on whose behalf such an enterprise might be engaged—what Benito Cereno calls "the negro" in Melville's story "Benito Cereno" (1855). The dominion of shadows in "The Conflict of Convictions" mimes the dominion of Melville's "negro" on the *San Dominick*.[50]

These connections between the African and the project of emancipation, on the one hand, and between the African and the corruption of the law, on the other, are visible in *Battle-Pieces* as well. In "The Swamp Angel" the Parrott gun, "planted in the marshes of James Island, and employed in the prolonged . . . bombardment of Charleston" (250), is represented as both emancipator ("And farther walls fall, farther portals" [108]) and as African ("There is a coal-black Angel / With a thick Afric lip" [107]), and as both the generator of law ("And he breathes with a breath that is blastment, / And dooms by a far decree" [107]) and the violator of it ("It comes like the thief in the glooming" [108]): it emancipates slaves by burgling homes. The African emerges as the figure for the deployment of force under the name of law (the gun that dooms by a far decree), and emancipation emerges as the name of the result of that deployment. "With law on her brow and empire in her eyes," imposing the law of emancipation by way of obliterating the law of the old Constitution, "America" looks like nothing so much as "the negro." The return of the light in "A Meditation" thus counts in some senses as the return of whites to the positions of centrality in the American political imaginary: *Battle-Pieces* is a proto-restoration collection as well as a Reconstruction collection, or, rather, the way in which it is a Reconstruction collection is by forecasting, and eagerly awaiting, the restoration.

It is in response to this conflation of America with the Negro that Melville's white America begins to emerge. If emancipation becomes the name for the presentation of force as law (the strapping of the term *decree* to the act of firing a gun), and if Africa seems to be the name of the nation on whose behalf it is practiced, then what is the alternative to Africa? What makes the *American* union? *Battle-Pieces* is notoriously indirect on this matter, presenting its most specific accounts of the content of the postwar nation only in a voice that lies at some remove from Melville's own. It is as if Melville wishes to stage the effects of a given logic as much as he wishes to prosecute an argument within it. But those effects and the logic that underwrites them are clear. The resolution of the war, on the account we receive in "A Meditation," lies in the nation's recognition that those who appear as "foemen" are in fact "brothers." The war ends with the rise of a "rebellion" against familial conflict, not with the suppression of the rebellion designed to secure the oppression of those who might become brothers:

> And something of a strange remorse
> Rebelled against the sanctioned sin of blood,
> And Christian wars of natural brotherhood.   (241)

In a world in which the state is merely a structure of racial domination (here, ironically, the racial domination of whites by Africans), racial solidarity becomes a way of neutralizing the problem it poses, becomes a way of imagining a kind of sociality whose "natural" status allows it to transcend the coercion of the political. "Who ever heard of a white so far renegade as to apostatize from his species almost, by leaguing in against it with negroes?" wonders Captain Delano.[51] In 1855 the union of the "species" that constitutes the white race itself constitutes something of a law. To betray it is to become a "renegade."[52] In 1866 that species is an alternative to the law. Those who find their identity within "natural brotherhood" are the only beings who can escape the dominion of the state. In 1855 the state looks like the engine of racial solidarity. In 1866 the state is the engine that racial solidarity must supersede. Melville's ongoing commitment to "rebellion," his refusal to let acts of force count as the law, to let them count as real decrees, prevents him from embracing the multiracial America of Reconstruction.

Putting the point this way allows us to see how Melville can situate his radical critiques of the state in the midst of a collection that is often committed to urgent celebrations of "LAW." For to say, as I just did, that race emerges in *Battle-Pieces* as an alternative to the law is slightly misleading, insofar as it suggests that there is some necessary connection between the state and the law. At the end of the day, while it is certainly true that racial solidarity supersedes the state in *Battle-Pieces*, it is not exactly true that it supersedes the law. Instead, we might say that racial solidarity constitutes a valid, and higher, law in the volume, one that is valid and higher, just like the natural law of figures such as Garrison and Stowe, precisely because it has no political embodiment. The "Founders' Dream" of Melville's "victory of LAW" thus joins the Liberia of Stowe's various "victories" for "Africa" on the rolls of racially unified states distilled from the project of keeping law from assuming any coercive form. Melville is no less committed to natural law than the abolitionists; he simply replaces the natural law of Christian justice with the natural brotherhood of the white race. This is why he can use the law itself as a standard against which to measure the failings of the emergent America of African civil rights, why it counts as critique, rather than description, for him to call the African a "thief" and counts as irony, rather than description, for him to call the Swamp Angel's missiles "decrees." And as Melville begins to critique and ironize legal institutions from the perspective of the idea of legality, we can begin to see the ways in which he can be loyal to the law only by resisting a "rapprochement" with the "authority" of "the state."[53]

The Reconstruction amendments would count as abolition's ultimate rapprochement with the "idea of the state" and as marks of its ultimate willingness to give its "loyalty" to the law's "command." *Command* is by no means a casual word in this connection, and the law in question here was hardly something separate from the slaveholders' Constitution itself. For as we will see, the Fourteenth Amendment did not merely connect the integration of slaves into the civil life of the nation with their integration into an already extant legal order; it understood that integration to entail the *enforcement* of that order. For Bingham the chief work of the privileges or immunities clause was to provide a mechanism for empowering Congress to secure the provisions of Bill of Rights against the legislation of states. The Fourteenth Amendment thus did not merely make citizens, nor did it merely apply the Bill of Rights to state action. Rather, it gave Congress the power, as Bingham put it, to "enforce the bill of rights." It served, as the *New York Times* summarized one of Bingham's speeches, "to arm the Congress . . . with power to enforce the Bill of Rights."[54] The amendment was in this sense like the Swamp Angel—a machine for the inter-articulation of force and law, for the conversion of decrees such as Stewart's due process clause into acts of coercion such as Ophelia's "positive" "tenets." Melville was never so loyal to the law as to allow it that force, or rather, he was too loyal to the law to allow it that force. He was only able to express his loyalty to a law that was, unlike the laws of the potentially emergent civil rights–based, multiracial America, without shadows.

Thoreau's Natural Constitution

Battle-Pieces probably constitutes the most emphatic literary evidence of the transformation of the antislavery legal radicalism of the 1840s into the anti–civil rights legal radicalism of the 1850s and 1860s. No other work more clearly demonstrates the ways in which the natural law of God's justice could become the natural law of white men. Thoreau's political essays, by contrast, constitute the most intense literary effort to preserve natural law as the instrument of God's justice. More than any other abolitionist operating in the broad Garrisonian paradigm, Thoreau recognized the danger that the natural law of justice could drift away altogether from the realm of human institutions.[55] We have seen that in many respects *Somerset* encouraged such an evacuation of natural right from the legal realm. The primary project of Thoreau's 1850s essays is to find a way for the two to be integrated into a single structure. These essays seek ultimately to produce a legal nature.

The John Brown essays reveal what is at stake in the manufacture and deployment of this legal nature with unusual precision.[56] Nothing is more readily apparent in these essays than Thoreau's disdain for the law and legal institutions. "Are laws to be enforced simply because they were made? or declared by any number of men to be good, if they are *not* good?" he asks at one point in "A Plea for Captain John Brown" (136). He continues the attack just a page later: "I do not believe in lawyers. . . . Let lawyers decide trivial cases" (137). In the slightly later essay "The Last Days of John Brown" Thoreau delights in the effects of the news of Brown's arrest: "The North, I mean the *living* North, was suddenly all transcendental. It went behind human law, it went behind the apparent failure, and recognized eternal justice and glory" (147). But these attacks on the law are never far removed from invocations of the law. The very form of "A Plea for Captain John Brown"—a plea—marks the insertion of Thoreau's antislavery thinking into a more legalistic context than we encounter in "Resistance to Civil Government." To be sure, Thoreau does not exactly present his plea as an ordinary legal filing: "I am here to plead his cause with you. I plead not for his life, but for his character—his immortal life" (137). But even as this maneuver distances Thoreau somewhat from the realm of "trivial cases" appropriate for lawyers, it also has the effect of adding new dimensions of life to the litigious mechanisms Thoreau ordinarily condemns. One would think, after all, that Brown's "character," to say nothing of his "immortal life," would be secure beyond any human pleading. Brown generally excites Thoreau precisely because he is able to "stand[] up serenely against the condemnation of mankind, rising up above them literally *by a whole body,*—even though he were of late the vilest murderer, who has settled that matter with himself" (125). From this vantage Thoreau's essay runs directly counter to the "sublime" "spectacle" of Brown's death. Brown settles matters with himself; he realizes that pleas are unnecessary. Thoreau attempts, by pleading, to settle the same matters with the population his hero had already transcended.

And toward the end of "A Plea for Captain John Brown" we can even begin to see Thoreau backing off from his most radical assaults on the idea of law. Only several sentences after he seems to discard the normative power of law ("Are laws to be enforced simply because they were made? or declared by any number of men to be good, if they are *not* good?"), Thoreau directs his critique of recent legal defenses of slavery at the interpretive practices of the judges rather than the instruments they interpret: "Are judges to interpret the law according to the letter, and not the spirit?" (136). And if the judges themselves are not to blame, then maybe the lawmakers are. Congress, Thoreau explains, is "a counterfeiting law-factory, standing half in a slave land and half in a free! What kind of laws for free men can you expect from that?" (137). The problem here would seem to stem from the *kind* of laws being produced in the United States, not with the fact that the United States produces laws. Indeed, the problem would seem to derive precisely from the fact that those laws are actually inadequately lawful, that they are "counterfeit" rather than real.

There remains, as always, an important sense in which Thoreau casts the law itself as his enemy. His claim that he does not "believe in lawyers" comes right on the heels of his complaint that American laws are counterfeit. But rather than focusing on the relationship between the subject and the law, as he did in "Resistance to Civil Government," in the Brown essays he is interested in what we might call the relationship between the law and its embodiment in various "human" institutions: "in cases of the highest importance, it is of no consequence whether a man breaks a human law or not" (137). And hence, rather than stressing the irrelevance of legal thinking as such to justice, he instead stresses the relevance of orders of law which transcend the state's legal apparatus. It is not that the law itself is trivial here; lawyers deal with "trivial cases" and "human law," but presumably what makes this law trivial is its relationship to some other kind of law. The law becomes the instrument of Thoreau's reformist visions as well as the object of their attentions.

Thoreau's accounts of natural law, that law beyond the human, are themselves essentially *legal*. Thoreau's God is a "Commissioner on [a] case" as well as the creator of the world (96). The cases argued in His court do not hinge merely on a set of moral principles, such as effect the standing of men in their private lives. God's jurisdiction overlaps with, and indeed supersedes, the state's. Positive law does not suspend moral considerations. Such considerations instead generate "prior case[s] on the docket" which judges, "appointed by God, ha[ve] no right to skip" (98). Thoreau never tires of condemning those who fail "to recognize a higher law than the Constitution, or the decision of the majority" (104), but the problem with "the Constitution" turns out to be only that it is not the "CONSTITUTION": "The question is not whether you or your grandfather, seventy years ago, did not enter into an agreement to serve the devil, and that service is not accordingly now due; but whether you will not now, for once and at last, serve God,—in spite of you own past recreancy, or that of your ancestor,— by obeying that eternal and only just CONSTITUTION, which He, and not any Jefferson or Adams, has written in your being" (103). The innumerable puns on the term *constitutional* in Thoreau's later reform essays, then, work less as a way of castigating constitutionalism as such than as a way of castigating the constitutionalism that takes the American Constitution as the prevailing standard for constitutional law. His complaint with "government," from this vantage, is ultimately a complaint with the notion that law is derived from something like "the decision of the majority" rather than from God himself.

But what does it mean to think of God as a lawmaker as well as a creator? The immediate payoff, of course, is that it puts questions of natural right back into the legal arena from which *Somerset* had exiled them. Where Mansfield erects an absolutely secure firewall between positive law and natural right, Thoreau ties the two together in a hierarchical structure with natural right on top. But the process of integrating nature and law is by no means as straightforward as the passages I have quoted up to now might imply. We know where to look for the Constitution. Where do we find the CONSTITUTION, and how do we read it once we have located it? From the perspective of Thoreau's political essays from the 1850s, the problem with *Somerset* is its tendency to render natural law wholly abstract, no more relevant to the organization of human society than the laws of nature themselves. But Thoreau's pieces themselves have a hard time keeping natural law wholly distinct from natural laws. Indeed, the *Reform Papers* testify to the difficulty of legalizing nature as much as they demonstrate the value of naturalizing law.

It would seem that we do not have to look very far for the CONSTITUTION. It is "written in your being." This account makes God's CONSTITUTION easily accessible, but it also makes it somewhat useless as a legal instrument. How can we "serve" or "obey" what is written in our beings? Or to put the point more forcefully, how could we *fail* to obey what is written in our beings? And if the CONSTITUTION is merely the constitution of the world, merely nature itself, in what sense can we understand it to be "just"? By contrast, if the CONSTITUTION is something other than nature, if it is a legal order that might go more or less "obeyed," then in what sense should we say that it is "eternal"? In the very next paragraph Thoreau will disparage the notion that we might respond to the "majority['s] vot[ing] the devil to be God" by "reinstat[ing] God" (103). But in what sense is he asking us to do anything else? The danger here is that the natural law constitution will always be either too strong or too weak—too strong in the sense that it would be impossible for it not to be enforced or obeyed, too weak in the sense that it might either bear no relation to, or be incapable of defining, human law.

This is hardly the only time these questions emerge in Thoreau's political writings. Thoreau is everywhere sensitive to the prospect that moral claims will lose their normative authority in legal reasoning. He frequently stages this evacuation of moral authority in terms of what we might call the retreat of natural law into the law of nature. In "Resistance to Civil Government," for instance, Thoreau explains his refusal to capitulate to the state's demand by insisting that "they only can force me who obey a higher law than I." The state, predictably enough, does not obey such a "higher law." Its demands come only because "it must help itself" and, just like any other being, "do as I do." We have already had an occasion to register Thoreau's tendency to reduce the state to the status of a person, neighbor, or friend. What is significant about this sequence is the way in which the image with which he makes this equation informs the meaning of the higher law with which he begins the sequence: "I perceive that, when an acorn and a chestnut fall side by side, the one does not remain inert to make way for the other, but they both obey their own laws, and spring and grow and flourish as best they can, till one, perchance, overshadows and destroys the other. If a plant cannot live according to its nature, it dies; and so a man" (81). There is a strange individualizing of seemingly general properties here. We would think that natural laws generally cover all plants; that a nature contains all of them rather than their each having a nature of its own. But just as each citizen exists on the same ontological plane as the state, so too does each organism exist on the same ontological plane as nature itself. More important than this massive leveling, however, is Thoreau's surprising suggestion that natural laws do *not* constitute, exemplify, or embody "a higher law than I." Indeed, the laws governing plants actually exemplify, instead, the more local legal orders of persons and governments. The state will attain its status as a part of a higher law than an individual only when it breaks out of the legal domain of natural things. Thoreau returns to an image of plant growth at the end of the essay, when he discusses the "really free and enlightened State" (89). This state recognizes "the individual as a higher and independent power" and in so doing follows a higher law than the acorn and the chestnut: "A State which bore this kind of fruit, and suffered it to drop off as fast as it ripened, would prepare the way for a still more perfect and glorious State, which also I have imagined, but not yet anywhere seen" (90). This higher state does not follow its own law; it "suffers" the laws of its members. The "higher" law here operates in terms of the natural world, but it requires, crucially, judgment and volition rather than simple growth and development.

It is hardly surprising that Thoreau's most significant interrogations of the relationship between natural law and the laws of nature emerge in the course of his discussions of slavery, but the interrogations themselves lead to some fairly surprising claims about the terms in which slavery can be attacked. There is never a question in Thoreau's essays about whether slavery is wrong. Rather than making an argument about the horror of slavery, Thoreau simply announces that such an argument is no longer necessary: "If [American citizens] vote," he claims in "Slavery in Massachusetts," "they do not send men to Congress on errands of humanity, but while their brother and sisters are being scourged and hung for loving liberty, while—I might here insert all that slavery implies and is,—it is the mismanagement of wood and iron and stone and gold which concerns them" (102). But even as Thoreau insists that there is no need to say what slavery "is" or what it "implies," "Slavery in Massachusetts" is nonetheless committed to filling in the gap he leaves here, committed, that is, to showing that it is easy to be confused about what slavery is and what it implies. "Again it happens that the Boston Court House is full of armed men," Thoreau explains at the beginning of the essay, "holding prisoner and trying a MAN, to find out if he is not really a SLAVE. Does anyone think that Justice or God awaits Mr. Loring's decision? For him to sit there deciding still, when this question is already decided from eternity to eternity, and the unlettered slave himself, and the multitude around, have long since heard and assented to the decision, is simply to make himself ridiculous" (92). But if it is so obvious that a "MAN" cannot be a "SLAVE" that it is entirely "ridiculous" even to sit in judgment of the matter, it is by no means as obvious *why* a man cannot be a slave. Thoreau will later address exactly this point, and he introduces his thoughts about the matter by attempting to unsettle the confident judgments about slavery which he has inspired at other moments throughout the essay. "Much has been said about American slavery," he contends, "but I think that we do not even yet realize what slavery is."

> If I were seriously to propose to Congress to make mankind into sausages, I have no doubt that most of the members would smile at my proposition, and if any believed me to be in earnest, they would think that I proposed something much worse than Congress had ever done. But if any of them will tell me that to make a man into a sausage would be much worse—would be any worse, than to make him into a slave—than it was to enact the Fugitive Slave Law, I will accuse him of foolishness, of intellectual incapacity, of making a distinction without a difference. The one is just as sensible a proposition as the other. (97)

It is not entirely clear, at least at first, exactly what Thoreau means to be adding to our sense of "what slavery is" here—that slavery entails denying a person his or her humanity? that the fugitive slave laws extended, rather than limited, slavery's reach? Some of the argument seems purely tendentious: is the Fugitive Slave Act really every bit as bad as the law that makes slavery in the first instance? What the passage clarifies about the nature of slavery does not lie at the level of what it says about slavery. It instead lies at the level of what the passage implies about how we talk about slavery. The sequence subtly indicates that our condemnations of slavery can proceed along two similar but by no means identical paths. On one of these paths the barrier between "MAN" and "SLAVE" is essentially moral. Making a man into a sausage is like making him into a slave in the sense that it counts as an assault on his moral standing as a person. We would condemn such congressional behavior, as Thoreau does in the early parts of this sequence, as ethically suspect—"something much worse than

Congress had ever done." On the other path the barrier between "MAN" and "SLAVE" is natural or physical or ontological. Making a man into a sausage is like making him into a slave in the sense that, ontologically speaking, a man simply is not either a sausage or a slave. We would condemn such congressional behavior, as Thoreau does at the end of this sequence, as nonsensical—"The one is as sensible a proposition as the other." Now, it is pretty obvious which of these two paths should be preferable to us. Making men into sausages or slaves is not merely silly. But the minute we choose the moral path we have to revisit our understanding of that moment, early in the essay, when Thoreau first raised the issue of the relationship between the "MAN" and the "SLAVE." For there Thoreau suggested not that it would be wrong to make men into slaves but that it was inconceivable that they could ever in fact be slaves: "trying a MAN, to find out if he is not really a SLAVE." The trial consequently earns his derision rather than his condemnation: the judge is ridiculous, not immoral. What is the point of this project of revision? To show how easy it is for us to route our moral judgments through ontological channels; to show how easy it is for us to *deny* that men are slaves in the place of *preventing* men from becoming slaves.

In staging this process whereby natural law folds into the law of nature, Thoreau is protecting the concept of natural law, not critiquing it. He is not attempting to dismiss considerations of nature from our legal universe so much as establish the terms on which they could be valuable within it. It is not as if Thoreau does not think that men have a natural right not to be slaves or that there is nothing about their nature which suggests that slavery is wrong. What concerns him is the difficulty of keeping natural law legal, of keeping it from either becoming wholly abstract moral calculation or wholly concrete physical principle. The problem lies in certain tendencies implicit in the invocation of natural law (a tendency exemplified by *Somerset* on the one side and by the laws of acorns on the other), not in an adherence to natural law— indeed, the problem is that there are tendencies in the invocation of natural law which militate against an adherence to it.

It is only from the perspective of this difficulty that we can begin to make sense of Thoreau's most powerful elaboration of the nature of natural law, the concluding paragraphs of "Slavery in Massachusetts":

> But it chanced the other day that I scented a white water-lily, and a season I had waited
> for arrived. It is the emblem of purity. It bursts up so pure and fair to the eye, and so
> sweet to the scent, as if to show us what purity and sweetness reside in, and can be ex-
> tracted from, the slime and muck of earth. I think I have plucked the first one that has
> opened for a mile. . . . I shall not soon despair of the world for it, notwithstanding slav-
> ery, and the cowardice and want of principle of Northern men. It suggests what kind of

laws have prevailed longest and widest, and still prevail, and that the time may come when men's deeds will smell as sweet. (108)

Thoreau invokes nature as a kind of legal order here ("what kind of laws have prevailed longest and widest"), a legal order that is not merely separate from positive human laws but, rather, in competition with them. The good news is that nature wins the competition. The bad news is that it is hard to figure either how it could be competing with human laws or by what criteria it has prevailed over them. What does it mean to say that the laws exemplified by this flower's blossom "still prevail . . . longest and widest" in the world? Prevail in relation to what? What "law" exactly is prevailing here? The law that flowers bloom each spring? The law that flowers smell good? The laws of natural purity as opposed to the "cowardice and want of principle of Northern men"? How could the natural laws at stake here not prevail? And what about the appearance of this flower testifies to the fact that moral laws, as opposed to mere natural laws, *have* prevailed? How can the laws of nature (flowers growing) become natural law (purity prevailing)?

Thoreau never quite meets the challenge of these questions, but he does present, with impressive clarity, the kind of world in which they would never arise. We can begin to grasp this world by observing the ways in which Thoreau distances this flower from human life at the same time that he assimilates it to it. Part of the flower's value lies in the way it demonstrates that nature's "integrity and genius" remained "unimpaired," by which Thoreau means something like uncontaminated. The flower "reminds me that Nature has been partner to no Missouri Compromise. I scent no compromise in the fragrance of the water-lily. . . . In it, the sweet, and pure, and innocent, are wholly sundered from the obscene and baleful" (108). Even as he produces this celebration of nature's removal from the world of human politics, however, Thoreau begins to bind the two together. The "sweet" and "pure" are *sundered* from the "obscene and baleful"; they are not merely separate from them. And before he is through, Thoreau will not only assimilate the laws of nature into a realm in which they can interact with human legal institutions (and prevail or be sundered); he will also combine them with human legal institutions into a single organism, or ecosystem, of law. At the conclusion of the essay Thoreau begins to suggest that natural law and positive law do not actually constitute competing alternative legal orders so much as alternative parts of a single larger operation: "Slavery and servility have produced no sweet-scented flower annually, to charm the sense of men, for they have no real life: they are merely a decaying and a death, offensive to all healthy nostrils. We do not complain that they *live*, but that they do not *get buried*. Let the living bury them; even they are good for manure" (109). This passage is strangely self-consuming. The "slavery and servility" that produce "no sweet-scented" flower turn out by the sequence's end to be good for the "manure" that "sweetness and purity" "reside in" and from which they can be "extracted." Humans at one and the same time produce nothing good and lay the groundwork for natural beauty. Sweetness "resides" in the world, which would imply that we have little to do with it, and sweetness can be "extracted" from that world, which would imply that we have a role in bringing it out.

It is for this reason that Thoreau can combine his celebration of nature's abstracted purity with a call to human action. Slavery and servility can produce no flowers; we should make them into manure. The paragraph that precedes these closing sentences presents an even more explicit exhortation and an even more explicit demonstration of that exhortation's tense relationship to Thoreau's celebration of nature's "unimpaired" "integrity": "So behave that the odor of your actions may enhance the general sweetness of the atmosphere, that when we behold or scent a flower, we may not be reminded how consistent your deeds are with it; for all odor is but one form of advertisement of a moral quality, and if fair actions had not been performed, the lily would not smell sweet. The foul slime stands for the sloth and vice of man, the decay of humanity; the fragrant flower that springs from it, for the purity and courage which are immortal" (109). It is tempting to compare this account of political reform to the advice Stowe gives her readers at the end of *Uncle Tom's Cabin*. Like Stowe, Thoreau calls for personal reform, not political reform. He dwells on the production of an "atmosphere" rather than the generation of laws, and he introduces a large number of intermediate agents between the individual and the political results he or she may seek. We are not asked to make good laws but, rather, told to worry about the "odor of [our] actions" and how it will relate to the world's "general sweetness."

What is strange about this demand, however, and what makes it ultimately a much more *political* demand than the one we found in *Uncle Tom's Cabin*, is Thoreau's inability to specify whether we should follow nature or instead produce it. On the one hand, we are told to be mindful of the extent to which our "deeds" are "inconsistent" with the "scent" of "a flower." On the other, we are told to "enhance the general sweetness of the atmosphere," which turns out to mean not that we should keep our behavior in accordance with the flower's sweetness so much as that we should use our behavior to *make* the flower's scent sweet in the first instance: "if fair actions had not been performed, the lily would not smell sweet." The lily's dependence on our behavior is what makes its appearance a "confirmation of our hopes." Why would our hopes be confirmed by the knowledge that natural beauty persists regardless of human misconduct? But the lily's independence from our behavior—its integrity—is what makes its appearance useful as a moral norm, what gives it the power to suggest that "the time may come when man's deeds will smell as sweet." The "prior cases" on God's docket require that we inhabit a nature that is both subject to our authority and wholly outside of it.

This characterization of Thoreau will no doubt seem slightly perverse. Recent criticism has almost uniformly taken Thoreau to be devoted to representing nature in all of its alterity. In what constitutes the most powerful of these readings, Sharon Cameron, for instance, has stressed that Thoreau's "lifelong inquisition of nature" was "not meant to anthropomorphize" the world he observed and encountered. By contrast, Thoreau sought, "as . . . witness or beholder, not as . . . explicator," to encounter and register nature as a set of "phenomena" wholly "disassociated from human significance." To be sure, not all of Thoreau's *writing* remains faithful to his inquisition. But for Cameron those writings that "illustrate Thoreau's struggle to 'represent' nature in the social forms that are receptive to it—the form of the essay, the homily, the didactic instruction"—actually constitute betrayals of his larger purpose: "In the concessions by which *Walden* is yarded—by which it makes nature available to an audience—*Walden* presents not nature but the seductive rapprochement of the natural and the social to which, put in the harshest terms, nature is sacrificed."[57]

Few scholars go so far as to join Cameron in imagining that all of Thoreau's published work somehow represents a betrayal of the primary purpose of his life. But Thoreau has nonetheless consistently been identified with projects of recording nature's alienation from the human world—from Stanley Cavell's claim that *Walden* seeks to make its reader occupy "the position of outwardness, outsideness to the world, distance from it, the position of the stranger,"[58] all the way down to Lawrence Buell's reading of *Walden* in terms of the "aesthetics of relinquishment."[59] These readings are usually constructed in terms of *Walden* and the *Journal*, and I do not mean to challenge them as accounts of those works here. They certainly are *not*, however, accurate accounts of Thoreau's project in his later political writings, which are almost uniformly directed toward revealing the immanence of nature, its location already within institutions that might well otherwise attempt to keep it out. In the *Journal* "the self is not to be empowered by nature," writes Cameron. "It is rather to be converted to nature."[60] In the *Reform Papers*, by contrast, nature is constantly being converted to the self, and this "seductive rapprochement of the natural and the social," far from "sacrificing" nature, actually comes instead to constitute it, and to save us.

Sumner's Transcendental Constitution

Thoreau's efforts to underscore the legal content of natural law, of course, do very little to establish natural law as American legal code. The relationship he established between nature and law could easily be transported into the domain of American law, however, and it was already being so transported by the early 1850s. It was not so difficult to reproduce the relationship between Thoreau's CONSTITUTION and his constitution as the relationship between the American Constitution and state and federal statutes. The key was to introduce the Constitution itself, as a written legal instrument, into the *Somerset* calculus.

The figure most responsible for developing this line of argument was Salmon P. Chase—the same Salmon P. Chase who would sit as chief justice of the Supreme Court from 1865 to 1873 and who would produce the opinion of the Court in *Texas v. White*.[61] But the document that gave the position its clearest, most prominent, and most forceful formulation was Charles Sumner's August 1852 speech before the Senate, published under the title "Freedom National, Slavery Local," urging the repeal of Fugitive Slave Act of 1850.[62] Much of Sumner's argument in "Freedom National" is devoted to the idea that Congress has no authority to enact laws protecting slavery. The provisions recognizing slavery in the Constitution, he explains, do not recognize it explicitly: "Slavery, I repeat, is not mentioned in the Constitution. The name Slave does not pollute this Charter of our Liberties." And even when it is indirectly recognized, Sumner goes on, it is not recognized in a way that gives the "*positive sanction*" that *Somerset* insisted slavery must receive before it can count as legally operative (3:106).

Since the Constitution hardly ignores slavery altogether, a great deal of this argument hinges on the exact meaning of *positive sanction*. The peculiar institution makes no fewer than three relatively direct appearances in the Constitution. The provisions are now well-known, not to say infamous:

1. Representatives and direct Taxes shall be apportioned among the several States which may be included in this Union, according to their respective Numbers, which shall be determined by adding to the whole Number of Free Persons, including those bound to Service for a Term of Years, and excluding Indians not taxed, three fifths of all other Persons. (Art. I, sec. 2)

2. The Migration or Importation of such Persons as any of the States now existing shall think proper to admit, shall not be prohibited by the Congress prior to the Year one thousand eight hundred and eight, but a tax or duty may be imposed on such Importation, not exceeding ten dollars for each Person. (Art. I, sec. 9)

3. No Person held to Service or Labour in one State, under the Laws thereof, escaping into another, shall, in Consequence of any Law or Regulation therein, be discharged from Service or Labour, but shall be delivered up on Claim of the Party to whom such Service or Labor may be due. (Art. IV, sec. 2)

Sumner does not rest his case, as some other antislavery constitutionalists would, on the fact that the word *slavery* simply does not appear in the Constitution. He couples his readings of the specific language of the Constitution with arguments, derived largely from Madison's diaries, about the way in which that language was generated and ratified in Philadelphia. Here he makes one general point and one specific point. The general point, which he elaborates in a number of contexts, is that slavery is never directly mentioned in the Constitution because the founders wished to protect the nation's "fundamental law" from the taint of slavery (3:176). "The record demonstrates," Sumner insists at one point, "that the word 'persons' was employed to show that slaves, everywhere under the Constitution, are to be regarded as *persons*, and not as *property*, and thus to exclude from the Constitution all idea that there could be property in man," and he then goes on to quote Madison's admission that he "thought it *wrong* to admit in the Constitution the idea that there could be property in men" (3:109).

Even if the Framers sought to avoid the "admission" that there could be property in men, however, they certainly did implicitly recognize the rights of the holders of such property. As Glen Loury has recently claimed, "No, they didn't put the word 'slavery' in the Constitution—true enough. They merely put the institution of slavery under the protection of the Constitution—rather a worse offense."[63] But the absence of the word *slavery* meant more to antebellum legal thinkers than it does to Loury. In *Dred Scott*, for instance, Taney felt compelled to maintain that the "the right of property in a slave" is not only "distinctly" but also "expressly" "affirmed in the Constitution" (451). Given that such "express" references to slavery were conspicuously lacking in the Constitution, one can only conclude that Taney somehow felt that "distinct" affirmations would prove insufficient. Indeed, Sumner's case looks fairly strong with respect to the apportionment and slave trade clauses, which seem more to acknowledge that slavery exists than to clothe its operations in any special federal or constitutional protection. But the fugitive slave clause is another matter entirely: in its insistence that those "held to service or labor in one state" cannot be emancipated ("discharged" from their service) "in Consequence of any Law or Regulation" of a state to which they flee, the clause seems not only to recognize the existence of slavery but also to implicate the federal government in its regulation. And indeed, the fugitive slave clause constitutes Taney's primary evidence for his strained insistence on slavery's express recognition in the Constitution: "The Government in express terms is pledged to protect it in all future time, if a slave escapes from his owner" (451–52). Sumner uses his second, more specific historical argument to neutralize this implication of the federal government in the maintenance of slavery. Sumner's key point in this regard is that the fugitive slave clause, insofar as it does not specifically empower Congress to participate in the return of fugitives, is actually "in form merely a *compact*" between the states (3:149), and consequently "no power is delegated to Congress over the surrender of fugitives from service" (3:148): "As a compact, its execution depends absolutely upon the States, without any intervention of the Nation" (3:188).

It may seem somewhat farfetched to imagine either that there would be declarations in the Constitution unenforceable by Congress or that the Constitution would contain some provisions that simply announced compacts between states: why announce the compact in the Constitution if there is no national or constitutional authority to enforce it? As we will see in the next chapter, however, the notion of an unenforceable legal order was hardly alien to the legal culture of antebellum America. And Congress's enforcement power with respect to the provisions listed alongside the fugitive slave clause in Article IV, Section 2, was the source of enormous controversy throughout the antebellum period. There is, after all, at least some good reason to think that Article IV, Section 2, really was designed merely to announce a compact between the states. As Sumner himself points out, the full faith and credit clause of Article IV, Section 1, was lifted from its place among the items in Section 2 when the Convention decided to give Congress the specific power to enforce it. "Adding to the recorded compact an express grant of power," he claims, "they testified not only to their desire for such power in Congress, but their conviction that without such express grant it would not exist. But if express grant was necessary in this case, it was equally necessary in all the other cases. *Expressum facit cesare tacitum*. Especially, in view of its odious character, was it necessary in the case of fugitives from service" (3:152–53). Sumner thus combines the limitations on congressional actions implicit in constitutional federalism (grants of power are necessary for Congress to assume authority) with the limitations on legal action implicit in the special legal status of slavery (slavery requires explicit positive law) to build a two-planked argument against congressional authority to pass laws orchestrating the return of fugitive slaves. Rather than simply holding the Constitution up for comparison against empty statements of natural right, he instead reveals the ways in which constitutional structure runs parallel to, and is buttressed by, common law antislavery principles. By locating *Somerset* within the practice of constitutional interpretation, he converts what might look like the document's silence about slavery into its renunciation of it.

Sumner, however, is not content simply to stress that Congress lacks the power to generate laws recognizing slavery or facilitating Southern efforts to enjoy its benefits. He also wants to say that Congress is actively forbidden from passing the kind of law which it has enacted with respect to fugitive slaves. "For every act of Congress," a legal historian has noted, "there are two constitutional tests. The first is whether the Constitution authorizes it; the second is whether the Constitution forbids it."[64] Sumner insisted that the Fugitive Slave Act failed both of these tests: "*first,* that it is a usurpation by Congress of powers not granted by the Constitution, and an infraction of rights secured to the states; and, *secondly,* that it takes away Trial by Jury in a question of Personal Liberty and a suit at common law" (3:144). And indeed, he devotes more of his energy to establishing the second of these claims than the first, and does so for good practical reasons.

Plausible though Sumner's claims about the fugitive slave clause's status as a mere compact may have been, there was an important sense in which they were stillborn. Congress had already weighed in, and weighed in early on (in 1793), on the question of whether it had the power to pass a fugitive slave law. And in the famous case of *Prigg v. Pennsylvania* (1842) the Supreme Court had ruled, without a single justice dissenting on this particular point, that it did have such a power.[65] Sumner himself admitted that he must "conced[e] to it [*Prigg*] a certain degree of weight as a rule to the judiciary on this particular point" (3:145). But in *Prigg* the Court had directly addressed only the question of whether Congress could pass a fugitive slave law, not the question of whether the one that it had passed might be otherwise unconstitutional. Regardless of whether the Court had implicitly admitted as much in *Prigg,*[66] or had instead felt that what Story's son called "the general question as to the Act of 1793" was not properly before it (3:146),[67] Sumner could claim that Story's opinion in *Prigg* "does not touch the grave question which springs from the denial of Trial by Jury" (3:145). And this "trial by jury," and the argument Stewart had made in relation to it, thus lie at the heart of Sumner's insistence that the federal government has no constitutional authority to participate in the return of fugitive slaves.

Like Stewart, Sumner understands legal procedure itself, not the content of any particular law at any point in time, to constitute the grounds for slave emancipation. Instead of being defrauded by the legal system under the fugitive slave law, fugitives, on Sumner's account, are "defrauded of [the] Trial" to which they are entitled (3:167). The shadow of the law, or what he calls the "shield of Law and Constitution" (3:189), is precisely what Sumner thinks fugitives need, not what makes them slaves. And Sumner's commitment to legal form inheres in the form of "Freedom National" as well as its content. The speech does not merely pursue an argument about the meaning of particular American laws and the value of legal procedure as such. It also presents itself as a performance within such a procedure, as the opening statement in a trial. Sumner represents his argument as a procedurally proper, or at least procedurally conspicuous, indictment of Congress's fugitive slave laws themselves: "Sir, in the name of the Constitution, which it violates, of my country, which it dishonors, of Humanity, which it degrades, of Christianity, which it offends, I arraign this enactment, and now hold it up to the judgment of the Senate and the world" (3:142).

Tellingly, this "arraignment" before the Senate and the world takes place according to a variety of legal orders, only one of which is the positive law of the Constitution. But even more telling is the way in which each of these orders seems to contain within it the tenets of all of the others. Rather than giving us the sense that the fugitive slave law is guilty of a number of crimes, Sumner instead gives us the sense that it is guilty of a single crime, one recognized at all levels of legal jurisdiction. The seamless compatibility between the various legal orders here should help us see that while Stewart only generates higher law results out of positive law provisions, Sumner's reliance upon the moral work of legal procedure has the effect of rewriting institutionalized law as a kind of higher law. The rules of justice are, for him, the rules of law: "Such is the rule of morals. Such, also, by the lips of justices and sages, is the proud declaration of English law, whence our own is derived" (3:194). If moral forces are the only source of true legal authority in Sumner's imagination, it is because the law itself has been defined as a moral force, not because it has been displaced by them. Sumner generates a legal order in which the "*the constitution and laws*" deserve the "*reverence*" Lincoln requested we give them in his Lyceum Address (1:36).

No doubt, issues of civil disobedience remain a part of Sumner's remarks, especially as a part of the first half of his argument, which amounts to an attack on a legal principle that had received both legislative and judicial approval. But rather than disobeying the law in the name of justice, he disobeys the act in the name of the law. Consider, for instance, his particular inversion of Phillips's resignation imperative: "By the Supreme Law, which commands me to do no injustice, by the comprehensive Christian Law of Brotherhood, *by the Constitution, which I am sworn to support,* I AM BOUND TO DISOBEY THIS ACT" (3:194). Resisting civil government in "Freedom National" is entailed by obeying the Constitution.[68] This general rewriting of civil disobedience as a kind of ultra-constitutionalism is nowhere clearer than in Sumner's account of the American Revolution, the paradigmatic act of transformative civil disobedience in American history. Sumner's most polemically aggressive suggestion is that the Fugitive Slave Act errs in exactly the same way in which the Stamp Act erred in the eighteenth century: "I come at once upon two chief radical objections to this Act, identical in principle with those triumphantly urged by our fathers against the British Stamp Act" (3:144). In making this comparison, he converts what might look like the American Revolution's natural law commitments into mere constitutional gestures. Rather than standing for the principle of no taxation without representation or for the rights to life, liberty, and the pursuits of happiness, for instance, the Found-

ing Fathers are instead said to have devoted themselves to a battle against "a usurpation by Parliament of powers not belonging to it" (3:169). And instead of fighting for
the right of self-determination, the right, in effect, to make the laws for themselves,
the colonists are instead understood to have fought for the right to be subjects of a legal regime including "the liberties of the Magna Carta."[69]

The Revolution thus stands as a battle for the Constitution in two senses—for the
British constitutional rights that the Stamp Act compromised and for the American
Constitution, which is better able to embody those general constitutional principles
than British law does. "The Stamp Act's violation of constitutional rights was ex-
posed," Sumner explains. "By resolutions of legislatures and of town meetings, by
speeches and writings, by public assemblies and processions, the country was rallied
in peaceful phalanx *against the execution of the Act*. To this great object, within the
bounds of Law and the Constitution, were bent all of the patriot energies of the land"
(3:172). The revolutionaries are "patriots" not to a nation but to a law—a law, in fact,
of the nation against which they are waging their revolution and a law that becomes
theirs (the "constitutional rights" become over the passage "the Constitution") only
in their removing themselves from that other nation's rule by way of submitting themselves to its law. It is only through this rewriting of the American Revolution as the
restoration of British constitutionalism, this description of the American Constitution as the realization of British law, that Sumner can come to ground his argument
in both "the intentions of our fathers and the genius of our institutions" (3:188). It is
possible, of course, to see a tension between this filial piety, represented in a commitment to fathers and their institutions, and the actual practice of the fathers, which
seemingly entailed a repudiation of their fathers' institutions. But Sumner has, in
effect, made the fathers' revolutionary activity itself a kind of filial piety. He will follow both the letter of their law and the example of it. The tension Lincoln posited in
the Lyceum Address between the Founding Fathers' example and their institutions has
altogether vanished.

Obviously, at least part of the polemical appeal of this recasting of the American
Revolution as a project of British constitutionalism is that it allows Sumner to position documents such as the Declaration of Independence within the social and legal
context of the English empire without thereby converting them into the racist instruments they become in someone like Taney's hands. But the significant payoff lies
at the level of the legal standing of natural law, not the political standing of documents
such as the Declaration. Consider again the moment in which Sumner announces that
he is sworn to disobey "THIS ACT." His invocation there of "Supreme Law" would
seem to point in the direction of natural law, but we can now see that there is also an
important sense in which Sumner rewrites the tension between natural and positive

law as the tension between the Supreme Law of the Constitution and the transitory law of the "ACT." Sumner announces early on that he means to prevent "mere legislation" from "fasten[ing] a new provision on the Constitution" (3:101). He wishes to protect the Constitution from slave-based amendments rather than amend it in the direction of his antislavery sentiment. It is not exactly as though the old structure of *Somerset* disappears here, as though there is no dual structure containing both something like natural law and something like positive law. That structure is simply understood as the structure of American constitutionalism: the Constitution plays natural law to the legislative acts' positive law. And once *Somerset* is replaced by this new structure, Thoreau's sense that any law contrary to natural right must be unlawful becomes legally binding: the higher law *is* a higher law. Insofar as Sumner's "fundamental law" is quite literally "the law of the land" (3:176)—insofar as the Constitution counts as both "the Supreme law of the land" and an expression of higher law—the positive law prerogatives that result in slavery in *Somerset* will have no purchase at the level of federal law. "The time will come when courts or Congress will declare," Sumner claimed, "that no where under the Constitution can man hold property in man" (3:132).

But if the Constitution's emergence as an agent of higher law is useful as a way of making "Freedom National," it is not so useful as a way of abolishing slavery altogether. The problem with this line of thinking, from the antislavery perspective, is that it is not really abolitionist. Insofar as Sumner's argument ratifies *Somerset*, it also begins to ratify the slave codes in the South. It is worth remembering in this respect that in his "First Inaugural Address" Lincoln, the president who would appoint Chase to the Supreme Court, acknowledged the "provision" that the federal government "shall never interfere with the domestic institutions of the States, including that of persons held to service," "to now be implied constitutional law" (2:222). Sumner acknowledged as much himself. States, not having all of their laws "under the Constitution" in the same way that the territories and the Congress did, might preserve the institution: "It may linger in the States as a local institution" (3:142). For many abolitionists this "lingering" itself, not the national government's participation in or aloofness from slavery, was precisely the problem to be addressed. The relevant question was not under what "special law" slavery existed but, rather, whether it existed at all. As Wendell Phillips said in response to Sumner: "Whenever slavery is banished from national jurisdiction, it will be a momentous gain, a vast stride. But let us not mistake the half-way house for the end of the journey. I need not say that it matters not to Abolitionists under what special law slavery exists. The battle lasts while it exists anywhere."[70] But to suggest that Sumner, Chase, Lincoln, and others were merely playing a shell game in which they changed the name of the code under which the existing evil operated is to miss the force of their great innovation. For as the Constitution becomes the nation's natural law, the states' capacity to enact slave codes becomes a function of their separation from the constitutional order rather than their authority within it. Lincoln allowed that state rights to generate slavery were "implied in constitutional law," but there was a sense in which Sumner would have suggested that those rights existed primarily because of a lapse in constitutional law. In the first chapter I claimed that Melville maintains that in order to understand emancipation as a part of the North's "victory of LAW" one must imagine that the Southern states' commitment to slavery marked their having already seceded from the Union prior to 1860, or, indeed, their having never been fully assimilated to it. Sumner's "Freedom Nation, Slavery Local" is the legal, or at least the political, expression of this imaginary history.

CHAPTER FOUR

Legal Sentences

Hawthorne's Sovereign Performatives and Hermeneutics of Freedom

Sentences

"Among human beings," Henry Thoreau insists roughly halfway into "Slavery in Massachusetts" (1854), "the judge whose words seal the fate of a man furthest into eternity, is not he who merely pronounces the verdict of the law, but he, whoever he may be, who, from a love of truth, and unprejudiced by any custom or enactment of men, utters a true opinion or *sentence* concerning him. He it is that *sentences* him. Whoever has discerned truth, has received his commission from a higher source than the chiefest justice in the world, who can discern only law. He finds himself constituted judge of the judge."[1] As we saw in the previous chapter, Thoreau's general project throughout "Slavery in Massachusetts" is to challenge the normative power of existing legal authorities by contrasting their dictates to those of God, to diminish the "verdict of the law" by juxtaposing it to "a true opinion" derived from a "commission from a higher source than the chiefest justice in the world." Such challenges to the law are hardly unusual enough to grab our attention, as Thoreau himself knows very well. He concludes the paragraph that opens with these observations by remarking that it is "strange that it should be necessary to state such simple truths" (98). But in the immediate antebellum period these "simple truths" had been given a special edge by the way in which the legal standing of slavery raised the possibility of a legal code wholly independent of moral judgment and of a realm of moral judgment without any normative authority. Although Thoreau finds it "strange" that it is "necessary to state such simple truths," stating them required, as we saw, considerable effort—effort that itself had to be supplemented before the moral considerations that interest Thoreau could find their way into anything resembling the sentences of American courts.

That effort was the subject of the last chapter. Here I will be less interested in how difficult it was to assimilate man's docket to God's in the 1850s than in what we might call Thoreau's literal point: that antebellum American courts failed to issue real sentences. The kind of normative authority he denies the state and attributes to "higher sources" is hardly as "simple" as the idea that "the fate of a man furthest into eternity" will be determined more by God than by the verdict of the law. As his obligingly italicized puns on *sentence* begin to make clear, Thoreau understands authoritative judgment in terms of an unusual mixture of responsibility and force. As much as Thoreau is interested in religious *wisdom* (such as the ability to "discern[] truth" or to "utter a true opinion"), he seems equally interested in religious *power* (such as the ability to "seal the fate of a man into the furthest eternity"). The religious "judge" does not merely describe the world as it exists; he also produces the world he describes. What God's judgments possess and the states lack is neither insight nor force but a particular combination of the two, a combination that is also a combination of the two meanings implicit in the idea of the *sentence*—"opinions" that can "seal the fate" of men. Saying what is "true" and making what he says become true, Thoreau's Godly judge issues what Judith Butler has called a "sovereign performative."[2]

One did not have to believe that divinely inspired judgment, and divinely inspired judgment alone, possessed this peculiar linguistic force to see that it was lacking, and indeed conspicuously lacking, in antebellum American constitutional legal theory and practice. The matter was especially pronounced with the very topic at hand in "Slavery in Massachusetts": the questions of interstate comity arising from the movement of slave masters and slaves from one state to another. The origin of "slavery in Massachusetts" was the Fugitive Slave Act of 1850 (91), and that act's own origins lay in a constitutional clause that was famously situated somewhere between sentences and *sentences*. Because, you will recall, the fugitive slave clause does not appear in the Article I list of congressional powers, Charles Sumner could insist in August 1852 that the provision was "merely a *compact* between the States . . . *conferring no power on the Nation.*" It followed, then, that Congress could pass no law with respect to fugitive slaves, and though Sumner acknowledged that the clause counted in some way as a "*prohibition* upon the States," outside of aggressive congressional enforcement such a prohibition was bound to seem as weak as the verdict of Thoreau's earthly judge.[3] In *Prigg v. Pennsylvania* (1842) the first major case about the constitutionality of a federal fugitive slave law, Justice Joseph Story brought up the possibility that the clause might, as he termed it, "execute itself" with "no aid from legislation" only to conclude that such a reading of the clause would render the rights of recaption it was designed to protect "shadowy and insubstantial." Should matters "be left to the mere comity of states to act as they should please," he explained, the clause would be "a delusive and empty annunciation."[4] Story did not need to appeal to the higher commission of God to conjure the possibility that American law might not "execute itself," that it might consist of sentences without the power to *sentence*.

In the case of the fugitive slave clause, the gap between what the law said and what it did had effects other than the ones Thoreau lamented: in the hands of Sumner or Chase the gap would bear antislavery fruit. But the difference between sentences and *sentences*, in principle, had no necessary political direction, and it was as often deployed as a means of protecting slavery as contesting it. What is striking is the *frequency* with which the tension between legal utterance and legal authority surfaces in the debates about slavery's constitutional standing.[5] The fugitive slave clause was hardly alone in standing in the intermediate space between the law's constative and performative realms. This intermediate space was central to the very idea of an antislavery reading of the Constitution, and as such antislavery constitutional thinking emerged as a powerful political force over the course of the 1850s, the politics of slavery came to hinge on the status of a series of "shadowy and insubstantial" legal declarations—legal utterances whose relationship to actual legal power was either highly attenuated or essentially opaque: (1) the due process clause of the Fifth Amendment; (2) the Declaration of Independence; (3) the Clayton Compromise (1848), the Utah and New Mexico Territorial acts (1850), and the Kansas-Nebraska Act (1854); and finally (4) Roger Taney's *Dred Scott* opinion. In this climate, in which it often seemed that there was a substantial gap between what the law said and what it did, the exact boundaries of the legal quickly lost their distinctiveness, and the exact nature of legal *agency* quickly came to seem like a problem.

The author who most clearly grasped what was at stake in the various antebellum debates about the relationship between legal rhetoric and legal power was Nathaniel Hawthorne, whose career unfolds as an extended meditation on the problem letters might have in carrying out legal offices. The most powerful of his meditations on this problem, *The Scarlet Letter* (1851),[6] dissects the relationship between Thoreau's sentencing "truth" and mere law with particularly acute precision. It stands as perhaps the most vital and prescient commentary on the consequences of the law's elusiveness in the 1850s. In the second half of this chapter I will build toward a reading of *The Scarlet Letter* by way of several of Hawthorne's early stories, most centrally "Edward Randolph's Portrait" (1837).[7] This particular story gives the tension between Thoreau's sentences and *sentences* narrative form: it culminates in a moment in which it is difficult to tell whether a governmental official is acting or writing. Hawthorne ultimately renders this tension central to the very nature of law—indeed, he makes law a name for the suspended relationship between writing and acting. And in so doing he begins to lay the groundwork for what could become an essentially hermeneutical form of antislavery constitutionalism.

In saying that Hawthorne laid the groundwork for this hermeneutical form of antislavery constitutionalism, I do not mean exactly to say that *The Scarlet Letter* amounts to an antislavery brief or that Hawthorne *meant* to participate in the construction of such an antislavery argument. Although recent scholarship has usefully expanded our understanding of the relationship between Hawthorne and antebellum slavery,[8] my aims remain more modest and abstract. I want to situate Hawthorne in a broad jurisprudential crisis, a crisis that was most pronounced with respect to the law of slavery but which was in no way simply reducible to problems of slave law. If the novel's account of the law's agency opened up possibilities for antislavery legal argumentation, Hawthorne himself did not take advantage of them. Indeed, even as *The Scarlet Letter* examines the centrality of hermeneutical forms of political agency to legal authority, it also testifies to their weakness. Before getting to Hawthorne's multivalent examination of the structures of legal agency, however, we will first need to see why such an examination would be urgent in the decades leading up to the Civil War. A thorough registration of the uncertainty surrounding the nature and origins of legal authority in antebellum America is an extensive enterprise, one that will take us from the outer limits of fringe antislavery constitutional thinking to the inner sanctums of legislative debate and judicial opinion.

Words and Bargains

In many respects what is most remarkable about antislavery constitutional thinking is that it existed at all. It is indeed hard to grasp, at least at first, exactly why antislavery thinkers would have thought it was possible to maintain that the Constitution was incompatible with slavery. Had the institution not persisted, and thrived, under the Constitution? In this sense antislavery constitutional theory had to begin with Thoreau's distinction between the law's sentences and its *sentences*. Whatever else one might be inclined to say about the Constitution's relationship to slavery, it would be difficult to maintain that the Constitution had *done* an enormous amount to threaten its survival or curtail its expansion. As we have already seen in "Freedom National," however, what the Constitution said about slavery—or, more precisely, how the Constitution talked about slavery—was another matter. The most significant early accounts of the Constitution as an abolitionist instrument succeeded, insofar as they succeeded at all, precisely by reorienting our understanding of the Constitution's meaning along these lines—by shifting our concern from what the document enacted to how it spoke of its enactments.

Foremost among these accounts, at least in matters of length and originality, is Lysander Spooner's tract *The Unconstitutionality of Slavery* (1845),[9] which is worth examining in some detail as an introduction to the problems inherent in the genre as a whole. Spooner's polemic represents only one of a spate of constitutional antislavery

arguments developed from the mid-1830s through 1861. But out of a roster including works by Frederick Douglass, William Goodell, Samuel Joseph May, George
Mellen, Gerritt Smith, and Joel Tiffany, *The Unconstitutionality of Slavery* attracted the
most notice—indeed, sufficient notice that Wendell Phillips saw fit to subject it to a
scathing book-length rejoinder.[10] For Spooner the Constitution became an antislavery document in part because, at least as he understood it, there could be no legal authority other than natural law. If Mansfield said that because slavery was repugnant
to natural law it must be created by local law, Spooner insisted that because slavery
was repugnant to natural law it could not be created or recognized by local law. Because "natural law" "is the paramount law," and because "being the paramount law, it
is necessarily the only law," Spooner insisted, "there is, and can be, correctly speaking,
no law but natural law." In effect he insists that, even legally speaking, Thoreau's C O N -
S T I T U T I O N must count as the American Constitution. But just as Thoreau's C O N -
S T I T U T I O N could only count as a constitution by virtue of its insertion into the
world of legal form, so too does Spooner's natural law require some adjustment before it can become the American Constitution. We might wonder, to cast the point in
terms of the details of Spooner's rhetoric, how natural law can be both the "paramount" law and the "only" law at the same time. If it is the only law, then how can
there be any other law in relation to which it would be paramount? And this question
takes on a somewhat greater force when Spooner follows his italicized claim that there
is no law but the natural law with an account of the natural law's comparative importance: "There is no other principle or rule, applicable to the rights of men, that is
obligatory in comparison with this, in any case whatsoever" (7).

The confusion is suggestive and important. Had Spooner simply announced that
only natural law could have any force, his argument would have done little to change
the nature of the antislavery debate. Almost no one doubted that natural law was opposed to slavery. What was in doubt was whether natural law was applicable in the
cases in which slavery was contested in American courts, and Spooner's glib assurances that natural law is always paramount do not exactly constitute an argument for
deploying it in a court of human law. So, unsurprisingly, Spooner backed away from
his insistence that natural law was paramount because there was no alternative legal
order. Instead, like Sumner, he made his natural law paramount by incorporating it
into the Constitution itself. Here he relied on two separate contentions—one a contention about the meaning of the Constitution, the other a contention about how we
should construe meaning from documents like the Constitution.

The first step in Spooner's argument about the meaning of the Constitution is to
challenge the notion that the Constitution *recognizes* slavery. Spooner sets about this
improbable task by calling attention to and insisting upon the importance of the na-

ture of early American state slavery laws. State legal institutions, he maintained, were incorporated into the national constitutional order only to the extent that they had been clearly "authorized or established by any of the fundamental constitutions or charters that had existed previous to" the founding of the nation in general and the ratification of the Constitution in particular (54). Because "slavery had no constitutional existence, under the State constitutions, prior to the adoption of the constitution of the Unite States," the Constitution could "*not* recognize it as a constitutional institution" (55). For slavery to count as lawful under the Constitution, then, the Constitution would have had to have "created or authorized slavery as a new institution" (56). And, Spooner insisted, "it is perfectly clear . . . that the constitution of the United States did not, *of itself, create or establish* slavery as a *new* institution; or give any authority to the state governments to establish it as a new institution" (55).

Spooner's reasons for feeling so confident on this point will only emerge later on in his argument, but before getting to them we might well wonder why slavery had to be a part of state constitutions for it to be recognized by the national constitution. Why did slavery have to have constitutional, as opposed, say, to statutory, standing in the states? Spooner does not say, but his later reference to the Constitution's supremacy clause suggests that he is relying on an old argument about the relationship between states and the nation, according to which the states had only limited sovereign existences prior to the emergence of the nation and consequently, like the federal Congress after the ratification of the Constitution, had only certain constitutionally enumerated sovereign powers when the United States's fundamental law was established. Although this argument received its most famous presentation in Webster's monumental "Reply to Hayne" address (1830), it probably received its most thorough elaboration in Story's *Commentaries on the Constitution* (1833):

> [The Declaration of Independence] was not an act done by State governments then organized, nor by persons chosen by them. It was emphatically the act of the whole *people* of the united colonies, by the instrumentality of their representatives, chosen for that among other purposes. It was not an act competent to the State governments, or any of them, as organized by their charters to adopt. These charters neither contemplated the case nor provided for it. It was an act of original, inherent sovereignty by [the people] themselves, resulting from their right to change the form of government, and to institute a new one, whenever necessary, for their safety and happiness.[11]

Even granting that prior to the ratification of the Constitution the states did not actually have the power to generate slavery, however, it is still not clear that they would not have the power to generate laws tolerating it after ratification. The point of the Tenth Amendment, it would seem, is to insist that states did not need constitutional authority "to establish" whatever institutions they thought desirable. (Or, to cast the argument from Story's perspective, the Tenth Amendment would seem to have given the states constitutional authority to do whatever they pleased so long as they did not violate an actual constitutional provision.) If the states had limited legal powers be-fore the ratification of the Constitution, the Constitution itself would seem to allow them a wide range of latitude.

Spooner responds to this prospect by adding to his claim that states are not au-thorized to establish slavery the second claim that the establishment of such an insti-tution would be in violation of particular constitutional guarantees. Slavery is both unauthorized and forbidden. Here is the argument's general outline: because the Con-stitution, at least as Spooner would have it, existed for the protection of all of the peo-ple of the United States at the time of its ratification (none of whom, constitutionally speaking, were slaves), the act of enslaving a person must count as an act of usurpa-tion by state authorities over the rights of citizens of the United States. Slavery thus constitutes, in a weird but telling inversion of Melville's account of the Civil War, an invasion of the national body politic by the slaveholding states:

> The constitution of the United States, at its adoption, certainly took effect upon, and
> made citizens of *all* "people of the United States," who were *not slaves* under the State
> constitutions. No one can deny a proposition so self-evident as that. If, then, the *State*
> constitutions, then existing, authorized no slavery at all, the constitution of the United
> States took effect upon, and made citizens of *all* "the people of the United States," with-
> out discrimination. And if *all* "the people of the United States" were made citizens of the
> United States, by the United States constitution, at its adoption, it was then forever too
> late for the *State* governments to reduce any of them to slavery. . . . If the State govern-
> ments could enslave citizens of the United States, the State constitutions, and not the
> constitution of the United States, would be the "supreme law of the land"—for no higher
> act of supremacy could be exercised by one government over another, than that of tak-
> ing the citizens of the other out of the protection of their government, and reducing
> them to slavery. (56)

The subjunctive mood of most of these sentences and the hyperbolically confident tone of those sentences that are not subjunctive (i.e., "No one can deny a proposition so self-evident as that") make the argument sound slightly tenuous. Just how many of these conditionals rest on false premises? Is it entirely fair to say that the Constitu-tion produces a national citizenship? Until the ratification of the Fourteenth Amend-ment, as we will see in the next chapter, no clear legal consensus had emerged about whether political subjects in the United States were chiefly citizens of states (and only citizens of the nation by means of their status as state citizens) or chiefly citizens of the nation (and only citizens of the states by means of their status as national citizens). Did the Constitution "take effect upon, and make citizens of *all* 'the people of the United States'"? In *Dred Scott,* as we have already seen, Taney would insist that racial discrimination was in fact central to the intentions of the Framers of the Constitution. And even if all of the people of the United States had been made citizens of the United States by the Constitution, would they therefore be immune from being reduced to slaves by any state? In *Strader v. Graham* (1851) Taney would strongly suggest that national civil standing might have no ultimate effect on state slave status.[12]

What is missing from this argument is the hint of any part of the Constitution which expressly forbids slavery. Spooner, of course, in the spirit of *Somerset,* would place the burden on the other side of the argument. But it is easy enough to see that his argument that the states cannot keep the inhabitants of the United States in slavery would benefit greatly from any indication in the Constitution that slavery was necessarily incompatible with American citizenship. Spooner appears to take up this challenge when he insists that "the constitution of the United States not only does not recognize or sanction slavery, as a legal institution, but . . . on the contrary . . . presumes all men to be free" (56–57). As should already be clear from his decision to address what the Constitution "presumes" rather than what it declares or establishes, however, Spooner ultimately does not locate an antislavery provision in the Constitution or generate a specific antislavery argument from any provision within it so much as surround the document in a general antislavery aura.

Part of the way in which he does this is by stressing the way in which slavery is mentioned in the Constitution only indirectly. This indirection counts as good reason for thinking that the Constitution itself should not be seen as the origin of slavery in the United States, but it is not exactly an account of why the Constitution should count as the origin of its exclusion.[13] Spooner thus must bolster his case by insisting that some parts of the Constitution seem incompatible with slavery, or, at the very least, compatible with freedom. He finds eleven such constitutional provisions (94–114). They stretch from the plausible but strained, such as the guarantee clause ("The United States shall guaranty to every State in this Union a republican form of government . . ."), which was to become such an important part of the federal mechanics of Reconstruction (105–14: "Mark . . . especially that this guaranty is one of liberty, and not of slavery")[14]; to the wholly fanciful, such as the copyright clause (96: "This power, then, on the part of Congress, to secure an individual the exclusive right to his invention and discoveries, is a power inconsistent with the idea that individual himself, and all he may possess, are the property of another"), and the post office clause (96: "The right to send and receive letter by post is a right inconsistent with a man's being a slave"). Now of course, none of these provisions counts as an unproblematic ground for thinking that the Constitution proscribes slavery: the mere quotation of Spooner's arguments is sometimes enough to render them ridiculous (I borrowed the technique from Phillips's review), So, Spooner moves from his list of moments in which the Constitution "presumes" freedom to his second major argument, an argument less about what the Constitution means than how we should read it. (Almost half of *The Unconstitutionality of Slavery* is devoted to an extended discussion of "Rules of Interpretation.") And here, no surprise, he seeks to make what little evidence he presented in the first section of the book count as definitive.

His fourteen rules of interpretation work in roughly three ways. One set of rules seeks to limit legal power of the Constitution's vague references to slavery by insisting that technical legal meanings (such as "slavery") cannot be derived from general verbal usages ("person[s] held to service of Labour"). Hence, for instance, the second rule prioritizes the actual words in a constitution over a general knowledge of its provisions ("the intention of the constitution must be collected from its words" [161]), and the fourth rule insists that those words must be grasped in their technical sense ("where *technical* words are used, a technical meaning is attributed to them" [168]). A second set of rules works to effect the conversion of Spooner's evidence that the Constitution "presumes" freedom into the basis for the claim that it precludes slavery. They do so by insisting that the meaning of specific provisions of a legal document be run through the filter of the document's overall tone. "A fifth rule of interpretation is, that the sense of every word, that is ambiguous in itself, must, *if possible,* be determined by reference to the rest of the document" (180). "A ninth rule of interpretation is, to be guided, in doubtful cases, by the preamble" (198). "A tenth rule of interpretation is, that one part of an instrument must not be allowed to contradict another, unless the language be so explicit as to make the contradiction inevitable" (199). In this world the Constitution's presumption of freedom combines with its vagueness about slavery so as to guarantee freedom. If the danger facing Spooner is that the general assertions of the importance of freedom in the Constitution might have no specific application (that provisions such as the guarantee clause might be "idle verbiage"), this second set of rules makes them necessarily consequential, or, as Spooner puts it, "full of meaning, . . . [a] meaning [that] is not only fatal to slavery itself, but . . . fatal also to all those pretences, constructions, surmises, and implications, by which it is claimed that the national constitution sanctions, legalizes, or even tolerates slavery" (114).

It is nonetheless hard to justify a massive exercise of judicial review on the basis of the Constitution's treatment of peripheral matters never explicitly linked to slavery. Spooner's third set of rules ties these general "presumptions of freedom" to a specific source of legal authority, albeit one that does not take the form of a provision in the

Constitution itself. If you cannot find antislavery declarations in a body of law, you might say that all techniques of legal reading are themselves devoted to the cause of freedom: freedom can be made a part of the interpretation of the law even if it cannot be said to be the content of the law. Spooner's final set of rules works in precisely this direction. They serve the function of giving his undeniable higher law claims purchase in the positive law domain in which he is less effective. He provides rules, that is, which make natural law "paramount" to positive law rather than simply separate from it. If his efforts to give positive law an antislavery form might not be wholly successful, he can nonetheless fall back on the notion that ordinary rules of interpretation might supplement his efforts and compensate for any of their shortcomings. Hence, for instance, rule 8: "An eighth rule of interpretation is, that where the prevailing principles and provisions of a law are favorable to justice, and general in their nature and terms, no *unnecessary exception* to them, or their operation, is to be allowed" (196). The twelfth rule is even clearer: "A twelfth rule, universally applicable to questions both of *fact and law,* and sufficient, *of itself alone,* to decide, *against slavery,* every possible question that can be raised as to the meaning of the constitution, is this, '*that all reasonable doubts must be decided in favor of liberty*'" (200). Spooner's rules of construction incorporate his higher law into his positive law. They save his positivist claims from their weakness by routing them through the authority of the higher law as well as the Constitution. And likewise, by routing his higher law through amorphous phrases in the Constitution ("the prevailing principles" that are "favorable to justice"), he gives it a constitutional purchase as well as a legal one.

It is for this reason that Robert Cover is only half-right when he suggests that "the substance of his [Spooner's] argument is natural law."[15] Spooner's argument does begin with the assurance that only natural law is relevant, and it does derive almost the entirety of its force from the strictures of natural law rather than from the provisions of the Constitution. But Spooner does not merely declare that natural law stands as the paramount legal authority; he also seeks to provide a *legal* framework in which natural law would become meaningful even in human courts and to establish that the Constitution should be understood in terms of that framework. After accurately claiming that "Spooner's constitution is amputated from any societal context," Cover approvingly quotes Garrison's rejection of *The Unconstitutionality of Slavery:* "Garrison condemned it most succinctly: 'The important thing is not the words of the bargain, but the bargain itself.'"[16] But Spooner does not simply present a strained reading of the words of the bargain; he also maintains that, legally speaking, those words, rather than the "bargain itself," are what matters. Following Garrison, we might say that Spooner's argument casts the Constitution as an instrument of freedom only insofar as the law's meaning follows from its words rather than its purpose. If the

Constitution's sentences are *sentences,* slaves might go free. Because they are merely "words," the "bargain" they enact leaves slavery intact.

Putting the point this way, however, probably gives Spooner's argument about the Constitution's words more credit than it really deserves. Garrison could easily have attacked Spooner on the interpretive grounds that he misunderstood the Constitution's words instead of challenging him on the theoretical grounds that he addressed the wrong dimension of the Constitution. Even if Cover mistakes the basic structure of Spooner's argument, he is certainly right that Spooner's argument was sufficiently grounded in natural law as to seem somewhat kooky, which is to say that it was insufficiently grounded in plausible constitutional doctrine to have any imaginable application in an American court. Even more down-to-earth accounts of the Constitution's hostility to slavery, however, were unable to avoid the structural problems between bargains and words on display in *The Unconstitutionality of Slavery.*

Legal Action (the Fifth Amendment)

At the close of the last chapter we saw that Sumner's translation of the *Somerset* paradigm into specifically constitutional terms had the effect of producing an actual legal structure for Thoreau's slightly more abstract legalized nature. We also saw that it had the effect of leaving slavery largely intact so long as it remained a "local institution." The Fifth Amendment could be deployed against slavery, but the amendment could not quite eliminate it—at least not in Sumner's hands. But Sumner's instrument for attacking the Fugitive Slave Act could also be an instrument for attacking slavery as such, and it was in fact used in exactly this way by prominent abolitionists, most notably Alvan Stewart.[17] The difference between Sumner's antislavery due process clause and Stewart's abolitionist due process clause is nothing more than the difference between a constitution composed of bargains and one composed of words. To recall Stewart's argument: the Fifth Amendment insists that "no person. . . . [shall] be deprived of his life, liberty, or property, without due process of law." Because slave status certainly entails the deprivation of liberty, it must result from a legal proceeding, attended to by the usual juries and grand juries, which results in a conviction. At least in a constitutional sense it cannot arise from the forms of inheritance in which it was generally conveyed in antebellum America. As soon as the slave is able to present his case, "the judge will be obliged under the oath, which he must have taken, to obey the Constitution of his country, to discharge the slave and give him his full liberty" (289).

At the level of syllogistic abstraction it is hard to quibble with Stewart's reasoning, but there is nonetheless a significant problem with his legal calculus. Since the nation's slave codes were housed at the level of state law, the judge would have been under

Stewart's obligation to free the petitioning slaves only insofar as the Fifth Amendment limited the legal authority of states. Prior to 1866, at least, it did not. Just three years before Stewart generated his brief, the Supreme Court had unanimously held in a Marshall opinion in *Barron v. Baltimore* (1833) that none of the provisions in the Bill of Rights "ought to be so construed as to restrain the legislative power of a state, as well as that of the United States."[18] Stewart's take on the Fifth Amendment was by no means self-evidently wrong. It is in fact quite easy to make a case that the Bill of Rights in general and the Fifth Amendment in particular had a wider range of application than *Barron* would allow. The amendment says that no person shall "be deprived of life, liberty, or property, without due process of law," not that "the Congress of the United States shall not deprive any person." It looks as much like the announcement of a general principle as the enactment of a particular kind of legal restraint.[19]

If Stewart had good reasons to construe the Fifth Amendment broadly, however, Marshall had better reasons for confining its scope. Even in purely rhetorical terms there might have been some reason to moderate the amendment's seemingly universal application. Marshall maintained, for instance, that all of the Constitution's limitations upon the powers of states are specifically enumerated (or as he puts it, "averred in positive words") and that as a consequence, its "general" language in fact refers exclusively to limitations upon congressional power. But the real case against Stewart's reading lies not at the level of the Constitution's language but at the level of the amendment's history. "It is universally understood, it is a part of the history of the day," Marshall notes toward the end of his opinion, "that the great revolution which established the constitution of the United States, was not effected without immense opposition," opposition that centered around fears that the federal government's power "might be exercised in a manner dangerous to liberty":

> In almost every convention by which the constitution was adopted, amendments to guard against the abuse of power were recommended. These amendments demanded security against the apprehended encroachments of the general government—not against those of the local governments.
>
> In compliance with a sentiment thus generally expressed, to quiet fears thus extensively entertained, amendments were proposed by the required majority in congress, and adopted by the states. These amendments contain no expression indicating an intention to apply them to the state governments. This court cannot so apply them.[20]

"What makes *Barron*'s holding compelling," writes the legal historian, Akhil Reed Amar, "is neither its technical parsing of Article I nor its use of lawyerly rules of construction nor even the narrow legislative history of the Bill of Rights in Congress. Rather, it is . . . the historical background of the Bill of Rights."[21] Indeed, we might even say that that historical background governs even Marshall's "use of lawyerly rules of construction," for it is that history that allows him to reverse the plain meaning of the amendment's words by shifting the burden from those who would like to narrow their seemingly universal reach to those who would like to apply that reach to a given set of governmental institutions and instrumentalities. History allows him, that is, to convert the amendment's bold statement of an unlimited principle into an absence of an "expression indicating an intention" to apply that principle to "the state governments."

The point here is certainly *not* that Marshall is wrong about how the Fifth Amendment should have been treated as a matter of constitutional law prior to the ratification of the Fourteenth Amendment.[22] It is, rather, that what the Fifth Amendment was designed to do was not identical to the constative meaning of the amendment's language and that Stewart could consequently have recourse to the Bill of Right's language even if he misunderstood its meaning. The gap between the Bill's words and its deeds counts as a problem as well as an opportunity, however, in "A Constitutional Argument." Stewart does not merely want to suggest that slavery is incompatible with the Constitution. He wants to deploy the Constitution to eradicate slavery. And his efforts to activate the Constitution as an antislavery instrument lead him to reproduce the tension between the amendment's agency and its language which is central to the plausibility of Marshall's historicist opinion in *Barron*.

Stewart's argument does not altogether ignore the historical background of the Fifth Amendment. His interest in the emancipatory power of due process has the advantage of allowing for the fact that there might have been slaves at the time of the Constitution's ratification without having that allowance count as an admission of the constitutionality of antebellum slavery. Stewart is not compelled, as Spooner was, to "amputate" the Constitution from its "social context." Indeed, like the Garrisonians and many recent historians, Stewart considered the Constitution to be a compact in which "the men of the free states [were] made partakers in the crime of slavery" (285). In conceding the Founders' acceptance of slavery, however, Stewart ultimately gives up fairly little. Indeed, and this is the source of his argument's greatest ingenuity, for Stewart this acknowledgment of the corruption of the Founding Fathers ultimately has abolitionist consequences. By his account at least, in licensing slavery, the Constitution assumed the authority to specify what Stewart calls its "mould"—the legal terms governing the institution. And these terms, as Stewart is quick to point out, are almost never met: "It would be fair to infer," he insists, that not one Southern slave has been "deprived of his liberty, by due process of law" (294). As to the question of why the amendment's abolitionist tendencies have yet to bear fruit, Stewart responds simply by saying that they have yet to be adjudicated: "The reason why these unasserted rights of the slave have lain dormant and unexamined seems to have arisen from the utter inability of one under the bonds of slavery, to take the very first step, which is to appear in a court of law, to vindicate his right for and to himself" (290–91).

Of course, matters were not so simple. Stewart insists that the due process clause was a response to provisions in the Constitution which implicated the Northern states in the slavery system ("The men of the free states being made partakers in the crime of slavery, out of courtesy, might firmly, as they truly did, insist that the Constitution should contain the only mould in which slaves should be run" [285]), but in fact the due process clause was already present in the Articles of Confederation, which, as Stewart himself notes, "said [nothing] on the subject of slaves" (284). Consequently, Stewart is led to produce a wholly fictional and almost entirely fantastic account of the deliberations in Philadelphia. "We may suppose," he begins his account of how Northern fears of lynch law, Northern abolitionism, and Southern interests in securing honest title in slaves meld into the due process clause (285). That the Founding Fathers sought to address slavery in the Fifth Amendment was highly unlikely even in the 1830s, and the publication of Madison's diary in 1840 was soon to demonstrate that slavery was far from their minds when they hammered out the Bill of Rights.[23] Stewart's account of the amendment looks skewed even without the light such historical data might shed. Are we really to "suppose" that Southerners, in their efforts to secure their title to slaves, agreed effectively to emancipate them? Or that Northerners simultaneously meant both to make themselves complicit in slavery through the fugitive slave provisions and to abolish the peculiar institution altogether?

Stewart responds to these difficulties by withdrawing, at least in part, his claim that the Fifth Amendment would effect emancipation in and of itself. After insisting that a slave need merely present his case before a judge in order to become free, Stewart goes on to claim that because of the Fifth Amendment "Congress . . . possesses the entire and absolute right to abolish slavery in every state and territory in the Union" (282). The notion that the Fifth Amendment expanded Congress's authority over state laws, of course, is no more sensible as a historical matter than the notion that the amendment applied to state slave legislation. *Dred Scott* would maintain that the Fifth Amendment *deprived* Congress of power over slavery even in the territories. But it is easy enough to see why this form of congressional emancipation would be appealing to Stewart. So long as some supplemental congressional action remains a part of the emancipatory mechanics, it is at least loosely plausible that the Constitution represented a sectional compromise. This plausibility comes at the expense of a coherent account of the precise location of emancipatory authority in American law. The Constitution that emancipates slaves does not also need to authorize Congress to emancipate them, and Stewart is less interested in suggesting that Congress can emancipate slaves than in saying that it must do so. Hence, he is ultimately unwilling to displace emancipatory authority entirely from the amendment to the legislature. Congress's emancipation provision, he says, would be merely "a declaratory act" (294). Stewart's Fifth Amendment stands as something on the order of the slave trade clause—a constitutional measure that was understood to effect the end of a given institution but which nonetheless required further congressional action. But when Congress outlawed the importing of slaves, it was not declaring the meaning of the Constitution. It was simply exercising one of its constitutional powers.[24] In Stewart's hands it is not quite clear where the abolitionist power resides. In the words of the Constitution? In the acts of Congress? In some combination of the two? Spooner's Constitution speaks and presumes freedom without enacting it. Stewart would seem to have added an account of legal action to the calculus, but he gives that action almost no concrete origin. Marshall's Fifth Amendment enacts a law; Stewart's Fifth Amendment and his Congress are merely able to declare one.

Legal Declarations (The Declaration of Independence)

As is so often the case with what we might call the argumentative environment of constitutional antislavery, these problems surrounding the relationship between legal utterance and legal agency receive their most focused and intense literary commentary in *Battle-Pieces*.[25] The possible tension between legal act and legal enactment is frequently foregrounded in Melville's poetry, which forever makes us wonder whether a declaration or the enforcement of it counts as decisive: "A white flag showed, the fight was won" (114). Is the order backward here? Was the battle won because the flag showed, or did the flag show because the battle was won? And while in this case declaration is aligned with enforcement, the state's declarations are not always so compatible with its actions. Perhaps the best examples of Melville's interest in the prospect of a tension between the state's uses of force and its uses of rhetoric emerge in those moments in which he is most directly concerned with suggesting that the very existence of the state counts as an act of domination. We have already had occasion to note the strange way in which Melville attributes Draconian qualities to states at precisely those moments in which they seem not to be doing anything at all. We are now able to see that, while from one perspective these moments make the state itself look like a form of oppression, from another they mark the prospect that the state may proclaim a kind of oppression without enacting it or, conversely, enact a kind of oppression without proclaiming it:

Power unanointed may come—
Dominion (unsought by the free)
And the Iron Dome,
Stronger for stress and strain,
Fling her huge shadow athwart the main;
But the Founders' dream shall flee.
Age after age shall be
As age after age has been,
(From man's changeless heart their way they win).   (17)

Even as Melville renders the dome a form of unanointed "power," he also elaborates a notion of a state without force. Notice how passive the dome remains throughout the sequence. The power comes; it is not deployed. The dome is first associated with Dominion by an appositive phrase—it is linked to Dominion without doing anything and without its connection to it elaborated by anything other than an effect of juxtaposition. And notice also that the dome's authority comes from its performing an action ("flinging" its shadow) which it cannot be plausibly imagined to perform. It is presented as the agent of an activity that we know must be engineered elsewhere. The dome's power lies simply in its existence. It becomes a kind of self-executing declaration, or what we might call a declaratory law. But in presenting us with such a declaration, Melville actually marks the distinction between the image of the state's authority and the practice of that authority; he presents us with a declaration *so* self-executing as to underscore the need of most declarations to be executed. The dome's authority here is, quite literally, metaphorical.

If the Iron Dome counts as an example of a declaration that carries force with it, Melville also gives us acts of force which carry declarations with them. And if his examples of declarations that carry force with them raise the prospect that there might be some tension between the declaratory and regulatory dimensions of a state's activity, his examples of acts of force which carry declarations with them suggest that the two dimensions might be in open conflict with one another. Consider, for instance, the last lines of "The House-Top":

Wise Draco comes, deep in the midnight roll
Of black artillery; he comes, though late;
In code corroborating Calvin's creed
And cynic tyrannies of honest kings;
He comes, nor parlies; and the Town, redeemed,
Gives thanks devout; nor, being thankful, heeds
The grimy slur on the Republic's faith implied,

Which holds that Man is naturally good,

And—more—is Nature's Roman, never to be scourged.   (87)

The sequence sets up a fairly elaborate set of interactions between what Draco does (he comes) and what he says (that the population requires his discipline). With respect to the former, Draco does not "parl[y]"; with respect to the latter he only "parlies" and indeed "parlies" "In code." Calvin's creed thus is not enforced; it is "corroborated." If the state's action here seems somehow both "cynic" (in its power) and "honest" (in its aspiration to oppose the power of "sway of self" to "take[ ]" a population [86]), it can take on this dual role because it is engaged in two separate activities. Melville's project is to reveal, and indeed to insist upon, the gap between the two of them: what the state does (eliminate subjection) is at odds with what it says (subjection is necessary). Hence, the brilliant confusions in the concluding lines: what "implies" the "grimy slur on the Republic's faith"? Wise Draco and his "black artillery" or the conditions that he is required to confront? Melville's state is rendered essentially contradictory here: its force compromises the very liberty it is enlisted to protect. And what allows it to assume this contradictory form is the fact that its claims and its actions can work in exactly opposite directions.

"The House-Top" is extreme in the way it elaborates the relations between what the state says and what it does. Melville is more often interested in the irrelevance of the government's statements to its actions than in the hostility between the two. *Battle-Pieces* sometimes produces something indistinguishable from the scenario we encounter in the difficulty *Barron* poses for Stewart's argument—a structure in which there appears to be a declaration of principle to which figures have no access and which has no consequences within the poetic world in which it is inserted:

Vainly she [the city of Charleston] calls upon Michael

(The white man's seraph was he),

For Michael has fled from his tower

To the Angel over the sea.   (109)

The parenthetical line here makes a declaration that the remainder of lines render useless; it gives the city a reason to "call" upon Michael, but it does not give him the power to provide the relief for which the people will appeal. Its status as parenthetical is crucial, for as we read along we feel it to be in slight tension with what follows it: that Michael has fled seems incompatible with the fact that he might be "The white man's seraph." It is in the course of resolving this potential conflict that we begin to feel the force of Melville's claim that Michael "was" a seraph he may no longer be. But we only feel it once we—unwarned, like the citizens of Charleston, by anything other than the marginality of seraphs to this scheme—encounter the fact of his having departed: Melville never actually says that Michael has left his post, nor does he give us an account of his departure. Declarations of protection do not count as enforceable sources of authority.

In the 1850s the great act of American declaratory antislavery law bore roughly the same relation to the American slave population as Melville's declaration of Michael's status bears to the population of Charleston. That great act of declaratory law, of course, was the Declaration of Independence, and, according to Abraham Lincoln at least, the nature of its provisions were in danger of being altered—altered so that its claim that "we hold these truth are self-evident: that all men are created equal" would become, as Lincoln put it in his 1857 "Speech on the 'Dred Scott' Decision" in Springfield, "We hold these truths to be self-evident that all British subjects who were on this continent eighty-one years ago, were created equal to all British subjects born and *then* residing in Great Britain."[26] "I believe the entire records of the world," Lincoln announced in his reply to Douglas at Galesburg, "from the date of the Declaration of Independence up to within three years ago, may be searched in vain for one single affirmation, from one single man, that the negro was excluded from the Declaration of Independence" (1:702). The rationale behind Lincoln's concern for the sanctity of the Declaration is readily apparent: the Declaration could obviously play a valuable role in the construction of a legal atmosphere of antislavery. But it could play that role only so long as it was understood to be an essentially legal document, and it is not entirely clear that we should understand it that way. What makes the Declaration anything other than what Thoreau called an "ornament" of the revolution (138)—a symbol of the emergence of the nation but not exactly a foundational instantiation of that nation's legal principles? Why not understand it as the origin of American legal authority (a statement that produces American sovereignty) rather than as an expression of that authority?

As the Declaration of Independence began to emerge as the guiding political text of American politics in the 1850s, however, it also began to emerge as a specifically legal text. That Taney even felt a need to explain how the Declaration could be assimilated to his account of the status of African Americans at the time of the nation's founding implicitly attributes to the document a legally binding force. And the Declaration's status as a legal instrument is even clearer in the Lincoln-Douglas debates, especially in Lincoln's demand that Douglas "come up and amend" the Declaration if he wished to persist in claiming that African Americans were not to be included in its claim "that all men are equal, upon principle" (1:269): "I adhere to the Declaration of Independence. If Judge Douglass and his friends are not willing to stand by it, let them come up and amend it. Let them make it read that all men are created equal except negroes. Let us have it decided, whether the Declaration of Independence, in this blessed year of 1858, shall be thus amended" (1:477). This is a truly remarkable suggestion. What would it mean to "amend" the Declaration of Independence? Would such an act count as a second revolution? Would it count as a new Declaration of Independence? By what mechanism could one amend such a document? Lincoln's suggestion can make sense only if we think of the Declaration as a statement rather than an action, if we conceive of it as, as Lincoln would put it in the Gettysburg Address, a "proposition" instead of a performative (2:536).

Of course, making the Declaration into a statement might make it plausible to think of it as being like a law in the sense that it would be subject to amendment, but it does not guarantee that it will actually have any regulatory force. In a speech in Chicago in July 1858, Lincoln challenged Douglas and Taney to remove the Declaration from "the Statute book": "If that declaration is not the truth, let us get the Statute book, in which we find it and tear it out!" (1:457). Lincoln gets the Declaration into legal code by making it an utterance as opposed to an act—something we judge in terms of its truth rather than its consequences. But in so doing he also robs the document of exactly the legal authority it might have just seemed to acquire. We want to know whether statutes are legitimate, not whether they are true. Perhaps unsurprisingly, then, as the Declaration became a part of the American legal apparatus, it was increasingly identified with parts of the Constitution, especially with the first amendments to the Constitution, which themselves bore an oblique relationship to direct legal authority. Within two paragraphs of his account of Douglas's need to amend the Declaration, Lincoln presents Jefferson's text as a kind of Bill of Rights: "They [African Americans] are not our equal in color; but I suppose that it does mean to declare that all men are equal in some respects; they are equal in their right to 'life, liberty, and the pursuit of happiness'" (1:477–78). Part of the point here, no doubt, is to associate the Declaration with certain rights so as to weaken what looks like the absolute character of its claims of equality. It is worth remarking, however, that Lincoln's reduction of the Declaration to a guarantee of particular rights has the effect of reconfiguring it in the terms of the Fifth Amendment. And if the Declaration of Independence shared with the Fifth Amendment a set of substantive concerns, it also shared with it the peculiar legal status of not being legally binding, of counting as a legal assertion more than a legal enactment. At other moments Lincoln more explicitly associates its status as an assertion of rights with its inability actually, as he puts it, to "confer" those rights:

> They [the authors of the Declaration] defined with tolerable distinctness, in what respects they did consider all men created equal—equal in "certain inalienable rights,

among which are life, liberty, and the pursuit of happiness." This they said, and this meant. They did not mean to assert the obvious untruth, that all were actually then enjoying that equality, nor yet, that they were about to confer it immediately upon them. In fact they had no power to confer such a boon. They meant simply to declare the *right*, so that the *enforcement* of it might follow as fast as circumstances should permit. They meant to set a standard maxim for a free society, which should be familiar to all, and revered by all; constantly looked to, constantly labored for, and even though never perfectly attained, constantly approximated, and thereby constantly spreading and deepening its influence, and augmenting the happiness and value of life to people of all colors everywhere. (1:398)

Again, Lincoln is as concerned with limiting the Declaration's scope as he is with defining its role. But the role he defined for it is nonetheless remarkable. His Declaration is designed to be the kind of legal instrument Spooner deployed to convert the Constitution into an antislavery document: an assertion without particular or specific purchase which nonetheless can be determinative of, or at least have an influence upon, the more specific provisions of the legal order of which it is a part. Standing as the source of "rights enumerated" but not necessarily enforced (1:512), the Declaration of Independence begins to look suspiciously like the Bill of Rights itself.[27]

The alignment of the Bill of Rights and the Declaration as similar structures of declared but unenforceable laws received its most straightforward embodiment in Thaddeus Stevens's description of the Fourteenth Amendment before the U.S. House of Representatives in 1866: "I can hardly believe that any person can be found who will not admit that every one of these provisions is just. They are all asserted, in some form or another, in our DECLARATION or organic law. But the Constitution limits only the action of Congress, and is not a limitation on the States. This amendment supplies that defect"[28] Stevens's claim that the Constitution limits only the action of Congress with respect to the Bill of Rights, of course, is wholly in keeping with the Supreme Court's ruling in *Barron*. What is strange here is that he acts as though the Constitution might also limit the actions of Congress with respect to the Declaration of Independence—or, rather, that he feels no need at all to distinguish between the conceivably enforceable provisions that constitute the Bill of Rights and the seemingly wholly declaratory Declaration.[29] The result of this indifference has been a great deal of confusion about what Stevens actually means here, with some, such as Raoul Berger, claiming that he means only that the Fourteenth Amendment secures equality before the law with respect to the clearly enumerated rights of "life, liberty, and property,"[30] and others, such as Akhil Amar, suggesting that he means that it secures the provisions found in the Bill of Rights. Each of these readings has the benefit of making Stevens's claim legally sensible, but neither has the benefit of recognizing that Stevens was treating the Bill of Rights as entirely of a piece with the Declaration. Such a treatment makes no sense from the perspective of the current world, in which the law's *sentences* seem to follow from its sentences. But it makes perfect sense from the perspective of the world of constitutional law in the 1850s, a world in which the boundaries between the Constitution and statutes, the Constitution and the Declaration of Independence, and the Constitution's legal meaning and the meaning of its words were profoundly unstable.

Constitutional Settlements (the Clayton Compromise and Dred Scott)

So far I have been addressing the relationship between legal utterance and legal agency in fairly abstract legal settings, in more or less theoretical outposts of nineteenth-century American constitutional structure. But by the end of the 1850s the problems we have been exploring would emerge in the far more prosaic settings of actual congressional statutes and actual Supreme Court decisions. The clearest evidence of the difficulty in separating declarations of the law from enactments of it in the 1850s lay in the systematic intertwining of legislative and judicial functions in the period. What is remarkable, and jarring, about Stewart's argument is the way it reverses the usual relationship between Congress and the Courts by endowing the legislature with what amounts to a judicial function. But Stewart was hardly alone in his uncertainty about Congress's relationship to the legislative power and authority with respect to slavery. Such uncertainty, indeed, was part and parcel of the sectional conflict's steady constitutionalization in the 1850s. Thoreau claimed that nineteenth-century American laws did not sentence people, but it is not really clear that nineteenth-century lawmakers always *wanted* their laws to sentence people.

Exactly what authority Congress had with respect to the regulation of the domestic institutions of the territories had become a serious source of sectional contention in the 1820 debates over the Missouri Compromise, and the conflict the question aroused only became more serious in the protracted struggles over the Wilmot Proviso in the 1840s. Indeed, by the end of the 1840s the question had begun to divide the Democratic Party as well as the nation, with extraordinary legislative results. Beginning in 1848, with the introduction of what is now known as the Clayton Compromise, Congress frequently dealt with the conflict it could not resolve by simply passing it along to the courts. The original Clayton proposal, which was never enacted, forbade the territorial legislatures in the Southwest from passing any legislation with respect to slavery, explicitly extended the rules of the Constitution to the territories in question, and provided for Supreme Court review of any controversy that may arise over slavery in them. "The bill," John Clayton happily announced, "leaves the entire question" of slavery in the territories acquired in the Mexican war "to the Judiciary." "It was thought by this means," he added, that "Congress would avoid the decision of this distracting question, leaving it to be settled by the silent operation of the Constitution itself."[31] Clayton, Thomas Corwin famously quipped, had proposed that Congress enact a lawsuit, not a law.[32]

Future congressional enactments with respect to slavery in the territories carried on the Clayton tradition, and indeed the passed versions of the Clayton lawsuit were actually less lawlike than their progenitor. The Clayton proposal did at least exercise congressional lawmaking authority over territorial slavery to the extent that it *prohibited* local governments from exercising authority themselves with respect to the matter. In the famous Compromise of 1850 and the infamous Kansas-Nebraska Act of 1854, Congress declined even that expression of will. The Utah and New Mexico bills of 1850 implicitly extended regulatory authority to territorial legislatures by saying nothing whatsoever on the subject. The Kansas-Nebraska Act explicitly announced that its "true intent and meaning" was "not to legislate slavery into any Territory or State, nor to exclude it therefrom, but to leave the people thereof perfectly free to form and regulate their domestic institutions in their own way, subject only to the Constitution of the United States."[33] This language left a number of questions unanswered, most importantly the question of *when* the people of a territory might acquire the authority to form and regulate their domestic institutions. But it was nonetheless at least somewhat plausible for Louisiana senator Judah P. Benjamin to claim in 1856 that Congress, or at least the Democratic majority in Congress, had reached the following compromise in 1854:

All agreed that it was prejudicial to the best interests of the country that the subject of slavery be discussed in Congress. All agreed that, whether Congress had the power or not to exclude slavery from the Territories, it ought not to exercise it. All agreed that, if that power was owned by us, we ought to delegate it to the people whose interests were to be affected by the institutions established at home. We therefore put that into the bill.

Then came the point on which we disagreed. Some said, as I say, Congress has no power to exclude slavery from the common territory; it cannot delegate it, and the people in the Territory cannot exercise it, except at the time when they form their constitution. Others said, Congress has the power; Congress can delegate it; and the people can exercise it. Still others said . . . that the power to legislate on that subject was a power inherent in every people with whom the doctrine of self-government was more than an empty name. . . . We said, in this bill, that we transferred to the people of that Territory the entire power to control, by their own legislation, their own domestic institutions, subject only to the provisions of the Constitution; that we would not interfere with them; that they should do as they pleased on the subject; that the Constitution alone should govern. And then, in order to provide a means by which the Constitution could govern, by which that single undecided question could be determined, . . . agreed that every question touching human slavery, or human freedom, should be appealable to the Supreme Court of the United States for its decision.[34]

We should not let Corwin's humor blind us to his insight. The Clayton Compromise was no doubt politically attractive to a Democratic Party divided between those who thought Congress could not regulate slavery in the territories and those who thought that it should not do so. But it is hard to see exactly what Congress thought it was accomplishing, or, to put it slightly more clearly, why it thought that the measure it had passed would accomplish the results legislators such as Clayton sought. For one thing, although the whole point of a measure such as the Kansas-Nebraska Act was to displace constitutional questions from the Congress to the courts, these bills' language implied that the relationship between the Constitution and the territories was itself subject to congressional prerogative. The very act of extending the rules of the Constitution to the territories would seem to suggest that in the absence of such an extension the Constitution would not apply there. And while there was good reason to believe that the Constitution did not necessarily follow the flag in the nineteenth century,[35] it is hard to reconcile Congress's claiming the right to settle that constitutional question with its principled claim to have left "every question touching human slavery" to the courts.

Along these lines, moreover, exactly what Congress meant to be leaving to the courts proves almost impossible to pinpoint. The various post-Clayton territorial acts allowed the courts to rule on the status of slavery in the territories independent of any regulation and to rule on Congress's authority to delegate regulatory authority to territorial governments. They did not allow the Court to determine whether Congress itself had the right to regulate slavery in the territories. In order for that matter to be in question Congress would have had to have regulated slavery, not passed such authority on to the courts and territorial legislatures. But whether Congress meant to confine the Court's authority to such a narrow domain is uncertain, not to say doubtful. We can register some of the problem here by noting the way in which Benjamin slides from the claim that the Kansas-Nebraska Act left the Court with a "single undecided question" of the territorial legislature's authority to the claim that the act allowed for the Court to consider "every question touching human slavery, or human freedom." Was the idea to give the court a single question or the whole panoply of questions regarding territorial slavery?

Insofar as Congress thought that it was enlisting the Court to settle the question of its authority over slavery in the territories, it was imagining that it could, quite literally, pass a lawsuit rather than enact legislation that would be subject to adjudication. Implicit in the hyper-deferential Clayton principle, in other words, is that Congress somehow controlled the courts' docket—that it was responsible for the courts' workload not in the indirect sense that it produced laws that they would interpret so much as in the direct sense that it simply placed legal problems before them for consideration. There is a weird mixture of hubris and modesty here: on the one hand, Congress seeks to regulate the way in which the courts will attend to its laws; on the other, it refuses to presume any answer to constitutional questions in the course of its discharging its duty. But of course, legislators cannot avoid the constitutional questions: each law they pass presupposes a variety of constitutional conditions—that Congress has the authority to pass such a measure, that the measure does not conflict with protected rights, and so on. Such questions arise whether or not Congress explicitly presents them to the courts. They arise not because Congress is engaged in something like Stewart's "declaratory" activity but, rather, because it is engaged in its legislative activity. What is ultimately most significant about the Clayton Compromise and its legacy is the way they testify to an immense, systematic confusion about the relationship between these two enterprises on the eve of the Civil War.

Given this backdrop, it was probably inevitable that the lawsuit with respect to slavery in the territories which finally emerged in the 1850s would be vexed by a series of irregularities. When Congress passes lawsuits, judges become legislators. The lawsuit Congress got was *Dred Scott*, which was not exactly the lawsuit it had proposed. Historians have frequently noted that the Court took up the question of slavery's status in the territories only after Congress had sought, in David Potter's words, to "rid itself of the vexing territorial issue" by "pass[ing] the responsibility" to determine slavery's status in the territories "on to the courts." While it is no doubt true that Congress did "foster a judicial resolution of the problem" in the "statutes of 1850 and 1854,"[36] it is not quite right to say that the Court threw its weight into the sectional conflict "only upon the explicit invitation of Congress."[37] Benjamin's expansive second formulation of what Congress had presented to the Court would make such a reading plausible. But it does not exactly follow from Benjamin's earlier narrower description of the compromises of the early 1850s, nor does it follow, in a legal sense, from the legislation Congress had passed. In effect Taney dealt with Congress's laws, not its lawsuits—with Congress's power to regulate slavery, not with the status of territorial slavery independent of congressional interference. What the Democrats most wanted to displace to the judiciary was the question of whether territorial governments might possess the authority Taney denied *Congress*. But in *Dred Scott* this issue was handled only in a famous aside, and it remained an important bone of contention all the way through the Freeport doctrine debates and the ultimate disintegration of the Democratic Party at Charleston in 1860.[38]

Controversy over the status of slavery in the territories would thus comfortably survive Taney's best efforts to suppress it. Clayton's "silent operation of the Constitution" ultimately became a version of Story's self-executing Constitution, with the rights it guaranteed no less "shadowy and insubstantial." The most important by-product of Taney's opinion was in all likelihood the Freeport doctrine, which held that the *Dred Scott* decision itself was something like the fugitive slave clause, of little value unless enforced by specific legislation—and in this case the legislation in question would likely have to come from exactly that body that had thrown the question before the Supreme Court in the first instance. Douglas, who did most of the insisting that further legislation was essential to secure the slave property *Dred Scott* seemed to protect, was certainly in no hurry to provide such legislation.[39] Nor were Northern Democrats alone in turning *Dred Scott* into something of a dead letter. If a figure such as Douglas took the principle of the opinion at face value but refused to give that principle actual legal content, the Republicans took the legal content of the case on board without conceding one iota to its principle. Lincoln's response was in many respects typical. Acknowledging that the Supreme Court's decisions on constitutional questions "must be binding in any case, upon the parties to a suit, as to the object of that suit," he nonetheless insisted that they commanded no more than "very high respect and consideration, in all parallel cases, by other departments of the government" (2:221). What this meant was that the Supreme Court's rulings did not constitute rules of what Lincoln called "political action" (1:542), and consequently "the policy of the government, upon vital questions, affecting the whole of the people" is not to be "irrevocably fixed by the decisions of the Supreme Court" (2:221). The Freeport doctrine converted *Dred Scott* into one of Thoreau's sentences—a statement of principle which amounts to nothing more than a statement. Lincoln converted it into an action—a resolution of a concrete and tangible dispute which produces no principle by which future cases should be resolved (no "evil effect[s] following it" [2: 221]). What neither allowed it to be is a *sentence*.

This gap between legal expression and legal agency in jurisprudential penumbra surrounding *Dred Scott* derives from the systematic inter-articulation of acts of legislation and acts of adjudication. The world in which Congress produces lawsuits and the Court enacts laws proved to be a world in which lawsuits settled nothing and no laws were enacted. It is worth noting in this regard that Nathaniel Hawthorne conspicuously locates the action of *The Scarlet Letter* in exactly such a world. We might be surprised that such eminent men of state as the governor actively participated in debates about the proper way to allocate the custody of Pearl, Hawthorne explains at the beginning of "The Governor's Hall": "At that epoch of pristine simplicity, however, matters of even slighter public interest, and of far less intrinsic weight than the welfare of Hester and her child, were strangely mixed up with the deliberations of legislators and acts of state. The period was hardly, if at all, earlier than that of our story, when a dispute concerning the rights of property in a pig, not only caused a fierce and bitter contest in the legislative body of the colony, but resulted in an important modification of the framework itself of the legislature" (101). Here the constitutional, legislative, and judicial dimensions of governance twirl into a messy tangle. A dispute of the "rights of property in a pig" invites a response from "legislators" as well as judges. Deliberations about a petty property dispute shade into deliberations about the constitution of the polity's representative body. Enacting laws becomes executing laws becomes adjudicating disputes becomes configuring governmental institutions. It is no easier to locate legal agency here than it is in Stewart's "Constitutional Argument." We might be able to determine who will make decisions in old Boston, but we will not be able to specify exactly what kind of decisions they will have made. Whether this confusion produces the same problems in *The Scarlet Letter* which it produced in late 1850s America will be the subject of the remainder of this chapter. Before we can properly address that question, however, we would do well to consider the way in which Hawthorne understands the nature of legal language. Hawthorne's engagement with this issue receives its clearest and most direct elaboration in his early stories, especially the *Legends of the Province-House* (1837–38). As a way of approaching *The Scarlet Letter,* I would like now to turn to one of those *Legends,* "Edward Randolph's Portrait," to register the intensity with which Hawthorne confronted the problem of the law's verbal power and the sophistication with which he accounted for it.

Official Letters
Signed Orders

Since neither "Edward Randolph's Portrait" nor *Legends of the Province-House* ranks among Hawthorne's most prominent work, it probably makes sense to start out with a little bit of background information.[40] *Legends* consists of a series of four tales about the old Province-House in Boston which served as the governor's mansion in colonial days before being reduced to a second-rate inn in the early decades of the nineteenth century. Each of the tales begins with the narrator's recounting a journey to the inn, where he regularly meets a Mr. Bela Tiffany. A veritable fixture in the bar, Mr. Tiffany regales the narrator with stories in which the Province-House serves as the gothic backdrop for important but unrecorded developments in the course of the gradual erosion of colonial authority in Boston on the eve of the Revolutionary War (the last of the tales actually comes from one of Mr. Tiffany's "loyalist" companions [667]). The *Legends* are the narrator's recitations of what he takes to be the most compelling of these stories. "Edward Randolph's Portrait" hinges on Thomas Hutchinson's deliberations with respect to the wisdom of inviting British troops into Boston to "overawe the insubordination of the people" on the eve of what would become the Boston Massacre (642). Mr. Tiffany frames the story of Hutchinson's fateful meditations with an account of a darkened old painting in Hutchinson's office in the Governor's House, a portrait of the infamous Edward Randolph. On the day of Hutchinson's decision the painting is either restored or repainted by Hutchinson's niece, Alice Vane, to reveal a horrific face that throws an "evil omen" over the scene of Hutchinson's final considerations. Faced with the question of whether Randolph's grisly image indicates Randolph's suffering after he "trampled on the people's rights" or instead merely represents the niece's "painter's art," "her tricks of stage-effect," and her "Italian spirit of intrigue," Hutchinson decides to discount the painting's putative warning. He signs an order inviting British troops into Boston to establish order and brings upon himself "the blood of the Boston Massacre" (649, 650).

These developments probably seem far removed from the legal crises surrounding slavery which I have been discussing thus far in this chapter, but we can begin to see their relevance to the discussion at hand simply by looking at the way in which Hawthorne's narrator first encounters the Province-House itself: "One afternoon, last summer, while walking along Washington street, my eye was attracted by a sign-board protruding over a narrow arch-way, nearly opposite the Old South Church. The sign represented the front of a stately edifice, which was designated as the 'OLD PROVINCE-HOUSE kept by Thomas Waite'" (626). The key word here is *represented*, and Hawthorne's use of it is arrestingly odd insofar as it forces us to pose the question of whether the sign marks the site of the "old edifice" or instead frames an image of the building—whether, that is, the sign *designates* the location of the "edifice" or *presents* a drawing of it. Of course, by the end of the sentence it is clear that the sign contains a sketch of a house rather than marking the place where the building stands: the quotation marks around the house's name strongly suggest, after all, that the sign is doing its designating in words and that the narrator is not alluding to a more general designation made by, say, the townsfolk. But however clear matters might become by the sequence's end, this way of using the word *represent* is counterintuitive, not to say nonstandard. The kind of representation Hawthorne describes is an activity we strongly associate with the activity of subjective agents such as people, not something we generally attribute to inanimate material: it would seem to make more sense to say that the sign presented a representation of a house than to say that it represented one. We might say that Hawthorne's use of *represent* leads us to believe that the sign is doing something, when in fact he means to say that it is saying something. And it thus forces us to register the difference between sentences and *sentences* even as it testifies to the instability of that distinction.

At its very outset "Edward Randolph's Portrait" returns us to the questions of representation implicit in the Province-House's "sign." In the legend's fourth paragraph Alice Vane asks Hutchinson "Is it known . . . what this old picture once represented?" (642). Is she asking what the picture represented to the people who have left it in what she will go on to call "such a conspicuous place"? Or is she asking what image appears on the canvas? The story's plot and its narrative climax hinge on the difference between these two ways of thinking about the painting's representational authority. And Hawthorne makes sure that we understand their centrality to the portrait's function in the story by incorporating them, and the problem of keeping them distinguished from one another, into his very account of what a portrait is. On the ensuing page we encounter this sequence: "The oldest inhabitant of Boston recollected that his father, in whose days the portrait had not wholly faded out of sight, had once looked upon it, but would never suffer himself to be questioned as to the face which was there represented" (643).

Part of the point here lies simply in the reiteration of the problem of "representation": does the man's father refuse to talk about how the face was represented or what face was represented? But the more important issue is that these problems with respect to the meaning of *representation* can also worm their way into the story's account of the nature of portraiture itself. What does the "oldest inhabitant" mean by the word *portrait*? We would expect, of course, for the term to apply to the physical artifact of the canvas and the paint upon it. This is the way we use the word when we say that a portrait hangs on the wall or, for that matter, when we claim that someone who owns the canvas of a portrait owns the portrait in a way that those who have reproductions of it do not. But here the term signifies what is represented, not the artifact that presents the representation. Which is why the narrator can assume that "the portrait had . . . wholly faded out of sight" and that only a few figures from the distant past "had looked upon it" even at the same time that he reports the responses of a group of people to the artifactual remains of the canvas and frame: the "dark old square of canvas" alone does not count as the portrait for him (643).

In dramatizing the difficulty of stabilizing the distinction between pictures and subjects, between saying things and things said, these early and seemingly trivial sequences lay out the intellectual terrain on which the story's narrative will eventually play itself out. The tension between the two possible "portraits," or pictures, only grows greater when what the narrator calls "the portrait" returns to the purview of the tale in the story's conclusion. "Within the antique frame," the narrator explains,

> which so recently had enclosed a sable waste of canvas, now appeared a visible picture, still dark, indeed, in its hues and shadings, but thrown forward in strong relief. . . . The whole portrait started so distinctly out of the back-ground that it had the effect of a person looking down from the wall at the astonished and awe-stricken spectators. The expression of the face, if any words can convey an idea of it, was that of a wretch detected in some hideous guilt and exposed to the bitter hatred, and laughter, and withering scorn, of a vast surrounding multitude. There was the struggle of defiance, beaten down and overwhelmed by the crushing weight of ignominy. The torture of the soul had come forth upon the countenance. It seemed as if the picture, while hidden behind the cloud of immemorial years, had been all the time acquiring an intenser depth and darkness of expression, till now it gloomed forth again, and threw its evil omen over the present hour. (649)

Here again, terms such as *picture* and *portrait* refer less to the representing object (the "sable waste of canvas") than the representation it contains. And this shift from our ordinary sense that portraits and pictures are representing things to the idea that they are represented things does not pass without difficulty. For starters, as the passage goes along, it begins to suggest that even some of the canvas's representational field will not actually count as the "picture" in question here. The prospect arises when the narrator suggests that "the whole portrait started so distinctly out of the back-ground." "Back-ground" is ordinarily something that we imagine to be within the painting's representational field, not a part of the material out of which that field is constructed. Casting the story of the emergence of the picture from its material context in terms of the emergence of the foreground from the background, the narrator intertwines the painting's subject with the painting's substance. And this overlap explains, perhaps, the way in which the narrator also intertwines his account of the picture's emergence from the "sable waste of canvas" with an account of the emergence of Randolph's "expression" from the picture. As the picture becomes the subject of a painting rather than the painting itself, the narrator finds it increasingly difficult to isolate his expressive agents: hence, the painting's emergence becomes the emergence of a figure within it which in turn becomes the emergence of a quality within that figure. And hence the emergence of the portrait from the canvas can also stand as something like the emergence of the subject from the portrait, a point that receives clear expression when the narrator suggests that "the whole portrait . . . had the effect of a person looking down from the wall at the astonished and awe-stricken spectators." The story's confusion about what counts as representation, as it were, turns into the suggestion that there is no such thing as representation: the emergence of the picture becomes the emergence of the person whom the picture is a picture of.

Garrison's complaint with Spooner hinged on the difference between bargains and words, on the difference between what the law is or does and what it says. We might say that Garrison insisted that the law's implicit content trumped its explicit meaning—that the bargain implied in the drafting of the nation's fundamental law was more important than the terms in which the deal was consummated. "Edward Randolph's Portrait" systematically breaks down the distinction between these two realms—as the portrait becomes its subject, the gap between what it means in virtue of its existence and what it means in virtue of its expressive content wholly erodes. And Hawthorne drives this point home by linking his account of the emergence of one kind of representation out of another kind with an account of the emergence of an implicit feature of Randolph's identity into the explicitly visible dimensions of his visage. Here is the ending of the paragraph that articulates the emergence of the picture from the canvas in terms of the emergence of Randolph from the picture: "Such, if the wild legend may be credited, was the portrait of Edward Randolph, as he appeared when a people's curse had wrought its influence upon his nature." The "appearance" of the portrait coincides with the appearance of Edward Randolph, which coincides, in turn, with the appearance of the "people's curse upon his nature," as Hutchinson will put it, "upon his face" (649). These matters coincide, that is, with the moment in which the implicit dimensions of Randolph's identity become the explicit matters of his appearance, the moment in which what Edward Randolph means is made identical to who Edward Randolph is. The tale of the emerging portrait is also the tale of how "inward misery of the curse work[ed] itself outward, and was visible on the wretched man's countenance" (645).

The drama surrounding Hutchinson's decision ultimately plays itself out in terms of this drama of the relations between what things mean and what they are. That decision revolves around Hutchinson's response to the newly visible portrait, and Alice Vane's participation in the restoration of the canvas gives immediate rise to a series of questions about the portrait's authenticity—questions, in effect, about whether what the painting is (i.e., a forgery) is more important than what it means (i.e., that colluding with British military might against New Englanders results in immense personal suffering). The selectmen quickly respond to the newly visible image in terms of its meaning. They treat it as "a warning from a tormented soul." But their language of warnings *from* specific agents already begins to suggest that the canvas might not be a record of Randolph's "torment" so much as a deployment of that myth for political purposes. Such, at any rate, is Hutchinson's first take on the refurbished painting and their interpretation of it. His initial response to the painting is to attribute its effects to the work of his niece and thus to deny that it can have any meaning whatsoever: "'Girl!' cried he, laughing bitterly, as he turned to Alice, 'have you brought hither your painter's art—your Italian spirit of intrigue—your tricks of stage-effect—and think to influence the councils of rulers and the affairs of nations, by such shallow contrivances? See here!'" (650).

Hutchinson does not conclude his thinking about the portrait with this emphatic dismissal of the painting's authenticity, however, and in his next set of remarks he seems to turn his resistance to the painting's implications in a new direction. He goes on to rebuff a selectman who pleads with him not to ignore the painting's warning: "Away! . . . Though yonder senseless picture cried 'Forbear!'—it should not move me!" (650). From one perspective this simply stands as an amplification of Hutchinson's earlier claim that the painting was nothing more than his niece's contrivance. At first he suggested that he took whatever effects the portrait may have in its current form to result from "tricks" and "shallow contrivances." Here he emphasizes the claim by giving it a specific content, as if to say, "I won't believe what that painting says, no matter how clearly it says it." Yet it is interesting that the way in which he emphasizes his earlier claim actually brings a new set of concerns into the debate. For in insisting that the painting would not move him even if it gave its message directly ("cried 'forbear'"), Hutchinson begins to make it seem as though his initial opposition to Vane's "stage-effects" lay in the way that they gave only implicit warnings, in the way that they only suggested what they might have simply said. The claim that the painting is not believable becomes, from this perspective, the two separate claims that (1) it is not clear enough, on the one hand; and (2) that it should not have any political force regardless of its clarity, on the other. The painting is "senseless," then, both in the sense that whatever "sense" it may have is a false sense (claim 2) and in the sense that it makes its point too obliquely (claim 1). His order to his niece ("See here!") thus stands as something more than an assertion of his authority: it also stands as an assertion of the literal; in signing the order, he will do something whose meaning will not be subject to the allegorical world of "warnings" and the like which seem to make up "Italian" and Puritan politics.

There is nothing particularly logical about Hutchinson's tendency to articulate his concerns about the painting's provenance in terms of its clarity. These two grounds for resistance might be complementary in this particular instance, but they are by no means identical and are in fact in many ways incompatible. If the painting is inauthentic, after all, it cannot really matter how clearly it gives its warning. Hutchinson resolves this tension, in effect, by simply abandoning his concern about his niece's role in the warning's appearance. But it is no accident that Hawthorne stages Hutchinson's inability to separate his complaints about what the painting is from what it means.

This inability to separate acts from meanings remains central to Hutchinson's dilemma even after he fully abandons any concern with the painting: "Casting a scowl of defiance at the pictured face (which seemed, at that moment, to intensify the horror of its miserable and wicked look,) he scrawled on the paper, in characters that betokened it a deed of desperation, the name of Thomas Hutchinson. Then, it is said, he shuddered, as if that signature had granted away his salvation" (650).

If Hutchinson's reasons for denying the portrait's authority earlier seemed to shift from questions of the painting's authenticity to questions of its clarity, here the lieutenant governor seems less to deny the painting's authority than simply to oppose it. What once looked like a lack of belief in the "pictured face" has become an act of "defiance" against it, and defiance at a time in which the picture, so long as we believe that it is authentic, reveals itself all the more as a warning by "intensif[ying] the horror of its . . . look." But those questions of agency which recede at the moment when Hutchinson defies the painting's warning instead of dismissing it return in the way he carries his defiance out. The narrator's description of Hutchinson's signature emphasizes the gap between its performative and constative dimensions. What is initially striking about the signature is that it means something other than what it says. This is the force, after all, of the narrator's introducing his account of Hutchinson's scrawl by noting that the way that it was written "betokened it a deed of desperation." Its verbal content and its expressive content (what it "betokens") are hardly identical. But by the end of the narrator's description of Hutchinson's signature we are more likely to be struck by his suggestion that Hutchinson is *writing*, that the lieutenant governor's signature's meaning would have something to do with its explicit content in any way whatsoever, than by his insistence that the meaning of the act is not reducible to the meaning of the letters Hutchinson writes. The narrator focuses so carefully on *what* Hutchinson writes that it begins to seem as though Hutchinson is doing something other than signing his name: "he scrawled on the paper . . . the name Thomas Hutchinson" (650). A signature must entail something more than the inscription of a name. We do not think of ourselves as writing our names when we sign a check: if the important thing were the "scrawling" of a name, then it would be possible for anyone to sign any name. And in its redundant account of what name Hutchinson writes, the narrator's account almost makes it seem as though Hutchinson has done just that, has signed someone else's name.

Hutchinson's explicit warning has become his written signature. The narrator's description here mimes Hutchinson's emphatic and absolute commitment to the explicit, to a writing whose meaning lies in what it says, not what it does or what it is. But in "Edward Randolph's Portrait" at least, no legal author can ever make recourse to such exclusively constative writing. Hutchinson's signature entails a policy as well as a set of graphemes, which is why the narrator so emphatically distinguishes be-tween the "deed" the signature betokens and what it says. But once we begin to put the point this way a peculiar paradox emerges. For Hutchinson's problem is not sim-ply that his writing acts as well as speaks; it is also that in thinking that his writing merely speaks he loses control over the meanings attributable to the actions his sig-nature will carry out. In attempting to say things rather than enact policies, Hutchin-son blinds himself not only to the effects of his actions but also to what those effects betoken. Hutchinson finds himself operating not only in the realm of action, we might say, but also in the realm of implicatory speech acts (signatures). And unlike Alice, the Italians, and the Puritans, he seems unable to control what such utterances will mean or how he will be said to relate to them. In seeking to represent things (such as his name or history) rather than have his actions represent, Hutchinson commits what the tale represents as his most significant mistake, namely his inability to grasp the *symbolic* importance of welcoming the troops. In insisting that legal writing is neces-sarily a form of action, then, Hawthorne is not suggesting that it is merely, or exclu-sively, a form of action. In the domain of the law all writing counts as action, and all action also counts as writing.

Penal Language

This is why Hutchinson circles from writer to actor and back to writer again. And it is also why Hawthorne often approaches the problem of Hutchinson's signature not from the perspective of that signature's necessary implication in the realm of action but, rather, from the perspective of that signature's necessary implication in the realm of language. The converse of Hutchinson's written signature is Boston's written pun-ishment. At the center of the narrative logic of *The Scarlet Letter* is the fantasy that the scarlet letter is something more than a letter. This fantasy first appears when Hawthorne initially encounters the "rag of scarlet cloth" which "assumed the shape of a letter" (31). It persists when Hawthorne "experience[s] a sensation not altogether physical, yet almost so, as of burning heat; and as if the letter were not of red cloth, but red-hot iron," after spontaneously "plac[ing] it on" his "breast" (32). And it re-ceives perhaps its most emphatic iteration in the moment in which Hester's discard-ing the letter results in "her sex, her youth, and the whole richness of her beauty, [com-ing] back from what men called an irrevocable past": "She had not known the weight, until she felt the freedom" (202). Despite the repeated invocations of *weight, sensa-tion, physical,* and *rag,* these passages testify less to the materiality of this signifier than to the efficacy that materiality entails. The letter that burns Hawthorne and burdens Hester is a letter that acts rather than speaks. It is a self-executing law, self-executing even to the point of driving itself to Hawthorne's breast without his having any initial idea about why it might belong there.

In this regard it makes sense that the letter would be associated, right from the first chapter, with what Hawthorne calls a "penal machine" (55). In these moments the letter itself *is* a penal machine. But these moments are as exceptional as they are emphatic, and the letter often comes across as a part in a much larger machine rather than an entire and independent disciplinary apparatus of its own. Since this larger machine itself includes actual machines, such as "that instrument of discipline," "the pillory," we might even find ourselves thinking that the letter takes its place *beside* the penal machine rather than *within* it. Indeed, the letter's primary function in Hawthorne's initial accounts of the Puritans' penal machinery is to model the other instrumentalities that machinery deploys. If the letter sometimes assumes the form of a penal machine, the pillory will likewise take on the qualities of a letter. "The very ideal of ignominy," Hawthorne maintains, "was embodied and made manifest" in the pillory (55). This "instrument" seems to represent justice as much as it enacts it.

And for this reason we should not be completely surprised that the pillory does not make ignominy so manifest that a "society . . . grown corrupt" might not "smile, instead of shuddering," in response to its workings and that the Puritans' larger penal apparatus crucially depends upon less mechanical "contrivance[s]" (56, 55). What ultimately ensures the efficacy of the "legal sentence[s]" of Boston is not the machinery by which they are carried out but the environment in which that machinery operates: "Even had there been no disposition to turn the matter into ridicule, it must have been repressed and overawed by the solemn presence of men no less dignified than the Governor. . . . When such men could constitute a part of the spectacle, without risking the majesty or reverence of rank and office, it was safely to be inferred that the infliction of a legal sentence would have an earnest and effectual meaning" (56). To be sure, this sentence is famously less "effectual" than "earnest." "The scarlet letter had not done its office" (166). But Hawthorne's point in cataloging the limits of the letter's office is not to challenge the authority of the "men" who would execute it so much as to register the limitations of the instruments on which that execution will ultimately depend. Insofar as their sentence must be understood in terms of what it "means" as well what it "inflicts," they can never be precisely sure how the sentence will be executed: "Such helpfulness was found in her,—so much power to do, and power to sympathize,—that many people refused to interpret the scarlet A by its original signification. They said it meant Able; so strong was Hester Prynne, with a woman's strength" (161). This sentence fails to *sentence* precisely because it is a sentence.

The disciplinary problems most critics have located at the heart of *The Scarlet Letter* derive directly from the way in which Hawthorne represents the law as an essentially hermeneutical activity.[41] Even in its most direct forms of action, deploying "instrument[s] of discipline, so fashioned to confine the human head in its tight grasp" (55), legal power remains tethered to the world of discourse. The law must serve as an "effectual agent in the promotion of good citizenship" by way of making various "ideals" "manifest." The point is not that Hawthorne insists upon the elasticity of moral reasoning—as when he issues his famously unpersuasive "moral" at the end of the novel (260). Nor is it that Hawthorne insists upon the limitations of our capacity to grasp the external world—as when he lists a range of "theories" about Dimmesdale's last moments for the readers' "cho[ice]" rather than simply telling us what happened (259). These epistemological problems surface in *The Scarlet Letter* as symptoms of Hawthorne's unwavering insistence that our relationship to the law be essentially epistemological, that legal agency be constituted as much around declaratory acts and regulatory ones.

The Scarlet Letter thus effectively outlines a world in which Spooner's Constitution can supersede Garrison's. There are *no* bargains in the penal scheme of Puritan Boston, only more or less effective uses of words: even the pillory stands as a form of speech. But we might think that Hawthorne clears the space for Spooner's way of reading the Constitution only at the expense of the Constitution's *legal* authority. The *A* comes to mean "Able" by a process tinged in illegitimacy. The "many people" who give it such a construction do so only by "*refusing*" to honor the letter's "original signification." The *A* is an impotent signifier, not an unstable one: it retains its "original signification" even as that signification loses its authority. Lest we miss the point, Hawthorne presents it to us in a concrete example on the letter's first appearance in the novel, in which Hester's construction of the *A* ("fantastically embroidered and illuminated upon her bosom" [54], "it had all the effect of a last and fitting decoration to the apparel which she wore" [53]) is marked less as a reinterpretation of the law than an affront to it: "She hath good skill at her needle, that's certain. . . . But did ever a woman, before this brazen hussy, contrive such a way of showing it! Why, gossips, what is it but to laugh in the faces of our godly magistrates, and make pride out of what they, worthy gentlemen, meant for a punishment?" (54).

In light of antebellum legal theory, however, this criticism may well be slightly overstated. "Construction is unavoidable," Francis Lieber explains in his monumental *Legal Hermeneutics* (1839). In the narrow sense what Lieber means by this dictum is that it is impossible for legislators to write laws that are not subject to abuse. Because "men who use words," Lieber continues, "even with the best intent and with great care as well as skill, cannot foresee all possible complex cases," and because "no absolute language, by which is meant that mode of expression which absolutely says all and every thing to be said and absolutely excludes every thing else, is possible, except in one branch of human knowledge, namely mathematics," "no human wisdom can possibly devise an instrument that may not be interpreted so as to effect any thing but that for which the constitution was established and its fundamental principles laid down." Hence, "interpretation of some sort or other is always requisite, whenever human language is used." But Lieber is not content simply to maintain that because legal codes have no mathematical form they will never escape "construction" or "interpretation." He also goes so far as to say that construction and interpretation should be definitive of the meaning of legal documents instead of the intentions of those who actually write them. The absence of an "absolute language" ensures that after some "lapse of time, we must give up either the letter of the law, or its intent, since both, owing to a change in circumstances, do not any longer agree." At such a moment the choice is clear. "The appeal to the motives of the utterers is, in most cases doubtful, in many, dangerous; because it lies in the nature of things that it must be difficult, or impossible, to arrive at them otherwise than from the words themselves." Because our best, indeed our only safe, route to the "motives" of legal speakers is the language they have used, such motives "must form . . . , in most cases, a subject to be found out by the text, not the ground on which we construe it."[42] From this vantage the contrarian Bostonians are not refusing to recognize the intentions of the *A*'s authors. They are, rather, properly recognizing the sublimation of those intentions into the letters by which they gave them voice.

This sublimation remains incomplete in *The Scarlet Letter*. Legal agency is dispersed into legal language, but it is not so thoroughly dispersed that the language becomes altogether free-floating. Hawthorne is as concerned with the authority of legal interpreters as he is with that of legal speakers. Of course, in conjuring a world in which the intentions of legislators are subsumed into the language of laws, Lieber does not deprive the law of its agency. He simply relocates that agency from legislator to the hermeneutical system in which the legislator's words are processed. In *The Scarlet Letter* that system constrains the authority of Hester and the townspeople no less than their leaders. The alternative to the self-executing scarlet letter is Hester's self-executing wedding. If a letter cannot determine social arrangements, perhaps sentiments could. "What we did had a consecration of its own. We felt it so! We said so to each other! Hast thou forgotten it?" (195). Hester's informal but loving liaison with Dimmesdale, however, is no more "consecrated" than her unloving but formal marriage with Chillingworth ("Thou knowest . . . that I was frank with thee. I felt no love, nor feigned any" [74]). The point becomes clear toward the end of the novel, in the sequence in which we learn that Hester's *A* is no longer performing the Puritans' office. Hawthorne attributes the development in part to "Hester's strength." He even goes so far as to say that her new status is entirely her production: "She was self-ordained a Sister of Mercy." But Hawthorne revokes the category of the self-ordained almost as soon as he introduces it. The sentence goes on: "or, we may rather say, the world's heavy hand so ordained her, when neither she nor the world looked forward to this result" (161). The state's not having absolute control over the process of ordination does not necessarily allow any given individual to assume the vacated office. It instead makes the relationship between acts and offices essentially opaque, the "result" of processes wholly divorced from any specific agent's intentions.

Self-Ordained

This oscillation between Hester's *assuming* authority and her *receiving* it returns us to the sequence from Thoreau with which I began this chapter and to what we might call the jurisprudential dimension of Thoreau's drive for a better judiciary. Thoreau's real judge possesses what initially looks like an almost entirely personal form of power. How exactly does a "human being" get to "seal the fate of a man into . . . eternity"? Simply by virtue of having "discerned truth" or having uttered "a true opinion or *sentence* concerning him." In coupling "true sentences" with "true opinions," Thoreau goes beyond dissociating the judge's power from "the enactment of men." In Thoreau's scheme such enactments do not merely lose their control over a person's access to the "truth" and the power that comes with it. They are also made antithetical to the kind of judgment he has in mind. As "true" becomes a property of a person's "opinion" as well as a property of his sentences, it begins to seem that the truth that interests Thoreau, like the consecration that interests Hester, has no foundation whatsoever outside of the person who proclaims it. Is a true opinion an accurate opinion or one that a person genuinely holds? Insofar as the worldly judge's opinions are necessarily devoted to something outside of himself, such as "the verdict of the law," it would seem that they can never quite be true.[43]

Intertwined with this entirely personalized account of the sentencing power, however, is another account of the origins of the religious judge's authority, one that seems to involve precisely the kind of delegation of power which the category of "true opinions" would seem to render obsolete. True sentences matter as well as true opinions, which is simply to say that while at times the religious judge seems to be the source of his own authority and power, at other times he seems wholly dependent on conditions that lie outside of himself. Although Thoreau's general tone implies a radical distinction between the secular and the religious judge, his actual descriptions of the two judges have the effect of blurring them together. The new judge dwells "among human beings" rather than legal clerics, but he is from the very beginning not simply a person but also "the judge." As it turns out, his claim to a judge's standing is ultimately no less formal than that of "the chiefest justice in the world." Over the course of this sequence, he "receive[s] his commission" and "finds himself constituted [a] judge." Thoreau may imply that commissions are irrelevant to, if not actually incompatible with, judgment; he nevertheless makes sure that his judge receives them. And after suggesting that the new judge merely possesses a higher version of the old judge's authority rather than a new kind of authority altogether, Thoreau slyly reconfigures the relationship between the two judges. When the new judge first appears, he and the judge who "merely pronounces the verdict of the law" both cast judgment on the same "man." They represent alternative, and more and less successful, ways of going about the same business—namely, the business of "seal[ing] the fate of a man . . . into eternity." But as Thoreau goes on, he places the judge who "merely pronounces the verdict of the law," not a random defendant, before the new judge's bench. The new judge goes from judging a man to judging the judge. The effect of the shift, of course, is to reproduce the relationship between the man and the secular judge as the relationship between the secular judge and the religious judge. The sequence as a whole thus works more to transfer the authority of the court from the secular judge to the religious judge than to suggest that the religious judge possesses his own distinct, and overpowering, form of judgment. The speaker of truth takes over the judge's role, along with its commissions and constitutions, rather than transcending them altogether.

And as he does so he takes on some of the very attributes of judicial weakness which initially seem confined to the world of the law's "mere verdicts." Consider again, for instance, the way in which Thoreau's citizen judge seems both to *produce* the sentences he enunciates and to count merely as their spokesman. On the one hand, his "words seal the fate of a man furthest into eternity"; on the other, he "has discerned truth." His power here seems to come at the expense of his agency, which is why it makes sense for Thoreau to link his authority to his having "received [a] commission from a higher source." This source is "higher," to be sure, "than the chiefest judge in the world," but it is also higher than the religious judge's own words. Although Thoreau initially stresses the new judge's power, by the end of the sequence the new judge has become strikingly passive. "He finds himself constituted judge of the judge" when he discerns truth, rather than constituting himself such a judge by discerning truth or by uttering his true opinions. He starts out using his opinions to determine the fate of others; he finishes up learning what status he has been given. Before he can "seal" another's fate, his own fate, as it were, must itself be sealed.

Thoreau and Hawthorne understand the ultimate origins of this partly seized and partly imposed authority in slightly different terms. For Thoreau the authority lies in the broadly moral and philosophical realm of moral "truth." For Hawthorne, even though Hester's Boston is a world in which "religion and law were almost identical" and "thoroughly interfused" (50), this sentencing authority inhabits the much broader realm of "the world" as a whole, which amounts to something along the lines of the "general" social "sentiment" to which Hawthorne attributes the law's "vitality" (231). The "custom" Thoreau condemns is in many ways what secures Hawthorne's ordinances. But this difference should in no way obscure what the two writers have in common. Starting with the law's curious dependence upon language as the vehicle of its power, they both construe legal agency as a double structure involving both the active assertion of authority and the passive reception of authority. For both of them the law stands as an exercise of force and an exercise of representation, and legal actors stand as both the sources of legal prerogative and the recipients of it.

This latter point about the essentially double nature of legal agency receives as emphatic and incisive elaboration in "Edward Randolph's Portrait" as the former point about the law's strange oscillation between language's constative and performative dimensions. Although the story hinges on a moment in which Hutchinson, despite his most zealous efforts, *acts* as the lieutenant governor, it turns out that his authority is no more absolute than Hester's. The point becomes clear in the story's insistent foregrounding of the way its narrative situates us in the middle of events that have already begun. Here is the first sentence of our introduction to Hutchinson: "The Lieutenant-Governor sat, one afternoon, resting his head against the carved back of his stately arm chair, and gazing up thoughtfully at the void blackness of the picture." It seems at this point as though the story's narrative line will begin here with his examination of the picture. But the next sentence sends us back a few moments: "It was scarcely a time for such inactive musing, when affairs of the deepest moment required the ruler's decision; for, within that very hour, Hutchinson had received intelligence of the arrival of a British fleet, bringing three regiments of from Halifax to overawe the insubordination of the people" (642). It is as if Hawthorne wishes us to experience a kind of belatedness, a sense in which what we consider the present is invariably caught up in developments from the past. This is not the only time Hawthorne produces this effect in "Edward Randolph's Portrait." The action of the story's second "scene" has also already begun when the narrator starts his account of it. Once again Hawthorne foregrounds the way in which the event he is interested in describing commences in the "meantime" of another set of actions: "Partly shrouded in the voluminous folds of one of the window-curtains . . . was seen the white drapery of a lady's robe. . . . Meantime, the chairman of the Selectmen was addressing to the Lieutenant-Governor a long and solemn protest against the reception of British troops into the town" (646–47).

This somewhat peculiar narrative technique alerts us to the problems of chronology and agency which lie at the center of the story's plot, a plot that is ultimately structured around the same peculiar temporality as the story's narrative. At the center of that plot is what looks like a moment of concrete political action: Hutchinson's decision to invite the British troops into Boston. But on closer inspection it turns out that the lieutenant governor's resolution is merely a ratification of a decision made before the story itself gets going. The troops whose entry Hutchinson ultimately authorizes, as Michael Colacurcio has noted, have in fact already been sent from Halifax "to overawe the insubordination of the people" well before Hutchinson even receives intelligence of their departure (642).[44] Hutchinson is not making policy here so much as going along with it, or in light of *The Scarlet Letter* we might say that he is making policy precisely *by* going along with it. And a similar chronological structure works with respect to the portrait itself, which, like the decision to summon troops, is not produced in the tale so much as realized. Vane and Hutchinson both devote themselves to the present articulation of previously enacted patterns: their present actions are in some senses nothing more than other figures' past ones.

This structure of agency may well constitute the most significant feature of Hawthorne's writing, and critics have long located it at the heart of his political imagination. Sacvan Bercovitch, for instance, sees *The Scarlet Letter* largely in terms of the novel's insatiable desire to "recast conflict and change into a triumph of the American ideology."[45] For Bercovitch what the novel steadfastly refuses to allow is the moment in which any being simply acts; it stands as a magnificent machine for rerouting agency through a set of formal structures that effectively reclaim it for the normative institutions it might seem to challenge. But *The Scarlet Letter* does not exemplify this process so much as anatomize it, and Hawthorne's interest is less in consensus as such than in the particular legal institutions that work through such divided and complicated structures. What Bercovitch calls the American ideology, Hawthorne might simply call the government of law. It is for this reason that Lauren Berlant is right to locate *The Scarlet Letter* in the context of what she calls the "estranged proximity" of the law to utopia. On the one hand, the mechanisms of law forever cast the law as utopian—as constructed in terms of what Berlant calls the "ahistorical values of ethics." On the other, the very nature of those mechanisms—the resolution of conflict, the application of precedent or historically authentic legal acts, and, crucially in *The Scarlet Letter,* the verbal manifestation of legal principle—testify to the law's necessary removal from the ahistorical domain of utopia. Whereas Berlant sees the law's estrangement from the "ahistorical values of ethics" as a cultural peculiarity of the "social life the novel [*The Scarlet Letter*] represents," however, Hawthorne understands this estrangement as a peculiarity of the law itself. The law and utopia "are in contradiction," from his perspective, but that contradiction is in some important sense the necessary condition of the existence of either of them: without its utopian pretensions legal activity might lack moral authority; without legal enactment utopian aspirations can have no politically concrete form.[46]

The problem *The Scarlet Letter* addresses is not the problem of the incompatibility of historical and moral accounts of normative justice. It is, instead, the problem of the law's multivalent and unpredictable relationship to the normative. The complexity of this relationship, of course, does not have to be a problem. In Spooner's deployment of Lieberian legal hermeneutics, the problem language poses to the exercise of legal agency becomes the opportunity for radical, and utopian, deployments of the Constitution. But in a world in which legal power was increasingly identified with the progressive results sought by figures such as Spooner, indirection at the core of legal agency could hardly be reassuring. John Bingham would take advantage of the opportunities Lieber's hermeneutics offered the antislavery jurist, and he would produce a constitutional guarantee of the legal agency that proves so elusive in the context of slavery in the territories or *The Scarlet Letter*. In the next chapter, when we finally take Bingham up directly, we will see how.

CHAPTER FIVE

John Bingham's Poetic Constitution

Why did Walt Whitman "love" Abraham Lincoln?[1] The last of the four poems of "Memories of Abraham Lincoln" gives us an oblique answer.[2] Here is the poem in its entirety:

> This dust was once the Man,
> Gentle, plain, just and resolute, under whose cautious hand,
> Against the foulest crime in history known in any land or age,
> Was saved the Union of these States. (339)

The image of Lincoln as "Gentle, plain, just and resolute" is hardly unconventional. Whitman's account of what Lincoln did, however, is a little more telling than his account of who he was. Emancipation is conspicuously absent from Whitman's presidential epitaph, which focuses exclusively on the Great Emancipator's conservative side.[3] And if Lincoln gets no credit for freeing slaves here, he also bears a curiously oblique relation to his Union-preserving achievement. Did Lincoln save "the Union of these States"? Not exactly. The Union "Was saved" "under [his] cautious hand"—the formulation leaves the agent of this salvation tantalizingly unspecified. But at the same time that Whitman attributes the Union's survival to something other than Lincoln's direct activity, he also implies that the nation was only saved by an untoward exercise of authority on the president's part. The poem's emphasis upon Lincoln's "hand" and its willingness to place the Union "under" that hand seem to conjure exactly the intensely personal presidential authority that the passive last line scrupulously eschews. It is almost as if the last line has to disown the power the poem has already deposited in its "resolute and just" hero, a figure who must be made as "cautious" as he is strong.

The Union's prosecution of the Civil War relied upon, if it did not in fact require, this mixture of passivity and authority: the conservative implications of restoring the Union to the integral form it possessed before Southern radicals dismembered it balanced the revolutionary implications of emancipation, carried out under the hand of the president in the form of a proclamation.[4] And the deployment of the law as an instrument of emancipation itself required a similar mixture of authority and passivity: the exercise of will involved in abolishing slavery needed to be tethered to some second external order of authority—nature, higher law—in order to escape assimilation into the very autocratic order that slavery so clearly exemplified. In the preceding chapters we have seen that sustaining an appropriate balance between will and obedience in the 1850s and 1860s was no mean task.[5] Indeed, *whether* will and obedience could be so balanced was itself a pressing question in the period. Whitman balances the two, in effect, by promiscuously committing himself to both. Passive resolve can look contradictory as well as balanced, however, and it was easy enough for Whitman's Lincoln to come off more as mystification than mystical. "This Dust was Once the Man" could thus become Melville's "The House-Top" or Brown's *Clotel*, in which the point is not to fuse the Union's authority with its passivity so much as to expose the tension between the two.

John Bingham's Fourteenth Amendment constituted the most effective, indeed the definitive, reconciliation of the Union's conservative and radical agendas. This chapter will outline the amendment's achievement by locating Bingham's efforts to accommodate the government's hand to its caution in the context of Whitman's celebrations of Lincoln in the final four poems of *Drum-Taps*. I will be especially interested in the way in which Bingham and Whitman engage issues of transformation. The most emphatic evidence of the limits of Lincoln's authority in "This Dust was Once the Man" is not Whitman's refusal to specify the deceased president as the agent of the nation's salvation. It is, instead, the fact that Whitman first presents him not as a president or even as a man but, rather, as "dust." Lincoln could not have transformed the nation any more radically than the war transformed him. Whitman's interest in Lincoln was strikingly *memorial*, as if the fact that Lincoln died was more important than anything the president might have done while living. Revolving around a scenario in which "the knowledge of death . . . walk[s] [on] one side of" the speaker while "the thought of death close-walk[s] [on] the other" (120–21), "When Lilacs last in the Dooryard Bloom'd" is downright morbid. But that Lincoln's death should concern Whitman as much as his life is wholly in keeping with Whitman's essentially naturalist account of the nation that survives the war. In *Drum-Taps* the solution to "the problems of freedom" is "Affection" (315). "Manly affection" "shall tie . . . and band" together "lovers" and "comrades" with chains "stronger than hoops of iron" (316). The irony that "hoops of iron" might carry in *Battle-Pieces* or *Clotel* is largely absent from *Drum-Taps*. What effects such a powerful "reconciliation" that foes are bound together without being enslaved is "Death": "For my enemy is dead, a man divine as myself is dead, / I look where he lies white-faced and still in the coffin—I draw near /

Bend down and touch lightly with my lips the white face in the coffin" (321). Lincoln does not preserve the Union in *Drum-Taps;* he enacts its preservation in his death. In mirroring the death of "my enemy," his end constitutes the basis for an unchallengeable sectional reconciliation.

This form of national reconciliation does not resolve the conflict between the Union and the Confederacy so much as conceal it. The Union is saved from a "crime" in "This Dust was Once the Man," but the felons are not exactly brought to justice; they are not even identified. More significantly, the Union is given no cause other than its own persistence; the Union outlasts the war rather than winning it. And for this reason we should hardly be surprised that Lincoln himself was hardly inclined to join Whitman in locating death at the center of the nation's postwar reconciliation. Lincoln may well have understood the North's effort entirely in terms of the preservation of the Union, but he valued the Union for *reasons*, reasons he was happy to articulate.[6] He was less opposed to secession as such than the danger secession posed to what the Union embodied. If death guarantees the Union's success in *Drum-Taps*, it takes on a slightly more threatening hue in Lincoln's greatest speech, in which, famously, what prevents the soldiers slain at Gettysburg from having "died in vain" is the prospect of a "new birth of freedom" (2:536). Lincoln's "new birth of freedom" restores exactly the *active* dimension of the Union's effort which Whitman's "dust" effectively excludes. And the "freedom" and "equal[ity]" that Lincoln's dead produce are thus slightly different from the "Liberty" and "Equality" inspired by Whitman's affection (316): Lincoln's freedom and equality are an achievement, the product of "work" that the dead soldiers had to leave "unfinished" (2:536), not the result of a natural tendency. The dead at Gettysburg inspire freedom and equality rather than exemplifying it, and Lincoln's goal is not to model "a just, and a lasting peace" on their fate but, rather, to "bind up the nation's wounds" through the inspiration of their example (2:687).

Like the last lines of "This Dust was Once the Man," however, the Gettysburg Address balances innovation against preservation and transformation against restoration. Freedom is the product of work, but it is also a product of a slightly more spontaneous-sounding "birth." Likewise, while a "birth of freedom" would produce something wholly new; a "new birth of freedom," paradoxically, feels somewhat less novel. Bingham's achievement, we will see, is precisely to combine transformation and restoration into a single endeavor. He finds a way to articulate the construction of a new nation after the Civil War as the restoration of the nation that war had ruptured and to articulate the postwar reemergence of the Union in terms of the creation of a more perfect polity. He provides the legal code for the work of Lincoln's "new birth." His Civil War does not transform men into dust. Binding the nation together with the law's vitality rather than the body's mortality, it transforms the constitution into the

Constitution, or, rather, it realizes the Constitution inhabiting the constitution. Whitman was famously dismissive of the idea that the United States's integrity could inhere in its laws. "Were you looking to be held together by lawyers," he asks in the parenthetical conclusion to "Over the Carnage Rose a Prophetic Voice," "or by an arrangement on a paper? or by arms? Nay, nor the world, nor any living thing, will so cohere" (316).[7] But the precarious balance Whitman and Lincoln seek to establish between arms and affection in the salvation of the Union was realized more easily in terms of an "arrangement on a paper" than by the flesh of the living beings who had to die in order for the nation to persist as a coherent "living thing." Replacing Whitman's dusty corpse with the living law, Bingham gives political form to Whitman's mystical "band" of "Sons of the Mother of all" (316, 315).[8]

Old New Law

In a famous article from the early 1970s Michael Les Benedict sought to provide a "detailed analysis of the theoretical framework within which the Republicans developed their program" for Reconstruction. Even though that program had "long" been considered "violative of the principles of American federalism" and a "radical departure from traditional constitutional forms," Benedict concluded that it had in fact been "framed by constitutional conservatives who envisioned little real alteration in national-state relations."[9] Benedict's claim did not fall on deaf ears,[10] but by the middle 1980s it was under direct assault. In 1987 Robert J. Kaczorowski maintained that "Congressional Republicans believed that the Thirteenth and Fourteenth Amendments and the Civil Rights Act of 1866 represented a revolutionary change in American constitutionalism,"[11] and by 1995 Christopher Eisgruber would proclaim that "the radicalism of the Fourteenth Amendment is breathtaking."[12] We can attribute at least part of this schismatic conflict to the death throes of consensus history: in the aftermath of Richard Hofstadter and Louis Hartz it was easy to imagine that historical political analysis consisted largely in determining whether a given agenda was radical or conservative, with the latter category swallowing up all of the various liberalisms that had the temerity to posit nonrevolutionary approaches to the nation's ills. Even so, there is quite a disparity between Benedict's staid preservationists and Eisgruber's breathtaking radicals. It is hard to imagine that they are speaking about the same legal enactment. Such diametrically opposed responses to a single measure would seem to require an explanation internal to the measure itself. Ruling out insanity on one side or the other, we are left with a text that *elicits* conservative and radical readings in equal measure. What gives the Fourteenth Amendment the power to accommodate itself so readily to the eyes of its beholders?

We can begin to answer this question by posing another: what was it about the measure that was new to the Constitution? This question should hardly be challenging in the case of an *amendment,* whose very occasion, after all, would seem to be its altering the organ to which it is attached. But in the case of the Fourteenth Amendment matters were less clear on this point than we might first imagine. The Fourteenth Amendment did not start out as an amendment; it started out merely as an enforcement measure for the Thirteenth Amendment, as the Civil Rights Act of 1866. Indeed, many prominent Republican members of the Thirty-ninth Congress envisioned the measure as nothing more than the Thirteenth Amendment's statutory form. The Thirteenth Amendment is divided into two sections: one declaring, "Neither slavery nor involuntary servitude, except as a punishment for crime whereof the party shall be duly convicted, shall exist in the United States, or any place subject to their jurisdiction," and another giving Congress the power to enforce the first. Our encounters with the fate of Stewart's due process argument and with Sumner's "Freedom National" address have already indicated that measures providing for congressional enforcement of constitutional declarations were anything but casual appendages in the 1860s, and we will see that the Congress's enforcement powers lie at the center of the Thirty-ninth Congress's sense of both the need for and the benefits of the Fourteenth Amendment. For now what is important to note is that the civil rights measure that eventually resulted in the Fourteenth Amendment was initially presented as something like one of Stewart's "declaratory" laws in support of emancipation. Lyman Trumbull urged support of the Civil Rights Act of 1866, for instance, on the grounds that it was "intended to give effect to that declaration [sec. 1 of the Thirteenth Amendment] and secure to all persons within the United States practical freedom."[13]

For Trumbull the act was not an expression of Congress's authority under the amendment so much as a requirement placed upon Congress in order to realize the amendment. In a debate over a weaker version of what became the Civil Rights Act he announced what his later version of the legislation would accomplish: "I give notice, if no one else does, I shall introduce a bill and urge its passage through Congress that will secure to those men [the freedmen] every one of these rights [he had just read a list of rights similar to the ones that would be enumerated in the Civil Rights Act of 1866]: they would not be freemen without them. It is idle to say that a man is free who cannot go and come at his pleasure, who cannot buy and sell, who cannot enforce his rights. These are rights which the first clause of the constitutional amendment meant to secure to all" (43). Even those who did not understand Congress's civil rights legislation of 1866 as a mere manifestation of the Thirteenth Amendment tended to understand the Fourteenth Amendment less as a revision of the Constitution than as a repetition, or if that is perhaps too strong, a realization of other provisions already within it. Throughout the congressional debates it was repeatedly emphasized that the amendment amended very little: it would "only have the effect to give vitality and life to portions of the Constitution that were probably intended from the beginning to have life and vitality, but which have received such a construction that they have been entirely ignored and have become as dead matter in that instrument"; it was to be seen "as more valuable for clearing away bad interpretations and bad uses of the Constitution than it is for any positive grant of new power which it contains" (66).

A sense of redundancy thus haunted the amendment from the outset, a sense of redundancy so strong that it is easy to wonder exactly why the Fourteenth Amendment had to assume the form of a constitutional amendment. Was it necessary to enact a measure that only specified what was implied in another amendment? If so, why was the measure not simply passed pursuant to the Thirteenth Amendment's enforcement clause? In order to answer these questions we will first have to determine exactly what "rights" Trumbull thought were implied by "practical freedom" and to assess their standing in the structure of antebellum constitutional law. Exactly what, then, did the amendment mean to accomplish? This question, of course, has stood at the heart of American constitutional jurisprudence from the moment the amendment was enacted, and it would be an act of shameless hubris on my part to insist that after all the years of searching and debate by leading jurists I have finally come up with the answer. There are indeed meaningful questions about whether such an answer can even be generated given the enormous difficulties the amendment's history and language pose. Determining legislative intent is always tricky. Is the intent of the author of the measure the relevant intent? If not, how can we know what those who voted for the measure meant to do with their votes? How do we understand measures enacted despite demonstrably incompatible accounts by legislators about their purposes and meanings? The problems are only compounded in the case of constitutional amendments, in which we need determine not only the intent of a relatively small number of legislators, who are likely to be fairly familiar with the meaning of any given measure and also likely to speak on the record about what they think that measure will accomplish, but also the intent of state legislators and electorates. And the problems are doubly compounded in the case of the Fourteenth Amendment: key provisions were drafted, proposed, and adopted behind closed doors; the amendment's language and effects were seen as vague and opaque even by many of those in Congress and the state legislatures who voted for its ratification; and given the opacity of that language and the open confusion it seemed to generate, it is difficult to know exactly what those people—many of whom, of course, were not lawyers or trained in the law to such an extent that phrases such as *due process of law* would count for them as what Raoul Berger calls "terms of art"—understood their votes to accomplish.[14]

I will not provide a definitive account of the intention of the framers and ratifiers here; I will not even provide a definitive account of who the relevant framers were. Instead, I will be chiefly concerned with the intentions of the amendment's primary author, John Bingham, and with those of several of the measure's leading congressional advocates and explicators. The debate has never really been about what they thought the Fourteenth Amendment meant. It has, instead, been about whether their thinking determines the measure's meaning and whether that thinking was sufficiently coherent and sound so as to be taken seriously as a matter of constitutional doctrine.[15] Consequently, I will not produce an account of the amendment which even takes a first step toward suggesting how we might resolve some of the thornier contemporary legal problems that are centered on debates about its meaning. Instead, I will insert the amendment into the set of jurisprudential problems that loomed prominently in the nation's political, legal, and literary culture in the 1850s; argue that these problems help clarify some of the amendment's most interesting features; and suggest that the amendment represents a stunningly effective way of resolving them.[16]

Here is the amendment's first section: "All persons born or naturalized in the United States, and subject to the jurisdiction thereof, are citizens of the United States and of the State wherein they reside. No State shall make or enforce any law which shall abridge the privileges or immunities of citizens of the United States; nor shall any State deprive any person of life, liberty, or property, without due process of the law; nor deny to any person within its jurisdiction the equal protection of the laws." The first thing to note about this section, as many legislators noted at the time and many legal historians have since pointed out, is its lack of novelty: with the single exception of its reference to "equal protection of the laws," all of the section's key phrases are borrowed from other sections of the Constitution—*privileges or immunities; due process of law; life, liberty, or property; persons born or naturalized;* and so forth. The outlying *equal protection of laws* itself derives from a foundational American political document—the Declaration of Independence.[17] The amendment is a reconfiguration of the already extant constitutional apparatus as much as it is the production of a new part of it. Bingham would maintain before the House that "every word of this proposed Amendment is today in the Constitution of our country" (1066), and if he was exaggerating slightly, he was not exaggerating very much. As Akhil Amar has put the point, "his colleagues understood that, even if he was literally wrong he was legally right."[18]

The second thing to note about section 1 is that its chief and most obvious effect is the removal of the primary obstacle to the force of Stewart's constitutional abolitionist position. No matter how opaque the amendment's language might seem, at the very least we can see that the amendment eliminates *Barron v. Baltimore* as a problem for Stewart's argument about due process: indeed, its clear and express point is to ensure that the protections Sumner would have provided fugitives would be available to all. It gives "Freedom National" a truly national range of operations. Legal historians have not tended to locate the amendment's due process language in such a narrowly antislavery frame of reference,[19] but we should not forget the provision's local historical emergence in the Thirty-ninth Congress as an enforcement measure for the Thirteenth Amendment. The Thirteenth Amendment, after all, proscribed all slavery other than the kinds that Stewart had imagined were allowed by the Fifth Amendment. The Fourteenth Amendment further realizes his claim by securing the freedom he mapped out with the vehicle he claimed should secure it—due process of law.

Section 1 not only extends to all persons the single and enumerated protection of due process but also guarantees all citizens the plural and general protection of the "privileges or immunities of a citizen of the United States." If it is fairly easy to get a general grasp on the due process clause, it is somewhat more difficult to understand the function of the privileges or immunities clause, more difficult in large part because the phrase has a more complicated constitutional pedigree than *due process of law.* What constitutes "due process" has *become* an enormously controversial topic within American constitutional jurisprudence,[20] but figures such as Stewart and Sumner invoked the term as if there were little doubt about what it meant. "And, on this subject," Stewart explained, "it is believed that no lawyer in this country or England, who is worthy of the appellation, will deny that the true and only meaning of the phrase, 'due process of law,' is an indictment or presentment by a grand jury, of not less than twelve, nor more than twenty-three men; a trial by a petit jury of twelve men, and a judgment pronounced on the finding of the jury, by a court."[21] Stewart's overemphatic assertion that such a construction is entirely uncontroversial can inspire doubt as well as confidence. And indeed it is unclear why there would be separate constitutional guarantees for jury and grand jury rights, in the parts of the Fifth Amendment which precede the due process clause and in the Sixth Amendment, if due process alone already guaranteed them. But the principal point here is simply that Stewart could appeal to this due process standard with little fear that it would be challenged. The chief question surrounding his argument was whether state slave codes had to meet this due process standard, not whether he had misconstrued the standard in the first instance.

The "true and only meaning" of the privileges or immunities clause was far less transparent. This provision, like the due process clause, has its origins in the Constitution itself, and it has a history, again like the due process clause, which placed it at the heart of debates about the legal status of slavery.[22] The relevant clause—the so-called comity clause—appears in Article IV, section 2, the very article and section, you might recall, which houses the Constitution's references to fugitive slaves: "The Citizens of each State shall be entitled to all Privileges and Immunities of the Citizens in the several States." On its face this provision seems simply to announce a principle of nondiscrimination. It proclaims that states are not allowed to discriminate in favor of their own citizens and against citizens of other states. Story glossed the clause in these terms in his *Commentaries:* "The intention of this clause was to confer on them [citizens of "each state"], if one may so say, a general citizenship; and to communicate all the privileges and immunities, which citizens of the same state would be entitled to under the like circumstances."[23] Shortly after the congressional ratification of the Fourteenth Amendment, the Supreme Court would hold as much in *Paul v. Virginia* (1869).[24] Subsequent legal historians have tended to agree with this stance. "The Comity Clause was inspired by Article IV of the Articles of Confederation, whose purpose was 'The better to secure and perpetuate mutual friendship and intercourse among the People of the different States of this Union,'" Charles Fairman explains in his history of the legal developments of Reconstruction; "but if a State did not choose to be generous or protective toward its own, neither Congress nor the Court could make it so under Article IV."[25]

But from early in the nineteenth century onward there was an alternative reading of the comity clause, one that focused more on its commitment to "the Privileges and Immunities of the Citizens in the several states" than on its commitment to "Citizens in each State." This alternative reading tended to understand the measure less as a protection against discrimination than as the assertion of a set of national rights to which everyone, regardless of their state citizenship, would be entitled—what Story somewhat ambivalently calls "a general citizenship." Such a reading of the clause strains its language somewhat, and indeed we will see in a moment that Bingham was willing to reformulate the clause completely in order to clarify its commitment to national citizenship. But this construction was nonetheless adopted by many respected jurists, most prominently by Bushrod Washington in *Corfield v. Coryell* (1823), a regular point of reference in the Fourteenth Amendment's ratification debates. *Corfield* is useful not only because it shows that the comity clause could be transformed into a general citizenship clause but also because it reveals the extent to which the notion of citizenship could bring a series of claims from natural law into constitutional jurisprudence. We have already seen Spooner's attempt, albeit a somewhat clumsily one, to deploy citizenship in this way in *The Unconstitutionality of Slavery.* In Washington's hands the process is subtler and more effective.

The privileges or immunities clause seems to *refer* to rights rather than instantiate them: the phrase *privileges or immunities of citizens of the United States,* insofar as it does not enumerate the relevant privileges or immunities, implies an already existing set of rights rather than producing a new bundle of them. But it is not entirely clear to what rights it refers—indeed, whether it refers to national rights or state rights is itself unclear. And consequently interpreters could comfortably turn to natural law principles for aid in elaborating the referenced but unnamed privileges and immunities. Even if "the Privileges or Immunities of Citizens in the several States" derive their *force* from the Constitution, in other words, they might derive their *content* from the domain of broader natural justice. Which is why Washington could "feel no hesitation in confining" his elaboration of privileges and immunities "to those privileges and immunities which are, in their nature, fundamental; which belong of right, to the citizens of all free governments" (551–52).

Washington's "confining" these rights to the rights of "the citizens of all free governments" unsurprisingly results in a list of rights far more expansive than the Court's later rulings, and indeed, as he goes on to devote a full page to listing these "fundamental" privileges and immunities, it is hard to see from what perspective he has confined himself at all. He covers everything from the right to travel to the right to vote. Nor may the difficulties implicit in his reasoning be confined to the extent of his "confined" list. His insistence that these privileges and immunities "have, at all times, been enjoyed by the citizens of the several states which compose this Union, from the time of their becoming free, independent, and sovereign," begins to sound like something of a stretch: the historical standard he invokes here is in strong tension with, if not direct contradiction of, the theoretical standard ("privileges and immunities which are, in their nature, fundamental") he had invoked earlier.[26] What do we do with a privilege or immunity that is "in nature, fundamental," but which has not always been "enjoyed by the citizens of the several states which compose this Union"? Or one that has always been enjoyed but which is not in nature, fundamental? Many of Washington's own examples, such as, say, the right to vote, only become privileges and immunities by one of the two standards he produces.

From the present perspective, however, neither Washington's expansive natural law sense of the range of constitutional privileges or immunities nor the tension between the theoretical and historical dimensions of his argument is as important as the attention he pays to the particular legal procedural rights that were later placed at the center of constitutional antislavery arguments. The rights "to claim the benefit of the writ of habeas corpus; [and] to institute and maintain actions of any kind in the courts of the state" take a prominent position in his "confined" list.[27] This attachment of the privileges and immunities of citizens in the several states to these procedural safeguards would become, in Bingham's hands, a claim that the Fourteenth Amendment was designed to subject state governments to the limitations placed upon Congress in the Bill of Rights. The due process clause freed Stewart's Fifth Amendment case for the reversal of state slave laws from the countervailing authority of *Barron;* the privileges or immunities clause removed the barrier that *Barron* imposed between the states and the rest of the Bill of Rights. Like Washington, Bingham understood the comity clause as a protection of national citizenship. In an address in early 1859 he glossed the clause in exactly these terms and in so doing inadvertently revealed the problems implicit in such a reading: "The citizens of each State, all the citizens of the United States, shall be entitled to 'all the privileges and immunities of citizens in several states.' . . . There is an ellipsis in the language employed by the Constitution, but its meaning is self-evident that it is 'the privileges and immunities of citizens of the United States in the several states' that it guarantees."[28] But unlike Washington, Bingham derived these national rights less from principles of justice and the "fundamental" concerns of "free governments" than from other parts of the Constitution itself. Shortly after the ratification of the amendment, in 1871, Bingham explained that "the privileges and immunities of citizens of the United States, as contradistinguished from citizens of a State, are chiefly defined in the first eight amendments to the Constitution of the United States."[29]

Hence, the purpose of the privileges or immunities clause was largely, if not quite simply, "to arm the Congress of the United States, by consent of the people of the United States, with the power to enforce the Bill of Rights as it stands in the Constitution today" (1088). Or as Thaddeus Stevens, the amendment's floor manager in the House put it shortly before the amendment came up for approval, "the Constitution limits only the actions of Congress" with respect to the privileges and immunities enumerated in the Bill of Rights "and is not a limitation on the States": "This amendment supplies that defect, and allows Congress to correct the unjust legislation of the States" (2459). After having enumerated the privileges and immunities declared in the first eight amendments, Senator Jacob Howard described the Fourteenth Amendment in similar terms:

> Now, sir, here is a mass of privileges, immunities, and rights, some of them secured by the second section of the fourth article of the Constitution, which I have recited, some by the first eight amendments of the Constitution; and it is a fact well worthy of attention that the course of decision of our courts and the present settled doctrine is, that all these immunities, privileges, rights, thus guarantied by the Constitution or recognized by it, are secured to the citizen solely as a citizen of the United States and as a party in their courts. They do not operate in the slightest degree as a restraint or prohibition upon State legislation. States are not affected by them . . . . The great object of the first section

of this amendment is, therefore, to restrain the power of the States, and compel them at all times to respect these great fundamental guarantees. (2765–66)

Whether or not their accounts of the amendment's function should be understood as definitive of the amendment's actual legal application, Bingham, Stevens, and Howard in effect do to Washington what Stewart does to Garrison: they constitutionalize and thereby give a positive law form to what look like a set of natural rights claims. Just as Sumner made commitments to matters such as due process of law count both as a kind of higher law (the general common law rights that the Fathers fought for) and a kind of positive law (the specific "genius institution" of the Constitution which they made to secure them), so too does Bingham work to ground his invocation of privileges and immunities in a specific higher positive law of constitutionalism rather than the more straightforward higher law of divine command.

The point here is not that higher law principles were irrelevant to Congress's consideration of the Fourteenth Amendment. They were indeed deeply relevant to it, but they always appeared as features of the U.S. Constitution itself, not as alternatives to it. For Bingham the amendment encompassed "all the sacred rights of person," but he discerned the rights less from philosophical considerations than legal ones: "those rights dear to freemen and formidable only to tyrants—and of which the fathers of the Republic spoke; after God had given them victory." If the amendment only protected the "essential provisions of your Constitution," you could at least rest assured that those provisions were "divine in their justice, sublime in their humanity" (1090). From this perspective the Fourteenth Amendment both embodies the legal thinking that structured Sumner's "Freedom National" address and installs it within the American legal system. Or indeed, it installs that thinking *as* the American legal system: it renders the Bill of Rights the nation's higher law by appealing to it as the standard of "all the sacred rights of person," and it renders that higher law a part of the nation's positive law by subjecting all legal enactments to its standard. To put the point more directly in Bingham's terms, the amendment effects a final combination of "the inborn rights of every person" and the "privileges and immunities of all citizens of the Republic," a combination so powerful that Bingham can proceed from one to the other as if they are essentially the same. The amendment gave Congress the power, he explained, "to protect by national law the privileges and immunities of all citizens of the Republic and the inborn rights of every person within its jurisdiction whenever the same shall be abridged or denied by the unconstitutional acts of any State" (2542).

We might nonetheless say that the amendment's fusion of American law with higher law is left somewhat incomplete. Bingham does, after all, mention them both: the privileges and immunities of citizens of the Republic do not simply entail the inborn rights of every person, even if they are thoroughly aligned with them. At the level of legal enactment this point manifests itself in the potential redundancy in the amendment's containing both a due process clause and a privileges or immunities clause. The amendment's account of the nation's higher law (privileges and immunities) is not identical with its account of the law as such (due process). And if commentators have seldom unpacked the amendment in these terms, debate about the amendment's meaning has nonetheless centered on the troublesome relationship between these two clauses. This debate has generally revolved around the question of whether the privileges or immunities clause was actually designed to incorporate the legal protections of the Bill of Rights against state law, and skeptics of incorporation have frequently grounded their objections in the problem of the Fourteenth Amendment's both directly applying specific language from the Fifth Amendment to the states and incorporating the Bill of Rights against them as a whole. Why would the amendment need to contain a clause that it was incorporating? If incorporation was really the goal of the amendment, why would its framers feel a need to draft a new due process clause rather than simply incorporating the old one in the privileges or immunities clause?[30]

This problem, it seems to me, is only imaginary. What prevents it from being real is the fact that the due process and privileges or immunities clauses protect different classes of people: due process is secured for every person, privileges or immunities only for every "citizen of the United States."[31] Given the immense value due process had acquired in the decades preceding the 1860s—given, indeed, that it had in many ways become synonymous with freedom itself—it is hardly surprising that the Framers of the Fourteenth Amendment would want to ensure that everyone, citizen and alien alike, would be entitled to it. And as we have already had occasion to see, the Fifth Amendment access that was so vital to the constitutional antislavery of Stewart and Sumner was chiefly an issue in regard to noncitizens. Part of the legacy of *Dred Scott* was to suggest that only aliens could be enslaved: from this perspective the incorporation of the Bill of Rights against the states alone would not have ultimately guaranteed freedom on Stewart's Fifth Amendment model.

But even if the potential redundancy implicit in the presence of two due process clauses in one Constitution turns out to be somewhat illusory, another question remains. Coming at the problem from the other side, we might ask not why a due process clause is necessary given that the Bill of Rights will be incorporated by the privileges or immunities clause but, rather, why a privileges or immunities clause is necessary given the presence of due process protection (protection of "law in its highest sense," in Bingham's formulation [1066]). If the Bill of Rights is understood to constitute the chief expression of the fundamental rights of free people, then why is a guarantee of legal due process not itself a guarantee of their protection? Lest the idea that due process itself might imply that the remainder of the Bill of Rights seems far-fetched, it is worth keeping in mind that Stewart's conception of due process itself already involved protections given specific enumeration elsewhere in the Bill of Rights. Nor should we neglect the fact that the Supreme Court itself has essentially endorsed this position by conjuring the Bill of Rights from the Fourteenth Amendment's due process clause. In the second half of the twentieth century the Court came to accept a modified version of the incorporation thesis in large part by deriving incorporation from the due process clause, instead of the privilege or immunities clause.[32] There are good historical reasons for the Court to deploy due process rather than privileges and immunities to effect the result Bingham had planned for the amendment.[33] For now I merely want to show why such an argument, though clearly contrary to Bingham's actual designs, proved to be plausible enough to become established, if nonetheless contested, constitutional doctrine: insofar as the Bill of Rights counts as the higher law of the United States it can begin to take on the identity of the higher law that due process had been said to secure and embody.

To put the point slightly differently, the potential redundancy in the Fourteenth Amendment's relationship to Bill of Rights, in general, and the Fifth Amendment, in particular, is the point of the Fourteenth Amendment as well as a problem for it. Bingham's project is to suspend the Bill of Rights between divine law and positive law. The amendment's attention to providing access to both a generalized realm of the law and a specific series of rights that had been implicitly associated with that generalized legal realm before the Civil War suggests ways in which the Fourteenth Amendment codifies both *the* law and *our* law. In codifying both, it might also seem, to the skeptics such as Berger and Melville, to drive a wedge between the two. But that wedge might also be called a bridge. In claiming the Bill of Rights as the United States of America's higher law, the amendment has the effect of making the Bill look like an expression of the law as such as well as a set of rights provided for American citizens. It configures the Bill as both "law in its highest sense" (the due process clause in the Fifth Amendment) and a body of discrete and specific protections and limitations (the privileges or immunities of citizens of the United States).

By stressing the Fourteenth Amendment's commitment to the already existing American legal order, however, I do not mean to suggest that it did no independent legal work. Bingham maintained that "every word of this proposed Amendment is today in the Constitution of our country" (1066). But if the Fourteenth Amendment used no new words, it would certainly seem to have used the old ones to new effect. A provision that, to use Stevens's phrase, "supplies that defect" of the Constitution which leaves the rights of citizens entirely subject to the regulation of states has profoundly changed the nature of American federalism. It insists upon the primacy of national citizenship to state citizenship; in authorizing "Congress to correct the unjust legislation of the States," it subordinates states to federal authority in ways entirely unimaginable from the perspective of *Barron*. These transformations mattered in the North as well as in the South. Bingham openly insisted that the measure would have an impact wherever states were denying citizens any right that the Bill of Rights provided them in relation to Congress. It would operate on all states, he acknowledged, not just Southern states, which have enacted "in their constitutions and laws . . . provisions in direct violation of every principle of our Constitution" (1065). The effect of the Fourteenth Amendment, from this perspective, is precisely the effect that Melville's *Battle-Pieces* predicts for Reconstruction: it manufactures the Union into a nation, a conglomeration of territories and zones and countries deprived of independent legal authority, altogether dominated by a hegemonic central power. The Fourteenth Amendment renders the Union's victory the defeat of the rights of states as such, rather than the defeat of those particular states' rights claims that undergirded the Confederate States of America.[34]

It is important, however, to stress the ways in which what we might call the radicalness of these transformations might be muted by the conservativeness of the means of effecting them. The Fourteenth Amendment might have altered the nature of American federalism, but it did so by simply invoking American constitutional law. Indeed, as we will see in a moment, for many the Fourteenth Amendment did not even count as the application of one branch of American law in a new context. It was, instead, simply a measure that allowed what had always been the law to be enforced. The framers could thus insist both that the amendment constituted a crucial commitment to natural rights and that it did nothing other than realize principles already embodied in American law: they could represent the act as both revolutionary and reactionary. Legal historian Andrew Kull maintains that the "great political advantage" of "Bingham's pleasant phrases" lay in the fact that these phrases were so vague and "malleable" that they "did not mean anything in particular."[35] But what makes the Fourteenth Amendment "malleable" is not its vague phrases but, rather, its essentially hybrid structure. Far from not "meaning anything in particular," it in fact meant two particular things: an application of the Constitution on the one hand and a transformation of it on the other. And it thereby embodied both of the enterprises implicit in the Union's efforts during the Civil War and Reconstruction. For if the effect of the measure was to transform the South rather than to restore it, it effected that transformation by way of including the South in the constitutional legal order and under the Union flag of liberty. And if the effect of the amendment was to restore Southern states to national law, it did so by invoking the set of legal principles that were seen as the chief weapon against the problems inherent in the old Southern legal ways. The "chameleon" Southern state meets its match in the chameleon legal order that the Fourteenth Amendment makes the Constitution.[36]

This happy resolution of the legal tensions that Melville locates at the heart of the war and its aftermath was not entirely uncontested, of course. From the most conservative perspective there was nothing chameleon about the Fourteenth Amendment at all. It is fairly easy to see ways in which even what seems to be the most conservative feature of the Fourteenth Amendment—its application of the Bill of Rights to the states—might be understood to count as a massive transformation of the very body of laws that it seemingly only enforces. From this perspective not only does the Fourteenth Amendment radically reorient the nature of the relationship between the states and the nation; it also radically alters the very law by which it claims to effect its primary reforms. As Akhil Amar has recently shown, in making the first eight amendments the vehicle for its restructuring of American citizenship, the amendment importantly reconfigures the meaning and function of the Bill of Rights. For starters, merely to make the limitations outlined in the first eight amendments limitations against the states is to fundamentally change their scope and impact. The Bill of Rights divorced from the federalist structure in which it was meant to operate is an almost unrecognizably different being from the one Madison proposed. We might think that those of its provisions that were designed to protect individual rights from the prerogatives of Congress—such as, say, the free speech parts of the First Amendment—could be fairly easily expanded to protect individuals from the prerogatives of their states. But substantial chunks of the initial Bill were designed to protect the rights of states, not their citizens, from the prerogatives of Congress. Think, for instance, of the Second Amendment. To turn those provisions against the very institutions they were designed to empower is to undo the Bill of Rights as much as it is to apply it.

And, more important, to understand the Bill of Rights as somehow in need of enforcement or application is also to have changed its nature. It is to imagine the Bill as a kind of declaration of rights rather than an enactment of them. It is to transform the Bill from a set of regulations (protection of specific entities in relation to other specific entities) into a set of propositions (announcements of what conditions justice requires). From the orthodox perspective, after all, the Bill of Rights could not have been "enforced" against the states; it was not the announcement of laws that might or might not be relevant in particular jurisdictions so much as the enactment of a set of laws within a particular jurisdiction, a set of laws that simply had no purchase in those domains in which they were allegedly left unenforced. In *Barron* the Court was not failing to apply the Bill of Rights against the states; it was indeed applying it, but the Bill was not a limitation upon the enactments of states. The Fourteenth Amendment, to put it differently, makes the first eight amendments into a form of higher law as well as enforcing the higher law they represent: it does not merely apply the amendments; it also makes them into things that can be applied.

One way to register the full force of this point is to note that the portion of the Fourteenth Amendment which was designed to effect the incorporation of the Bill of Rights against the states was in fact already a provision of the pre-1866 Constitution. *Barron* had held that the Bill of Rights did not apply to the states, but it would seem, on the face of it, that the whole point of the comity clause is to limit the behavior of states. Even on its most conservative construction the comity clause is specifically directed at state action. Why, then, would a repetition of the comity clause in an amendment count as a ground for subjecting the states to the provisions in the Bill of Rights if they had not been subjected to them by it before? On the logic of the constitutional theory Bingham elaborates, there would be no reason to produce a new constitutional measure to enforce the Bill of Rights. Such a measure is already in place.

Of course, Bingham recognized as much, and like many Republicans in the 1860s— radical, conservative, and moderate—he thought that *Barron* had been wrongly decided.[37] But here we must recall the location of the comity clause, namely its position in what the antislavery constitutionalists had been devoted to claiming was a list of compacts, such as the fugitive slave provision, unenforceable by Congress. The Bill of Rights could thus be said to apply to states, but Congress had no authority to enforce it against them. Stevens claimed that the "Constitution limits only the actions of Congress," but Bingham insisted that it limited the states as well. Stevens maintained that the Bill of Rights had not applied to the states prior to the ratification of the Fourteenth Amendment. Bingham insisted, by contrast, that Congress could not enforce the Bill of Rights against the states: "There was a want hitherto, and there remains a want now, in the Constitution of our country, which the proposed amendment will supply. . . . It is the power of the people, by express authority of the Constitution, to do that by congressional enactment which hitherto they have not had the power to do, and have never even attempted to do; that is, to protect by national law the privileges and immunities of all citizens of the Republic and the inborn rights of every person within its jurisdiction whenever the same shall be abridged or denied by the unconstitutional acts of any State" (2542). If on Stevens's account the Fourteenth Amendment merges the two legal orders whose tense interaction and juxtaposition so interests Melville, on Bingham's account the two have been merged all along. The Fourteenth Amendment gives the merger the *force* of law, not the standing of law.

It was for this reason that Minnesota congressman Ignatius Donnelly could wonder how anyone could actually oppose an early version of the Fourteenth Amendment. "Why should this not pass?" he asked. "Are the promises of the Constitution mere verbiage? Are its sacred pledges of life, liberty, and property to fall to the ground through lack of power to enforce them? . . . Or shall that great Constitution be what its founders meant it to be, a shield and a protection over the head of the lowliest and poorest citizen in the remotest region of the nation?" (586). And likewise, Congressman James Brooks of New York could claim that he wanted a recorded vote on an early version of the Fourteenth Amendment because he sought a permanent record of those congressmen who were actually opposed to the rule of the Constitution. "And I want it understood," he explained, "who are opposed to enforcing the written guarantees of the Constitution" (813). Donnelly and Brooks were not interested in expanding the Constitution's authority; they were interested in rendering the Constitution authoritative. Earlier chapters should have prepared us well for the prospect that "idle verbiage" could take the place of "sacred pledges" in antebellum constitutional structure, but many members of Congress found it hard to conceive of such an abstract legal order. Indeed, a healthy chunk of the debate over the measure revolved around Bingham's having to explain to members of Congress that without the Fourteenth Amendment Congress had no power to secure the rights enumerated in the first eight amendments. Indiana congressman James Wilson, for instance, expressed disbelieving shock at the idea "that at the mercy of the States lie all the rights of the citizen of the United States . . . that revolted South Carolina may put under lock and key the great fundamental rights belonging to the citizen" (1294).

If Stevens's account makes the restoration of the South seem identical to the Reconstruction of it, Bingham's account is actually able to make the conquest of the South identical to the restoration of it. This point becomes visible once we consider the Supreme Court's most prominent affirmation of Bingham's notion that Article IV provisions constituted unenforceable compacts: Taney's unanimous opinion in *Kentucky v. Dennison*. *Dennison* held that, though states had entered in a "compact" through Article IV, section 2, which required that they return fugitives from justice to the states from which they had fled, "there is no power delegated to the General Government . . . to use any coercive means to compel" a governor of a state to abide by the terms of the compact. Article IV, section 2, was, Taney insisted, "declaratory of the moral duty which this compact created when Congress had provided the mode of carrying it into action. The act does not provide any means to compel the execution of this duty . . . nor is there any clause or provision in the Constitution which arms the Government of the United States with this power."[38] This claim flies in the face of Story's opinion in *Prigg*, of course, and it also seems to entail Sumner's position with respect to the unconstitutionality of fugitive slave legislation. To find such reasoning in an opinion penned by the author of the opinion of the Court in *Dred Scott* is startling. The legal historian Paul Finkelman has suggestively accounted for the incompatibility between this opinion and Taney's usual stance on matters pertaining to slavery by noting that Taney may well have sought to use *Dennison* to signal his position on the constitutional status of secession, which, by analogy, would constitute a violation of the "compact" dimension of the Constitution but which would also be essentially immune to any federal remedy ("does not provide any means to compel the execution of this duty").[39] In effect Taney would give secession roughly the form it occupies in *Battle-Pieces:* a great crime but one that can only be addressed by further crime. And from this perspective Bingham's reading of the Constitution makes the maintenance of the Union identical with the expansion of civil rights. If emancipation and the guarantee of federal civil rights represent a transformation of the legal relations between the states and the federal government, so too does the very restoration of the Union. "Law on her brow and empire in her eyes." Melville's puzzle now points to a distinction that makes no sense: the law upheld by the Civil War is no different from the law imposed by Reconstruction. If the Union's compact forbade secession, it also, and in the very same legal instrument, forbade slavery.

The difference between Stevens's account of the Fourteenth Amendment and Bingham's is the difference between Stewart's two different accounts of emancipation under the Fifth Amendment: for Stevens the Constitution alone does the work; for Bingham the Constitution enables the work to be done by others. But whereas Stewart's bifocal account of constitutional emancipation emerged from a radical absence of legal agency in antebellum America, the Fourteenth Amendment could be said to mark the arrival of a surplus of that agency. So it would have seemed to Taney; so it did seem to Melville; and so it has seemed to the many commentators, such as Raoul Berger, who find the judicial activism carried out under the auspices of section 1 of the Fourteenth Amendment to clash with the congressional activism contemplated by section 4.[40] But rather than marking a surplus of agency, we might instead regard the measure as finally engineering the doubled structure of agency we find in *The Scarlet Letter* or "Slavery in Massachusetts," a structure in which the law is both said and done, in which the legal agent both receives his commission and enforces his decision. In this respect Bingham might seem less to have transformed American constitutional jurisprudence than to have made it possible in the first instance.

He makes it possible by giving that jurisprudence normative weight, by securing the letter of the Constitution as the law of the land. And he also makes it possible by making constitutional reasoning central to American legislative activity, by locating determinations of what count as the fundamental rights of free persons and citizens of the United States at the heart of the Congress's enterprise. The Fourteenth Amendment is thus both the result of and the occasion for what Larry Kramer has recently called "popular constitutionalism."[41] The amendment is premised on an elaborate counter-judicial reading of the Constitution. Jacobus tenBroek has noted that the major clauses of section 1 "were the product of . . . a popular and primarily lay movement which was moral, ethical, religious, revivalist rather than legal in character."[42] Bingham's amendment effectively rewrites the Constitution in that religious movement's idiom, or to put it slightly differently, it retrospectively casts that movement as a legal movement as well as a revivalist one. At the same time, the amendment also invites such reformulations in the future, invites efforts to infuse legal forms with moral content. That the Supreme Court wasted little time in monopolizing the legal agency conferred by the amendment should not obscure the ways in which Bingham made it newly possible for the Constitution to count as a terrain of action as well as declaration.[43] After 1868 American legal sentences would finally, once again, *sentence.*

Ever Returning

About a third of the way into "When Lilacs Last in the Dooryard Bloom'd" Whitman begins to show us how the nation was saved under Lincoln's hand. In "Lilacs" Lincoln's authority is slightly more explicit than it is in "This Dust was Once the Man," or at least it seems that way at first. In this poem Lincoln is at least explicitly identified as "powerful," though Whitman's formulation—"Oh powerful western fallen star!" (8)—grants that power equivocally. The power comes to Lincoln in symbolic form, and it comes to him only in his "fallen" state. The nation lives "under" its president only in some astronomical sense. Exactly why Whitman links Lincoln's fall to his power becomes clear in the fifth and sixth sections of the poem, in which we witness the power of his "coffin." In section 5 the coffin itself "journeys" "Over the breast of the spring, the land, amid cities" (32, 26). It roams "Amid lanes and through old woods" (27), "Amid the grass in the fields" (28), through "the yellow-spear'd wheat" (29), and through the "apple-tree . . . orchards" (30). In effect Lincoln's journey to "where it [his corpse] shall rest in its grave" is a journey that recombines the various "lands" dispersed by the "foul crime" of secession (31). In case we miss this point Whitman gives it a more explicit form in the next section, in which the "processions" of mourners, "long and winding" (37), are analogized to the "show of the States themselves" upon the flag and in which the "dirges through the night" effectively unite "thousands of voices rising strong and solemn" (36, 39). In death Lincoln's form "envelop[es] man and land" (98), just as death itself "envelop[es]" Whitman "with the rest" of the nation (117).

Alongside this account of Lincoln's authority, however, stands another, one that is, quite literally, muted by talk of this overwhelmingly powerful dirge. It turns out that Lincoln has been reaching out to Whitman for some time prior to his apotheosis:

Oh western orb sailing the heaven,

Now I know what you must have meant as a month since I walk'd,

As I walk'd in silence the transparent shadowy night,

As I saw you had something to tell as you bent to me night after night,

. . . .

As the night advanced, and I saw on the rim of the west how full you were of woe

As I stood on the rising ground in the breeze in the cool transparent night,

As I watch'd where you pass'd and was lost in the netherward black of the night,

As my soul in its trouble dissatisfied sank, as where you sad orb,

Concluded, dropt in the night, and was gone.   (55–65)

It is remarkable that Whitman never learns exactly what the orb has "to tell" here, but it is even more remarkable that he folds his account of that message into his account of the orb's natural motion. Almost as if self-consciously undoing Thoreau's efforts to derive moral messages from nature, Whitman simply dissipates meaning into physical processes. Lincoln "concludes" not with a message but with the simple fact of his passing. Of course, Lincoln did leave the world prematurely, and in other hands what would be mourned here would not be Lincoln's death itself so much as his not having had a chance to give us the full benefit of his wisdom about how the nation could be reunified. But it is not at all clear that the word *concludes* here is in any way ironic. Death does the work that Lincoln's insight might have done. Fifty lines later Whitman will walk along between "the knowledge of death" and "the thought of death" (120, 121), before "chant[ing] for thee [delicate death], . . . [and] glorifying thee above all" (145). His poem stands, in the end, as a celebration of Lincoln's conclusion.

Or rather, the end of his poem *contains* a celebration of death in the form of a "*chant of fullest welcome*" (144). Whitman's lone voice "tallying" the "chant of death" synthesizes the "thousand voices rising strong and solemn" with "dirges through the night" (200, 128, 39). The poem becomes a performance of the uniting authority it lodges in Lincoln's death,[44] and "the tally" of Whitman's "soul" itself comes to embody the nation reunited at the Civil War's conclusion, a nation defined by its newfound knowledge of and thoughts about death. While the "myriads" of "battle-corpses" become the "debris . . . all the slain soldiers of the war" (176, 179),

The living remain'd and suffer'd, the mother suffer'd

And the wife and the child and the musing comrade suffer'd,

And the armies that remain'd suffer'd.   (182–84)

After Lincoln's death armies suffer casualties, not defeat—and indeed foes are united in their *joint* suffering. And in a world made whole by the thought and knowledge of death, Whitman's suffering renders him representative, representative of the wife and child as well as the musing comrade. He can present himself as an emblem of the united nation.

"Lilacs" is a record of the process whereby Whitman assumes such a representative position, not an instance of his having assumed it. It is a brief for poetry's capacity to unite, not an example of it. Indeed, the poem is rather an account of *death*'s capacity to unite. It is only after the dirge has been sung by thousands that Whitman himself can convert it into his chant. And in this regard we would do well to note the extent to which Whitman's chant emphatically *says* that it is a chant: what the chant most forcefully reiterates is that it is a celebration of death (135–62). Just as Whitman himself never gives voice to what Lincoln wished to tell him, he also never exactly gives voice to death's "carol" (128). The poem repeatedly displaces words with death. We might say that it records death's conquest of the word, or, rather, that it registers the word's absolute dependence upon death. In "Lilacs" poetry requires death, which is just a tricky way of saying that Whitman's power in the poem is absolutely dependent upon Lincoln's power, which is in turn absolutely dependent upon nature's.

Whitman thus bears to Lincoln something like the relation the Thirty-ninth Congress bore to the Bill of Rights. And it is tempting to see in Whitman's peculiar mixture of deference and authority something on the order of the peculiar mixture of deference and authority which underwrites an amendment that simultaneously restates the law and completely transforms it. But to cast the Fourteenth Amendment in these terms is to miss some of its force, indeed to miss its *poetic* force. What Whitman's poetry observes and describes, Bingham's compendium of "pleasant phrases" actually does. As "it is dislocation and detachment from life of God, that makes things ugly," Emerson maintains, "the poet, who re-attaches things to nature and the Whole,—re-attaching even artificial things, and violations of nature, to nature, by a deeper insight,—disposes very easily of the most disagreeable facts."[45] It is hard to imagine a clearer account of Bingham's achievement than this description of poetic agency. If Whitman chronicles the apotheosis of the horror of the Civil War into the beauty of the restoration, Bingham effects exactly the reattachment Emerson has in mind. In his hands our "artificial" legal regime, with all of its violations of nature, finds its way back to the protection of God and nature. His constitutional vision readily disposes of the "disagreeable fact" that the Constitution was "ugly" enough to countenance slavery. If the Fourteenth Amendment posits the Bill of Rights as the nation's fundamental law, it also establishes the Bill in that position. The Fourteenth Amendment says something about the Constitution. It also does something to it. It stands as precisely the voice that never can appear in "Lilacs"—the voice that unifies the nation. And if from one perspective such a voice might seem so powerful as to threaten the integrity of the objects it commands, from another it is nothing more than a repetition of the voice that brought them into being in the first instance.

To say that poetry is involved in the precarious balance between restraint and power in Bingham's amendment is not necessarily to praise his achievement. What looks like a towering success from the perspective of *Drum-Taps* looks like nothing more than manipulative deceit from the perspective of *Battle-Pieces*. Consider, for instance, the poem "Gettysburg: The Check (July, 1863)," the second greatest account of the meaning of the Civil War produced in relation to Gettysburg. The poem might initially seem to fit comfortably within the framework that I elaborated in the first chapter of this book. Melville's first account of the result of the battle stresses the role of God and right in the North's triumph:

> Dagon foredoomed, who, armed and targed,
> Never his impious heart enlarged
> Beyond that hour; God walled his power,
> And there the last invader charged.   (84)

But as the poem goes along, the force that repels the South begins to look somewhat less divine:

> Surged, but were met, and back they set:
> Pride was repelled by sterner pride,
> And Right is a strong-hold yet.   (85)

If "Right is a strong-hold" here it is a stronghold because the strong hold it, not because it possesses any moral strength: the North and South meet on a morally neutral field—pride was repelled by sterner pride—and the North simply happens to possess more force ("sterner") at the point of confrontation. "God walled his power" might mean as much that He walled His own power from the field of the conflict as that He walled the Confederate army's power against the North. When right and might combine here, their combination looks wholly contingent.

What makes "Gettysburg" slightly different from the poems I discussed in the first chapter is that it presents a second alternative to force as an explanation for the North's victory. If the divinity of the North's cause does not "foredoom" Dagon's charge, neither does might alone. Something else leads the North to victory, namely the fact that Gettysburg is already the monument that the battle will eventually make it:

> Sloped on the hill the mounds were green,
> Our centre held that place of graves,
> And some still hold it in their swoon,

And over these a glory waves.
The warrior-monument, crashed in fight,
Shall soar transfigured in loftier light,
A meaning ampler bear;
Soldier and priest with hymn and prayer
Have laid the stone, and every bone
Shall rest in honor there.   (85)

Two processes are at work here, one having to do with the monumental status of the graves in question, the other having to do with the moral status of the Northern army. The Northern army both defends and produces a graveyard; it preserves a monument and transfigures its meaning. Rather than suggesting that the dying soldiers produce a new monument or change the monument that is already there, Melville indicates that they merely alter the setting in which the already existing monument will appear. These soldiers are doing Bingham's work—transforming by way of defending. And in so doing, they endow their cause with the moral dimension it had seemed to have lost. It acquires a "glory" worthy of soldier and priest; it gives the monument a "loftier" "meaning," not just a new one. Here we get a merger of the formal and moral, and we get it precisely around an enterprise involving renewal and re-creation. We get the Fourteenth Amendment.

But it is crucial for us to note exactly how this happy reconciliation comes to pass. The loftier light in question here is loftier than the light that shined at the end of the day of battle, a light that took the place of soldiers in death ("The evening sun / Died on the face of each lifeless one, / And dies along the winding marge of fight / And searching-parties lone" [85]). Just as the context for the conflict comes to count as the result of the conflict, so too does the language surrounding the battle's setting become the language surrounding the battle's result. The poem thus *enacts* the process whereby context becomes result as much as it describes it. The soldiers' mixture of re-creation and preservation is a poetic effect, one produced from outside the scene by a linguistically talented observer, not an actual condition of the battle scene. And so too is the moral glow that comes to surround their triumph. It is a glow made out of words, not deeds. The triumph represented by the Fourteenth Amendment is from this vantage only a poetic triumph, only a triumph because of linguistic manipulation. It does not reconcile the Union's two goals; it simply glosses the tension between them so efficiently that it becomes invisible. As a legal enactment, it does precisely what the word *law* does: unite enterprises rhetorically when they cannot be united theoretically. It would be tempting to suggest that Bingham can do what Whitman can only describe precisely because he possesses the legislator's legal power rather than the poet's rhetorical power. But from Melville's perspective at least, Bingham's achievement requires rhetorical authority no less than political force. It is only because the law is made of sentences that the Fourteenth Amendment could ultimately restore its *sentencing* authority.

In a classic article from 1975 Thomas Grey asked whether "we have an unwritten Constitution." What prompted the question was the appearance of a set of cases, largely in the arena of reproductive rights,[46] in which the Supreme Court had, in John Hart Ely's terms, violated "its obligation to trace its premises to the charter from which it derives its authority."[47] These cases hinged on the meaning of the Fourteenth Amendment, and in them the Court often seemed less bound by the actual words in the amendment than by a nebulous set of "fundamental values" somehow contained in the amendment without being directly expressed there.[48] The history I have charted in this book has little to say about how cases such as *Roe v. Wade* should be decided, and the problem is not simply that reproductive rights did not weigh heavily on the minds of the members of the Thirty-ninth Congress. Despite its centrality to the future progress of almost all branches of constitutional jurisprudence, the Fourteenth Amendment is remarkably retrospective in its orientation. As relatively conservative commentators such as Andrew Kull and relatively liberal judges such as Chief Justice Earl Warren have maintained, its history cannot even definitively settle the constitutional controversies arising from the persistence of racial inequality and racial discrimination in the United States.[49] Kull goes so far as to suggest that the Fourteenth Amendment did not even address what was the most pressing civil rights question of the mid-1860s.[50] The problems the amendment solved were the problems of *Texas v. White* (1869) and the *Prize Cases* (1863), not the problems of *Brown v. Board of Education* (1954) and *Plessy v. Ferguson* (1896).

But if the history I have been recounting can tell us little about how to resolve the legal conflicts that have arisen under the Fourteenth Amendment, it can tell us a great deal about the theoretical nature of the conflicts the amendment would occasion and the rhetorical terms in which they would be engaged. What it can tell us, in particular, is that what Grey and Ely consider a problem for Fourteenth Amendment jurisprudence is in fact the nature of Fourteenth Amendment jurisprudence. Bingham's proposal was carefully poised on the line between the written and the unwritten, the line between natural right and positivist formality. The measure works by way of a baroque set of textual references, but it also invokes a realm of fundamental justice. It claimed fealty to the Constitution "as written" yet completely revamped the Constitution's meaning. In this regard we might say that Grey's complaint is as predictable as *Roe's* natural law penumbras. What the Fourteenth Amendment established was a studied interaction between the U.S. Constitution and its moral aspirations, a tricky dialog between justice in the abstract and formal code. But the Thirty-ninth Congress did not set up this interaction by avoiding the Constitution's writing. It was able to establish the interaction, in fact, only because the Constitution is written. The Fourteenth Amendment depends on the life in the Constitution's words, and it in turn gives those words renewed vitality. It is in this sense that the amendment's achievement is a poetic achievement. The Civil War required that the Constitution become a poem; Bingham's amendment gives it that form. Because poems are tricky sources of authority, however, the Thirty-ninth Congress's legacy is a Constitution whose meaning seems to reside both within and beyond its words. That is the Civil War's great curse and its great blessing.

1. Herman Melville, *Battle-Pieces and Aspects of the War* (1866; rpt., New York: Da Capo, 1995), 30.

2. Abraham Lincoln, *Speeches and Writings, 1832–1865* (New York: Library of America), 2 vols., 2:232; hereafter cited in parentheses in the body of the chapter.

3. The phrase is Lyman Trumbull's, *Congressional Globe,* 39th Cong., 1st sess. (1866), 43.

4. Ibid., 1066.

5. William Lloyd Garrison, "Prospectus to the Liberator Volume VIII," *Liberator,* Dec. 12, 1837.

6. The standard history of the development of American constitutional law from the 1830s through the 1860s remains Harold M. Hyman and William M. Wiecek, *Equal under the Law: Constitutional Development, 1835–1887* (New York: Harper and Row, 1982). See also William M. Wiecek, *The Sources of Antislavery Constitutionalism in America, 1760–1848* (Ithaca: Cornell University Press, 1977); Phillip S. Paludan, *A Covenant with Death: The Constitution, Law, and Equality in the Civil War Era* (Urbana: University of Illinois Press, 1975); Jacobus tenBroek, *The Antislavery Origins of the Fourteenth Amendment* (Berkeley: University of California Press, 1951); and Earl M. Maltz, "Fourteenth Amendment Concepts in the Antebellum Era," *American Journal of Legal History* 32 (1988): 305–46.

7. In addition to tenBroek, *Antislavery Origins,* see also Howard J. Graham, "The Early Antislavery Backgrounds of the Fourteenth Amendment," *University of Wisconsin Law Review* (1950): 497–507; and Raoul Berger, *The Fourteenth Amendment and the Bill of Rights* (Norman: University of Oklahoma Press, 1989).

8. Any plausible effort to make sense of the Fourteenth Amendment must flow from tenBroek's *Antislavery Origins,* and in many respects my argument is simply a refinement of his pioneering work. Whereas tenBroek is interested in tracing the meaning of particular legal clauses to a group of "fanatical reformers" "who knew little and cared less about the erudition and the ancient uses of the law" (116), however, I will suggest that the basic thinking encapsulated in those phrases had a plausible, if not exactly a legitimate, legal foundation and that the people who enshrined them in the Constitution actually cared quite a bit about "ancient uses of the law" even if they had a somewhat peculiar understanding of what those uses were.

9. Paul W. Kahn, *The Cultural Study of Law: Reconstructing Legal Scholarship* (Chicago: University of Chicago Press, 1999), 19–20. The concept of arguments "internal" to the law is also crucial to Ronald Dworkin, *Law's Empire* (Cambridge, Mass.: Harvard University Press, 1986), esp. 49–65, from which Kahn seems to derive it. The two, however, differ about the value of such internal study, with Dworkin insisting that internal understandings are the only possible understandings of the law and Kahn suggesting that the unstated assumption that the law should be studied internally has radically deformed the practice of legal scholarship in the United States.

10. Andrew Kull, *The Color-Blind Constitution* (Cambridge, Mass.: Harvard University Press, 1992), 81.

Introduction

1. *Liberator,* July 21, 1854.

2. "On the Constitution and the Union," *Liberator,* Dec. 29, 1832.

3. Ibid.

4. For an account of the debates that led the society to adopt this position, see Henry Mayer, *All on Fire: William Lloyd Garrison and the Abolition of Slavery* (New York: St. Martin's Press, 1998), 324–29.

5. Abraham Lincoln, *Speeches and Writings, 1832–1865* (New York: Library of America), 2 vols., 1:32–33; hereafter cited in parentheses in the body of the chapter.

6. *Liberator,* July 21, 1854.

7. Garrison, "Constitution and the Union."

8. Ibid.

9. The most powerful discussion of the relationship between Lincoln and the Declaration appears in Harry V. Jaffa, *Crisis of the House Divided: An Interpretation of the Issues in the Lincoln-Douglas Debates* (New York: Doubleday, 1959), 363–86. See also Jaffa, *New Birth of Freedom: Abraham Lincoln and the Coming of the Civil War* (New York: Rowman and Littlefield, 2000), 73–152; and Garry Wills, *Lincoln at Gettysburg: The Words That Remade America* (New York: Simon and Schuster, 1992).

10. *Liberator,* May 24, 1854.

11. Eric Foner, *Free Soil, Free Labor, Free Men: The Ideology of the Republican Party before the Civil War* (New York: Oxford University Press, 1970), 73. The most thorough account of this "transition" probably remains Richard H. Sewell, *Ballots for Freedom: Antislavery Politics in the United States, 1837–1860* (New York: Oxford University Press, 1976).

12. For another version of this basic point, see George Fredrickson, *The Inner Civil War: Northern Intellectuals and the Crisis of the Union* (New York: Harper and Row, 1965), 113–29. Actual emancipation, Fredrickson maintains, "forced" abolitionists "into denying their own philosophy of reform" (128). See also Amy Dru Stanley, *From Bondage to Contract: Wage Labor, Marriage, and the Market in the Age of Slave Emancipation* (Cambridge: Cambridge University Press, 1998), 1–59.

13. Eric Foner, *Reconstruction: America's Unfinished Revolution, 1863–1877* (New York: Harper and Row, 1988), 244.

14. *Congressional Globe,* 39th Cong., 1st sess., 1090.

15. The Supreme Court had held as much in *Barron v. Baltimore* (37 US [7 Pet.] 243 [1833]). Despite the Court's ruling, however, many prominent constitutional thinkers remained in doubt on this point through the 1840s and 1850s.

16. The argument for incorporation stems from Hugo Black's dissent in *Adamson v. California*, 332 US 46, 120 (1947), and has been powerfully elaborated in William Winslow Crosskey, *Politics and the Constitution in the History of the United States* (Chicago: University of Chicago Press, 1953); Michael Kent Curtis, *No State Shall Abridge: The Fourteenth Amendment and the Bill of Rights* (Durham: Duke University Press, 1986); Richard L. Aynes, "On Misreading John Bingham and the Fourteenth Amendment," *Yale Law Journal* 103 (Oct. 1993): 57−104; and Akhil Reed Amar, *The Bill of Rights: Creation and Reconstruction* (New Haven: Yale University Press, 1998). The case against incorporation can be found in Charles Fairman, "Does the Fourteenth Amendment Incorporate the Bill of Rights?" *Stanford Law Review* 2 (1949): 5−139; Louis Henkin, "'Selective Incorporation' in the Fourteenth Amendment" *Yale Law Journal* 73 (1963): 74−90; Raoul Berger, *Government by Judiciary: The Transformation of the Fourteenth Amendment* (Cambridge, Mass.: Harvard University Press, 1977; and *The Fourteenth Amendment and the Bill of Rights* (Norman: University of Oklahoma Press, 1989). For commentary about the conflict, see Pamela Brandwein, "Dueling Histories: Charles Fairman and William Crosskey Reconstruct 'Original Understanding,'" *Law and Society Review* 30 (1996): 289−399; and Michael J. Perry, *We the People: The Fourteenth Amendment and the Supreme Court* (New York: Oxford University Press, 1999), 15−87.

17. *Congressional Globe,* 42nd Cong., 1st sess., 84.

18. *Congressional Globe,* 39th Cong., 1st sess., 2459.

19. Ibid., 1090.

20. Lewis Perry, *Radical Abolition: Anarchy and the Government of God in Antislavery Thought* (Ithaca: Cornell University Press, 1973), 71, 79−80.

21. *Liberator,* Dec. 12, 1837.

22. It is true that the Thirteenth Amendment merely reprises the language that, from the time of the Northwest Ordinance forward, had conventionally prohibited slavery in United States code. But the notion that slavery would be subjected to legal standards rather than abolished altogether was not simply a matter of the amendment's phrasing. On the one hand, as we will see in later chapters, the Thirteenth Amendment's commitment to legal process responds to a number of developments in antislavery discourse in the 1840s and 1850s. On the other, the Thirteenth Amendment was only one of a number of emancipation amendments before Congress in 1865, and not all of them retained the legalist commitments of the old Northwest Ordinance. Charles Sumner, for instance, proposed that Congress pass an amendment declaring that "no person can hold another as a slave" (qtd. in Don E. Fehrenbacher, *The Slaveholding Republic: An Account of the United States Government's Relations to Slavery,* completed and ed. Ward M. McAfee [New York: Oxford University Press, 2001], 331). The most thorough discussion of the development of the Thirteenth Amendment can be found in Michael Vorenberg, *Final Freedom: The Civil War, the Abolition of Slavery, and the Thirteenth Amendment* (Cambridge: Cambridge University Press, 2001).

23. Qtd. in Amar, *Bill of Rights,* 187.

24. *Congressional Globe,* 39th Cong., 1st sess., 1090.

25. See James Madison, *Notes of Debates in the Federal Convention of 1878* (1840; rpt., Athens: University of Ohio Press, 1966).

26. Robert M. Cover, *Justice Accused: Antislavery and the Judicial Process* (New Haven: Yale University Press, 1975), 7. See also David Brion Davis, *The Problem of Slavery in Western Culture* (Ithaca: Cornell University Press, 1966), 3–28, 391–482; and *The Problem of Slavery in the Age of Revolution, 1770–1823* (Ithaca: Cornell University Press, 1975), 255–342, 469–522. For a discussion of the specifically constitutional, as opposed to more broadly legal and jurisprudential, crisis slavery occasioned in the nineteenth century, see Mark E. Brandon, *Free in the World: American Slavery and Constitutional Failure* (Princeton: Princeton University Press, 1999).

27. See Jacobus tenBroek, *The Antislavery Origins of the Fourteenth Amendment* (Berkeley: University of California Press, 1951), 57–93.

28. *Somerset v. Stewart,* 20 Howells State Trials 82, 98 Eng. Rep. 499, 510.

29. See, e.g., Charles Sumner, "Freedom National, Slavery Local" (1852), in *The Works of Charles Sumner,* 15 vols. (Boston: Lee and Shepard, 1870–83), 3:92–196.

30. See Don E. Fehrenbacher, *The "Dred Scott" Case: Its Significance in American Law and Politics* (New York: Oxford University Press, 1978), 188–208, 449–550.

31. Max Farrand, ed., *The Records of the Federal Convention of 1787,* rev. ed., 4 vols. (New Haven: Yale University Press, 1937), 2:417.

32. Fehrenbacher, *"Dred Scott" Case,* 27.

33. Henry David Thoreau, "Slavery in Massachusetts," in *Reform Papers,* ed. Wendell Glick (Princeton: Princeton University Press, 1973), 92. All future references to Thoreau's essays will be to this edition and will appear in parentheses in the body of the chapter.

34. Qtd. in Edmund Wilson, *Patriotic Gore: Studies in the Literature of the American Civil War* (New York: Oxford University Press, 1962), 3.

35. See Ralph Waldo Emerson, "Address to the Citizens of Concord" (1851) and "The Fugitive Slave Law" (1854), in *Emerson's Antislavery Writings,* ed. Len Gougeon and Joel Myerson (New Haven: Yale University Press, 1995), 53–72, 73–89; and "Slavery in Massachusetts," 91–109.

36. Melville, *Battle-Pieces,* 259.

37. "I regarded such laws as the regulations of robbers, who had no rights that I was bound to respect" (Harriet Jacobs, *Incidents in the Life of a Slave Girl* (1861), in *Slave Narratives,* ed. Henry Louis Gates Jr. [New York: Library of America, 2000], 930).

38. The best account of these developments in Douglass's career is Robert S. Levine, *Martin Delany, Frederick Douglass, and the Politics of Representative Identity* (Chapel Hill: University of North Carolina Press, 1997), 18–143.

39. Nathaniel Hawthorne, *The Scarlet Letter* (1850; rpt., Columbus: Ohio State University Press, 1962), 31.

40. Many recent students of the relationship between law and literature have called for forms of synthetic analysis which could move beyond what Shoshana Felman has called the "thematic," forms of analysis which could "illuminate reciprocally not just the themes, the thematized meanings of the literary narratives of crime and trial, but (most important) the structure and process of these narratives; and not just the structure and process of the stories but their actual impact, their historical reception" ("Forms of Judicial Blindness, or the Evidence of What Cannot Be Seen: Traumatic Narratives and Legal Repetitions in the O. J. Simpson Case and in Tolstoy's *Kreutzer Sonata,*" *Critical Inquiry* 23 [Summer 1997]: 739). I do not share Felman's interest in issues such as "legal haunting," nor do I share her sense that the proper study of literature and law requires that we distinguish between examinations of "meaning" (litera-

ture) and examinations of "truth" (law). But I do share her interest in those moments in which the legal and the literary are so intertwined that their "structures and processes" seem to be implicated in one another. Rather than thinking that such moments take us beyond an analysis of literary "reflection" upon legal matters (739), I would be inclined to say that they simply reveal the depth of that reflection.

41. Dworkin, *Law's Empire* (Cambridge, Mass.: Harvard University Press, 1986), 229.

42. All references to Emerson's essays will be to Ralph Waldo Emerson, *Essays: First and Second Series* (New York: Library of America, 1990), and will appear in parentheses in the body of the chapter.

43. *Congressional Globe,* 39th Cong., 1st sess., 1090.

44. Daniel Aaron, *The Unwritten War: American Writers and the Civil War* (New York: Knopf, 1973), xviii.

45. Edmund Wilson, "Abraham Lincoln: The Union as Religious Mysticism," *Eight Essays* (New York: Doubleday, 1954), 202.

46. Robert A. Ferguson, *Law and Letters in American Culture* (Cambridge, Mass.: Harvard University Press, 1984), 271–72.

47. Brook Thomas, *Cross-Examinations of Law and Literature: Cooper, Hawthorne, Stowe, and Melville* (Cambridge: Cambridge University Press, 1987), 12.

48. Ferguson, *Law and Letters,* 200.

49. Gregg D. Crane, *Race, Citizenship, and Law in American Literature* (Cambridge: Cambridge University Press, 2002), 1–11.

50. Ibid., 11, 8.

51. See, e.g., Eric J. Sundquist, *To Wake the Nations: Race in the Making of American Literature* (Cambridge, Mass.: Harvard University Press, 1993), 175–82. We might also note, in passing, that invocations of the "divine" did not always work in the reactionary ways Crane's formulation would seem to imply.

52. *Dred Scott v. Sandford* 60 US (19 Howard) 393 (1857).

53. Fehrenbacher, *"Dred Scott" Case,* 123.

54. See, e.g., Albert J. Von Frank's claim that the corruption of slavery could be "cured only from a vantage point outside and above it, . . . from the direction of the ideal or abstract" (*The Trials of Anthony Burns: Freedom and Slavery in Emerson's Boston* [Cambridge, Mass.: Harvard University Press, 1998], xvi). Other examples are Jane Tompkins, *Sensational Designs: The Cultural Work of American Fiction, 1790–1860* (New York: Oxford University Press, 1985), 122–47; and Saidiya V. Hartman, *Scenes of Subjection: Terror, Slavery, and Self-Making in Nineteenth-Century America* (New York: Oxford University Press, 1997).

55. For exceptions to this general trend (i.e., accounts of how the moral domain of human right might be read out of and into American positive law), see Anthony J. Sebock, "Judging the Fugitive Slave Act," *Yale Law Journal* 100 (1991): 1835–54; and Christopher L. M. Eisgruber "Justice Story, Slavery, and the Natural Law Foundations of American Constitutionalism," *University of Chicago Law Review* 55 (1988): 273–327; John Stauffer, *The Black Hearts of Men: Radical Abolitionists and the Transformation of Race* (Cambridge, Mass.: Harvard University Press, 2003); and esp. Fehrenbacher, *Slaveholding Republic.*

56. Sundquist, *To Wake the Nations,* 154, 175, 176, 178, 176.

57. Donald does not simply condemn Charles Sumner's thinking about slavery as repres-

sive or racist because it took place within an avowedly constitutional framework, for instance, but he does adduce Sumner's refusal to "join Garrison and Phillips in denouncing the Constitution as a proslavery document and desiring the disruption of the Union" as a sign of his conservative inclinations. "The basic influences of [Sumner's] life," he explains, "had all been conservative" (*Charles Sumner and the Coming of the Civil War* [New York: Knopf, 1960], 228). Foner also represents constitutional antislavery as a kind of dilution of the abolitionist's moral message, a "painful" retreat from a full-bore commitment to racial justice (Foner, *Free Soil*, 73).

58. Wald's concern about the "contingency of personhood upon the law" emerges in the course of a critique of Lincoln's efforts to redefine the United States of America during the Civil War. Wald condemns those efforts for failing, in her terms, to produce "an equal place for black subjects within a reconstructed narrative" of the nation. But the figure she opposes to Lincoln, Frederick Douglass, counts as more "radical" and less "limited" than the great emancipator not because he manages to produce a powerful multiracial alternative to Lincoln's limited white republic but because he refuses to allow his personhood to be defined entirely in terms of normative legal plotlines in the first instance. Wald champions Douglass for insisting that his status lies "betwixt and between" the various legal narratives that constitute Americans. Whereas the force of Lincoln's rhetoric is to "suggest[] that human minds [. . .] as well as 'the people' have been formed by the Constitution," Douglass refuses to be wholly shaped in its image. His achievement lies in his evasions of the "symbolic identit[ies]" and "enslavement" that the law provides and which Lincoln's greatest rhetorical moments enabled (Priscilla Wald, *Constituting Americans: Cultural Anxiety and Narrative Form* [Durham: Duke University Press, 1995], 23, 72, 21, 69, 100, 66).

59. I do not mean to deny that the Thirteenth and Fourteenth amendments did not satisfy the ambitions of those who were making the most radical demands for black civil rights in the 1860s. But there is little evidence that the amendments were considered too moderate because they were overly committed to legal accounts of civil freedom and civil rights. The moderation of Reconstruction lay in the scope of its efforts, not in the fact that it thought that legal terms might be instrumental in, if not necessary to, the task at hand. Whereas scholars such as Wald and Sundquist suggest that legal expressions of civil rights would actually be hostile to the rights of African Americans, radicals such as Stevens maintained that they were merely insufficient. We might say that Bingham's commitment to the Constitution limited the range of options he was willing to explore or embrace, and in that sense his constitutionalism hampered the rights of freedmen. But it is by no means clear that constitutionalism had to have this effect. Sumner was no less committed to constitutional postwar remedies than Bingham, but he was able to reconcile them quite easily with his rather more radical take on how the South should be treated after the war. Even radicals such as Stevens, who wanted to rewrite the Constitution as much as they wanted to enforce it, nonetheless had less in common with Garrison than Lincoln. Stevens could only just bear to support Bingham's amendment, and he considered the Civil War a "fortunate chance" because it had "broken up for awhile the foundation of our institutions." He certainly did not think, however, that the application of the "just" provisions of the Bill of Rights to the states was much of a problem. And if he thought that the Fourteenth Amendment was a little too loyal to the "foundation of our institutions," he had no interest in replacing those institutions with a superinstitutional form of government; he merely hoped that the institutions might be more thoroughly "remodeled" (*Congressional Globe*, 39th Cong., 1st sess., 3148). Le-

galism was one of the languages of American civil rights in the 1860s, and no one seemed to object to its serving in that capacity (for discussions relevant to this point, see David Herbert Donald, *Charles Sumner and the Rights of Man* [New York: Knopf, 1970], 132–61, 218–67; and Foner, *Reconstruction*, 228–332). The scholar who comes closest to producing a critique of the Fourteenth Amendment on the grounds of its commitment to citizenship and civil standing is Saidiya V. Hartman, who complains that the Fourteenth Amendment proceeded as if racial "differences didn't inhabit the text [of the Constitution] or the law was uninvolved in their production" (*Scenes of Subjection*, 181). But it is ultimately unclear whether Hartman is critical of the amendment's commitment to the "neutrality of law" or of Reconstruction's practical inability to "enact [the] blindness" to racial difference on which the amendment depends (181). In light of Fehrenbacher's *Slaveholding Republic,* moreover, what Hartman calls the "racialized" status of the Constitution begins to look more like an effect of nineteenth-century "enactment" than anything necessary or central to constitutional order as such.

Chapter One • Victory of LAW

1. Herman Melville, *Battle-Pieces and Aspects of the War* (1866; rpt., New York: Da Capo, 1995), 272, 259; hereafter cited in parentheses in the body of the chapter.

2. I say "declared officially ratified" because the question of how and when an amendment became ratified in the aftermath of the Civil War was the source of considerable dispute and debate. Did an amendment need the support of three-fourths of all states in the Union (including those in the former Confederacy)? Or did one merely require the support of three-fourths of those states recognized by Congress as states for the purposes of having their representatives allowed to participate in congressional activity? The political conflict this question produced was central to the congressional debates about both the Thirteenth and Fourteenth amendments. For a discussion of these matters, see Bruce Ackerman, *We, the People, II: Transformations* (Cambridge, Mass.: Harvard University Press, 1998), 99–254.

3. William Dean Howells produced the first instance of the former critical concern in his review of *Battle-Pieces,* in which he ventriloquized, "Is it possible—you ask yourself, after running over all these celebrative, inscriptive, and memorial verses—that there has really been a great war, with battles fought by men and bewailed by women? Or is it that Mr. Melville's inner consciousness has been perturbed, and filled with the phantasms of enlistments, marches, fights in the air, parenthetic bulletin boards, and tortured humanity shedding, not words and blood, but words alone?" (*Atlantic Monthly* 19 [1867]: 252–53). The proximity between Melville and the war has remained a staple topic of the criticism ever since. It animates among other things the ever vexatious question of the relationship between Melville's verse and the various reported documents on which it explicitly and implicitly relies (see, e.g., Willard Thorpe, "Introduction," in *Herman Melville: Representative Selections* [New York: American Books, 1938]; Richard Harter Fogle, "Melville and the Civil War," *Tulane Studies in English* 9 [1959]: 61–89; and Joyce Sparer Adler, "Melville and the Civil War," *New Letters* 40 [1973]: 99–117). And it persists in the ongoing question of whether the poems are really about the war at all. Stanton Garner, for instance, has recently argued against "the assumption that [Melville] was disengaged from and only marginally aware of the greatest national convulsion in American history as it occurred around him" (*The Civil War World of Herman Melville* [Lawrence: University Press of Kansas, 1993], 389);

while Elizabeth Renker, by contrast, suggests that Melville was so "disengaged from" the Civil War that it "is only of secondary importance to" *Battle-Pieces* (*Strike through the Mask: Herman Melville and the Scene of Writing* [Baltimore: Johns Hopkins University Press, 1995], 101); and Timothy Sweet suggests that the volume could not ever apprehend the war directly: "To write poetry about war is, in some sense always to aestheticize it; poetry necessarily evades 'the real war' . . . because it is only a representation" (*Traces of War: Poetry, Photography, and the Crisis of Union* [Baltimore: Johns Hopkins University Press, 1990], 180).

At the same time that critics have had a hard time understanding the relationship between the poems and the events to which they refer, they also have been struck by what is usually characterized as an uneasy relation between the poems and the various forms in which they do their referring. For descriptions of this uneasiness, see Robert Penn Warren, "Melville the Poet," in *Selected Essays* (New York: Random House, 1958); Richard Harter Fogle, "Melville's Poetry," *Tulane Studies in English* 12 (1962): 81–86; Edmund Wilson, *Patriotic Gore: Studies in the Literature of the American Civil War* (New York: Farrar, Straus, and Giroux, 1962), 323–29; Daniel Aaron, *The Unwritten War: American Writers and the Civil War* (New York: Knopf, 1973), 75–90; John Seelye, *Melville: The Ironic Diagram* (Evanston: Northwestern University Press, 1970), 130–51; and Clark Davis, *After the Whale: Melville in the Wake of "Moby Dick"* (Tuscaloosa: University of Alabama Press, 1995), 107–24.

Two prominent recent considerations of Melville's verse effectively bridge these two avenues of inquiry by taking up the theme of poetic irregularity and difficulty in the context of the epistemological problems that are often seen as central in Melville's work. See William C. Spengemann, "Melville the Poet," *American Literary History* 11 (1999): 569–609; and Rosanna Warren, "Dark Knowledge: Melville's Poems of the Civil War," *Raritan* 19 (1999): 100–121. Spengemann suggests that it is precisely *Battle-Pieces'* irregularity that marks its poetic achievement insofar as it represents "a form and style appropriate to an utterly ambiguous and unknowable world" and thus does what "what neither faith nor philosophy nor fiction could do: make some sense of a nonsensically fragmented world without pretending that the world itself makes sense" (580, 599). Warren similarly contends that Melville's "inwrought, crabbed, ponderous, grimed verse" "engage[s] the reader" in a "struggle" for knowledge (100, 102), which, as she sees it, resists "conventional poetic solutions" and "ready-made judgment" (103, 110). Later in this chapter I will challenge Spengemann's and Warren's contentions that the poems are devoted to making claims about the difficulty of understanding the world and evince a hostility to commonplace forms of knowledge.

4. Critics who have attempted to understand Melville's Civil War poetry in terms of its political context tend to conceive of that context in more expansive terms than the relatively narrow ones that I plan to take up. George Fredrickson sees Melville's Civil War poetry as a symptom of the North's disaffection for "antislavery humanism" after the war (*The Inner-Civil War: Northern Intellectuals and the Crisis of the Union* [New York: Harper and Row, 1965], 183–89). Carolyn L. Karcher understands *Battle-Pieces* in terms of Melville's lifelong interest in slavery (see *Shadow over the Promised Land: Slavery, Race, and Violence in Melville's America* [Baton Rouge: Louisiana State University Press, 1980], 258–307). And though Michael Rogin takes up a number of the concerns I will address later in this chapter, including the relationship between the poems' formal awkwardness and their legalistic thematics, he too locates the poems in a far broader historical sphere than the one I am introducing here, one that is more interested in the status of "the state" and its "authority" than it is with the more narrow Reconstruction issues of

the states and their rights which I will foreground (Michael Paul Rogin, *Subversive Genealogy: The Politics and Art of Herman Melville* [New York: Random House, 1983]).

5. I should stress at the outset that a concern with Melville's interest in the legal grounds on which Reconstruction should proceed is different from a concern with the particular Reconstruction policies he favored. I am less interested, that is, in what Melville would have done had he been a senator in 1866—though his "Supplement" perhaps speaks more to that issue than any other—than in what he thought would have made whatever policy he recommended count as a lawful policy. As we will see, it is the latter concern—a concern with what makes a law lawful rather than a concern about what makes a law good—in which the poems are ultimately most invested. For an analysis of Melville's response to incipient Reconstruction *policy,* see Carolyn L. Karcher, "The Moderate and the Radical: Melville and Child on the Civil War and Reconstruction," *ESQ* 43 (1999): 187–257.

6. Ackerman, *Transformations,* 100, 99, 117, 118. Cf. Fredrickson, *Inner Civil War,* 53–64.

7. When Secretary of State Seward announced that the Thirteenth Amendment had officially been incorporated into the Constitution, twenty-seven of the thirty-six states comprising the Union had ratified the measure. Southern states seeking restoration to the Union under Johnson's presidential Reconstruction program accounted for eight of the twenty-seven ratifications. As Johnson himself frequently insisted at the time, unless the Southern states were considered to be a part of Union, the amendment, at the time of its becoming a part of the Constitution at least, would have had the support of only nineteen of the twenty-seven Northern states and would not have had the necessary three-fourths for ratification. See Ackerman, *Transformations,* 100–109, 120–59.

8. Ibid., 109.

9. Abraham Lincoln, *Lincoln: Speeches and Writings, 1859–65,* ed. Don E. Fehrenbacher, 2 vols. (New York: Library of America, 1989), 2:699; hereafter cited in parentheses in the body of the chapter.

10. The "chameleon" image comes from Justice Grier's dissent in the case that eventually held that secession was unconstitutional, *Texas v. White* 74 US (7 Wall.) 700 (1869), at 740; hereafter cited in parentheses in the body of the chapter.

11. Rogin, *Subversive Genealogy,* 267, 275.

12. 67 US (2 Black) 635 (1863), 670; hereafter cited in parentheses in the body of the chapter.

13. They arise even more forcefully two sentences later, when Lincoln insists that Southern leaders "accordingly . . . commenced by an insidious debauching of the public mind" and "invented an ingenious sophism, which, if conceded, was followed by perfectly logical steps, through all the incidents, to the complete destruction of the Union" (2:255). It is worth pointing out in passing that Lincoln's account of these conspiratorial activities has the effect of making Southern leaders look like Melville's Southern soldiers: both can only relate to the law in terms of its relationship to some end they have independent of the law itself. The soldiers see legal documents as the stimulus for fires; Lincoln's conspirators see legal arguments as the stimulus for revolt. For neither, however, do the means law makes available (even if those means are simply available by virtue of the fact that legal documents are printed on paper) work toward legal ends. For now I am interested only in the consequences of Lincoln's implicit admission that not all Southerners who profess to be lawful are simply being disingenuous, that at least some mean to follow the law rather than use it.

14. The problem is not even that they have a bad account of which country is their country—North or South—for the figures Lincoln had in mind here actually saw the Confederacy itself as a lawful development under the Constitution of the United States. Perhaps the most remarkable confirmation of this way of thinking about the South came in the form of former Confederate vice president Alexander Stephens's *A Constitutional View of the War between the States* (Philadelphia: National Publishing Co., 1868), which endeavored to prove that the Southern acts of secession were constitutional and that Northern efforts to protect the Union were not (he dedicated the volume to precisely those people Lincoln considered his strongest allies, "All true friends of the Union under the Constitution of the United States" [iii]). We might think that the point of the Confederacy was to escape the Constitution (or at least to insist that it was inapplicable in Southern locales), but Stephens thought of the Constitution as something that could be invoked to protect nascent nation. Stephens imagined the Constitution, that is, to be one of the legal foundations of the Confederacy, not a legal foundation that Southern states had abjured.

15. 74 US (7 Wall.) 700 (1869).

16. Even if we think that the country in question here is unmistakably the country of the Northern troops, we still cannot be sure which way the appeal should go. The speaker could understand the needs of the Union in terms of the value of secession. Sometimes, as we will see later on, Melville will hint that the country could be made better by the eradication of the South, not a commitment to maintaining it in the Union. Likewise, were the speaker to value the Union precisely because of its refusal to impose its law on states that wished to avoid it, the call of the country could be made to go hand in hand with the justice of secession; there were, after all, plenty of people in the North who valued the Union precisely for this reason throughout the 1860s. My point is not to stress either of these readings, however, but rather to point out that the passage's refusal to identify which country is "their country" and which cause is the "just one" makes its initial pro-Union valences begin to look somewhat equivocal under more careful scrutiny.

17. In his "Supplement" Melville actually goes so far as to suggest that it makes no sense to compel Southerners to acknowledge the rightness of Northern legal claims: "Some of us are concerned because as yet the South shows no penitence. But what exactly do we mean by this? Since down to the close of the war she never confessed any for braving it, the only penitence now left to her is that which springs solely from the sense of discomfiture; and since this evidently would be a contrition hypocritical, it would be unworthy in us to demand it" (260).

18. The person who comes closest to taking this position is Andrew Johnson. In his first annual address to Congress (given in December 1865) Johnson explained that "it is manifest that treason, most flagrant in character, has been committed. Persons who are charged with its commission should have fair and impartial trials in the highest civil tribunals of the country, in order that the Constitution and the laws may be fully vindicated, the truth clearly established and affirmed that treason is a crime, that traitors should be punished and the offense made infamous, and, at the same time, that the question may be judicially settled, finally and forever, that no State of its own will has the right to renounce its place in the Union" (*Presidential Messages and State Papers,* ed. Julius W. Muller, 10 vols., [New York: Review of Reviews, 1917], 6:2046–47; all future quotations from Johnson will be from the sixth volume and will be cited in parentheses in the body of the chapter). Leaving aside for the moment the question of why these tri-

als would "vindicate" the law rather than merely allowing it to operate (Johnson seems to think that the war has placed the law in need of vindication rather than in a state of suspension) and also leaving aside the question of how much Johnson was ultimately committed to seeing that these persons "charged" with treason "be punished" (he would eventually extend pardons to many of them), what is most interesting about this proposal is that by the time it was made in late 1865 it already constituted a conservative response to the secession crisis. James G. Randall has suggested that "the Government's action was never so severe as the words of the radical statesmen" on the subject of the "traitors" in the South would lead one to expect (*Constitutional Problems under Lincoln* [1926; rpt., Urbana: University of Illinois Press, 1951], 73). But by the end of the war Lincoln's cavalier extension of the pardon to most Southerners who were willing to take an oath of loyalty ensured that the "severe" action taken by the Union would be directed against the Southern states rather than the "traitors" who populated them.

19. For detailed discussions of Lincoln and habeas corpus, see Mark E. Neely Jr., *The Fate of Liberty: Abraham Lincoln and Civil Liberties* (New York: Oxford University Press, 1991); Dean Sprague, *Freedom under Lincoln* (Boston: Houghton Mifflin, 1965); James M. McPherson, "Lincoln and Liberty," in *Abraham Lincoln and the Second American Revolution* (New York: Oxford University Press, 1991), 43–64; and James G. Randall, *Constitutional Problems under Lincoln*, 118–39. For an extended defense of Lincoln's actions with respect to habeas corpus and the other constitutional issues raised by Randall and others, see Daniel Farber, *Lincoln's Constitution* (Chicago: University of Chicago Press, 2003), esp. 92–114, 176–95.

20. *Ex Parte Merryman* 17 Fed. Cas. 144, 153 (D. Md. 1861).

21. Qtd. in Randall, *Constitutional Problems*, 1–2.

22. The most famous of these is his June 12, 1863, letter to Erastus Corning, which was published in the *New York Tribune.* There Lincoln not only argued that he had the right and the duty to suspend habeas corpus, but he also claimed that he "th[ought] the time not unlikely to come when I shall be blamed for having made too few arrests rather than too many" (458). His argument was relatively simple. The Constitution provides that "the privilege of the writ of habeas corpus shall not be suspended unless when, in cases of rebellion or invasion, the public safety may require it" (457). The South's secession certainly constituted a "rebellion," and the public safety was certainly at risk. Hence, habeas corpus could be suspended. As far as that goes, this argument seems entirely unobjectionable. What was more objectionable to Taney was the idea that the president, rather than Congress, should be the agent of its suspension. (Taney's position that Congress has the authority to suspend the writ has essentially become the law.) And there is even a problem with the idea that Congress should be able to suspend it, for the privilege of the writ would hardly count for all that much if the Congress could suspend it at its pleasure simply by declaring that its suspension was made necessary by civil strife. For a detailed discussion of these matters, see William F. Duker, *A Constitutional History of Habeas Corpus* (Westport, Conn.: Greenwood, 1980).

23. The most thorough history of the Supreme Court in the Reconstruction period is Charles Fairman's three-volume contribution to the *Oliver Wendell Holmes Devise History of the Supreme Court, Reconstruction and Reunion, 1864–88* (New York: Macmillan, 1971–88).

24. 71 US (4 Wall.) 2 (1866) at 120–21.

25. 71 US (4 Wall.) 277 (1867); 71 US (4 Wall.) 333 (1867).

26. Field wrote an opinion for each case (the opinions run more or less identical argu-

ments). Miller wrote a single dissent (in which the other Republican justices, Chase, Swayne, and Davis, joined) for the two cases. To keep matters relatively simple, I will join the Republicans and discuss the two cases together and at the same time.

27. It is easy to exaggerate the Court's commitment to restoring the authority of the judicial branch in the immediate postwar period. While it was willing to overturn test oaths and military trials, it famously went well out of its way to avoid making any pronouncement on the legality of the very mechanism of Reconstruction itself—the idea that Southern states could be held under federal military authority pending their ratification of various state constitutional provisions and federal constitutional amendments. The important cases in this regard are *Mississippi v. Johnson* 71 US (4 Wall.) 475 (1867), *Georgia v. Stanton* 73 US (6 Wall.) 50 (1868), and *Ex Parte McCardle* 74 US (7 Wall.) 506 (1869), in which the Court repeatedly sought procedural grounds to avoid ruling on the constitutionality of Reconstruction measures. Matters were particularly embarrassing with respect to *Ex Parte McCardle,* in which the Court's postponement of its decision allowed Congress to pass an act that was later held to limit the Court's jurisdiction over the matters in dispute. "By postponement of this case," Grier explained, "we shall subject ourselves, whether justly or unjustly, to the imputation that we have evaded the performance of duty imposed on us by the Constitution, and waited for legislative interposition to supersede our action, and relieve us from responsibility" (qtd. in David P. Currie, *The Constitution in the Supreme Court: The First One Hundred Years, 1789–1888* [Chicago: University of Chicago Press, 1985], 307). The Court would eventually decide that it had been wrong to think that the Congress could limit its appellate jurisdiction in such a matter, in *United States v. Klein* 80 US (13 Wall.) 128 (1872).

28. Qtd. in Fairman, *Reconstruction and Reunion,* 216, 218.

29. Currie, *First One Hundred Years,* 296.

30. Qtd. in Robert M. Cover, *Justice Accused: Antislavery and the Judicial Process* (New Haven: Yale University Press, 1975), 119–22.

31. *Congressional Globe,* 39th Cong., 1st sess., 3148.

32. Qtd. in Cover, *Justice Accused,* 120.

33. Qtd. in ibid., 121.

34. *Congressional Globe,* 39th Cong., 1st sess., 1310.

35. After all, any claim that the Union was perpetual would be an advance over the Constitution's silence with respect to the matter. It seems at least as plausible that the Articles of Confederation's guarantee of perpetuality was intentionally omitted from the Constitution as it does that it was silently incorporated. Along the same lines, moreover, the mere invocation of the Articles tends to pose a problem for any claim of the Union's perpetual standing: since it had not been ratified in accordance with the Articles' amendment procedure, the Constitution itself testifies to the ease with which the Articles' guarantee of perpetuality might be waived (and, presumably, legally waived). And as a final concern, even if we grant that the Articles' provisions had been silently incorporated into the Constitution, we may well still wonder what the relationship between perpetuality and perfection is. Is it not at least possible, especially given the absence of a clause guaranteeing that the alliance would be perpetual, that it was precisely because the Constitution was not perpetual that it was more perfect than the Articles? (For recent commentators who have found the Constitution unpleasantly conservative in its values and strictures, the fact that it is itself something of an improper amendment to the Articles can emerge as a valuable

fact: if our very Constitution counts as a formally innovative revision of the law, then what is to stop us from revising it without recourse to the obstructionist formal procedures it provides for its own revision? The most interesting recent response to this question lies in Bruce Ackerman, *We the People I: Foundations* [Cambridge, Mass.: Harvard University Press, 1991] and *We the People II: Transformations,* which argue that we should understand first the Reconstruction amendments and then the New Deal as wholly new constitutional orders.)

The flimsiness of Chase's position here makes a little more sense of Lincoln's and Grier's willingness to claim that the war itself determined the legality of secession: the constitutional argument against it is hardly straightforward. "The best argument," David Currie explains, "was based upon an important change of language from the Articles to the Constitution: while the former were a 'firm league of friendship' among 'sovereign[]' states, the latter was 'the Supreme law of the Land'" (313). This was the argument of the most important treatise on constitutional law in the antebellum period, Joseph Story's *Commentaries on the Constitution of the United States* (Boston: Hilliard, Gray and Co., 1833), 318–22. But as Currie himself notes, it is not entirely clear that even this argument really holds up, for the question secession poses is not the question of what law should be supreme (state or Constitution) so much as the question of whether a state must remain under the Constitution in the first place. As Currie puts it, "while it is scarcely the most natural inference, it would not have been wholly inconsistent for the Framers to require that states respect federal law only so long as they chose to remain in the Union" (313). Given the widespread efforts to connect the Union's cause to the idea that the law should reign supreme, however, it is telling that Chase chose to omit the standard and strongest argument on behalf of his position when it revolved precisely around the idea of the law's authority.

36. Randall, *Constitutional Problems,* 71.

37. A good instance of this account is Foner, *Reconstruction,* 176–280.

38. *Congressional Globe,* 37th Cong., 2nd sess., 2189.

39. Ibid., 2299. This is a slightly bizarre claim, however, for it would seem to suggest that only the military defense of secession, not the act of secession itself, would count as treason. Needless to say, someone like Lincoln was much more committed to the secession's status as something inherently treasonous. He was even willing to call those people who merely refused to denounce secession traitors: "The man who stands by and says nothing when the peril of his Government is discussed, cannot be misunderstood. . . . [H]e is sure to help the enemy" (2:458).

40. It is interesting in this regard that while Art is aligned with metrical matters, the rules are aligned with matters of "rhyme"—interesting because the poem's metrical scheme is wholly consistent but only half of its lines are specifically connected to a rhyme scheme (and that scheme does not evolve). In this regard it is also interesting that the one moment of metrical difficulty in the poem comes in its penultimate line, in which the poem's syntax produces a caesura much stronger than the simple breaks we found in other lines; this moment of difficulty comes as a result of the emergence of a tension between the poem's formal regularity and its substantive content, a tension between its poetic rules and its logical ones, and it comes at precisely the moment in which the poem attempts to extrapolate from Dupont's victory a claim about LAW's victory: it is as if the poem reminds us here with a gap between form and content that its own expressions of the connection between the two of them might be somewhat troublesome.

41. Hence, Rogin will be interested in ways in which Melville's commitment to poetic success—his commitment to "confinement" and producing "the intensity of language under compression"—comes at the expense of "the vitality of [Melville's] early fiction" and "contaminates" *Battle Pieces*' "political message" (*Subversive Genealogy*, 278-79).

42. Obviously, at the moment in which I produce a distinction between the act of describing a poem and the act of summarizing one I reintroduce those terms that I claim are the subjects of Melville's poetry: form and content. What formalist critics have taken to be the form of Melville's poems, I am suggesting, is actually their content. And in doing this I might ultimately be taken to be suggesting that the poems do effect the reconciliation between form and content whose failure I have been arguing they merely stage: on the account I have been elaborating, what they mean seems to have a great deal to do with how they mean. To this charge I will ultimately plead guilty: I do think that the form and the content of Melville's poems work toward a single meaning. The reason my argument has revolved around the distinction between form and content in the poems is that the meaning I think they work toward is the meaning that form and content are separate and conceivably incompatible properties of both the law and a work of art. In other words, I think that the poems represent the separation between form and content even if they do not embody it.

Chapter Two • Shadows of Law

1. Harriet Beecher Stowe, *Uncle Tom's Cabin* (1852; rpt., New York: Modern Library, 1996), 13; hereafter cited in parentheses in the body of the chapter.

2. References to Herman Melville, *Battle-Pieces and Aspects of the War* (1866; rpt., New York: Da Capo, 1995), will appear in parentheses in the body of the chapter.

3. I am led to this formulation by Michael Paul Rogin's description of shadows in *Battle-Pieces* (*Subversive Genealogy: The Politics and Art of Herman Melville* [New York: Knopf, 1983], 267–78). Still a foundationally important reading of the shape of Herman Melville's career, *Subversive Genealogy* maintains that *Battle-Pieces* represents Melville's "imaginative rapprochement" with the "authority" of "the state" (267). On Rogin's account this "rapprochement" is marked not merely by Melville's newfound commitment to the law's "power to endure and command loyalty" but also by his adoption of a conservative racial politics (275). If "the young Melville" of the 1840s and 1850s "had a liberating political purpose[] and . . . peopled his tales with a variety of racial and social types," Rogin argues, the older postwar Melville was willing not only to embrace the law but also to sanction "the exclusion of blacks" from the purview of both his artistic landscape and the nation whose Civil War it sought to delineate (278). I will argue, by contrast, that what enables the "young Melville" of the early multicultural fictions to become the older Melville of the white Union is in fact the persistence of Melville's anxiety about the law, not his acquiescence before the state's emergent force.

4. For an alternative account of this transition, see George Fredrickson, *The Inner Civil War: Northern Intellectuals and the Crisis of the Union* (New York: Harper and Row, 1965), 183–98.

5. See Aileen S. Kraditor, *Means and Ends: Garrison and His Critics on Strategy and Tactics, 1834–1850* (New York: Pantheon, 1969); Lewis Perry, *Radical Abolitionism: Anarchy and the Government of God in Antislavery Thought* (Ithaca: Cornell University Press, 1973); Richard H. Sewell, *Ballots for Freedom: Antislavery Politics in the United States, 1837–1860* (New York: Ox-

ford University Press, 1975), 3–79; and John Stauffer, *The Black Hearts of Men: Radical Abolitionists and the Transformation of Race* (Cambridge, Mass.: Harvard University Press, 2002), 8–
44, 134–81. For a different and suggestive approach to Garrison's relation to his rhetoric, one
that focuses on its implications for white subjectivity rather than black rights, see Christopher
Castiglia, "Abolition's Racial Interiors and the Making of White Civic Depth," *American Literary History* 14 (Spring 2002): 32–59.

6. David Brion Davis, *The Problem of Slavery in the Age of Revolution, 1770–1823* (Ithaca:
Cornell University Press, 1975), 164; hereafter cited in parentheses in the body of the chapter.

7. William Blackstone, *Commentaries on the Laws of England*, 5 vols. (1765–69; rpt., Chicago:
University of Chicago Press, 1979), 1:127, 1:423–24.

8. *Somerset v. Stewart* 98 Eng. Rep. 499 (1772). On *Somerset*'s significance, see William M.
Wiecek, "*Somerset:* Lord Mansfield and the Legitimacy of Slavery in the Anglo-American
World," *University of Chicago Law Review* 42 (1974): 86–146; Robert M. Cover, *Justice Accused:
Antislavery and the Legal Process* (New Haven: Yale University Press, 1975), 58–94; Davis, *Prob-
lem of Slavery in the Age of Revolution*, 469–522; Don E. Fehrenbacher, *The "Dred Scott" Case:
Its Significance in American Law and Politics* (New York: Oxford University Press, 1978), 31–58;
and Paul Finkelman, *An Imperfect Union: Slavery, Federalism, and Comity* (Chapel Hill: University of North Carolina Press, 1981), 70–180.

9. By the 1850s Southerners often challenged *Somerset*'s authority by citing the slightly later
case *The Slave, Grace*, decided by Lord Stowell in 1826. In early 1858, for instance, Judah Benjamin regaled the Senate with a long-winded account of how the errors of *Somerset*, produced
by Mansfield's inability to withstand the "spirit of fanaticism," were ultimately corrected by the
"resplendent genius" Stowell (*Congressional Globe*, 35th Cong., 1st sess., 1067–72). How did
Stowell correct Mansfield? *Somerset* had held that a slave became free simply by virtue of leaving the legal domain in which his slave status had been formalized. Mansfield certainly implied,
if he did not say so directly, that once a slave left a slave territory that slave was henceforth forever free. Stowell insisted, by contrast, that the emancipatory effects of slave transit were not
necessarily permanent. Should a slave return voluntarily to slave territory he or she would return as a slave. The difference between the two cases is subtle, perhaps a little more subtle than
someone like Benjamin grasped. Stowell openly acknowledged that a "slave could not be taken
from this country in irons and carried back to the West Indies, to be restored to the dominion
of his master" (*The Slave, Grace*, 2 Haggard Admiralty 94 [1827], 106–7). To be sure, *Slave, Grace*
did at the very least mitigate some of *Somerset*'s wholesale castigation of the slave system. Stowell maintained Mansfield's "observations to the foundation of the whole system of slavery"
amounted to nothing more than dicta (127), and his opinion certainly limited the extent to
which freedom could be considered man's default condition. Nonetheless, *Slave, Grace* did nothing to alter the core contention of *Somerset:* that positive law was a prerequisite for slavery. In
discarding some of the moral reasoning that informed Mansfield's holding and in changing one
of that holding's practical effects, Stowell did little to challenge the holding itself. For more extended discussion on this point, see Finkelman, *Imperfect Union*, 181–284. See also Fehrenbacher, *"Dred Scott" Case*, 48–73, 397–99.

10. *Dred Scott v. Sandford* 60 US (19 Howard) 393 (1857), 624.

11. I have taken this passage from the report in the *Scot's Magazine* (43 [1772]: 298–99),
which provides a slightly more detailed record of Mansfield's opinion than the one printed in

the *English Reports.* I was alerted to this report by Davis, *Problem of Slavery in the Age of Revolution,* 476–77, n. 12.

12. [Anthony Benezet], *A Short Account of that Part of Africa, inhabited by Negroes . . .* , 2nd ed. (Philadelphia, 1762), qtd. in Davis, *Problem of Slavery in the Age of Revolution,* 317.

13. All references to Thoreau's essays will be to Henry David Thoreau, *Reform Papers,* ed. Wendell Glick (Princeton: Princeton University Press, 1973), and will be made in parentheses in the body of the chapter.

14. Qtd. in Cover, *Justice Accused,* 153.

15. William Lloyd Garrison, "Prospectus to the Liberator Volume VIII," *Liberator,* Dec. 12, 1837.

16. Henry C. Wright, "Ballot-box and Battle-field. To voters in the United States government," *Liberator,* Mar. 25, 1842. "The greatest wrong I could do to the cause of human freedom would be to violate [the "law of love"] to abolish slavery. By its violation the slave is a slave. Shall I violate it to relieve him? NEVER."

17. Ibid., Sept. 30, 1842.

18. Ibid.

19. For a discussion of Garrison's resistance to the compatibility of abolition and the state, see Wiecek, *Sources of Antislavery Constitutionalism,* 228–48.

20. This emphasis on voting and governmental agency, coupled with Mansfield's emphasis upon positive law, might lead us to believe that the principal enemy of freedom within this logic is statutory law and that other legal orders, such as the common law, might remain immune from the taint of slavery. As we will see later on, the statutory authority of democratic governments was subject to special scrutiny, but in this context it is important to remember it was far from the sole source of complaint. Garrison's universal emancipation required more than the simple rejection of statutory authority. A long-standing custom is no less a matter of the dominion of man, after all, than a recent statute. Nor did Mansfield understand his invocation of positive law in exclusively statutory terms. The most complete record of Mansfield's opinion carefully assimilates slavery's positivist origins into the broader legal realm of custom and precedent. In this report Mansfield follows his remark that slavery can only "take its rise from *positive* law" with the claim that "the origin of it can in no country or age be traced back to any other source: immemorial usage preserves the memory of positive law long after all traces of . . . its introduction are lost; and, in a case so odious as the condition of slaves, must be taken seriously" (*Scots Magazine,* 298–99). Insofar as "Mansfield's concept of positive law included 'immemorial usage,'" Davis notes, he "was not saying, as commonly interpreted, that slavery was so odious that it can only be supported by statutory law. He was simply maintaining that the character of slavery is such that the law must be 'taken seriously'" (Davis, *Problem of Slavery in the Age of Revolution,* 477, n. 13). It is hard to know whether this more complete report of Mansfield's opinion was accurate, and harder still to say how well it was known in antebellum America. But whatever the reason, American abolitionists tended to associate slavery not simply with statutory authority but with the whole of what Thoreau called "civil government." There is an indiscriminate quality to the abolitionist assault on the law: judges, executive officers, legislators, voters—all were appropriate targets.

21. For a slightly less aggressive reading of the relationship between slavery and government in "Resistance to Civil Government," see Barry Kritzberg, "Thoreau, Slavery, and Resistance to Civil Government," *Massachusetts Review* 30 (Winter 1984): 535–65.

22. Ralph Waldo Emerson, *Essays and Lectures* (New York: Library of America, 1983), 559.

23. Lawrence Buell, *The Environmental Imagination: Thoreau, Nature Writing, and the Formation of American Culture* (Cambridge, Mass.: Harvard University Press, 1995), 38.

24. See, e.g., Foner, *Free Soil, Free Labor, Free Men: The Ideology of the Republican Party before the Civil War* (1970; rpt., New York: Oxford University Press, 1992), 103–49; Perry, *Radical Abolitionism;* Wiecek, *Sources of Antislavery Constitutionalism;* Ronald G. Walters, *The Antislavery Appeal* (Baltimore: Johns Hopkins University Press, 1976); and Sewell, *Ballots for Freedom.*

25. Cf. Fredrickson, *Inner Civil War,* 184–87.

26. Cf. Rogin, *Subversive Genealogy,* 276–78.

27. See Ann Douglas, *The Feminization of American Culture* (New York: Knopf, 1977), 2–9, 297–309; Philip Fisher, *Hard Facts: Form and Setting in American Fiction* (New York: Oxford University Press, 1985), 87–127; Tompkins, *Sensational Designs,* 122–47; Thomas, *Cross Examinations,* 113–37; Karen Sanchez Eppler, *Touching Liberty: Abolition, Feminism, and the Politics of the Body* (Berkeley: University of California Press, 1993), 14–49; Gillian Brown, *Domestic Individualism: Imagining Self in Nineteenth-Century America* (Berkeley: University of California Press, 1990), 13–60; Lynn Wardley, "Relic, Fetish, Femmage: The Aesthetics of Sentiment in the Work of Stowe," *Yale Journal of Criticism* 5 (1992): 165–91; Joshua D. Bellin, "Up to Heaven's Gate, Down in Earth's Dust: The Politics of Judgment in *Uncle Tom's Cabin,*" *American Literature* 65 (1993): 275–95; Marianne Noble, "The Ecstasies of Sentimental Wounding in *Uncle Tom's Cabin,*" *Yale Journal of Criticism* 10 (1997): 295–320; Lora Romero, *Home Fronts: Domesticity and Its Critics in the Antebellum United States* (Durham: Duke University Press, 1997), 70–88; and Gregg D. Crane, *Race, Citizenship, and Law in American Literature* (Cambridge: Cambridge University Press, 2002), 56–86.

28. Thomas, *Cross-Examinations,* 130.

29. Crane, "Dangerous Sentiments: Sympathy, Rights, and Revolution in Stowe's Antislavery Novels," *Nineteenth Century Literature* (1996): 182. While I share Crane's interest in locating Stowe's representations of slavery and sentiment in the context of a particularly legal crisis in antebellum America, I dispute his suggestion that once we place Stowe's within the history of natural rights thinking we will understand her commitment to sentiment to be a legal strategy rather than an expression of a strategy to avoid the legal. For Crane locating Stowe's sentimentalism in a legal context allows us to see the extent to which the novel means to function within the legal domain that sometimes seems the object of its polemic. For me it allows us to see why the novel wishes to depart from that legal domain. And hence, if Crane complains that Stowe's readers have read her "as though [she] were castigating the legal system of slavery from an anarchist position" (182), I will complain that they have tended not to realize the extent of her anarchism. Just as I differ with Crane about the status of law in Stowe's work, I also differ with him about the relationship between law and the racial segregation *Uncle Tom's Cabin* often seems to accept. Whereas Crane understands Stowe's inability to fashion sentiment into a coherent jurisprudence to result from her "inability to imagine natural rights fully as the moral consensus and fundamental entitlement of a racially diverse community" (181), I will suggest in the next chapter that the causality in fact works the other way—that her inability to imagine a racially diverse community is a result of her willed refusal to fashion a civil order out of her sentimental commitments.

30. "Nor will . . . God hold them guiltless who, with the elective franchise in their hands,

and the full power to speak, write and discuss, suffer this monstrous system of legalized cruelty to go one from age to age" (*A Key to Uncle Tom's Cabin* [Boston: J. P. Jewett and Co., 1853], 115).

31. Orlando Patterson, *Slavery and Social Death: A Comparative Study* (Cambridge, Mass.: Harvard University Press, 1982), 13, 22.

32. Brook Thomas has astutely noted that the sentiment that Stowe places in opposition to the workings and law of slavery was actually understood by some antebellum jurists to be an integral component of those workings and that law. See Thomas, *Cross Examinations*, 115–16; and Mark Tushnet, *The American Law of Slavery, 1810–1860* (Princeton: Princeton University Press, 1981), 11–43.

33. As George puts it in his conversation with Mr. Wilson: "Look at my face,—look at my hands,—look at my body . . . ; why am I *not* a man, as much as anybody?" (159).

34. Critics have claimed both that the body is central to Stowe's conception of personhood (Romero, *Home Fronts*, 82–83) and that the body is irrelevant to that conception (Karen Sanchez-Eppler, *Touching Liberty: Abolition, Feminism, and the Politics of the Body* [Berkeley: University of California Press, 1993], 113). My point is merely that in *Uncle Tom's Cabin* neither the radical identification of persons with their bodies nor the radical disarticulation of personal identity from its biological forms leads in the end to anything that can plausibly count as the liberation of the person from slavery.

35. For accounts of the "power" of Stowe's sentimentalism in the context of abolition efforts, see Tompkins, *Sensational Designs*, 132–35, 139–46; and Brown, *Domestic Individualism*, 13–38; for more skeptical accounts of this power and her commitment to radical politics, see Douglas, *Feminization of American Culture*, 297–309, Romero, *Home Fronts*, 81–89; and Joan D. Hedrick, *Harriet Beecher Stowe: A Life* (New York: Oxford University Press, 1994), 251–52. See also Lauren Berlant, "Poor Eliza," *American Literature* 70 (1998): 635–68.

36. Stowe's tendency to represent liberty in terms of passivity might initially look somewhat odd, but it is worth noting that this connection between freedom and the loss of agency actually has a pretty strong pedigree within the tradition of Anglo-American liberalism. Steven Knapp has suggested, for instance, that on Locke's account of "liberal agency" "settling on any particular option can look more like the betrayal of freedom than its fulfillment" and that consequently "the purest expression of freedom would seem to be the capacity to refrain from deciding [or acting] at all" (*Literary Interest: The Limits of Antiformalism* [Cambridge, Mass.: Harvard University Press, 1993], 103).

37. Philip Fisher, *Hard Facts*, 108, 107.

38. In describing the sentimental as a rhetorical strategy available for selection by interested agents, I am obviously departing from some of the most powerful recent accounts of sentimentalism, most especially those of Lauren Berlant, "Poor Eliza," *American Literature* 70 (1998): 635–68; Lori Merish (*Sentimental Materialism: Gender, Commodity Culture, and Nineteenth-Century American Literature* [Durham: Duke University Press, 2000]); and Glenn Hendler, *Public Sentiments: Structures of Feeling in Nineteenth-Century Literature* [Chapel Hill: University of North Carolina Press, 2001). For Berlant, Merish, and Handler sentiment is a normative cultural force, not a rhetorical or philosophical stance available to subjects within a culture.

39. This is not say to say that sentimentalism could not be used as a weapon in the fight against slavery, nor is it to say that sentimentalism was not the instrument that ultimately

brought about emancipation. Although I have severe reservations about Berlant's claim that American identity itself was ultimately produced as a structure of affect (the nation made a "state of feeling") by the power of nineteenth-century sentimentalist poetics, for the present purposes I am less interested in making claims about the political consequences of the invocation of sentimentalism in texts such as *Uncle Tom's Cabin* than the jurisprudential reasons sentimentalism would be appealing to their authors in the first instance. See Berlant, "Poor Eliza."

40. Sometimes this tension is understood in terms of the novel's celebration of nonviolence and its producing accounts which would seem to inspire violent and revolutionary responses (see, e.g., Thomas, *Cross Examinations*, 113–25; Crane, "Dangerous Sentiments," 194–204; and Bellin, "Up to Heaven's Gate," 275–83). On my account Stowe is less interested in violence than action—or to put it slightly differently, Stowe refuses to distinguish between violence and action. And consequently her concern is less with the dangers of revolutionary politics than with the dangers of politics as such.

41. Bellin, "Up to Heaven's Gate," 282–91; Crane, "Dangerous Sentiments," 183.

42. See Tompkins, *Sensational Designs*, 132–33; and Brown, *Domestic Individualism*, 40–41.

43. In contrast to the reading I am putting forth, Gillian Brown reads *Uncle Tom's Cabin* as an expression of an "activist feminine program for abolition." Her example of the way in which the feminine might be active, however, works less to reveal the "activist" authority of women than the attenuated nature of the authority they wield: "the most brutal man cannot live in constant association with a strong female influence, and not be greatly controlled by it" (qtd. in Brown, *Domestic Individualism*, 36). Here the actual woman herself disappears behind the authority of her powers of "association," and, likewise, what "controls" men at the moment of abolition is not some other person but rather a generalized "influence." For women to "exploit" their authority in *Uncle Tom's Cabin* is for them to dissipate themselves (36). Marianne Noble claims that "political transformation through feelings was precisely the reaction that sentimental authors sought to provoke" ("Ecstasies of Sentimental Wounding," 295). This claim remains true only so long as we stress the ambivalence implicit in *provoke*—so long, that is, as we understand *provoke* to be in some meaningful way opposed to *effect*—and only so long as we understand the political transformation in question to be less a transformation of the political domain than of the relevance of that domain to the persons who might live within it.

44. Cf. Noble, "Ecstasies of Sentimental Wounding," 295–320.

45. Hedrick, *Harriet Beecher Stowe*, 235.

46. All future references to William Wells Brown, *Clotel; or, The President's Daughter: A Narrative of Slave Life in the United States*, ed. Robert S. Levine (1853; rpt., Boston: Bedford, 2000), will appear in parentheses in the body of the chapter.

47. We have already encountered a number of these readings with respect to *Uncle Tom's Cabin*. See, e.g., Thomas, *Cross Examinations*, 113–25; Bellin, "Up to Heaven's Gate," 275–83; and Crane, "Dangerous Sentiments," 194–204.

48. All references to Harriet Beecher Stowe, *Dred: A Tale of the Dismal Swamp* (1856; rpt., New York: Penguin, 2000), will appear in parentheses in the body of the chapter.

49. See, e.g., Hedrick, *Harriet Beecher Stowe*, 234–36.

50. *Liberator*, July 21, 1854.

51. The tradition would also include works such as Martin Delany's *Blake; or, The Huts of Africa* (1861), Thoreau's John Brown essays, and Frederick Douglass's "The Heroic Slave" (1853).

The best discussion of this tradition is Robert S. Levine, *Martin Delany, Frederick Douglass, and the Politics of Representative Identity* (Chapel Hill: University of North Carolina Press, 1997), esp. 82–85, 144–223.

52. See, e.g., Guilia M. Fabi, "The 'Unguarded Expressions of the Feelings of Negroes': Gender, Slaver Resistance, and William Wells Brown's Revisions of *Clotel,*" *African American Review* 27 (Winter 1993): 639–54; Peter A. Dorsey, "De-Authorizing Slavery: Realism in Stowe's *Uncle Tom's Cabin* and Brown's *Clotel,*" *ESQ* 41 (1995): 256–88; Werner Sollors, "A British Mercenary and American Abolitionists: Literary Retellings from 'Inkle and Yarico' and John Gabriel Stedman to Lydia Maria Child and William Wells Brown," in *Formations of Cultural Identity in the English Speaking World,* ed. Jochen Achilles and Carmen Birkle (Heidelberg: Carl Winter Universitatsverlag, 1998), 95–123; and Lee Schweninger, "*Clotel* and the Historicity of the Anecdote," *Melus* 24 (Spring 1999): 21–36.

53. Robert Reid-Pharr, *Conjugal Union: The Body, the House, and the Black American* (New York: Oxford University Press, 1999), 38. For Reid-Pharr the novel's interest lies in Brown's "meditation on the tragedy and promise of American republicanism, tragedy and promise that . . . are immediately apparent in the distinctly American, distinctly hybrid body of the mulatto" (38). For other accounts of the significance of racial hybridity in *Clotel,* see Paul Gilmore, "'De Genewine Artekil': William Wells Brown, Blackface Minstrelsy, and Abolitionism," *American Literature* 69 (Dec. 1997): 743–80; and Adeleke Adeeko, "Signatures of Blood in William Wells Brown's *Clotel,*" *Nineteenth Century Contexts* 21 (1999): 115–34.

54. See, e.g., Elisa Tamarkin, "Black Anglophilia; Or, the Sociability of Antislavery," *American Literary History* 14 (Fall 2002): 444–78, and the sources cited therein. Unlike Tamarkin, I think this Anglophilia is more a matter of polemic than sociability.

55. References to *Running a Thousand Miles for Freedom,* as well as references to *Narrative of the Life of Frederick Douglass* and *Narratives of William W. Brown,* will be to the editions in, *Slave Narratives,* ed. Henry Louis Gates Jr. (New York: Library of America, 2000).

56. *Liberator,* Dec. 29, 1932.

57. Garrison, "An Address to the American Colonization Society," in *Selections from the Writings and Speeches of William Lloyd Garrison* (Boston: R. F. Walcut, 1852), 45.

58. James Boswell, *The Life of Samuel Johnson, LL. D.* (1787), qtd. in David Brion Davis, *The Problem of Slavery in Western Culture* (Ithaca: Cornell University Press, 1966), 3.

59. Edmund Morgan, *American Freedom, American Slavery: The Ordeal of Colonial Virginia* (New York: Norton, 1975).

60. Abraham Lincoln, *Speeches and Writings,* ed. Don E. Fehrenbacher (New York: Library of America, 1989), 2 vols., 1:398; hereafter cited in parentheses in the body of the chapter.

61. For another account of Jefferson's role in the novel, see Ann duCille, "Where in the World Is William Wells Brown? Thomas Jefferson, Sally Hennings, and the DNA of African-American Literary History," *American Literary History* 12 (Fall 2000): 443–62.

62. Cf. Ryan Simmons, "Naming Names: *Clotel* and *Behind the Scenes,*" *CLA Journal* 43 (Sept. 1999): 19–37.

63. For a brilliant discussion of the import of antebellum black invocations of Revolutionary ideals, see Eric J. Sundquist, "Slavery, Revolution, and the American Renaissance," in *The American Renaissance Reconsidered,* ed. Walter Benn Michaels and Donald Pease (Baltimore: Johns Hopkins University Press, 1982), 1–33.

64. David Herbert Donald, *Charles Sumner and the Rights of Man* (New York: Knopf, 1970), 208.

65. *Dred Scott v. Sandford*, 410.

66. Harry V. Jaffa, *Crisis of the House Divided: An Interpretation of the Issues in the Lincoln-Douglas Debates* (New York: Doubleday, 1959). See also, Jaffa, *New Birth of Freedom: Abraham Lincoln and the Coming of the Civil War* (New York: Rowman and Littlefield, 2000).

67. Davis is reluctant ever to let liberty interests sustain a separate viable standing in the defenses of slavery. Hence, sentences such as "The defense of slavery, or even of slave trading, could easily be conflated with a defense of liberty and public order" (*Problem of Slavery in the Age of Revolution*, 260). My first point is that such a defense of slavery did not have to be *conflated* with a defense of liberty; it could be seen as an extension of it. And my second point is that the invocation of freedom in the context of the defense of slavery was in no way required in recourse to the realm of such practical considerations as the "public order."

68. For another account of Brown's attitudes toward the state's role in moral instruction, see Robert S. Levine, "'Whiskey, Blacking, and All': Temperance and Race in William Wells Brown's *Clotel*," in *The Serpent in the Cup: Temperance in American Literature*, ed. David S. Reynolds and Debra J. Rosenthal (Amherst: University of Massachusetts Press, 1997), 93–114.

69. For another, and slightly different, take on this sequence's significance, see Christopher Mulvey, "The Fugitive Self and the New World of the North: William Wells Brown's Discovery of America," in *The Black Columbiad: Defining Moments in African American Literature and Culture*, ed. Werner Sollors and Maria Diedrich (Cambridge, Mass: Harvard University Press, 1994), 99–111.

70. The literature covering Douglass's relationship to manhood is at this point voluminous, not to say exhaustive. See, in particular, Houston A. Baker Jr., *The Journey Back: Issues in Black Literature and Criticism* (Chicago: University of Chicago Press, 1980), 32–47; William J. Andrews, *To Tell a Free Story: The First Century of Afro-American Autobiography* (Urbana: University of Illinois Press, 1986), 214–39; Joseph Fichtenberg, *Faith and Method in American Autobiography* (Philadelphia: University of Pennsylvania Press, 1989), 116–61; Stephanie A. Smith, "Heart Attacks: Frederick Douglass's Strategic Sentimentality," *Criticism* 34 (1992): 193–216; Wald, *Constituting Americans*, 14–105; Russ Castronovo, *Fathering the Nation: American Genealogies of Slavery and Freedom* (Berkeley: University of California Press, 1995), 194–99; Levine, *Delany, Douglass*, 99–143; Ann Fabian, *The Unvarnished Truth: Personal Narratives in Nineteenth-Century America* (Berkeley: University of California Press, 2000), 79–116; and Hartman, *Scenes of Subjection*, 17–112, 115–124.

71. Cf. Wald's claim that this sequence indicates the "fragility of [Douglass's] identity and the importance of a name" (*Constituting Americans*, 85).

72. For a discussion of this form of judgment in antislavery religious and legal discourse, see Crane, *Race, Citizenship, and Law*, 56–86.

Chapter Three • Constitutional Disobedience

1. Harriet Beecher Stowe, *Dred: A Tale of the Great Dismal Swamp* (1856; rpt., New York: Penguin, 2000), 460.

2. All references to Thoreau's essays will be to Henry David Thoreau, *Reform Papers*, ed.

Wendell Glick (Princeton: Princeton University Press, 1973), and will be made in parentheses in the body of the chapter.

3. Martin R. Delany, *Blake; or, The Huts of America, a Novel* (1861–62; rpt., Boston: Beacon, 1970), 39. If Delany's account of natural freedom seems slightly casual, it may well be because he does not really think that it is necessary. Religion frequently appears in *Blake* in the mode of an instrument, a political tool, not a foundational set of beliefs. (See, e.g., Henry's response to Mammy Judy: "Don't talk to me of religion! What's religion to me? . . . Put my trust in the Lord! I've done so all my life nearly, and of what use is it to me?" [16]). And in this regard it is telling that Delany invokes God's presence in nature with respect not only to the *right* of revolution but also to the "scheme" and "plan" Henry hopes to implement (39). Floyd J. Miller reminds us in his introduction to the Beacon edition of *Blake* that Delany treats religion with, at best, "a certain amount of ambivalence" (xxiv). Even if Delany does not believe that God's explicit endorsement was necessary for the slave revolution, however, he certainly posits that others would believe as much.

4. Ralph Waldo Emerson, "Address on the Emancipation of the British West Indies" (1844), in *Emerson's Antislavery Writings*, ed. Len Gougeon and Joel Myerson (New Haven: Yale University Press, 1995), 7.

5. See Lewis Perry, *Radical Abolitionism: Anarchy and the Government of God in Antislavery Thought* (Ithaca: Cornell University Press, 1973), 18–92.

6. For other examinations of Thoreau's interest in law, see Robert C. Albrecht, "Conflict and Resolution: 'Slavery in Massachusetts,'" *ESQ* 72 (1973): 179–88; Carl S. Smith, "Law as Form and Theme in American Letters: An Essay in Law and American Literature," in *Law and Literature: A Collection of Essays*, ed. Carl S. Smith, John P. McWilliams, and Maxwell Bloomfield (New York: Knopf, 1983), 1–44; Michael Mayer, "Civil Disobedience and the Problem of Thoreau's 'Peaceable Revolution,'" in *Approaches to Teaching Thoreau's "Walden" and Other Works*, ed. Richard J. Schneider (New York: MLA, 1996), 150–54; and "Thoreau and Black Emigration," *American Literature* 53 (Nov. 1981): 380–86. For other examinations of Thoreau's treatment of slavery, see Barbara Ryan, "Emerson's 'Domestic and Social Experiments': Service, Slavery and the Unhired Man," *American Literature* 66 (Sept. 1994): 485–508; Barry Kritzberg, "Thoreau, Slavery, and Resistance to Civil Government," *Massachusetts Review* 30 (Winter 1984): 535–65.

7. All references to *Dred Scott v. Sandford* 60 US (19 Howard) 393 (1857) will be made in parentheses in the body of the chapter.

8. William M. Wiecek, *The Sources of Antislavery Constitutionalism in America, 1760–1848* (Ithaca: Cornell University Press, 1977), 239–40.

9. David M. Potter, *The Impending Crisis, 1848–1861*, completed and ed. Don E. Fehrenbacher (New York: Harper and Row, 1976), 130

10. See Potter, *Impending Crisis*, 130–44.

11. See, most prominently, Avery Craven, *The Coming of the Civil War* (1942; rpt., Chicago: University of Chicago Press, 1957).

12. Abraham Lincoln, *Speeches and Writings* (New York: Library of America, 1989), 2 vols., 2:128; hereafter cited in parentheses in the body of the chapter.

13. See Fehrenbacher, *"Dred Scott" Case*, 45–47, 123–26, 133–40, 142–60; and William W. Freehling, *The Road to Disunion: Secessionists at Bay, 1776–1854* (New York: Oxford University

Press, 1990), 211–566. Freehling maintains that this higher law doctrine had been percolating in Southern politics almost from the beginning of the Revolution.

14. See Potter, *Impending Crisis*, 138–39.

15. Alvan Stewart, "A Constitutional Argument on the Subject of Slavery" (1837), in Jacobus tenBroek, *Equal under Law* (New York: Collier, 1965), 286–87; hereafter cited in parentheses in the body of the chapter.

16. Stewart relied upon two highly dubious assumptions, one historical, the other doctrinal. The historical claim was that the Fifth Amendment's due process clause was actually a result of a compromise between the South and the North: "The men of the free states being made partakers in the crime of slavery, out of courtesy, might firmly, as they truly did, insist that the Constitution should contain the only mould in which slaves should be run, and if they were not made in that mould, with all its forms, they could not exist" (ibid., 285). The doctrinal claim was that the Fifth Amendment applied to the laws of states as well as Congress (the Supreme Court had specifically rebuffed this position in *Barron v. Baltimore* [1833] only a few years before Stewart produced his essay). As Robert M. Cover has explained, Stewart's argument "requires nothing more than a suspension of reason concerning the origin, intent, and past interpretation of the" Fifth Amendment (*Justice Accused: Antislavery and the Judicial Process* [New Haven: Yale University Press, 1975], 157).

17. Cf. Thomas R. R. Cobb, *An Inquiry into the Law of Negro Slavery in the United States of America* (Philadelphia: T. and J. W. Johnson and Co., 1858).

18. Potter, *Impending Crisis*, 130–31. Another of the "gratuitously obnoxious provisions" he mentions—the act's prescribing a larger payment to a presiding justice when an alleged fugitive was ruled a slave than when he was determined to be free—probably was gratuitously obnoxious.

19. Harold M. Hyman and William M. Wiecek, *Equal Justice under Law: Constitutional Development, 1835–1875* (New York: Harper and Row, 1982), 149.

20. Charles Sumner, *The Works of Charles Sumner* (Boston: Lee and Shepard, 1870–83), 15 vols., 3:189; hereafter cited in parentheses in the body of the chapter.

21. Wendell Phillips produced perhaps the most important version of this attack in his "The Philosophy of the Abolitionist Movement" (1853), in *Speeches, Lectures, and Letters* (1868; rpt., Boston: Lee and Shepard, 1902). From Phillips's perspective Sumner's efforts to undo the Compromise of 1850 were "very mistaken" because the "battle" of abolitionists "lasts while [slavery] exists anywhere." Merely fighting for the federal government to withdraw from the enforcement of slavery was not to be "enlisted for the whole war" (142).

22. He would deal with state slave proceedings in a later case, *Ableman v. Booth* (62 US [21 Howard] 506 [1858]), and figures such as Abraham Lincoln understood the "slave power" largely in terms of a fear that he would eventually do the same kind of work with respect to proceedings in free states. See Paul Finkelman, *An Imperfect Union: Slavery, Federalism, and Comity* (Chapel Hill: University of North Carolina Press, 1981), 313–43.

23. See Priscilla Wald, *Constituting Americans: Cultural Anxiety and Narrative Form* (Durham: Duke University Press, 1995), 20–24, 40–63, for a discussion of some the cultural implications of this finding.

24. For formulations of these lines of criticism, see Fehrenbacher, *"Dred Scott" Case*, 335–

88, and the sources cited therein; and David P. Currie, *The Constitution in the Supreme Court: The First Hundred Years, 1789–1888* (Chicago: University of Chicago Press, 1985), 263–72, and the sources cited therein.

25. Fehrenbacher, *"Dred Scott" Case*, 360. See also Gregg D. Crane, *Race, Citizenship, and Law in American Literature* (Cambridge: Cambridge University Press, 2002), 152–53.

26. For another account of the ways in which the invocation of natural law could reinforce rather than challenge the slave regime, see Eric J. Sundquist, *To Wake the Nations: Race in the Making of American Literature* (Cambridge, Mass.: Harvard University Press, 1993), 163–82.

27. Fehrenbacher, *"Dred Scott" Case*, 351.The earliest commentary on this point appeared almost immediately on the case's heels, in W. A. Leonard's essay "Negro Citizenship," *New Englander* 15 (Aug. 1857): 345–65, 478–526.

28. Harriet Beecher Stowe, *Uncle Tom's Cabin* (1852; rpt., New York: Modern Library, 1996), 158–59.

29. See Fehrenbacher, *"Dred Scott" Case*, 434–52. Taney does not merely insist that African Americans have no civil standing in the United States. He also maintains that they have no civil standing anywhere else and that because they have no civil standing anywhere else they can *never* have civil standing in the United States. Taney is keen throughout his opinion to suggest that were states to have the authority to confer the right to sue in federal courts on their black citizens they would in effect assume the naturalization authority that the Constitution, at least as Taney would have it, exclusively vests in Congress. But he ultimately suggests not merely that states cannot naturalize Africans but also that Congress itself cannot. American naturalization law, he reasoned, only allowed the naturalization of foreigners (of figures such as, in George's terms, "the Irishman, the German, the Swede" [616]), and since slaves and slave descendants weren't actually citizens of some other nation, they weren't eligible for naturalization: "And this power granted to Congress to establish an uniform rule of *naturalization* is, by well-understood meaning of the word, confined to persons born in a foreign country, under a foreign government. It is not a power to raise to the rank of a citizen any one born in the United States, who, from birth or parentage, by the laws of the country, belongs to an inferior and subordinate class" (417).

"What this meant, though Taney never explicitly said so," Fehrenbacher somewhat melodramatically explains, "was that *American Negroes, free and slave, were the only people on the face of the earth who (saving a constitutional amendment) were forever ineligible for American citizenship*" (357). Since as George puts it, "African *nationality*" still remains to be "develop[ed]" (614, 615), it is perfectly appropriate for Taney's "subordinate class" of persons who are citizens of no place at all. George says that he does "*not want*" American citizenship; he wants "a country, a nation, of [his] own" (616). Taney suggests that insofar as that country of his own is undeveloped, George cannot have American citizenship whether he wants it or not. What he can have instead counts for freedom in *Uncle Tom's Cabin* and guarantees slavery in *Dred Scott*. It keeps George from being "owned" by the law and keeps open the possibility that he will be owned by someone else.

30. See, e.g., Marion J. Russell, "American Slave Discontent in Records of High Courts," *Journal of Negro History* 31 (1946): 418–19.

31. Currie, *First Hundred Years*, 271.

32. *American Insurance Company v. Canter* 26 US (1 Pet.) 511 (1828), 546.

33. For an alternative reading, one that emphasizes Taney's "deference to power" rather than his efforts to dissolve that power before a mystified and abstracted notion of natural right, see Crane, *Race, Citizenship, and Law,* 152.

34. See *Dorr v. US* 195 US 138, 146–49 (1904).

35. Carl Brent Swisher, *The Taney Period, 1836–64,* vol. 5 of the *Oliver Wendell Holmes Devise History of the Supreme Court of the United States* (New York: Macmillan, 1974), 508.

36. Fehrenbacher, *"Dred Scott" Case,* 384. Potter and Corwin think otherwise and think that the due process claim was a central feature of Taney's argument. See Potter, *Impending Crisis,* 276–77; Edward S. Corwin, "The Doctrine of Due Process of Law before the Civil War," *Harvard Law Review* 24 (1911): 366–85, 460–79.

37. Don E. Fehrenbacher, *Prelude to Greatness: Lincoln in the 1850s* (Stanford: Stanford University Press, 1962), 122.

38. Fehrenbacher, *Prelude,* 121.

39. See Potter, *Impending Crisis,* 333–40.

40. Jefferson Davis, *Jefferson Davis, Constitutionalist: His Letters, Papers, and Speeches,* ed. Dunbar Rowland, 10 vols. (Jackson: Mississippi Dept. of Archives and History, 1923), 3:284–332. In the face of Democratic fire over the Freeport doctrine, Douglas himself frequently cited Davis's remarks.

41. Potter, *Impending Crisis,* 338.

42. I cite the versions of Douglas's remarks in the Lincoln-Douglas debates included in Lincoln's *Speeches and Writings.*

43. Davis, *Papers,* 3:332.

44. Ibid., 3:344–45.

45. Fehrenbacher, *"Dred Scott" Case,* 500–501.

46. References to Herman Melville, *Battle-Pieces and Aspects of the War* (1866; rpt., New York: Da Capo, 1995), will appear in parentheses in the body of the chapter.

47. See George Fredrickson, *The Inner Civil War: Northern Intellectuals and the Crisis of the Union* (New York: Harper and Row, 1965), 189–98.

48. In a passage from his "Supplement" which I quoted in the first chapter, Melville includes himself among "those of us who always abhorred slavery as an atheistical iniquity" and who "gladly . . . join in the exulting chorus of humanity over its downfall" (268)—note that it is an "atheistical iniquity," not an unlawful one.

49. See Michael Paul Rogin, *Subversive Genealogy: The Politics and Art of Herman Melville* (New York: Random House, 1983), 267–78; Carolyn Karcher, *Shadow over the Promised Land: Slavery, Race, and Violence in Herman Melville's America* (Baton Rouge: Louisiana State University Press, 1980), 258–307.

50. Herman Melville, *The Complete Stories of Herman Melville,* ed. Jay Leyda (New York: Random House, 1949), 352.

51. Ibid., 295.

52. For more on the way racialism and the law operate in *Benito Cereno,* see Sundquist, *To Wake the Nations,* 154–82.

53. Cf. Rogin, *Subversive Genealogies,* 275.

54. Qtd. in Akhil Reed Amar, *The Bill of Rights: Creation and Reconstruction* (New Haven: Yale University Press, 1998), 187.

55. For an account of the ways in which Emerson worked through a similar set of problematics, see Eduardo Cadava, *Emerson and the Climates of History* (Stanford: Stanford University Press, 1997).

56. For accounts of the larger context in which Thoreau produced these pieces, see Robert C. Albrecht, "Thoreau and His Audience: 'A Plea for Captain John Brown,'" *American Literature* 32 (Jan. 1961): 393–402; and Michael Meyer, "Thoreau's Rescue of John Brown from History," *Studies in the American Renaissance* (1980): 301–16.

57. Sharon Cameron, *Writing Nature: Henry Thoreau's Journal* (New York: Oxford University Press, 1985), 12, 75, 23, 24.

58. Stanley Cavell, *The Senses of Walden* (New York: Viking, 1972), 53–54.

59. Lawrence Buell, *The Environmental Imagination: Thoreau, Nature Writing, and the Formation of American Culture* (Cambridge, Mass.: Harvard University Press, 1995), 169.

60. Cameron, *Writing Nature*, 89.

61. The classic discussion of Chase's legal and political philosophy is Eric Foner, *Free Soil, Free Labor, Free Men: The Ideology of the Republican Party before the Civil War* (1970; rpt., New York: Oxford University Press, 1995), 73–102. See also Richard H. Sewell, *Ballots for Freedom: Antislavery Politics in the United States, 1837–1860* (New York: Oxford University Press, 1976), 149–53, 219–22.

62. For a discussion of the local circumstances in which the address was drafted and delivered, see David Herbert Donald, *Charles Sumner and the Coming of the Civil War* (New York: Knopf, 1960), 224–37.

63. Glenn C. Loury, *The Anatomy of Racial Inequality* (Cambridge, Mass.: Harvard University Press, 2002), 120.

64. Fehrenbacher, *"Dred Scott" Case*, 44.

65. For good discussions of the legal issues at stake in *Prigg*, see ibid., 43–54; and Finkelman, *Imperfect Union*, 126–45, 313–44.

66. As Fehrenbacher suggests when he says that Story's majority opinion "coolly ignored . . . the argument from counsel for Pennsylvania that the law of 1793, in certain of its provisions, violated personal rights guaranteed by the privileges-and-immunities clause, by the Fourth Amendment, and by the due-process clause of the Fifth Amendment" (*"Dred Scott" Case*, 44).

67. As Sumner contends by way of evidence from a recently published biography of Story which maintained that Story would have "still considered" the question of the constitutionality of the Act of 1793 "an open one" (Sumner, *Works*, 3:146).

68. There are moments in which Sumner seems to make claims like those we have seen developed by Garrison, as, for instance, when he quotes Algernon Sidney's remarks on the eve of his execution: "I value not my own life a chip; but what concerns me is, that *the law* which takes away my life may hang every one of you, whenever it is thought convenient" (ibid., 3:143). But Sumner is less horrified that "*the law*" might have this power than he is that the state might misuse it: the power he fears is not the power to hang; it is the power to hang "whenever it is thought convenient." And so he follows this complaint about the power of the law with a two-page-long complaint that the Fugitive Slave Act does not provide adequate procedural safeguards (3:143–45).

69. Samuel Adams, qtd. in ibid., 3:170.

70. Phillips, "Philosophy of the Antislavery Movement," 142.

Chapter Four • Legal Sentences

1. Henry David Thoreau, "Slavery in Massachusetts," in *Reform Papers*, ed. Wendell Glick (Princeton: Princeton University Press, 1973), 98; hereafter cited in parentheses in the body of the chapter.

2. See Judith Butler, *Excitable Speech: A Politics of the Performative* (New York: Routledge, 1997), 77–101.

3. *The Works of Charles Sumner*, 15 vols. (Boston: Lee and Shepard, 1870–83), 3:186–87.

4. *Prigg v. Pennsylvania* 41 US (16 Peters) 539 (1842), 613, 612, 614.

5. Thomas Gustafson has usefully cataloged the variety of ways in which American culture was beset by linguistic difficulty in the 1840s and 1850s. I mean to make a considerably narrower point about the particular difficulties surrounding the efficacy of legal language in the period. See Gustafson, *Representative Words: Politics, Literature, and the American Language* (Cambridge: Cambridge University Press, 1992), 1–15, 301–47. His discussion of linguistic sovereignty is especially suggestive (372–95).

6. All references to Nathaniel Hawthorne, *The Scarlet Letter* (1850; rpt., Columbus: Ohio State University Press, 1962), will appear in parentheses in the body of the chapter.

7. All references to Hawthorne's short fiction will be to the versions printed in Nathaniel Hawthorne, *Tales and Sketches* (New York: Library of America, 1982).

8. See, e.g., Jean Fagan Yellin, "Hawthorne and the American National Sin," in *The Great American Tradition: Essays and Poems for Sherman Paul*, ed. Daniel H. Peck (Baton Rouge: Louisiana State University Press, 1989), 75–97; Yellin, "Hawthorne and the Slavery Question," in *A Historical Guide to Nathaniel Hawthorne*, ed. Larry J. Reynolds (Oxford: Oxford University Press, 2001), 135–64; Jennifer Fleishner, "Hawthorne and the Politics of Slavery," *Studies in the Novel* 23 (Spring 1991): 96–106; Deborah L. Madsen, "A Is for Abolition: Hawthorne's Bond Servant and the Shadows of Slavery," *Journal of American Studies* 25 (Aug. 1991): 255–59; Jay Grossman, " 'A' Is for Abolition? Race, Authorship, and *The Scarlet Letter*," *Textual Practice* 7 (Spring 1993): 13–30; Leland S. Person, "The Dark Labyrinth of Mind: Hawthorne, Hester, and the Ironies of Racial Mothering," *Studies in American Fiction* 29 (Spring 2001): 33–48.

9. All references to Lysander Spooner, *The Unconstitutionality of Slavery*, vol. 3 in *The Collected Works of Lysander Spooner*, 5 vols. (Boston: Bela Marsh, 1860), will appear in parentheses in the body of the chapter.

10. Wendell Phillips, *A Review of Lysander Spooner's "Unconstitutionality of Slavery"* (1847). For accounts of these various works, see Jacobus tenBroek, *The Antislavery Origins of the Fourteenth Amendment* (Berkeley: University of California Press, 1951), 66–94; Aileen S. Kraditor, *Means and Ends in American Abolitionism: Garrison and His Critics on Strategy and Tactics, 1834–1850* (New York: Pantheon, 1969), 186–95; William M. Wiecek, *The Guarantee Clause of the U.S. Constitution* (Ithaca: Cornell University Press, 1972), 159–65; and *The Sources of Antislavery Constitutionalism, 1870–1848* (Ithaca: Cornell University Press, 1977); Richard Sewell, *Ballots for Freedom: Antislavery Politics in the United States, 1837–1860* (New York: Oxford University Press, 1976), 88–95; Lawrence J. Friedman, *Gregarious Saints: Self and Community in American Abolitionism, 1830–1870* (Cambridge: Cambridge University Press, 1983), 68–95; Earl M. Maltz, "Fourteenth Amendment Concepts in the Antebellum Era," *American Journal of Legal History*

32 (1988): 305–46; Richard L. Aynes, "On Misreading John Bingham and the Fourteenth Amendment," *Yale Law Journal* 103 (Oct. 1993): 57–104, 68–80; and John Stauffer, *The Black Hearts of Men: Radical Abolitionists and the Transformation of Race* (Cambridge, Mass.: Harvard University Press, 2002), 8–44, 135–81.

11. Joseph Story, *Commentaries on the Constitution of the United States* (Boston: Hilliard, Gray and Co., 1833), 157–58.

12. In dicta in *Strader v. Graham* Taney insisted that in determinations of the slave status of any person before them state courts were bound by neither the laws of other states (the question "depended altogether upon the law of the State" in which the proceeding was taking place "and could not be influenced by the laws" of any other state) nor, amazingly, the laws of the federal government ("The ordinance in question [the Northwest Ordinance, which forbade slavery in the Northwest territory], if still in force, could have no more operation than the laws of Ohio in the state of Kentucky") (51 US [10 How.] 82 [1851] 97). Presumably, states would have been bound by the Constitution itself, which, in its fugitive slave provisions, would have forbidden the emancipation of any fugitive (but not necessarily any domiciled slave). They would thus be less bound by claims of federal citizenship, which was subject to congressional regulation through the naturalization clause, than the Constitution's specific claims about slavery. It is certainly hard to imagine a Taney-led Court coming to any other conclusion.

13. For example: "To assert, therefore, that the constitution *intended* to sanction slavery, is, in reality, equivalent to asserting that the *necessary* meaning, the *unavoidable* import of the *words alone* of the constitution, come fully up to the point of a clear, definite, distinct, express, explicit, unequivocal, necessary and peremptory sanction of the specific thing, *human slavery, property in man.* . . . Now, who can, in good faith, say that the *words alone* of the constitution come up to this point? . . . Not even the name of the thing, alleged to be sanctioned, is given" (59).

14. He passes over the fact that the guarantee is extended to the states, not to the persons inhabiting them. It is for this reason that many thought that the point of the guarantee clause was to guarantee that the federal government would protect state governments from insurrections by their own citizens. Insofar as the clause's assurances are directed to the states themselves rather than the persons within them, it is unclear that they could be used as a way of changing state law rather than restoring it. From this perspective the Reconstruction Acts may have actually constituted a violation of the guarantee clause rather than an enforcement of it, as many Democrats were fond of pointing out in the late 1860s. See J. G. Randall, *Constitutional Problems under Lincoln* (New York: D. Appleton, 1926), 405–33.

15. Robert M. Cover, *Justice Accused: Antislavery and the Judicial Process* (New Haven: Yale University Press, 1975), 156.

16. Qtd. in Cover, *Justice Accused*, 157.

17. References to Alvan Stewart, "A Constitutional Argument on the Subject of Slavery" (1837), in Jacobus tenBroek, *Equal under Law* (New York: Collier, 1965), will be cited in parentheses in the body of the chapter.

18. *Barron v. Baltimore*, 32 US (7 Peters) 243 (1833), 247.

19. Stewart was hardly alone in his ignorance of or hostility to *Barron*. At various moments John Calhoun, Abraham Lincoln, and Stephen Douglas, among others, advanced arguments built around the notion that the Fifth Amendment applied to the states. In the next chapter we will see that many members of the Thirty-ninth Congress were simply astounded that the Bill

of Rights had no bearing on state legislation. Both Amar (*Bill of Rights*, 145–56) and Wiecek (*Origins*, 266–68) provide arguments for why so many antebellum legal thinkers were unaware of *Barron*.

20. *Barron v. Baltimore*, 250.

21. Amar, *Bill of Rights*, 144.

22. For an excellent defense of Marshall's opinion, see Amar, *Bill of Rights*, 140–45.

23. See James Madison, *Notes of Debates in the Federal Convention of 1878* (1840; rpt., Athens: University of Ohio Press, 1966).

24. Taney seems, somewhat implausibly, to have thought that the slave import clause constituted evidence that the Constitution "expressly affirm[s]" property rights in slaves. He follows his insistence that there is "express" constitutional recognition of slavery by noting "the right to traffic in it, like an ordinary article of merchandise and property, was guaranteed to the citizens of the United States" (*Dred Scott v. Sandford* 60 US [19 Howard] 393, 451–52). For Fehrenbacher's counterargument, see *The "Dred Scott" Case: Its Significance in American Law and Politics* (New York: Oxford University Press, 1978), 380–81.

25. References to Herman Melville, *Battle-Pieces and Aspects of the War* (1866; rpt., New York: Da Capo, 1995), will appear in parentheses in the body of the chapter.

26. Abraham Lincoln, *Speeches and Writings*, 2 vols. (New York: Library of America, 1989), 1:400; hereafter cited in parentheses in the body of the chapter.

27. It is along these lines that Garry Wills would eventually claim the chief result of the Civil War was to install the Declaration of Independence within operative machinery of American political institutions, to establish it "as a way of correcting the Constitution itself without overthrowing it" (*Lincoln at Gettysburg: The Words that Remade America* [New York: Simon and Schuster, 1992], 147). The origin of Wills's argument is Sumner's eulogy of Lincoln, "The Promises of the Declaration of Independence, and Abraham Lincoln" (*Works*, 9:367–428).

28. *Congressional Globe*, 39th Cong., 1st sess., 2459 (1866).

29. For discussions of the status of "declaratory" law in the practice of legal interpretation in antebellum America, see Amar, *Bill of Rights*, 147–56; tenBroek, *Equal under Law*, 126–31.

30. See Raoul Berger, *The Fourteenth Amendment and the Bill of Rights* (Norman: University of Oklahoma Press, 1989), 31–36.

31. *Congressional Globe*, 30th Cong., 1st sess., 950 (1848).

32. David M. Potter, *The Impending Crisis, 1848–1861*, completed and ed. Don E. Fehrenbacher (New York: Harper and Row, 1976), 116.

33. *Congressional Globe*, 33rd Cong., 1st sess., app. 231 (1854).

34. *Congressional Globe*, 34th Cong., 1st sess., 1093 (1856).

35. Cf. *Dorr v. US* 195 US 138, (1904).

36. Potter, *Impending Crisis*, 271.

37. Wallace Mendelson, "Dred Scott's Case—Reconsidered," *Minnesota Law Review* 38 (1953): 16.

38. Here is the aside: "And if Congress itself cannot do this [forbid slavery]—if it is beyond the powers conferred on the Federal Government—it will be admitted, we presume, that it could not authorize a territorial government to exercise them. It could confer no power on any local government, established by its authority, to violate the provisions of the Constitution" (451). It is easy enough to see why this pronouncement would hardly settle the matter. For one

thing, having nothing to do with the court's actual holding in the case, it is pure dictum. For another, it is at least possible to maintain, as Benjamin himself acknowledged, that territorial governments derived their authority to regulate slavery from the Constitution, or from the nature of democratic government, rather than from Congress. And further still, as we have already seen, "the provision of the Constitution" the territorial government might be violating in its regulation of slavery, the due process clause of the Fifth Amendment, was itself held as an established feature of constitutional doctrine not to limit the authority of any governmental body other than Congress. Taney's claim is indeed a "presum[ption]" based on hopes of what others might "admit[]," not a definitive argument.

39. In one of the case's many ironies he managed to avoid such obligations, in effect, by recurring to the uncertain status of the one question Congress seemed especially eager to put before the Court in the 1850s: do territorial legislatures have constitutional power to exclude slavery from their precincts? Douglas had no great interest in condemning Taney's opinion. He simply neutralized it. In his notorious *Harper's* essay from 1859 he maintained that territorial legislatures possessed police power authority over slavery as a matter of constitutional right; and that, short of that, Congress could confer legislative authority to territorial legislatures even if it could not itself exercise it. The narrow Clayton lawsuit became in effect a way of avoiding the implications of the judicial resolution that the broader version of that lawsuit had invited. Stephen A. Douglas, "The Dividing Line between Federal and Local Authority: Popular Sovereignty in the Territories" (1859), in, *In the Name of the People: Speeches and Writings of Lincoln and Douglas in the Ohio Campaign of 1859,* ed. Harry V. Jaffa and Robert W. Johannsen (Columbus: Ohio State University Press, 1959), 58–125.

40. Although there has been relatively little commentary about *Legends of the Province-House,* they play an important role in one of the truly classic works of Hawthorne criticism, Michael J. Colacurcio's magisterial *Province of Piety: Moral History in Hawthorne's Early Tales* (Cambridge, Mass.: Harvard University Press, 1984), 389–482, to which my reading is heavily indebted.

41. From the time of Henry James's *Hawthorne* (New York: Harper and Brothers, 1879) on, the critical history of *The Scarlet Letter* has largely been a history of assessments of how the novel represents and confronts plurality. James addresses the plurality in aesthetic terms, concerning himself with whether Hawthorne seeks "purity" or "harmony" (108, 114), as does Richard Chase in his account of the tension between *The Scarlet Letter*'s "unity" as "*a novel*" and Hawthorne's inability to "share" with his characters "their imperfect humanity" (*The American Novel and Its Tradition* [1957; rpt., Baltimore: Johns Hopkins University Press, 1980], 70, 68, 87). In D. H. Lawrence's reading of the novel as "a marvelous allegory" of "perfect duplicity," the plurality James sees "impregnate[ing]" (110) the novel's style becomes Hawthorne's chief ethical theme (*Studies in Classic American Literature* [New York: Albert and Charles Boni, 1930], 147). What Lawrence considers duplicity, F. O. Matthiessen considers "life"; and in *American Renaissance* Hawthorne's achievement is precisely to recognize "the mixed nature of life" and to find a mode of address appropriate to it, the "fertile" "device of multiple choice" (Matthiessen, *American Renaissance: Art and Expression in the Age of Emerson and Whitman* [New York: Oxford University Press, 1941], 254, 276). For Leslie Fiedler the novel's plurality results not from Hawthorne's insight but from his limitations, from his need to stifle the "passion" implicit in his story, a process that produces a "peculiar tension" between the novel's "passion analogues" and "the dispassionate quality of the actual text" (*Love and Death in the American Novel,* rev. ed. [1960; rpt.,

New York: Stein and Day, 1966], 229). R.W.B. Lewis gives the thematics of plurality a more precisely social or anthropological dimension in his account of the novel as an expression "of the inevitable doubleness in the tribal promise" (*American Adam: Innocence, Tragedy, and Tradition in the Nineteenth Century* [Chicago: University of Chicago Press, 1955], 111); while Nina Baym gives Lewis's "tribal promise" an explicitly feminist hue, noting that the "self-expression" that always represents "a threat to the community" must "necessarily" be especially "repress[ed]" in *The Scarlet Letter* because it proceeds from a "young and female" subject (*The Shape of Hawthorne's Career* [Ithaca: Cornell University Press, 1976], 141, 127]; and Michael Ragussis inverts the terms of the Lewis-Baym analysis by suggesting that self-expression is precisely the mechanism by which Puritan repression takes place ("Family Discourse and Fiction in *The Scarlet Letter*," *ELH* 49 [1982]: 863). Like Matthiessen, Richard Brodhead sees the novel's achievement precisely in its capacity to suspend several versions of its narrative without subordinating any one to another: "Thus he allows us to participate in both versions of his novel's experience, and also to frankly recognize each *as* a version. . . . He allows us to construct our own conclusion" (*Hawthorne, Melville, and the Novel* [Chicago: University of Chicago Press, 1973], 65, 68); but as we will see at the end of the chapter, Sacvan Bercovitch contends that this strategy of suspension is exactly how the novel prevents the "construction" of alternative conclusions: "Ambiguity is a function of prescriptiveness" (*The Office of the Letter* [Baltimore: Johns Hopkins University Press, 1991], 22). By recognizing legal agency's centrality to *The Scarlet Letter* we will begin to see why the novel has seemed both repressive and liberal, tolerant and puritanical.

42. Francis Lieber, *Legal Hermeneutics; or, Principles of Legal Interpretation and Construction in Law and Politics* (1839; rpt., St. Louis: F. H. Thomas, 1880), 110, 29, 170, 29, 110, 102, 119.

43. Lest it seem that I am making too much of this distinction between true sentences and true opinions, it is worth noting that Thoreau was operating in a legal climate in which antislavery jurists frequently stressed the difference between their "true opinions" about slavery and the legal opinions their offices obliged them to produce. Thoreau's rhetoric here almost directly tracks what had become a standard feature of a slavery adjudication in the 1830s and 1840s. Consider, for instance, these lines from Judge Bissell's dissent from a fugitive slave case in 1837: "As a citizen and as a man, I may admit the injustice and immorality of slavery; that its tendencies are all bad; that it is productive of evil, and of evil only. But as a jurist, I must look at that standard of morality, which the law prescribes" (*Jackson v. Bullock* [12 Conn. 39 (1837)]). Robert Cover provides an extensive compendium of such passages and a rigorous analysis of the "retreat to formalism" they represent in *Justice Accused*, 119–30.

44. See Colacurcio, *Province of Piety*, 406–23.

45. Bercovitch, *Office of the Letter*, xiii, xvi.

46. Lauren Berlant, *The Anatomy of National Fantasy: Hawthorne, Utopia, and Everyday Life* (Chicago: University or Chicago Press, 1991), 60; see also Charles Swann, *Nathaniel Hawthorne: Tradition and Revolution* (Cambridge: Cambridge University Press, 1991), 76–87.

Chapter Five • John Bingham's Poetic Constitution

1. Walt Whitman, "When Lilacs Last in the Dooryard Bloom'd," l. 71, in Whitman, *Leaves of Grass*, ed. Sculley Bradley and Harold W. Blodget (1965; rpt., New York: Norton, 1973), 332. Future references to "Lilacs" will be given by line number in parentheses in the body of the chap-

ter. Future references to other poems in *Leaves of Grass* will be given by page number in the body of the chapter.

2. This section closes *Drum-Taps* in the post-1881 editions of *Leaves of Grass*. In the 1871 and 1876 editions the four poems comprising "Memories of President Lincoln" were grouped together as "President Lincoln's Burial Hymn" in the "Passage to India" annex.

3. Whitman himself was opposed to slavery and had actively supported the Wilmot Proviso. See Gay Wilson Allen, *The Solitary Singer: A Critical Biography of Walt Whitman* (Chicago: University of Chicago Press, 1955), 89–91; and David S. Reynolds, *Walt Whitman's America: A Cultural Biography* (New York: Knopf, 1995), 111–72, 350–85.

4. For a thoroughgoing effort to situate Whitman in the political context of the 1850s and 1860s, see Betsy Erkkila, *Whitman the Political Poet* (New York: Oxford University Press, 1989).

5. For a discussion of the broader history of this tension in American legal theory, see Paul W. Kahn, *Legitimacy and History: Self-Government in American Constitutional Theory* (New Haven: Yale University Press, 1993), 3–170.

6. Hence, though he claimed to proceed with "malice toward none" and with "charity for all," he also claimed to proceed with "firmness in the right" (Abraham Lincoln, *Speeches and Writings*, 2 vols. [New York: Library of America, 1989], 2:687; future references to Lincoln will be made in parentheses in the body of the chapter).

7. Cf. Kerry Larsen's powerful, *Whitman's Drama of Consensus* (Chicago: University of Chicago Press, 1988), which maintains that *Drum-Taps* represents a "confused flight from advocacy" (222).

8. Timothy Sweet condemns Whitman for "detach[ing] wounds and deaths from the body (often without explicitly acknowledging them) and attach[ing] them to the discourse of the state" (*Traces of War: Poetry, Photography, and the Crisis of the Union* [Baltimore: Johns Hopkins University Press, 1990], 15). While it is no doubt at least partly true that Whitman attaches "wounds and deaths" to the "discourse of the state," it is not at all clear to me that he thereby detaches them from the body. And while Sweet thinks that Whitman's verse works to make "the individual body disappear into ideology" (15), it seems more plausible to me that it makes ideology disappear into the discourse of the body. For a powerful rejoinder to Sweet, see Mark Maslan, *Whitman Possessed: Poetry, Sexuality, and Popular Authority* (Baltimore: Johns Hopkins University Press, 2001), 114–36.

9. Michael Les Benedict, "Preserving the Constitution: The Conservative Basis of Radical Reconstruction," *Journal of American History* 61 (June 1974): 66. See also Benedict, *A Compromise of Principle: Congressional Republicans and Reconstruction, 1863–1869* (New York: Norton, 1974).

10. Other versions of Benedict's core contention may be found in Charles Fairman, *Reconstruction and Reunion*, 2 vols., vols. 6–7 of *The Oliver Wendell Holmes Devise History of the Supreme Court*, ed. Paul Freund (New York: Macmillan, 1971–88); Harold Hyman, *A More Perfect Union: The Impact of the Civil War and Reconstruction on the American Constitution* (New York: Knopf, 1973); Philip Shaw Paludan, *A Covenant with Death: The Constitution, Law, and Equality in the Civil War Era* (Urbana: University of Illinois Press, 1975); Herman Beltz, *Emancipation and Equal Rights: Politics and Constitutionalism in the Civil War Era* (New York: Norton, 1978); and *A New Birth of Freedom: The Republican Party and Freedman's Rights, 1861–1866* (Westport, Conn.: Greenwood, 1976).

11. Robert J. Kaczorowski, "To Begin the Nation Anew: Congress, Citizenship, and Civil Rights after the Civil War," *American Historical Review* 92 (Feb. 1987): 47. See also Kaczorowski, "Revolutionary Constitutionalism in the Era of the Civil War and Reconstruction," *New York Law Review* 61 (Nov. 1986): 863–940.

12. Christopher L. Eisgruber, "The Fourteenth Amendment's Constitution," *University of Southern California Law Review* 69 (1995): 101.

13. *Congressional Globe,* 39th Cong., 1st sess. (1866), 43. Hereafter references to the *Congressional Globe* for this Congress and this session will appear in parentheses in the body of the chapter.

14. Raoul Berger, *The Bill of Rights and the Fourteenth Amendment* (Norman: University of Oklahoma Press, 1989), 92. For a good account of these difficulties, see William E. Nelson, *The Fourteenth Amendment* (Cambridge, Mass.: Harvard University Press, 1988). See also Lino A. Graglia, "'Interpreting' the Constitution: Posner on Bork," *Stanford Law Review* 44 (1992): 1019–51, 1033–34.

15. The most important argument about the Fourteenth Amendment in the twentieth century is Hugo Black's dissent in *Adamson v. California* 332 US 46 (1947), 68. Black relied almost entirely on Bingham's claims about the Fourteenth Amendment, and insofar as this opinion has been the touchstone for all further debate, that debate tends to focus on Bingham's legal competence and his representative status. Those who are skeptical of Black's views include Charles Fairman, "Does the Fourteenth Amendment Incorporate the Bill of Rights?" *Stanford Law Review* 2 (1949): 5–127; and Berger, *Bill of Rights and the Fourteenth Amendment.* Those who have joined him include William Crosskey, *Politics and the Constitution in the History of the United States* (Chicago: University of Chicago Press, 1953); Michael Kent Curtis, *No State Shall Abridge: The Fourteenth Amendment and the Bill of Rights* (Durham: Duke University Press, 1986); Richard L. Aynes, "On Misreading John Bingham and the Fourteenth Amendment," *Yale Law Journal* 103 (Oct. 1993): 57–104; and Akhil Reed Amar, *The Bill of Rights: Creation and Reconstruction* (New Haven: Yale University Press, 1998).

16. Debate about the meaning of the Fourteenth Amendment has often hinged on whether the measure was designed to proscribe racial distinctions tout court (as Justice Harlan suggested in his *Plessy* dissent) or to protect certain enumerated or vaguely referenced "affirmative rights." In my analysis such considerations take a back seat to questions regarding the structure of rights under than Constitution. Even Andrew Kull, who believes that the crucial task before the Thirty-ninth Congress was "affording a federal guarantee of what Sumner liked to call equality before the law" (86), ultimately acknowledges that Congress's "paramount object" was not to specify the nature of civil equality in the United States but, rather, to guarantee "natural rights of citizens against infringement by the states" (87). For Kull's interesting and suggestive account of this dimension of the debate, see *The Color-Blind Constitution* (Cambridge, Mass: Harvard University Press, 1992), 67–87.

17. See Robert J. Reinstein, "Completing the Constitution: The Declaration of Independence, the Bill of Rights, and the Fourteenth Amendment," *Temple Law Review* 66 (Summer 1993): 361–411.

18. Amar, *Bill of Rights,* 283.

19. This is one of the primary reasons Berger discounts tenBroek's brilliant analysis of the Fourteenth Amendment's antislavery antecedents. See Berger, *Fourteenth Amendment,* 90–95.

20. The classic discussion of antebellum due process remains Edward S. Corwin, "The Doc-

trine of Due Process of Law before the Civil War," *Harvard Law Review* 24 (1911): 366–85, 460–79. For cogent accounts of the complicated standing of due process in post-Reconstruction constitutional law, see Alexander M. Bickel, *The Least Dangerous Branch: The Supreme Court at the Bar of Politics* (New Haven: Yale University Press, 1962), 199–243; John Hart Ely, *Democracy and Distrust: A Theory of Constitutional Review* (Cambridge, Mass: Harvard University Press, 1980); and Lawrence Tribe, *Constitutional Choices* (Cambridge, Mass.: Harvard University Press, 1985), 3–46.

21. Alvan Stewart "A Constitutional Argument on the Subject of Slavery" (1837), in Jacobus tenBroek, *Equal under Law* (New York: Collier, 1965), 283.

22. It is clear, for instance, that at least one of the reasons Taney was adamant that African Americans could not count as citizens is that he wanted to guarantee states a wide latitude for racial discrimination and that he felt that were African Americans to count as citizens the comity clause would radically restrict the states' efforts to subordinate them: "For if they [African Americans] were . . . entitled to the privileges and immunities of citizens, it would exempt them from the operation of the special laws and from the police regulations which they [the large slaveholding States] considered to be necessary for their safety. It would give persons of the Negro race, who were recognized as citizens in any one State or the Union, the right to enter every other State whenever they pleased, singly or in companies, without pass or passport, and without obstruction, to sojourn there as long as they pleased, to go where they pleased at every hour of the day or night without molestation, unless they committed some violation of law for which a white man would be punished; and it would give them the full liberty of speech in public and private upon all subjects upon which its own citizens might speak; to hold public meetings upon public affairs, and to keep and carry arms wherever they went. And all of this would be done in the face of the subject race of the same color, both free and slaves, and inevitably producing discontent and insubordination among them, and endangering the peace and safety of the State" (*Dred Scott v. Sandford* 60 US [19 Howard] 393 [1857], 416–17).

23. Joseph Story, *Commentaries on the Constitution of the United States* (Boston: Hilliard, Gray and Co., 1833), 674.

24. *Paul v. Virginia,* 75 US (8 Wall.) 168 (1869).

25. Fairman, *Reconstruction and Reunion,* 2:587.

26. 6 F. Cas. 546 (C.C.E.D. Pa. 1823) (No. 3230), 551–52 (1823).

27. Ibid., 551.

28. *Congressional Globe,* 35th Cong., 2nd sess., 984 (1859); see Maltz, "Fourteenth Amendment Concepts," 339–42; Amar, *Bill of Rights,* 174–80, 187–97.

29. *Congressional Globe* 42nd Cong., 1st sess., 84 (1871).

30. The most forceful version of this argument appears in Berger, *Fourteenth Amendment and the Bill of Rights,* 91–92. See also Ely, *Democracy and Distrust,* 27; and Douglas Laycock, "Taking Constitutions Seriously: A Theory of Judicial Review," *Texas Law Review* 59 (1988): 343–421, 348.

31. As Akhil Amar has put the point: "By incorporating the rights of the Fifth Amendment, the privileges-or-immunities clause, under the precedent of *Dred Scott,* would have prevented states from depriving 'citizens' of due process," Amar explains. "Bingham, Howard, and their colleagues wanted to go even further by extending the benefits of state due process to aliens. But for this, a special clause—speaking not of 'citizens' but of 'persons'—was needed" (*Bill of Rights,* 172). An earlier version of more or less the same argument may be found in Aynes, "On Misreading John Bingham," 68–80.

32. The original elaboration of a due process–based incorporation is Black's dissent in *Adamson v. California,* 332 US 46, 68.

33. Chief among them being that the Supreme Court produced an extraordinarily narrow reading of the privileges or immunities clause the first time it had a chance to rule on the matter in the seminal *Slaughthouse Cases,* 83 US (16 Wall.) 36 (1873).

34. Many legal historians have resisted the incorporationist reading of Fourteenth Amendment precisely because that reading implies these far-reaching changes in the nation's constitutional federal structure. They are inclined to ignore the direct evidence of Bingham's claim that the amendment should be understood as entailing these consequences because many state legislators voted to ratify the measure without acknowledging that they were in effect voting to have chunks of their state legal codes rendered unconstitutional. The most important elaboration of this claim appeared in the first systematic effort to prevent Bingham's account of the amendment from being a definitive one, namely Charles Fairman's essay "Does the Fourteenth Amendment Incorporate the Bill of Rights?" "If it was understood, in legislatures that considered the proposed Amendment, that its adoption would impose upon the state governments the provisions of the federal Bill of Rights, then almost certainly each legislature would take note of what the effect would be upon the constitutional law and practice of its own state" (82–83). But Amar points out that "many key provisions" of the amendment "received relatively little attention during ratification, simply because there was so much else to talk about" (*Bill of Rights,* 202). To Amar's analysis I would like to add only two considerations: (1) The radical effects of the Fourteenth Amendment's incorporationist tendencies were often not recognized by those who supported it not because they did not understand that the amendment would perform some form of incorporation but, rather, because they thought that incorporation was unnecessary, that states were in fact already bound by the Bill of Rights. They may have concluded that Congress might not have had the power to enforce the provisions of the Bill of Rights against the states, just as it could not enforce the other provisions in Article IV, section 2, but that the states had nonetheless entered into a compact to abide by them. Later on we will see that Bingham understood the states' relation to the Bill in roughly these terms. (2) Insofar as the Bill of Rights had come to be understood as the codification of a generalized code of legality, many thought that it was already an implicit feature of law wherever it might exist. In this regard it is useful to return for a moment to Sumner's "Freedom National." From the perspective of Fairman's analysis what is strangest about Sumner's argument is that he never contemplates the prospect that the states, rather than the federal government, might deny alleged fugitives due process of the law. This topic does not come up, in part, because many Northern states, the one he represented most prominent among them, had already explicitly provided the forms of legal process he recommended. But it also does not come up because Sumner seems to think that state common law necessarily entails the legal protections the Bill of Rights enumerates. "Without any express legislation" by Congress "the whole proceeding" to determine if a given person is a fugitive slave, he claims, "may be left to the ancient and authentic forms of the Common Law, familiar to the framers of the Constitution, and ample for the occasion" (3:190). The prospect that state legislatures might have any control of the proceeding simply never arises here. And when it does arise several sentences later the legislatures emerge as wholly subject to the common law Sumner imagines the Fifth Amendment to constitutionalize: "If, from ignorance or lack of employment, these processes have slumbered in our country, still they belong to the great arsenal of the Common Law, and continue, like other

ancient writs, *tanquan gladius in vagina,* ready to be employed at the first necessity. They belong to the safeguards of the citizen. But in any event, and in either alternative, the proceeding would be by 'suit at Common Law,' with Trial by Jury" (3:190). Sumner does not directly claim that states are subject to the provisions in the Bill of Rights here, but he certainly never contemplates that they might ignore them.

35. Kull, *Color-Blind Constitution,* 69.

36. The term *chameleon* comes from Justice Grier's dissent in *Texas v. White* 74 US (7 Wall.) 700 (1869), at 740.

37. For accounts of this tendency in Republican constitutional thinking, see Amar, *Bill of Rights,* 145–62; Aynes, "On Misreading John Bingham and the Fourteenth Amendment," 71–74.

38. *Kentucky v. Dennison,* 65 US (24 How.) 66 (1860), 109–10, 107.

39. Paul Finkelman, "States' Rights North and South in Antebellum America," in *An Uncertain Tradition: Constitutionalism and the History of the South,* ed. Kermit L. Hall and James W. Ely Jr. (Athens: University of Georgia Press, 1989), 146. See also Aynes, "On Misreading John Bingham and the Fourteenth Amendment," 74–79.

40. See Berger, *Government by Judiciary: The Transformation of the Fourteenth Amendment* (Cambridge, Mass.: Harvard University Press, 1977). See also Bickel, *Least Dangerous Branch,* esp. 98–111, 113–98; John Hart Ely, *Democracy and Distrust;* and Ronald Dworkin, *Freedom's Law: The Moral Reading of the Constitution* (Cambridge, Mass.: Harvard University Press, 1996).

41. Larry D. Kramer, *The People Themselves: Popular Constitutionalism and Judicial Review* (New York: Oxford University Press, 2004), esp. 207–26.

42. TenBroek, *Equal under Law,* 116.

43. See Kramer, *People Themselves,* 3–9, 227–54.

44. My thinking here is informed by Mark Maslan's brilliant reading of Whitman in terms of "the process whereby" the "speaker" in Whitman's poems becomes "representative" (*Whitman Possessed,* 122). In this regard, see also Kerry Larson, *Whitman's Drama of Consensus;* and M. Wynn Thomas, *The Lunar Light of Whitman's Poetry* (Cambridge, Mass.: Harvard University Press, 1988).

45. Emerson, "The Poet," in *Emerson: Essays and Lectures* (New York: Library of America, 1983), 455.

46. *Roe v. Wade* 410 US 113 (1973); *Doe v. Bolton* 410 US 179 (1973).

47. John Hart Ely, "The Wages of Crying Wolf: A Comment on *Roe v. Wade,*" *Yale Law Journal* 82 (1973): 949.

48. Thomas C. Grey, "Do We Have an Unwritten Constitution?" *Stanford Law Review* 27 (1975): 703–4.

49. Kull, *Color-Blind Constitution,* 86–87; *Brown v. Board of Education* 347 US 453 (1954), 492–93: "In approaching this problem, we cannot turn the clock back to 1868 when the Amendment was adopted, or even to 1896 when *Plessy v. Ferguson* was written. We must consider public education in the light of its full development and its present place in American life throughout the Nation."

50. Kull maintains that the amendment was popular precisely because it avoided the question of whether the nation needed "a federal guarantee of what Sumner liked to call equality before the law" (Kull, *Color-Blind Constitution,* 86).

114, 138, 174–92, 231n16; and antebellum poetics, 14–15, 194–97; and Bill of Rights, 4–9, 185–86, 188, 201n16, 231n15, 232n31, 233n34; and citizenship, 180–84; and comity clause, 180–84; and due process, 179–80; and higher law, 184, 186–89; hybrid structure of, 187–92, 196–98; potential redundancy of, 177–79, 184–86; and popular sovereignty, 191–92; and unwritten law, 197–98

Freehling, William, 95

Freeport Doctrine, ix, 9, 104–9, 156

Fugitive Slave Act of 1850, 73, 127, 133

Fugitive slave clause, 108, 124–27, 189–90

Fugitive slaves, x

Garrison, William Lloyd, viii, 17, 18, 48–49, 52, 55–56, 59–60, 96, 113, 184; on the Constitution, 1–4; on the Declaration of Independence, 2, 70, 74; on sectional conflict 1, 2–3; on Lysander Spooner, 141–42, 161, 172; on "universal emancipation," 5–6; on voting, 52–54

Grey, Thomas, 197

Grier, Robert, 23–25, 37–38

Guarantee clause, 139, 226n14

Habeas corpus, 28, 209n22

Hawthorne, Nathaniel, x–xi, 156–68, 169–72; on interrelation of acts of legislation and adjudication, 156–57; on legal hermeneutics, 166–68; on penal language, 164–66; on political agency, 171–72; representation, 158–64. Works: "Edward Randolph's Portrait," 134, 157–58, 159–64, 170–71; *Legends of the Province-House*, 157–59; *The Scarlet Letter*, 11, 134–35, 156–57, 164–68, 171–72, 191

Higher law, 2–3; and citizenship, 65–66, 99–102, 138–39; and common law, 7–8, 49–51, 93–94, 127–31; and Constitution, 7–8, 18, 175–76, 184–92, 194–98; and laws of nature, 51, 91–93, 114–15, 117–123; and legal agency, 114–17; and legal procedure, 96–98, 127–28; and racial inequality, 17–18, 110–14, 212n3; and slavery, 17–18, 31–32, 49–52; and universal values, 16–18

Howard, Jacob, 183–84

Jackson, Francis, 52

Jacobs, Harriett, 10, 15

Jaffa, Harry S., 77

Jay, John, Jr., 31

Jefferson, Thomas, 75, 78, 89–90

Johnson, Andrew, 29, 32, 38–39, 208n18, 209n19

Johnson, Samuel, 74–75

Kaczorowski, Robert J., 176

Kahn, Paul W., viii

Kansas and Nebraska Act of 1854, 134, 153–54

Karcher, Carolyn, 112

Kentucky v. Dennison, 190–91

Kramer, Larry, 191–92

Kull, Andrew, ix, 187, 197, 231n16

Lecompton Constitution, 105

Levine, Robert, 72, 87

Lieber, Francis, 9, 31, 166–67, 172

Lincoln, Abraham, vii, 2, 6, 9, 17, 20, 38, 75–78, 90, 95, 130, 156, 192–94, 207n13; and Declaration of Independence, 149–51; as emancipator, 2–6, 174–76; and Freeport Doctrine, 104–9; Gettysburg Address, 175–76; and habeas corpus, 27–30, 209n22; Lyceum Address, 2, 12–15, 128–29

Locke, John, 216n36

Loury, Glenn, 125

Madison, James, 6, 8, 125, 145, 188

Magna Carta, 129

Mansfield, Lord (William Murray), 49–52, 93, 109, 136, 214n20

Marriage, and slavery, 79–82

Marshall, John, 103, 143–44, 146

Maslan, Mark, 230n8

May, Samuel, 78

McLean, John, 31–32, 42

Melville, Herman, 10, 19–46, 47–48, 131, 138, 146–49, 189; on agency of legal language, 146–49; on civil status of African Americans, 47–48, 110–14; on Civil War as constitutional crisis, 22–27; deployment of parentheses in, 39–45; on emancipation as form of slavery, 57–59, 112–14; as poet, 21–22, 45–46, 195–97; on relations between poetic form and truth, 39–42; on slavery, 33–35, 57–59; Southern legal claims in Civil War, 22–27. Works: "America," 23, 33–34, 58–59, 112; "Armies of the Wilderness," 23, 25; *Battle-Pieces*, vii–viii, ix–x, 19–46, 47–48, 110–14, 146–49; "Benito Cereno," 112–13; "Conflict of Convictions (1860–61)," 57–59, 111–12, 146–47;